In the Long Run We're All Dead

Timothy Lewis

In the Long Run We're All Dead:
The Canadian Turn to
Fiscal Restraint

UBCPress · Vancouver · Toronto

09 08 07 06 05 04 03   5 4 3 2 1

Printed in Canada on acid-free paper

National Library of Canada Cataloguing in Publication Data

Lewis, Timothy, 1966-
    In the long run we're all dead : the Canadian turn to fiscal restraint /
    Timothy Lewis.

    Includes bibliographical references and index.
    ISBN 0-7748-0998-1 (bound); ISBN 0-7748-0999-X (pbk)

    1. Deficit financing – Canada – History. 2. Budget deficits – Canada – History.
3. Fiscal policy – Canada – History. I. Title.
HJ8513.L48 2003   339.5'23'0971   C2003-910026-X

Canadä

UBC Press gratefully acknowledges the financial support for our publishing
program of the Government of Canada through the Book Publishing Industry
Development Program (BPIDP), and of the Canada Council for the Arts, and
the British Columbia Arts Council.

This book has been published with the help of a grant from the Canadian
Federation for the Humanities and Social Sciences, using funds provided by the
Social Sciences and Humanities Research Council of Canada.

Printed and bound in Canada by Friesens
Set in Stone by Brenda and Neil West, BN Typographics West
Copy editor: Jacqueline Larson
Proofreader: Judy Phillips
Indexer: Noeline Bridge

UBC Press
The University of British Columbia
2029 West Mall
Vancouver, BC V6T 1Z2
604-822-5959 / Fax: 604-822-6083
www.ubcpress.ca

For Blaise and Talia, the loves of my life

Contents

Preface:
In the Long Run

The great economist John Maynard Keynes famously observed in his 1923 *A Tract on Monetary Reform* that '*in the long run* we are all dead.' As Donald Moggridge has noted in *Keynes and the Contemporary World*, Keynes's comment was most immediately directed at some oversimplified uses of the quantity theory of money. This marvellous phrase has also been deployed to vindicate active short-run government stabilization policy. But Keynes's aphorism can have wider application. This book is entitled *In the Long Run We're All Dead,* in part because it is concerned with Keynesianism, but also because it specifically pertains to the long life and slow death of Keynesian ideas and policy regarding deficit finance.

The project began to take form in the mid-1990s. It emerged out of my confusion regarding how Canadian politics, particularly in Ottawa, had become organized around the fiscal position of governments, and my concomitant dissatisfaction with existing explanations of the Canadian turn to fiscal restraint. Deficits were everywhere, and contrary to Keynesian era norms, everywhere impugned. Governments moved in different ways, but with dogged determination, to eliminate their fiscal shortfalls. My goal was to specify precisely the ideas about deficit finance that were carrying the day with governments, the forces that supported the selection of these ideas over others, and the consequences of the selection of these ideas.

I was convinced that an adequate account of deficit's disrepute required much better theorizing and deeper historicizing than analysts had provided. Typically, the questions were not rigorously framed. Theory that could allow us to understand immediate events was notable only by its absence. My aspiration was to approach the problem from a disinterested stance that would allow theory to be built. I also thought a proper historical perspective was necessary. One reason to historicize deficit finance was to reveal the contemporary contempt in which fiscal deficits are held as historically contingent rather than objectively necessary. More important,

I was of the view that deficit elimination in the 1990s did not emerge out of nowhere. To understand Chrétien it was necessary to understand Mulroney; to understand Mulroney it was necessary to understand Trudeau; and to understand Trudeau it was necessary to understand the Keynesian era.

Three findings that I did not specifically anticipate bear particular mention here. The first is that ideas can persist and have a causative role in political outcomes long after the socio-economic factors that supported their selection in the first place expire. The conditions on which Canadian Keynesianism were posited had largely passed from the scene by the mid-1970s. Yet Keynesian notions regarding deficit finance continued to inform federal budgeting until 1984. Indeed, in my view, a 'Keynesian touch' remained in Ottawa's discourse and fiscal policy throughout the Mulroney years. Only in the very long run did Keynesian ideas about deficit finance die.

Second, there is Canada's overriding economic liberalism. Living next to the United States, Canadians tend to overlook it. Economic liberalism can take different forms, as this book will demonstrate. But rare indeed, outside of war, are the moments when Canada has dissented from liberal economic arrangements in the Anglo-American tradition. When violations of liberal precepts have occurred, the resulting backlashes have restored the liberal tradition and taken the offending policies off the table. Canada does have Tory and socialist ideological strains, which have been much noted by commentators. But Canada is, to its core, a country of economic liberalism, regardless of which party has held office.

Third, my research helps us to understand the character of linkages between international competition and globalization on the one hand, and domestic political outcomes on the other. As this book makes clear, the trajectory of ideas in Canada regarding deficits and the embodiment of those ideas in policy was informed by developments in the global political economy. But in the end, the capacity of these ideas and their cognate policies to capture the state remains very much a matter of domestic politics. Whatever imperatives economic globalization may enjoin, they can usually be realized only through the mediation of domestic institutions and political actors. The relevance of globalization to domestic politics resides not in its capacity to determine outcomes but in its capacity to alter calculations of the costs and benefits of domestic policy choices and partisan alternatives. The global economy tends to punish certain policies and actors while rewarding others. Just as important, perceptions of its consequences can aid or hinder different policy choices and political options. Because economic globalization changes the resources available to domestic political actors, it tilts the playing field of domestic politics in one direction or another; but it does not (indeed in its current form it cannot) simply determine the results of the game.

In what is said to be a global world, the study of a particular country can seem quite 'old economy.' But states are not going to disappear any time soon. This book was written because Canada is interesting and worthwhile and, if well governed, has prospects in the twenty-first century.

I would like to thank a number of people who have been involved in this project at various stages of its development. Stephen Clarkson, my thesis supervisor at the University of Toronto, devoted enormous amounts of time to my work and offered much needed personal support. David Cameron and Susan Solomon, the other members of my dissertation committee, were also helpful in ways that went beyond their substantial direct contributions to my work. Paul Barber, Neil Bradford, Robert Campbell, Rupert Gordon, Jeff Loucks, Craig McFadyen, Mel Watkins, and David Wolfe also read parts or all of what became this book. Their comments have resulted in a much-improved final product. Any errors, of course, remain my own.

I would also like to thank my family and friends for their love and support while I was all too focused on this project. My parents have been with me through thick and thin. My wife, Blaise Clarkson, and my brother, Andrew Lewis, have been important in ways I cannot begin to express.

In the Long Run We're All Dead

1
Fiscal Politics

Ideas in Politics: Questions and Issues

> The ideas of economists and political philosophers, both when they are
> right and when they are wrong, are more powerful than is commonly
> understood. Indeed, the world is ruled by little else. Practical men, who
> believe themselves to be quite exempt from any intellectual influences,
> are usually the slaves of some defunct economist ... I am sure that the
> power of vested interests is vastly exaggerated compared with the gradual
> encroachment of ideas.[1]
>
> *– John Maynard Keynes*

What are the relationships among ideas, politics, and policy? Specifically,
what is the precise content of the ideas embodied in political discourse
and in public policy? What factors determine the selection of certain ideas
over others at different times? And what results flow from the selection of
particular ideas? Changes in Canadian fiscal policy and political rhetoric
since the mid-1970s offer an opportunity to better understand the political role of ideas. Put differently: Was Keynes right about his own ideas?

Canada's postwar Keynesianism assumed that, and behaved as if, Ottawa
was the leader in macroeconomic policy. During Canada's postwar era,
and through to 1984, federal governments typically presented deficit
finance in Keynesian terms as a sound policy tool that could compensate
for cyclical economic underperformance. However, persistent rather than
countercyclical deficits emerged in the mid-1970s under Pierre Trudeau's
Liberal governments. The federal government's public view changed when
Brian Mulroney's Progressive Conservatives took power in 1984. The Mulroney administration presented deficit finance, for the most part, as the
sworn enemy of good economic performance. Yet the Mulroney governments did not attain their stated fiscal policy goals. Jean Chrétien's

Liberals, elected in 1993, adopted and hardened the Mulroney critique. Chrétien and his finance minister, Paul Martin, succeeded where Mulroney failed. It was they who slew the federal deficit dragon that had, on the argument of Liberals, Tories, and Reformers alike in the 1990s, been terrorizing the land for nearly a quarter-century.

The culmination of these changes was a major shift in the focus of Canadian politics. The 1990s were the decade of *fiscal politics* in Canada. To an extent unprecedented in the postwar era, Canadian politics was about the fiscal position of the country's governments. Although this is primarily a story about the federal government, provincial politics in the 1990s were also organized to a large degree in terms of provincial finances. By the end of the decade, the budgets of almost all the provinces were balanced or nearly balanced. Provinces are supporting characters in the story. And this fiscal orientation was not confined to elites. Canadians were largely voting for parties they believed would best exercise fiscal responsibility and exorcise fiscal demons. It became close to impossible to get elected anywhere in Canada if a party's commitment to budgetary balance was not credible.

This book is about the public life of the winning ideas regarding deficit finance propounded by Canada's federal government. The book aspires to answer three specific questions:

1   What was the content of these ideas at various points in time? By closely examining budget documents, other materials put out by the federal government, and federal policies, I plan to identify and detail Ottawa's public position on deficit finance.
2   What caused changes in the ideas that Ottawa championed? An investigation of the political and economic conditions that support the selection of some ideas over others makes it possible to identify linkages between ideas and the environments in which they thrive.
3   What were the consequences of these changes? The fiscal politics that apprehended the country's collective psyche and the concomitant restructuring of the state's economic role were the most significant results.

Once we have tackled these queries, partial answers to more general questions regarding the role of ideas in politics, and the nature of political change, will emerge.

Three key issues are central to this book's answers to the questions it poses. One recurrent issue is *Canadian public policy*. The priority of fiscal concerns in Canada emerged in part from a policy history and environment that circumscribed the range of viable fiscal options and pushed the Chrétien government to give deficit elimination pride of place. Policies like the Canada-United States Free Trade Agreement structured future possibilities. In turn, the budgetary position of the Canadian government was the country's most salient ongoing issue in the 1990s. Fiscal policy was important not only in itself but also with respect to its impact on other policy fields. Social policy, economic policy, public administration, federal-provincial relations, and a host of other areas were deeply shaped by the primacy and scope of the fiscal question.

Ideological change regarding the role of the state in the economy is also a central issue. The ideological strand that dominated the Western world in the postwar years has been called 'embedded liberalism.' This liberalism sees the economy as embedded in society. The state's economic role is to protect society and the economy from the economy's own worst tendencies, even as the state promotes economic activity by helping markets to function. Embedded liberalism is to be contrasted with 'neo-liberalism,' which inverts these priorities. The role of the neo-liberal state is to facilitate economic change and to discipline both itself and society so that neither interferes with market functions. These are ideal types, and elements of both varieties of liberalism can always be identified over the time frame with which we are concerned. Nonetheless, since Brian Mulroney took office, neo-liberal ideology has increasingly supplanted the embedded liberalism that supported postwar Keynesianism in Canada. These ideological categories describe visions of the state role in the economy, to which approaches to deficit finance are closely linked. Accounting for change in winning ideas regarding deficit finance means considering their relationships to ideological currents and the state's economic role.

The third central issue is the public policy literature concerned with the connections between *interests, ideas, and institutions.* The book will develop theory regarding these relationships, and thereby account for the interests that ideas rationalize, the institutions in which ideas are entrenched, and the other ideas with which fiscal notions compete and cooperate. These relationships are usually reciprocal. Ideas may be the children of vested interests, but they also inform an actor's understanding of his or her interests and the best means to their realization. Institutions carry ideas, but ideas provide part of the context in which institutions function.

I have introduced the subjects this book addresses, the questions it aspires to answer, and the issues it pursues. Why is this formulation superior to previous efforts to understand the Canadian turn to fiscal restraint?

Ideology over Analysis: Competing Explanations of Fiscal Restraint

There have been very few sustained or persuasive explanations of Canada's turn to fiscal restraint. In part this is because analysts have not been sufficiently disinterested. Instead of trying to understand ideational change, commentators have usually used the ideas that should be under the micro-scope to either applaud or condemn the changes at hand. As such, insuffi-cient conceptual rigour and historical nuance are brought to the table. Indeed, even the questions I have just formally stated have rarely been put forward as explicit matters for investigation. As such, identifying schools of thought on the issue is a somewhat creative exercise.

On one side of the debate are organizations like the C.D. Howe Institute, the Fraser Institute, the *Globe and Mail* editorial board, and also the governments that have taken a serious crack at deficit reduction or elimi-nation. On the other side are groups like the Canadian Centre for Policy Alternatives and writers such as Linda McQuaig. The former group has a lot in common with the 'liberal continentalist' school which has won so many political battles in Canada over the last twenty years. The latter group shares much with the 'interventionist nationalist' school which has suffered so many setbacks. But it is too simple to describe this as a 'right' versus 'left' debate. Bob Rae's NDP government in Ontario and Roy Romanow's NDP government in Saskatchewan were in the same camp as the Mulroney Progressive Conservatives with respect to the broad desir-ability of deficit reduction. I prefer to categorize these views in terms of their assumptions. The former group I call the 'objectivists,' the latter the 'subjectivists.' Objectivists share the view that Canadians and their gov-ernments became so focused on fiscal issues because of the reality of the problem. Deficits were a real issue so people took the issue seriously. Sub-jectivists argue that the deficit 'problem' was at best grossly exaggerated. The focus on fiscal issues resulted from the ideological capture of people and governments by powerful vested interests.

The Objectivist Argument
The objectivist story is that the political salience of deficits flowed in a *mechanistic* fashion from the *objective* basis of the problems created by fiscal shortfalls. Deficits and debt levels were so high that they would soon, if they had not already, seriously impair the well-being of Canada and Canadians (government of Canada fiscal data are provided in the Appendix, pp. 208-13). This harsh reality necessarily led, or would lead, Canadians and their governments to a well-founded focus on the deficits that increased the debt. Objectivist reasons that these fiscal gaps were unsustainable include: the resulting inflation; the ever-increasing share of federal spending taken up by debt interest payments; the prohibitively high interest rates that would be required to continue to sell Canadian bonds; skewed market decision making and interference with private capital formation; reduced business confidence; and the ineffectiveness of deficit finance in enhancing economic performance. Presently, and into

the foreseeable future, a rising debt load and high deficits would be severely punished. Realizing this, Ottawa inevitably acted, or would soon act, to rectify the problem.[2]

The defining characteristic of the objectivist position is that the centrality of deficits to political consciousness and behaviour follows in an unmediated fashion from the obvious and deep problems with fiscal shortfalls. The language of this argument is in the terms that deficits 'must' or 'have to be' rectified because the problems they elicit are, argued Finance Ministers Michael Wilson and Paul Martin both, 'real' not 'ideological.'[3] For the objectivists, this reality is the cause of fiscal issues being thought about and acted upon.

The objectivist account contains important insights. The argument embraces the basic data around which debates about fiscal questions are constructed. As long as there is public sector budgeting, there will be revenues, expenditures, and the excess of one over the other. Canadian finance ministers have interpreted deficits and surpluses differently, but they have never spoken as if the fiscal position was irrelevant. The numbers matter. At a minimum, they are the starting point for analysis and debate. Similarly, the emphasis on 'objectivity' makes salient at least parts of the real world financial market context that informs the budgetary decisions of policy makers.

But just as the objectivist view highlights some things, it obscures others. What the objectivists shield from sight are nothing less than *politics*. The salience of deficits, as well as action to eliminate them, cannot simply emerge from objective conditions. Consciousness and behaviour are functions not simply of an external reality but also of what that reality is understood to be, and of reactions to that understood reality. 'Reality' does not speak for itself. It is politically mediated.

First, even though there is a reality within which budgeting occurs, it does not follow that this reality will be recognized. Both misunderstandings and predispositions make it more or less difficult to see different things. For example, it is now well understood that economic performance in Western industrialized countries suffered a secular decline that seems to have started roughly with the first OPEC oil price shock in 1973. But Canadian policy makers, operating on what turned out to be outdated assumptions about economic performance in the mid-1970s, did not quickly recognize this reality. Policy responses were therefore less than optimal. Second, even if reality is fully grasped, political responses to it are indeterminate. Much can get between a stimulus and a response. Among the things that may intervene are ideology, political commitments, and the relative power of actors to impose their views. The responses a Keynesian or a post-Keynesian or a monetarist would script, and would be able to script, to the secular decline in economic performance beginning around 1973 were very different. Politics, then, *mediate* between reality and outcomes. Politics are part of the reality that must be explained and cannot be assumed away. The salience of deficits as a problematic is political to the core.

Indeed, it might be thought that measuring the deficit, at least, is an objective exercise. But even the selection of deficit measures has a political component. Broadly speaking, the federal fiscal balance is measured in three different ways, depending on the actuarial purposes of the measurer. The Public Accounts, the National Accounts, and the Financial Requirements/Surplus generate different measures of the 'deficit.'[4] In the 1990s, the Public Accounts deficit, which excludes so-called nonbudgetary transactions, exceeded the National Accounts deficit and the Financial Requirements/Surplus, sometimes by over \$10 billion. The Public Accounts number is the one most commonly used in political debate in Canada, although in the United States the usual number is closer to a National Accounts figure. And the Public Accounts themselves are indeterminate because what is counted as a budgetary transaction changes over time. Unemployment Insurance (as it was then called) was moved from the nonbudgetary to the budgetary side of the equation in 1986. In the early 1970s, the finance minister would point out that the Public Accounts did not really give an accurate picture of the government's fiscal position because it excluded the government's Unemployment Insurance deficit, which helped stimulate the economy.[5] In the latter half of the 1990s, the Employment Insurance Account served to reduce the Public Accounts deficit substantially. In other words, there is no Archimedean point from which *the* fiscal position can be determined. Governments emphasize the 'deficit' that best serves their political purposes.

Regardless of the measurement system, Canada was in the red for more than twenty years, and its debt was mounting. But the indeterminacy of the deficit indicates that neither the arithmetic nor the objectivity of the problem can determine political consciousness. Otherwise, deficit consciousness in Canada (at least with respect to the federal government) would have evaporated the day Ottawa balanced its books. Similarly, by 1999 Alberta's assets exceeded its liabilities when the Heritage Fund was included. It had no net debt. According to the objectivist argument, fiscal concerns in the province should have disappeared. Yet the orientations and behaviour in the Albertan and Canadian governments, both of which remained concerned with protecting their fiscal positions, demonstrates that numerical realities are not the end of the story.

The absence of politics and nuance from the objectivist account is reflected in its inability to coherently bring the issues of timing and party into the theory. The argument that deficit reduction was necessary has been propounded for rather a long time; the federal government itself began making the case in 1984. Nothing about this perennial 'necessity' explains why the 1995 budget was the one that broke the federal deficit's back. The focus and political conditions necessary for the task did not spontaneously emerge with the 'objective' problem. Similarly, the party holding power and the direction from which opposition parties attack the government appear to have some explanatory power with respect to fiscal visions and behaviour. But for the objectivists, history marches forward in an inevitable direction while political actors fall beneath its feet. Yet, as I hope to demonstrate, the Mulroney Tories and the Chrétien Liberals are relevant to the story. The objectivist case is too sweeping to say anything specific about how parties may have generated public support for their fiscal agendas, or about the different pressures to which different parties are subject, but which those parties also try to manipulate.

As Louis Pauly argues, 'Corporate financiers, as well as representatives of national governments, among the largest borrowers of international capital, use the language of inevitability to obscure the notion that other normative choices are conceivable. It is the language of what Karl Polanyi called "the self-regulating market."'[6] As Pauly notes, this discourse disguises the fact that such markets are not inevitable but very much the creation of concerted state action. Without state support of property rights and market stability, none of this would be possible.[7] The objectivist case is part and parcel of a specific economic model and accompanying vision of the role of the state. As such, it cannot go outside itself and explain the political dominance in the 1990s of that economic model and that vision regarding the state's role. An adequate account cannot be wedded to an underlying normative position. The subjectivists make the same error from the opposite direction.

The Subjectivist Argument
For their part, the subjectivists argue that the government's fiscal position became salient not because deficits were in fact so important but because this point of view was constructed through the manipulations of empowered interests. The subjectivists are typically of the view that the deficit problem was at best grossly exaggerated – it certainly did not merit the label of 'crisis' – or at least easily fixed by looser monetary policy. For the subjectivists, any deficit problem was more a matter of 'ideology' than 'reality.' Widespread fiscal consciousness resulted from a sort of ideological capture of the state and the public. One of the main villains orchestrating it all was the business community, of which the mass media is presented as either a part or a tool. Also complicit was the mainstream economics profession, as represented not only in the academy but also in think tanks and state institutions like the Department of Finance and the Bank of

Canada. Political parties too were responsible, for either pacing change or for capitulating to it. These groups colluded, intentionally or not, to foster a fiscal consciousness because it furthered their economic and ideological interests.[8]

The strength of the subjectivist position resides in its crediting the salience of these anti-deficit ideas to politics. The subjectivists understand that power imbues publicly debated ideas about fiscal issues specifically, and the role of the state in the economy generally. These debates are not neutral. In addition, the subjectivist focus on the role of monetary policy and the Bank of Canada is an important feature of which no analyst should lose sight. But ironically, the subjectivist case, which emphasizes the importance of constructed ideas, cannot take those ideas very seriously. One could hold to the idea that the fiscal situation was a problem only if one saw advantage in the view or was under the thrall of a false consciousness. There are two major difficulties with this stance.

First, since the ideas underlying deficit reduction are assumed to be without merit, the subjectivists do not analyze and unpack their content: what this fiscal vision makes more visible and more obscure, what it presupposes, and the way these ideas hang together or fall apart. Instead of explaining the salience of these ideas, for the most part the subjectivists caricature them as patently absurd. Second, since the life of these ideas is said to be only about interest or false consciousness, the subjectivists are driven to the wildly implausible assumption, at least implicitly, that all who ascribe to these fiscal views are either Machiavellian or fools. But it was and is possible for a reasonable person to take the position that the deficit was a real problem. The argument was reasonably coherent. Sincere and intelligent people have been persuaded. Subjectivists cannot account for the sincere or intelligent position that the fiscal condition posed a problem as that problem was defined by the federal government. Neither, then, can they account for much of what needs to be explained regarding the public viability of these ideas about deficit finance. In particular, they cannot explain why public statements and policy built around deficit elimination would have wider resonance.[9]

The subjectivist position hides other factors that it should strive to explain. By reducing anti-deficit views to mere ideology, the subjectivists tend to ignore the relevance of the prejudices of market actors and voters. For example, if bond traders believe that high debt and persistent deficits make a country's bonds riskier, they will tend to behave accordingly, even if their belief is entirely a function of ideological capture.[10] If voters think the country will go to hell if the deficit is not eliminated, they too will tend to act accordingly. In dismissing these possibilities as prejudice, the subjectivists ignore the political relevance of bias. That ideas are operative parts of the political world ends up being strangely ignored by those whose focus is on the political construction of ideas.

Like the objectivists, the subjectivists paint with too broad a brush to explain change or its timing. The business community has hectored Ottawa about the federal government's fiscal position since the mid-1970s. But the federal government did not accept this critique until 1984. Nor did a more general fiscal consciousness emerge until the 1990s, and Ottawa did not move to eliminate the deficit until 1995. This long lag goes unexplained. So too with related change regarding the party in power and the party system. The subjectivists must sweep these categories under the rug of ideological capture. In addition, sociological categories like patriarchy, for example, have lasted rather a lot longer than contemporary concerns with fiscal shortfalls, and so can hardly have been a cause in any immediate sense of the turn to fiscal restraint.[11]

If the language of the objectivists is that of inevitability, the language of the subjectivists is that of ideology. Refusing to ground anti-deficit ideas and deficit elimination in truth, for the most part the subjectivists neglect to ground these ideas and policies in history. The subjectivist case is also bound up with a specific economic model and vision of the state's economic role. But their preferred approach has clearly been on the defensive in Canada since at least the mid-1980s. Fighting for its life, the subjectivist position cannot go outside itself and account for its political weakness. As with the objectivists, the subjectivists take a normative position on dominant political and economic currents. This limits their ability to explain precisely what should be at issue.

Theorizing Fiscal Politics

A full account of the public life of the winning ideas about deficit finance understands economic and fiscal reality as politically mediated. It takes seriously, without simply embracing it, the view that deficits are problematic. It also draws on 'inside' accounts that tell the story of the mid-1990s in Ottawa well.[12] But this account is more than a combination of the strengths of other positions. The turn to fiscal restraint has emerged in conjunction with cognate changes in the global political economy, ideology, domestic policy, and a specific experience of economic decline. The linkage, I will argue, between change in winning fiscal ideas and these politico-economic factors is that the latter have functioned to alter dominant conceptualizations of the economic and political interests of citizens, business, and the state. These changing conceptualizations of interests have resulted in political opportunities for parties propounding changed visions of the role of the state in the economy. New visions of the state's economic role have not been kind to fiscal shortfalls. The now dominant ideas about deficits have reinforced both the state role and the underlying interests that supported these ideas in the first place.

Ideas, Interests, and Institutions

This broad sketch of a process of change must be located in a theoretical framework. I take the trite position that ideas, interests, and institutions all matter as explanatory variables. But as Hugh Heclo notes, it is not crucial on which of these factors the analysis first focuses. What matters is that the analysis grasp their interrelationships.[13] I cut into the chain by treating interests as the engine driving change. I then examine the ideas that publicly support and privately rationalize interests, and finally explicate the entrenching of those interests and ideas in institutions. But more interesting are the dynamic linkages between the factors.

There may be such a thing as an objective economic interest. But the political relevance of an interest depends on how it is conceptualized. In Max Weber's classic formulation, 'not ideas, but material and ideal interests, directly govern men's conduct. Yet very frequently the "world images" that have been created by "ideas" have, like switchmen, determined the tracks along which action has been pushed by the dynamic of interest.'[14] Interests drive and energize politics. However, the direction the political train takes is deeply conditioned by ideas, which provide interests with their political meaning. Just as a physicist would argue that speed without direction is meaningless, an 'interest' in itself is politically meaningless. An 'interest' does not specify either how the interest is understood by those who hold it, or what strategy will be seen as best realizing the interest.[15] The interest must be conceptualized, however inchoately, to be politically meaningful. When I refer to interests, unless modified by the adjective 'objective,' I mean the operating construction of what those interests are and how they are best realized. Ideas and interests are politically inseparable.

The resulting approach to the role of ideas is on the one hand cynical, but on the other hand ascribes to ideas a fairly wide autonomy in certain circumstances. The approach is cynical to the extent that ideas are treated as a dependent variable, or in other words, when the factors that determine the selection of ideas are being considered. With Weber, ideas become practical roughly insofar as they serve as weapons in political struggles between groups, and roughly insofar as they rationalize individual interests.[16] That is, ideas are selected in the first instance approximately to the extent they have an instrumental value. But this approach ascribes autonomy to ideas to the extent that, over time, ideas can function as intervening and on occasion as independent variables with explanatory value regarding outcomes. With Weber and also with Keynes, ideas, once selected and embedded in minds and institutions, can act as a filter through which circumstances are understood and responses scripted. Ideas can display a remarkable tenacity and persist long after the material and interested circumstances that supported their selection in the first place have expired.

Heclo argues that governments not only 'power,' but that they also 'puzzle.'[17] This is true, but the distinction overstates the dichotomy between these concepts in a political context. Puzzling is informed by the relative power of competing ideas. Puzzling will be done, when a set of ideas is entrenched, in terms of those ideas. Such puzzling is evidence of those ideas' power, of their political and policy relevance. To the extent puzzling occurs under conditions of uncertainty, the uncertainty is usually a reflection of the diminishing relative power, and therefore diminishing relevance, of formerly dominant ideas. This is not to say that disciplines and ideas have no internal integrity or developments; it is to argue that to the extent ideas are in the political realm, they are necessarily caught up in power relations. Ideas are subject to, but also contain and transmit, power and power relations.

In principle, institutions can also drive change. They inform interests and support some ideas over others. Bureaucratic work is intimately related to policy outcomes and must be considered. In addition, tools of institutional analysis are important for analyzing the turn to fiscal restraint. Sometimes it is necessary to disaggregate the state and focus on its discrete aspects to understand results. The concept of path dependencies is also important. Policies shape not only subsequent policy decisions but also politics. As such, I am not challenging scholars who have sought to 'bring the state back in.'[18] There is no effort 'to take the state back out.'

But there are limits to the explanatory power of institutional analysis. Institutions are at least as subject to change in socio-economic and political conditions as they are likely to pace such change.[19] In addition, scholars in the field acknowledge that structural institutional analysis is particularly effective at explaining differences across nations and continuity within a country.[20] It is less strong with respect to similarity across jurisdictions and change within a country. These limits apply as well to rational choice analysis of institutional structures, which cannot in itself explain why results in a country change while the relevant structural forms remain constant.[21] The concern here is change within Canada. The limits of institutional analysis for understanding the problem at hand are, therefore, case specific as well as theoretical. And common outcomes across jurisdictions weaken an institutionalist case. The American government turned to deficit elimination at about the same time as its Canadian counterpart, and each balanced its budget in the late 1990s. Given the profound differences in the institutions that determine the budgetary process in the two countries, domestic institutions cannot explain the convergence. Institutional structures matter here, but not as much as the environment in which they reside.

Viability and Beyond

The interactions between ideas, interests, and institutions support or oppose the 'viability' of a set of ideas. Peter Hall argues that the viability of a set of economic ideas is determined by economic, political, and administrative factors. Economic viability is based on the relationship of the ideas to existing theory, to the nature of the national economy, and to international constraints. Political viability relates the ideas to the overall goals of ruling political parties, to the interests of potential coalition partners, and to collective associations with similar interests. Administrative viability links the ideas to the administrative biases and relative power of relevant agencies, and to structural capacities to generate information.[22] Hall argues that the more viable a set of ideas is in these three senses, the more likely it is to be adopted as policy.

Hall's approach is particularly apposite because it was developed out of a comparative study of the selection of Keynesian ideas across nations (although his study excluded Canada). But there are two related weaknesses with respect to the concept of viability. One is that viability operates by exclusion. It tells us which ideas are not viable and therefore will not be selected. But in principle there can remain a number of viable ideas from among which the concept of viability cannot determine the winner. The outcome is underdetermined by the concept. That a foetus is viable does not mean it will live. As is often the case with the historical institutionalism to which it relates, viability provides us with the necessary but not sufficient conditions for the selection of ideas. We require a move beyond viability to determine which among a set of viable ideas will be embraced.

Hall has, in fact, developed another concept that provides analytical assistance in understanding the selection of ideas and, especially, policies. He argues that there are three 'orders' at which policy change can occur. First-order policy change entails changes in the settings of given policy instruments. Increasing the deficit would be a first-order policy change. Second-order change refers to change in the instruments of policy. Taking the deficit instrument off the table would be a second-order policy change. Second-order change typically also involves changes in the settings of instruments. Finally, third-order policy change entails change in the hierarchy of goals behind policy. Replacing unemployment with inflation as the pre-eminent policy concern, and pursuing balanced budgets and direct tax reductions rather than macroeconomic efforts to reduce unemployment, would be examples of third-order change. Third-order change is usually accompanied by changes in instruments and their settings.[23] Hall's concept of orders assists in categorizing policy changes, which in turn allows us to better understand their character. I will use the concept of orders of policy change extensively to describe the nature of various policy shifts – but since it is basically a classification scheme, the concept does not in itself explain why change occurs.

Hall's answer to the conundrum of viability's insufficiency as an explanatory tool, I suspect, relates to third-order change and his definition of ideas. He is really concerned not so much with specific ideas as with the adoption of a whole 'policy paradigm.'[24] Drawn from Thomas Kuhn's notion of a scientific paradigm, a policy paradigm is a third-order change containing fundamental value judgments and goals regarding the state role in the economy. If ideas are defined at this broad level, the notion of viability is probably strengthened. During a period when the dominant approach to regulating the economy is up for grabs, perhaps only one alternative can be viable. If the only choices are Keynesianism or monetarism, then if just one of these is viable, by default it will be selected. But this, in my view, exposes the second weakness of 'viability.' If the concept is bound up with the notion of a policy paradigm, then it will tend to obscure the existence and persistence of ideas that do not fit within the dominant paradigm. As I will argue, Keynesian ideas about deficit finance persisted long past the nominal end of the Keynesian era in 1975, and even past the neo-liberal turn with Brian Mulroney in 1984. But if Mulroney's policy paradigm, which amounted to a third-order change from the Trudeau era, was more 'monetarist,' the concept of viability would not allow us to see the continuation of now subordinate Keynesian ideas inconsistent with the policy paradigm. To put the point differently, the use of deficit finance in certain economic circumstances was one component of Keynesianism. With the fall of the Keynesian paradigm, if the paradigm is really all that matters, then Keynesian notions about deficit finance should have been simultaneously extinguished. But they were not. I am concerned with these paradigms and the ideologies in which they participate. But I am also concerned with ideas about deficit finance specifically. So it is necessary to go below the paradigms, and here viability is an insufficient concept.

I therefore return to the relationships between interests and ideas to explain the selection of ideas about deficit finance from the range of viable ideas. Ideas resonate when they are framed in ways that participate in the interests of actors, remembering that I refer to interests as imbued by understandings of both the content of the interests and the strategies to realize them. Ideas tend to be selected when there is political opportunity in articulating ideas that speak to these interests. As Robert Reich argues, when 'questions' (such as whether the deficit should be eliminated) 'catch on,' 'even before the question is asked, the public (or a significant portion of the public) seems already to be searching for ways to pose it – to give shape and coherence to events that seem random and unsettling – and thus to gain some measure of control. Rather than responding to pre-existing public wants, the art of policy making has lain primarily in giving voice to these half-articulated fears and hopes, and embodying them in convincing stories about their sources and the choices they represent.'[25] Reich's enterprise is in part an effort to carve out a fairly wide autonomy for ideas. But in my view these random and unsettling half-articulated fears and hopes about the state role in the economy are a function of changing interests. These interests are what get people searching for the question in the first place. Politicians can either present new ideas or repackage old ones at moments when interests are under stress, when old understandings of interests are weakening because expectations regarding those interests are no longer being realized. As expectations are disappointed, the sense of lost control increases. And by mediating between interests on the one hand and ideas as embodied in platforms, policy, and discourse on the other, political figures and political parties become an important part of the analysis. One limitation of approaching the problem through the relationships between ideas, interests, and institutions is that these categories do not account for the role of political leadership. Such leadership comes into play when it articulates issues in ways that mobilize interests into politically coherent forms through rhetoric that credibly deploys ideas.

Concepts

Fiscal Politics

Earlier I referred to the 1990s as the decade of 'fiscal politics' in Canada to indicate the extent to which the federal government's fiscal position permeated politics. I use the term 'fiscal politics' to capture the political importance of this fiscal consciousness. The restraint of the 1990s was sufficiently coherent, specific, and historically unusual that it can be meaningfully named. *Fiscal politics*, or *fiscalized politics*,[26] or the *fiscalization of politics*, refer to a situation in which politicians, officials, organized interests, and the general public alike are highly conscious of the state's fiscal position in the sense that deficits (and perhaps also debt) are conceptualized as intrinsically inimical public policy. This is more than simply being aware of the situation. Fiscal consciousness matters because it is politically meaningful. Fiscal politics exist when a substantial portion of politics, whether fiscal in nature or not, is *charged* with this fiscal awareness. Politics becomes energized by, and organized and debated in terms of, the state's fiscal position. Fiscal politics are fully operative not only when political actors must at least appear responsive to fiscal concerns but also when political rhetoric situated in terms of fiscal control is generally persuasive and mobilizing. Fiscal considerations have always mattered, but have not always been primary. Nearly every federal activity, whether a proposed or existing policy initiative or human resources issue, had to be justified in fiscal terms by 1995. To a great extent, the merit of a decision was determined by its fiscal impact; its intrinsic value was a secondary consideration. Neither social nor economic nor industrial nor foreign policy escaped this new structure of justification. Such are the circumstances that constitute fiscal politics.

When I describe fiscal politics as operative, I will also use the word 'entrenched.' This characterization is chosen to capture the point that fiscal politics was an enduring cause of outcomes. Fiscal politics did not become entrenched autonomously. But upon politics locking in on these fiscal ideas and norms, fiscal politics was entrenched in the sense that it was not only a cause but also would not easily be dislodged. The ideas that characterized fiscal politics became anchored in and diffused throughout the Canadian political system. The idea that deficits were intrinsically bad gained pride of place for political reasons; once entrenched as the key notion of fiscal politics, the idea acted autonomously as an independent variable.

The term fiscal politics is broad enough to cover debt, deficits, budgetary balance, and surpluses. Fiscal politics became entrenched in Canada in the mid-1990s. But looking back, it is possible to identify some of its constituent elements in earlier discourse and behaviour. When I describe the movement toward fiscal politics, I will refer to 'early' or 'premature' moments in the evolution toward entrenchment. In the mid- to late 1990s, fiscal politics was primarily about the (Public Accounts) deficit. Evidence of this politics is found in the extent to which budgets were occupied with both rhetoric and action against fiscal shortfalls. Looking forward, it is not so much that an entrenched politics is dislodged as that it recedes. Fiscal politics will become more of a background condition than an explicit battleground – a process already in motion. Just as what was once the surface of a tree becomes an inner ring, fiscal politics will no longer *charge* or dominate our experience of politics. But it is contained within and continues to shape the explicit exterior. At the turn of the millennium, the discussion turned to the distribution of expected future surpluses. The notion of distributing the surplus presupposes that deficits are out of the question. Fiscal politics recedes, but budgeting remains informed by its norms.

It is important not to exaggerate change. Politics are politics. Politicians try to get elected. Pork-barrelling, patronage, strategy, ambition, and the

like are enduring features of the political game. Fiscal politics has not over-
turned the political process. But it has tilted the field on which the game
of politics is played. The fiscalization of politics restructured both how the
game could be won and who would be likely to win it. Understanding this
was critical to political success in Canada in the 1990s and into the
twenty-first century.

Public Utterances and Fiscal Rhetoric
The primary source materials used for this project are budget documents.
Budget speeches, supporting papers, and other government documents
are all employed. This material is buttressed by interviews with key
finance ministers, Finance officials at the deputy minister and assistant
deputy minister levels, and senior Bank of Canada officials. A wide range
of secondary sources is also canvassed.

A challenge in using public documents as a primary source, as even a
political novice knows, is that there is often a gap between what the political actor says and what the actor actually believes. However, content
analysis of government documents is still the best measure of the belief
systems of those elites within the state who are responsible for a policy
area.[27] Interviews are also a partial way of getting at individual and corporate belief. But my primary concern is not belief in itself. Belief is relevant
primarily to the extent it informs the public selection of ideas by governments. Rather, I am concerned with the public life of ideas, in no small
part because speech constructed for public consumption provides access
to power relations.

That political talk has to be modified for public consumption, whether
that public resides on Saskatchewan's wheat farms or in New York's financial markets, indicates that governments and other political groups are
subject to forces that require them to shape presentations of their policy
and political goals. That governments and others bother to modify their
political talk also indicates the flipside of this coin, that governments can
use these forces for their own purposes. Were it not for power relations
there would be no political rhetoric to interpret. Rhetoric exists in a country where, to paraphrase Pierre Elliott Trudeau, we count heads instead
of breaking them because no actor is omnipotent and power is distributed
throughout the political system.[28] Were it otherwise, politicians would
not have to craft their statements for public consumption because there
would be no forces, nor indeed political opponents, who could frustrate
their goals. Similarly, there would be no need to manipulate because there
would be no forces to use. To put the point in more formal terms, if truth
were uncontested there would be no need for rhetoric, for persuading
people of the truth or the value of a position. But insofar as truth is contested – insofar as it is political – it becomes a matter of power.[29] From this

springs the need to shape language into forms that can be heard, and to use language as a tool to realize goals. If the object is to understand politics and the power of ideas, public rhetoric is a crucial place to look.[30]

Governments more than any other political actor are conscious of the political impact of their statements. There is a word for a government's comments when they are not vetted for positioning: gaffe. Just about everything a government puts on paper and releases publicly has been written and rewritten in terms of its political impact. This is even more the case with budgets, which are vetted and refined over and over again for precisely these purposes. None of this means the government will get its political read 'right.' But the 'read' is based on an assessment of the political factors that determine the success of ideas and policies. My focus on the public statements of *governments* flows from the emphasis on tracing the *winning* ideas about deficit finance. Competing ideas always exist, and the competition has to be described. But there are winners and losers. Since Canada's fiscal position is a matter of public policy, the winning ideas are those expressed in word and deed by the authors of the policy; in this case, the federal government, particularly the minister of finance and the Department of Finance.[31] By understanding that in which the winning fiscal rhetoric participates, we open a window on wider political dynamics and the reasons that deficits are being described in one way or another. When fiscal rhetoric as a critique of deficit finance takes centre stage, it suggests rhetoric shaped in these terms is persuasive and mobilizing. When rhetoric resonates in this way, it usually means the speech activates something in its audience. This resonance is implied by the notion of an operative fiscal politics, and it is part of why I emphasize fiscal rhetoric.

There is another reason these public documents are so important. Public speech is the primary way governments have of communicating their views. Public speech is the only way to reach the mass public. But to a surprising extent, public statements are also how governments communicate with themselves and with other governments. Particularly with respect to broad priorities, Throne Speeches and budgets signal to officials where their own and where other governments aim to go. These documents also become resources in intragovernmental and intergovernmental negotiations. Similarly, they are used by interest groups to anchor their claims. Authoritative public utterances are distributed throughout the political system. Imbued as they are with strategic positioning, they are very much the stuff of power and politics.

The Role of the State in the Economy
David Wolfe has written that most arguments about deficit finance are really debates about the relationship between state and economy in late capitalism. Wider values are at stake than a narrow consideration of fiscal

policy first suggests.[32] As with policy paradigms, a government's vision of the state role in the economy is intimately related to, although not coextensive with, its conceptualization of debt and deficits. If, as with Trudeau's Liberals, the state is viewed as capable of creating a 'just society' through its interventions, there will be fewer ideational limitations on its actions. Deficits seem relatively unproblematic in the context of this social project. Fiscal shortfalls may even be seen as a way of accelerating progress. If, as at times with the Chrétien Liberals, the state is conceived as an irresponsible laggard with little direct capacity to improve economic performance, fiscal shortfalls are more salient as an example of and reason for the state's failings. Visions of the role of the state do not emerge autonomously, but they are politically normative. Paul Martin's budgets in the mid-1990s legitimated policy actions, such as eliminating the deficit, which were consistent with the wider vision of the state's role. As always with these issues, the causal arrows point in two directions. A government's view of deficits and debt will also inform its vision of the state's purposes and functions.

The argument that follows asserts that there have been important changes in the role of the Canadian state in the economy. It relates these changes, as both cause and effect, to fiscal politics and conceptualizations of deficit finance. But it is important to recognize that these changes do not necessarily imply that the state's role has been shrunk or diminished. Rather, as Stephen Clarkson and I have argued elsewhere, it has shifted.[33] This role was once relatively consistent with embedded liberal norms. It now converges more with neo-liberal orderings. Shifting from the one to the other required strong and concerted state action; and a neo-liberal state is not a state that has withered. These ideological categories are useful ways of describing the state's role. But if used normatively by the analyst they obscure the actual content of change. Nuance and investigation, rather than ideology, are required to understand these changes and how the state might further evolve.

Chapter 2 historicizes the contemporary disrepute of deficit finance by identifying earlier circumstances when deficits were accepted and even applauded. The chapter also describes the Keynesian era that Canada has since largely repudiated. Chapter 3 examines the character of economic decline, and reinterprets the 1975 policies said to mark the end of the Keynesian era. Chapter 4 investigates fiscal policy and rhetoric under Trudeau. Chapter 5 describes the relationships between change in the international political economy, evolving corporate interests, and Mulroney's political project. Chapter 6 analyzes the changes Mulroney wrought and explains his failure to control the deficit in spite of vociferous rhetoric in favour of deficit reduction. Chapter 7 identifies the political and economic conditions that made government organized around balanced budgets politically successful. Chapter 8 explains Chrétien's success in eliminating the deficit in the wake of the Mulroney years. Chapter 9 brings the book to an end with reflections on the meaning of neo-liberalism and political legitimacy. It also assesses Canada's prospects as a new 'politics of the surplus' emerges.

2
Deficit Finance in Historical Perspective

The contemporary political consensus against deficit finance impoverishes our imagination and our memory. The opprobrium attached to deficits makes it difficult to conceive of circumstances in which rational people could see value in fiscal shortfalls. It encourages us to forget that there were times before Pierre Trudeau when Canadian governments conceptualized deficits as useful. Or, if we recall these times, we misremember by imagining the thinking to have been ill informed. Impairing imagination and memory gives the current disrepute of deficit finance a timeless quality; we have this thing figured out and will not fall into irresponsible and ignorant error again. But the current consensus is a contingent rather than a timeless view. There have been at least three identifiable moments or circumstances when deficit finance was respectable in Canada. Historicizing dominant currents about these fiscal matters compels us to investigate the factors that have supported the winning views. Otherwise we are writing Whig history from the point of view of the late twentieth and early twenty-first centuries.

The three roles Canadian governments have propounded for deficit finance are: to promote the inseparable goals of nation-building and economic development; to fight world wars; and to stabilize the business cycle. From at least the creation of the province of Canada in 1840 to the end of the nineteenth century, deficit finance was conceptualized as a necessary mechanism for importing the foreign capital thought essential to developing the country. From 1914-18 and 1939-45, deficits were vindicated as indispensable to Canada's war efforts. After the Second World War, deficit finance was presented in Keynesian terms as an instrument that could bring economic growth and employment up to 'high' levels when economic slowdowns occurred. I will briefly discuss the first two roles to give a flavour of the place deficit finance has held in Canada's evolution. The Second World War also provides much of the context from which Canadian Keynesianism emerged. The Keynesian era will be treated in greater detail because to understand change in public ideas regarding deficit finance since 1975, one has to understand the rhetoric and policy of Canada's post-Second World War Keynesianism.

Developing the British North American Hinterland

Canada's place in the international economy, and the accompanying definitions of national purpose and nationalism, have always been proximate to visions of the country's fiscal policy.

Budgetary deficits and public debt have a long and noble place in Canadian history. Even before Confederation, economic development in the Province of Canada and the rest of British North America depended upon public debt. This dependence was related to Canada's position as a hinterland economy of the British Empire. Canada's role was to supply raw materials to Britain for manufacture. The colony would use the proceeds of its sales to buy British products. Canada's dominant (English) business class saw its and Canada's prospects in terms of the imperial centre. So did the government.[1]

The trick was that Canada's role in the international economy as a supplier of raw materials to Britain required the creation of a transportation infrastructure to move the commodities from the interior of the vast new land to the British metropolis. The extremely high costs of developing first the canals and then the railways needed for these purposes required access to capital beyond that which was thought to be available domestically. Certainly the revenue instruments of the province were inadequate to the task. Tariff revenues and liquor and tobacco taxes were not sufficient. The province turned to foreign capital and incurred substantial foreign debt to support the annual deficits being run to pay for the infrastructure. The primary source of capital was Britain, the world's first industrial economy and the greatest capital exporter the world has known.[2]

The operative model of economic growth was dynamic. It held that the surplus population emigrating from the United Kingdom could be used to enhance the trade of products of the soil for the manufactures of Britain. Building public works, particularly the transportation infrastructure, would provide the immigrants with jobs. Eventually they would have the cash to purchase lands, preferably near the transportation facilities, on which they would work to produce more commodities for exchange with the home country.[3] This conceptualization of development anchored the continued willingness of the province to run deficits and incur debt. The strong economy that this process was expected to build would, it was thought, pay back these early investments.[4] So far from being inimical to a well-functioning economy, deficit finance was seen as integral to building one.

Changes in party, government, and minister made little difference to the basic orientation of Canada to this policy.[5] Indeed, even the Baldwin-Lafontaine introduction of responsible government in 1848 altered little regarding economic and financial policy. The biggest change was the move to building railways rather than canals by the end of the decade.[6] The centrality to this vision of building a transportation system implied that the state would play a central role in its financing. From this arose the legitimacy of deficit finance. That British capital needed to be secured acted as a limit on the extent of deficit financing. But the centrality of state-raised capital to economic development also meant that if the price of raising capital was deficits, debt, and high interest payments, then the price was viewed as reasonable. It was not that deficits were conceptualized as serving an intrinsic economic function so much as that they were a necessary epiphenomena of the state's accepted role in developing the economy and the country. This was not the Keynesian justification of running deficits to stabilize downswings in the business cycle; but neither was it consistent with the balanced budgets demanded by the English norms of Gladstonian sound finance. A different political and economic context resulted in a different approach to deficit finance.

There is more to the story, of course, than the vision of the economy and the state role therein. Part of what supported the model of growth was immediate material interest, graft, and corruption. Public office and private profit existed in a symbiotic relationship in nineteenth-century Canada. The line between business and politics was often blurred.[7] Sir John A. Macdonald, Canada's first prime minister, resigned his office largely because his telegram to Montreal capitalist Sir Hugh Allan requesting 'another ten thousand' was discovered.[8] After a five-year hiatus, he returned as prime minister in 1878. The transportation elites made a killing overbuilding railways and saddling the country with more debt than was necessary. The economic vision, however coherent and compelling in its own terms, was a handy rationalization of quite a lucrative enterprise. The vision and the graft helped keep the government of the day in power, particularly Macdonald's post-Confederation Conservatives. Indeed, Macdonald criticized the first Ontario premier, John Sandfield Macdonald, for the latter's defeat in 1871. Sandfield's mistake, said Sir John A., was being too thrifty with public finances in running a budgetary surplus! Such restraint meant he kept the Cabinet too small and his government was not able to dole out enough jobs.[9] The dominant approach was challenged both on grounds of economic vision and opposition to corruption by George Brown's *Globe* and the urban commercial and rural agrarian interests represented by the Liberal Party before the 1890s. But these interests were consistently defeated. The Macdonald-Cartier alliance of French-Canadians and the Roman Catholic Church in Lower Canada, English Canadian merchants and businessmen in Montreal, Upper Canadian moderate reformers who fought for responsible government, and the remnants of the Family Compact, was the stronger coalition. Wilfrid Laurier's Liberals did not take office until they adopted and refined Macdonald's old approach.[10]

The state's role was intimately attached to nation-building, and public debt was a central reason for Confederation. In 1866, the Americans cancelled the Reciprocity Treaty with Canada. This was one economic reason to look east and west rather than south. In addition, in 1866, the aggregate debt of the British North American colonies was $96 million net, of which $50 million was directly linked to spending on, or borrowing for, the railways. Debt interest charges accounted for 29 percent of colonial spending. It was also becoming difficult to float long-term bond issues in London. Short-term funding could be got only at 8 percent interest.[11] A financial crisis was recognized. The most significant remedy was Confederation, which would consolidate the debts of the colonies and create a better credit instrument managed by the new federal government. The fiscal arrangements were a crucial part of the Confederation deal. Ottawa assumed provincial debts. It also provided provinces with annual per capita grants of 80 cents, annual grants 'in support of Government and Legislation' heavily weighted in per capita terms in favour of the Maritime provinces, and a special grant to New Brunswick.[12] But such a crisis did not mean that outstanding debt and persistent deficits should be eliminated. Rather, the debt consolidation would permit funding the further capital projects conceptualized as necessary to continuing Canadian economic development:

> By filling out the union to its broadest bounds it was hoped to provide the widest possible base for the economic expansion that was confidently expected to be in the offing. Cheap and rapid transportation was the key to the continued discovery and development of raw materials for export which had been the basis of expansion of the pioneer economy of British North America. It was to be the function of the new national government to assume the whole burden of pressing forward this expansion by opening the West and building an all-Canadian route to the Maritime Provinces. A commercial empire beckoned, and a national government to carry the heavy expense of unlocking the door by railways was essential.[13]

The project of economic development was national because of the continuing need in British North America for the financing that a national government could best acquire. The 1879 National Policy of Sir John A. Macdonald, based on immigration, railways, and tariffs, continued an established Canadian vision. Modern nation-states were being created in Europe at around the same time (particularly Germany and Italy at the beginning of the 1870s), in part because the nation-state was seen as the appropriate unit for political and economic development.[14] Canada, while taking its own specific trajectory, participated in this pattern.

This is not to argue that the results were necessarily optimal. Gordon Laxer views the size of the debt accumulated by the Canadian government and its predecessors as an important factor in the high level of foreign ownership in the Canadian economy. The divide between the French and the English prevented populist alliances that otherwise would have more effectively opposed the high borrowing by elites.[15] Harold Innis, Canada's greatest political economist, saw debt as incidental to the imperatives of staples-led growth. The transportation necessary to get raw materials to Great Britain made debt the natural concomitant of staples growth. The resulting debt was paid by a tax on Canadian consumption: the tariff.[16] Often tariff policy in the nineteenth century had much more to do with government revenues than trade considerations.[17]

But for better or for worse, the vision that accepted deficits and debt won the day. There is a certain irony in the contumely that the winning vision in the 1990s attached to deficits. Without the debt and deficits accrued in the nineteenth century, the Canada we know today and over whose fiscal policy we currently argue would not exist. Absent these levels of debt, Canada may have done better. But we cannot understand the Canada people currently value unless we understand Canada's fiscal policy in the nineteenth century. To forget this past is to forget the basis in deficits and debt of Canadian economic and national development.

War Financing

First World War
The model of economic development I just described continued into the twentieth century. Laurier built railways whether Canada needed them or not.[18] But a long period of economic growth brought on by the worldwide recovery from the extended slump of 1873-96 and the prewar wheat boom brought about more substantial tariff revenue which lessened the need for state debt to finance capital expenditures.[19] By 1913, the country had spent the previous seventeen years constructing the capital facilities which were both cause and effect of Prairie expansion. The long economic expansion came to an end by the midsummer of that year. The First World War helped solve the problem by stimulating Canadian exports to Britain and pulling the economy from its moribund condition.[20]

Canada's path has always been intimately related to the country's links with the dominant metropoles of a particular era. This is so in political, economic, and cultural terms. The United States has always been important to Canada, and after the Second World War, it was increasingly the country that Canada orbited. But before the Second World War, Canada looked more to Great Britain. It was not only the staples economy that tied Canada to the mother country; the cultural linkages born of loyalism and emigration from the United Kingdom to Canada were strong. When England declared war against Germany in 1914, Canada's cry, as articulated by former prime minister Laurier, was 'Ready, aye, ready!' Or at least this was the cry in English Canada. Less 'ready, aye, ready,' were many of the French-Canadians, whose ancestors had fought and lost to the English on the Plains of Abraham. Canada followed Britain into the war automatically, as dominions were not then autonomous in foreign policy, although the extent of Canada's involvement was domestically determined.[21] The French-English cleavage nearly fractured the country around the conscription question in 1917.[22] Nonetheless, Canada's commitment of both troops and equipment had to be funded.

There were three alternatives for financing the war: taxation, printing notes, and borrowing.[23] Ninety percent of federal revenues were from customs duties and excise taxes at the start of the war.[24] Over the course of the war the government's tax capacity grew. Consumption taxes were introduced in 1915 under the Special War Revenue Act. A retroactive business profits tax emerged in 1916, in part as a response to resistance against war profiteering. 1917 saw Canada's first national income tax on individuals and corporations.[25] But there was great reluctance to increase tax burdens lest Canada have difficulty attracting the immigration it still sought to fill out the new country. Budget speeches almost annually advertised Canada as one of the world's lowest tax countries, although without adequate statistical evidence.[26] With respect to issuing notes, inflation was used to pay for the war effort. It served its purpose, but could be stretched only so far.[27] This left borrowing. Initially, Canada financed its war contribution with British capital. But in 1915, when the pound sterling fell in New York, the British announced that they would no longer support Canada's war expenditures. The government of Canada was pleasantly surprised to learn that the country could finance itself. High wheat exports, low private investment, increasing incomes, and profits expanded by inflation allowed Ottawa to meet its borrowing needs domestically.[28] Most of the loans were made by business, which was benefiting the most from the war economy.

The fiscal consequence was that Ottawa spent $2.2 billion more than it took in from 1914 to 1920. Of this, $1.7 billion went to the war effort, $350 million to railways and public works, and $110 million was lent to other governments. About $2 billion of this debt was raised domestically.[29] The government did continue to spend on public works. The railways were not finished when the war started, and not to finish them would mean there was no chance of recouping substantial investments.[30] Deficits and debt were vindicated by the First World War effort and by more persistent strands in Canada's strategy for economic development.

The Second World War
The First World War was funded on the notion that succeeding generations should and could bear some of the financial burden. With the Second

World War this view was supplanted in normative terms by a 'pay-as-you-go' approach.[31] The requirements for the two wars were very different. The scale of the Second World War was much greater. First World War expenditures were probably no greater than 10 percent of national income. Second World War spending was nearly 50 percent of national income.[32] In addition, the First World War required only intensifying and shifting economic activity. As J.J. Deutsch observed in 1940, the Second World War effort required detailed planning, centralized direction, and effective coordination to realize the necessary industrial capital investment and labour training.[33] The existence of a more mature tax system helped. But pay-as-you-go or not, substantial borrowing was still a crucial feature of Canada's Second World War effort.

The Second World War economic context was also different because Canada was still recovering from the Great Depression when the war started in 1939. Culturally, though, the context was similar. English Canada was not quite as attached to the United Kingdom as it was in 1914. The country was perhaps not quite as unreflective in joining this war. With Canada now formally independent of Britain (courtesy of the 1931 Statute of Westminster), rather than join the fray contemporaneously, Liberal prime minister Mackenzie King waited until after the British declared war on Hitler. But join the battle Canada did, and again French Canada felt itself dragged into an English war. The cleavage was particularly manifest, as in the First World War, on the question of conscription.[34]

In 1939 there was still a lot of slack in the Canadian economy. There was not much competition for resources between the private sector and the state's war effort. But as resources became more scarce, competition for them started to emerge.[35] The war tax system was designed to empty the private purse so that people and materials were not diverted from the war effort, which was understood to take priority.[36] By design, the tax system raised a lot of money and repressed private economic activity. In addition, Ottawa signed 'tax rental agreements' with the provinces in 1942, which gave the federal government full control over the personal income tax system. Ottawa set and collected all the taxes. Provinces were paid a 'rental' fee for giving up their tax capacity.[37] Ottawa's command of tax policy under conditions of emergency federalism was close to plenary. Nonetheless, as Harvey Perry argued in 1955, the tax system probably cannot fund all of an important war. The destruction of incentives, the disruption of private arrangements (such as postwar retirement savings), and inequitable outcomes all constrain use of the tax instrument.[38] To the extent taxation could not do the job, and notwithstanding the 'pay-as-you-go' approach, borrowing from the Canadian public at the lowest possible rates of interest was the government's solution.[39] Ottawa's revenues increased ninefold from 1939-40 to 1945-6. Yet receipts were only 58.7 percent as great as expenditures.[40] Substantial deficits were incurred. By the end of the war, the debt-to-GNP ratio was over 100 percent, a figure not approached before or since.

Neither world war was fought by Canada for economic reasons. Deficits were not a result of a new vision of the state role in the economy, although the Second World War in particular did contribute to a different understanding of state economic capacity (a matter to which we will return). The point is only that when things held fundamental and dear, like liberty, a better life, and not least Great Britain, were seen to be at stake, the necessary financial arrangements were made without much dissent. When Canadians had more fundamental concerns, deficit finance was just fine to the extent it was instrumental to realizing those goals.

The Keynesian Era

The economic impact of the Second World War can be understood only in terms of its relationship to the Great Depression by which it was preceded. In the years leading up to the 1929 crash, Gladstonian orthodoxy was the rule of the day in Canada and elsewhere. Deficits were inherently suspect, and virtue resided in balancing the budget. When the Depression hit, these norms continued to govern Canadian fiscal policy. Economic activity ground to a halt, so revenues declined and some spending increased. The policy response was to raise taxes and cut expenditures to get the budget back in balance. Precisely when the economy needed more lubrication in the system, Ottawa was taking money out to realize austere fiscal goals. These moves were accompanied by Prime Minister R.B. Bennett's increases in tariff rates. Tariffs were heightened both to raise revenues and to leverage more access to foreign markets where tariffs were also increasing.[41] Tariff increases such as Bennett's (and the American 1930 Smoot-Hawley tariff) manifested an economic nationalism, in Canada and elsewhere, which undermined the liberal trading order that had been built before the First World War. Conservative fiscal policy and nationalist trade policy in a time of worldwide depression left the Western world ripe for liberal Keynesian ideas.

Keynes, the General Theory, and the Second World War

England's John Maynard Keynes was, in the estimation of no less an authority than John Kenneth Galbraith, the most influential economist of the twentieth century. Galbraith's view is also that Keynes was one of the three or four greatest economists ever. He shares the stage with only Scotland's Adam Smith, Germany's Karl Marx, and perhaps also David Ricardo.[42] By the 1930s Keynes was already of the highest intellectual reputation. He was a part of the 'Bloomsbury' group, which included Virginia Woolf and Lytton Strachey, among others – a circle of intellectuals who devoted their leisure to the higher pursuits.[43] In addition to his experience in and linkages with the British Treasury, he had an outsider's political influence;[44] he had written among the leading works on monetary theory;[45] and his brilliant and prescient *Economic Consequences of the Peace,* published in 1919, had darkly warned in type if not name of the Hitlerian politics that could arise from the terms the Allies imposed on Germany's First World War surrender.[46]

Yet none of these credentials would match the impact of Keynes's *The General Theory of Employment Interest and Money,* published in 1936.[47] Spurred on by the view that the fiscal orthodoxy of the 1930s was not helping things (and was actually making them worse), Keynes challenged what he called the 'classical' school of economics that influenced much government policy, summed up by what Keynes called the 'Treasury view.' If I may grossly oversimplify a sweeping analysis, Keynes attacked a number of classical precepts. Chief among them was the conventional wisdom, called 'Say's Law,' that supply creates its own demand. The idea here is that producers pay for their factors of production, so suppliers and workers will have the money to buy whatever producers put on the market. Keynes argued that there is no reason to believe this nostrum. There is no necessary connection between decisions to save now and spend later. That I am paid for my labour does not mean I shall be willing or able to consume supply when it comes onto the market. I may, for example, hoard my money or go bankrupt. There would be full employment only if it happens to be supported by sufficient demand in the economy. Since Say's Law was specious, full employment could not be assumed; it was for Keynes a contingent rather than necessary circumstance.[48] What classical economics regarded as normal was really just a special case. Keynes's remedy was straightforward. Since supply does not create its own demand, sometimes the state would have to create demand to ensure full employment. Demand could be stimulated by monetary or fiscal policy. Increasing public investment and running budgetary deficits could constitute stimulative fiscal policy. Unemployment was the great economic issue of the Great Depression; Keynes's answer to the problem required reform rather than revolution.[49]

Coming as it did from so forceful an intellect, and in an economic situation crying out for an articulate remedy, the *General Theory* prompted a sea change in economic ideas. Foreign students flocked to Cambridge (England) to study under the master. While they often ended up working with Keynes's colleagues instead, his ideas dominated the intellectual climate. These disciples returned to their home countries to take positions in academia and government. In Canada, Robert Bryce was the primary example. He studied at Cambridge and later found work in Ottawa's Department of Finance. He would eventually become a long-serving deputy minister, and Clerk of the Privy Council. Other Canadian Keynesians would infiltrate the Canadian bureaucracy and bring public life to Keynes's thought. W.C.

Clark, W.A. MacIntosh, Louis Rasminsky, A.F.W. Plumptre, and J.J. Deutsch were among the Canadian converts.[50]

As powerful as Keynes's thought was in its own terms, and as compelling as it may have been in the economics profession, there is no such thing as a pure idea in politics. The political reception of ideas depends on not only the ideas but also the politico-economic context into which they are introduced. Keynes's ideas were received differently in different countries. 'Proto-Keynesian' policies could be identified in some countries before 1936. Swedish economists of the 'Stockholm school,' particularly Gunnar Myrdal, anticipated some of Keynes's work.[51] This early Keynesianism suggests that the favourable reception of Keynes's thought had much to do with the harmony between his ideas and conditions in political economies. The horrific economic performance that accompanied fiscal orthodoxy during the Great Depression helped discredit that orthodoxy, and was one factor that gave political life to Keynesian alternatives. By 1939 public authorities were beginning to recognize that the policies of most countries in the 1920s and 1930s had been, in Keynesian terms, perverse.[52] In Canada, the Rowell-Sirois Commission recommended what Neil Bradford describes as 'technocratic Keynesian' solutions to the economic malaise.[53] Roosevelt's New Deal in the United States, while not really Keynesian in nature, legitimated a more proactive state role in the economy.[54]

But the Second World War was as crucial as anything else to the favourable reception of Keynesian thought. Financing the war with borrowed money provided deficits with some legitimacy. More important, the war increased the state's capacity to influence the economy. The state grew exponentially relative to GNP, and institutions were built to handle the load.[55] That the war economy performed well legitimated the state's expanded economic role. The Second World War also increased the potential of, and the expectations for, the Canadian economy. Real GNP was 50 percent greater in 1946 than in 1939.[56] And part of the acceptance of Keynesianism resided in the view that Canadians did not fight the Second World War to come home to depression conditions. There was great anxiety about an economic relapse in the early postwar years. Peter Hall's argument with respect to the reception of Keynesian thought across nations applies to Canada. The Great Depression tore down the panaceas of classical economics. The Second World War built up the edifices and expectations that propelled Keynesian ideas forward.[57]

Keynesianism and the Keynesian Welfare State
Unless I say otherwise, I refer not to the *General Theory* or to what went on in Keynes's head when I refer to Keynesian policy or to Keynesianism. By these terms I refer to what Canada counted as Keynesian policy or ideas, since this book is concerned with the politics of ideas. Although Keynes's

basic thrust could not be missed, the precise policy implications of the *General Theory* were unclear.[58] There have been vociferous debates over just what Keynes understood the *General Theory* to entail.[59] As Galbraith has remarked, 'unlike nearly all of Keynes's other writing, this volume is deeply obscure; perhaps had it been otherwise and had economists not been called upon to debate his meaning and intentions, it would not have been so influential.'[60] Most think the *General Theory* was a moderate or even conservative program to save capitalism, but some argue that Keynes was describing a radical socialization of investment. Resolving this debate is not our concern here. What matters to this book's subject is how the ideas were actually received. Even if Canadian Keynesianism was only, to borrow the language of Keynes's colleague, Joan Robinson, a 'bastard Keynesianism,'[61] it is this form of Keynesianism and change from it that must be explained.

Narrowly construed, Robert Campbell states, 'the term "Keynesianism" is normally taken to imply the countercyclical use of fiscal and monetary tools to even out the business cycle and perpetuate high rates of employment.'[62] On the fiscal (taxing and spending) side, for a Keynesian, when the economy is underperforming so that employment falls below what is deemed its highest feasible level, the government's responsibility is to use its policy tools to increase aggregate demand and restore employment. One way to do this is to run budgetary deficits by increasing spending and/or cutting taxes. By this mechanism the state puts more money into the economy than it removes. The demand effects of this stimulus would be multiplied by the injection being spent more than once. This is the Keynesian 'multiplier.' By contrast, when the highest feasible employment level has been reached and inflation threatens, the government is to snuff out demand in excess of that required for high employment, and to pay down the debt accumulated when deficits were run. A mechanism for so doing is to incur budgetary surpluses by increasing taxes and/or reducing spending. With a surplus the state takes more out of the economy than it adds. The budget, then, should not necessarily be balanced in any one year, but should rather be balanced over the course of the business cycle.

Both 'discretionary' measures and 'automatic stabilizers' can be used for these purposes. Discretionary measures are intentional spending or tax moves designed to respond to an anticipated or actual deviation from high levels of growth and employment. If unemployment has gone up 1 percent, the government may decide to put money into, for example, a public works project to stimulate the economy. In the late 1960s and early 1970s, the budgets of Liberal Finance Ministers Mitchell Sharp and Edgar Benson responded to the Economic Council of Canada's argument that the difficulty in forecasting economic performance, and the lags between discretionary initiatives and their effects, imposed constraints on stabilization policy. Sharp and Benson both held that this was an argument not against discretion, but rather in favour of exercising it more precisely. As such, they would introduce initiatives not only at budget time but also throughout the fiscal year.[63] This 'fine tuning' approach was emblematic of discretionary Keynesian measures. 'Automatic stabilizers,' by contrast, are built intentionally but operate automatically. All things equal, (Un)Employment Insurance payouts increase to some degree as unemployment increases; revenues decline as the economy slows and fewer people are working. Economic stimulation will occur as a by-product of a slowdown to the extent that the fiscal structure is designed to be responsive to cyclical variation in the economy.[64] For example, in 1950 and 1951 Liberal Finance Minister D.C. Abbott argued that demand management was built into the tax structure because revenues were now very sensitive to changes in employment and income.[65] The deficits that come from automatic stabilization are sometimes described as 'passive.' To the extent deficits emerge from discretionary measures they are sometimes called 'active.'[66]

The Keynesian approach to monetary policy, and the connections between fiscal and monetary policy, are equally crucial. There is probably more debate regarding what constitutes Keynesian monetary policy than Keynesian fiscal policy. As with so many issues, Keynes vacillated (within limits) regarding the role of monetary policy.[67] The most common view is that monetary policy (as Campbell's definition of Keynesianism suggests) should, like fiscal policy, be used to even out the business cycle. A variant on this theme is that policy is more Keynesian to the extent fiscal policy is made a priority over monetary policy.[68] Fiscal expansion will work only if monetary policy accommodates fiscal policy by expanding the money supply to prevent the contractionary increase in the interest rate that can be expected to follow from the increased demand for funds created by government borrowing. Indeed, a fall in the interest rate may be necessary, in Keynes's argument, to offset any rise in the price of capital goods following from demand expansion.[69] In some contrast, the American economist Paul Krugman argues that the Keynesian prescription is to use monetary policy as the first method of stimulation. In the short run more money means more demand. Fiscal measures are to be employed only if the economy has fallen into a 'liquidity trap' where people will hoard rather than spend money. In this circumstance the government must do the spending for people through fiscal measures.[70] Finally, the *General Theory* also argues that monetary policy should be expansive enough to keep the long-term rate of interest below the rate of return on investment in capital. This will ensure that investment is productive rather than speculative. However, fiscal policy will probably also be necessary because long-run interest rates cannot stabilize the business cycle.[71] The common thread in these views is that monetary policy should be developed and implemented with a view to stabilizing the *real* economy.

Keynesianism puts a higher priority on maintaining high levels of employment than on fighting inflation. The normative basis for this preference, beyond the output lost due to unemployment, was the human and economic costs of Depression-era unemployment levels.[72] This does not mean that Keynes himself was unconcerned with inflation.[73] He wrote about its dangers often.[74] The *General Theory* itself expresses concern about 'true inflation,' or inflation resulting from demand expansion when full employment has already been reached. In this circumstance, for Keynes, all the effects of demand expansion would be inflationary rather than real, and hence unjustified.[75] Still, it is probably fair to say that a little inflation was relatively less important to those who developed their views in the Depression's wake or to those trained in economics based on solutions to Depression-era concerns. The empirical basis for the notion that inflation and unemployment are tradeoffs is the Phillips Curve (Figure 1). In 1957 the British economist A.W. Phillips observed that countries with lower levels of unemployment tended to have higher levels of inflation. Those with lower levels of inflation had higher levels of unemployment.[76] This tradeoff is not a strict prediction of Keynesian theory, but it fits with the Keynesian focus on unemployment, and extended the willingness of Keynesians to stimulate the economy in the face of inflation. The Phillips Curve defined the price of low unemployment as a bit of inflation, a price that, before the inflationary 1970s, did not seem particularly dear. As Krugman argues, the Phillips Curve increased the ambition of the Keynesian prescription by moving it from 'expand the economy up to full employment' to 'expand the economy up to the point where you think that the cost of higher inflation outweighs the benefits of lower unemployment.'[77]

Nonetheless, there are circumstances when Keynesian policy, whether of the immediate postwar or Phillips Curve variety, focuses on inflation. If employment reaches what is believed to be its maximum level, there would be no slack in the economy. Extra demand would simply translate into price increases, so a Keynesian would not support limitless expansion. Alternatively, if the costs of inflation outweigh the benefits of lower unemployment, a Phillips Curve Keynesian would not support further demand expansion. In addition, Keynesian economists have been known to recommend policy mixes, such as 'easy money' and 'tight budgets,' which do not necessarily pull in the same direction, but which are viewed as facilitating both employment growth and inflation control.[78] Indeed, Keynesian justifications for fighting inflation appeared during the postwar era. For example, the Korean War created inflationary pressures. Liberal Finance Minister Abbott argued that the economy was at full employment. Balancing the budget rather than running a deficit was presented in 1951 as a way of keeping inflation in check.[79]

Keynesianism also has political implications broader than those strictly suggested by the narrow policy definition with which we began. First, it was a technocratic solution to the economic problems of the Depression that shielded liberal democracy and capitalism from too deep an extension of the political domain into the economy. By the appropriate application of sound macroeconomic management and technical expertise, the economy could be made to perform optimally.[80] Second, Keynesianism provides an economic anchor to full employment, labour unions, and high wages insofar as each contributes to the aggregate demand levels seen as required for optimal economic performance. Social security is supported for similar reasons, including its function as an automatic stabilizer of demand.[81] Providing social programs and other political commitments with the legitimacy of sound economics was a powerful vindication of the welfare state. In 1946 Liberal Finance Minister J.L. Ilsley championed public investment, social security, Unemployment Insurance, old age pensions, and health care on the social justice grounds that they provided a reasonable standard

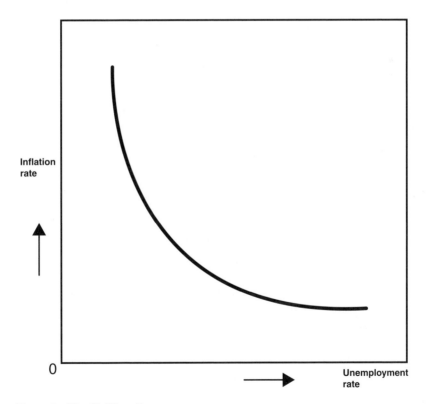

Figure 1   The Phillips Curve

of economic security for all Canadians. But he also justified these measures in terms of their role as part of an effective anti-Depression policy that would maintain full employment and high national incomes.[82] Edgar Benson's 1971 budget, twenty-five years later, was redolent with Ilsley's language. The stimulative measures recently used, said Benson, contributed not only to equity and justice. They also built stronger safeguards against slowdowns in demand growth, and added new dimensions to the structures of automatic stabilization.[83] Of course, Benson's rhetoric applied to a much more mature social assistance system than did Ilsley's. But the structure of the argument was the same, and spanned Canada's Keynesian era.

Persistent as they were, these conceptualizations helped to expand the social security system. The amalgam of macroeconomic and social policies that developed coalesced into what is often called the postwar 'Keynesian welfare state.' Keynesian conceptualizations also made it more difficult to dislodge the Keynesian welfare state once it was in place. Keynesian norms limit, or at least rationalize limits upon, the extent to which retrenchment should be pursued. In 1968, for example, Finance Minister Benson refused to pursue deeper inflation reduction for fear that doing so would damage the economy.[84] As we shall repeatedly observe, there are always two ways to interpret Keynesian rhetoric used to constrain retrenchment. One is that decision makers mean what they say. The other is that they do not want to cut spending for political reasons but need to cloak this in legitimating (Keynesian) garb. It is usually a bit of both. But if retrenchment was politically difficult in the Keynesian era, this was in part because of widely held conceptions of the state's role and responsibilities. Whether due to belief or rationalization, Keynesian ideas either won out or fought an effective rearguard action because they were reinforced by a sympathetic political context.

In its turn, the Keynesian welfare state tended to embed economic life in social relations. Its normative prescriptions were presented as protecting both the economy and society from the economy's own worst tendencies.[85] The Keynesian welfare state was the domestic policy that operationalized the postwar era's 'embedded liberalism.' The international dimension of embedded liberalism was found in the Bretton Woods arrangements that were the basis of the postwar international economic order. This order was in part designed to protect the policy autonomy of states to manage demand and provide social security.

Embedded Liberalism and the Postwar International Order
Drawing on the work of the economic historian Karl Polanyi,[86] John Ruggie has coined the term 'embedded liberalism.' He argues that the economic liberalization of the postwar international economic order was embedded within social relations. Strong economies were to be built, but the

social fabric was not to be subject to economic imperatives.[87] More precisely, the major parties at Bretton Woods were England and the United States. Harry Dexter White was the lead American negotiator. The ubiquitous John Maynard Keynes represented the English. Although the goals and interests of each country were somewhat different, the broad objective was still to build a multilateral economic order in which the pursuit of domestic stability would be safeguarded and supported. But at the same time, the pursuit of national goals would not trigger the mutually destructive high tariff beggar-thy-neighbour policies of the interwar period. 'This was the essence of the embedded liberal compromise: unlike the economic nationalism of the thirties, it would be multilateral in character; unlike the liberalism of the gold standard and free trade, its multilateralism would be predicated upon domestic interventionism.'[88] The Bretton Woods institutions, the World Bank and the International Monetary Fund (IMF), along with the General Agreement on Tariffs and Trade (GATT), were designed to realize these goals. Exchange rates would be fixed. Trade would be opened and liberalized over time. Capital movements, particularly of 'speculative' rather than 'productive' capital, would be controlled.[89]

Exceptions to the general liberalization thrust were permitted to allow countries to maintain their domestic policy autonomy. Protecting the balance of payments was viewed as particularly important. If flows of money could be kept in reasonable equilibrium, market actors could not exercise excessive influence over policy choices. For example, in addition to capital controls, the GATT permitted quantitative restrictions on imports to safeguard the balance of payments. Explicitly included were balance-of-payments difficulties arising from the domestic pursuit of full employment.[90] When a country requested an adjustment in its pegged exchange rate on the grounds that domestic policy was causing a disequilibrium, the IMF could not block the request.[91] The exchange rate would be adapted to domestic goals, not the other way around. Canada, parenthetically, was exceptional in that the Canadian dollar floated in the 1950s.[92] Keynesian and other domestic policies were seen to require international agreements that limited the power of financial actors to punish states for the pursuit of high employment. Keynesianism was anchored in an international framework of embedded liberal ideology and in institutions that protected domestic policy autonomy to engage in welfare measures and countercyclical fiscal and monetary manoeuvres. Such policies were conceptualized as being in the interests of justice. But they were also in place to ensure that the state action viewed as necessary to maximizing economic performance would not be frustrated. Indeed, William Beveridge, the 'father' of the welfare state, thought domestic full employment was a necessary condition for a continuing multilateral order. Otherwise, depression in one country would spill into the others.[93]

The concept of embedded liberalism must be taken as an ideal type. The postwar order was full of classical liberal strands. The Americans, and New York financial capital in particular, were less than fully persuaded of the virtues of the policies constituting the embedded liberal compromise that, on the whole, won the day. Sylvia Ostry goes so far as to argue that, while there may have been compromise, there was no consensus because the Americans never bought in.[94] Ruggie takes a more optimistic view. He agrees that the Americans were less enthusiastic than others. But he argues that the differences were over the form and depth of state intervention to attain domestic stability, rather than over the legitimacy of the goal.[95]

Given the gap between British and American preferences, Canada played an important role as a broker between the leading players. Canadian negotiators were sympathetic to Keynes's more ambitious proposals. But they advocated positions closer to the American view because of concerns that anything more would be defeated in the American Congress.[96] This was perhaps an early example of the postwar eclipsing of Britain by the United States as the dominant foreign nation in Canada's calculations and politics. Canada was an enthusiastic participant in the creation of the postwar international order, which was viewed as important to Canada's interests for a number of reasons. It would ensure Canada of markets for its exports and access to crucial imports. In tying the United States to a multilateral order, Canada would have allies should American protectionism and isolationism arise. International cooperation would elide the need for Canada to choose between the declining British metropolis to which it was traditionally attached and the ascending American metropolis into whose orbit Canada was increasingly drawn. Finally, it was thought that full employment could be effectively pursued only through an international framework of law and order.[97]

The Reception of Keynesianism in Canada

This was the international context within which domestic Keynesianism was to function. How in fact were Keynesian ideas received and Keynesian policies applied in Canada? Broadly speaking, in discursive terms, the postwar era in Canada was somewhat Keynesian. The language of classical budgeting persisted in postwar fiscal rhetoric. In addition, the federal government described its fiscal tools as legitimately deployed to pursue economic goals beyond stabilization policy. But Keynesian rhetoric, as we have seen, took its place in these budgets. This was an important and demonstrable change. Canada's implementation of Keynesian policy was probably less robust than Ottawa's Keynesian rhetoric. The government did not play quite as good a Keynesian game as it spoke. It is well recognized in most academic accounts that Canada's Keynesianism has been exaggerated in popular discussions.[98] Before the Keynesian 'revolution,' 'the grave consequences of going into the red, by simple analogy with personal finance, could be felt in the Anglo-Saxon bone marrow, so there was no need to specify them logically.'[99] Even after Keynes, Keynesian economists bemoaned their failures in educating the mass public, and governments, as to the appropriate role of fiscal deficits.[100] Canadian Keynesianism was circumscribed because of Canada's bounded substantive commitment to Keynesian procedures, the structure of the country's economy, Canada's extensive use of non-Keynesian policies, and the relative ineffectiveness of federal demand management. I will consider each of these factors in turn.[101]

Bounded Keynesian Commitments

Written by W.A. MacIntosh, the 'official' reception of Keynesian thought in Canada came in the Department of Reconstruction's 1945 White Paper.[102] Canada's commitment to Keynesianism was defined in this document. It emphasized the manipulation of aggregate demand to maintain high levels of employment, and it explicitly identified consumption, investment, government spending, and net exports as the constituents of aggregate demand. The White Paper was distinctly Canadian in its emphasis on the export portion of the equation. But in part due to Canada's trade dependence, it pulled back half as much as it pushed forward. Paralleling both American and British experience,[103] the White Paper commitment to attaining *high* levels of employment[104] was watered down from the King government's 1943 Throne Speech commitment to reach *full* employment after the war.[105] The Canadian White Paper argued that the federal government's capacity to achieve full employment was circumscribed by the open nature of the Canadian economy, the constraints imposed by the federal system, and the seasonal nature of some economic activity.[106] The 1945 employment commitment was timid and restrained.[107]

As we shall see in the next section, there was truth in the claim that the openness of the Canadian economy was a problem for Keynesian arrangements. But the federal government dwarfed the provinces in its fiscal capacity in 1945 and for years after. The federal system argument was particularly weak at that time. Indeed, as Campbell argues, Canadian Keynesianism was focused on Ottawa in part because it was in a clear position of economic dominance over the provinces.[108] Had the government really been committed to full employment, whatever difficulties Canada's situation created for attaining the goal would have been presented as a reason not for restraint but for a more aggressive state role.

The King Liberals, however, were a bourgeois party uncomfortable with extending the state as far as the White Paper implied would be necessary to attain full employment. The dominant (Anglo-American) tradition was liberal-democratic and capitalist. This was reflected in the fact that the

Liberals continued to hold office. Canadian business was never deeply persuaded of the merits of Keynesianism. It was at best acquiescent, even to moderate Keynesianism, and at points overtly hostile.[109] There were socialist strands in Canadian political discourse, particularly in light of the Depression.[110] Business could not politically avoid an at least nominally Keynesian solution, due to the return of soldiers who had not fought to relive the Depression and who expected a better life, somewhat more active unions, and the rise of the 'socialist' Cooperative Commonwealth Federation.[111] It could, though, shape the content of Keynesianism, and a moderate Keynesianism that was not committed to full employment was the least intrusive way of the state extending itself into the economy. The Liberal coalition included not only social interests but also strong representation of business concerns.[112] The CCF's ascending popularity in 1943 pushed the Liberals leftward. The full employment commitment in the Throne Speech was a matter of tactics.

The Liberals were trusted to save rather than overthrow the Canadian orthodoxy. Campbell describes what resulted as an 'optimistic' Keynesianism. The Canadian approach was pretty sanguine about the ability of the private sector to generate economic growth. Government assistance would be confined to fine-tuning macroeconomic aggregates and to building in piecemeal fashion the welfare state. The state would not interfere with private decision making. Investment would not be socialized. Campbell properly argues that Canadian Keynesianism cannot be understood outside of how it functioned to maintain and even strengthen liberal democratic and capitalist traditions.[113] The institution building that characterized continental Europe did not occur. A circumscribed state was liberal capitalist Canada's norm. Given that the prevailing discourse and the orientation of the governing party primarily reflected the values of a liberal democratic and capitalist society, Canada was unlikely to embrace a more robust Keynesianism that might consider socializing investment. Optimistic Keynesianism offered the possibility of sidestepping the stark choice between laissez-faire and a socialist system. To put the point in ideological terms, Canada was going to be liberal. Embedding that liberalism was as radical a change as ideological parameters permitted.

The character of Canadian Keynesianism was also related to the character of the labour movement. I have noted that Keynesianism legitimates unions and high wages. Full employment, as the Polish economist Michael Kalecki argued in 1943, weakens the bargaining position of capital.[114] Labour has an interest in full employment because it strengthens labour's bargaining power. That Canada backed off the full employment goal and that the governing party was not a labour party reflected Canadian labour's relative weakness. Mackenzie King was no real friend to the working class; he was actually a hired management gun for the Rockefellers in his earlier life.[115] Canadian labour was willing to cede control of business decisions to management in exchange for free collective bargaining, and was not mobilized into the centre of the party system. Instead, labour legitimated state supervision of private bargaining. This was in contrast to the more 'social democratic' experiences in Western Europe.[116] In addition, as Stephen McBride argues, the notion that technocratic Keynesian macroeconomic management was enough to keep the economy rolling demobilized political activism.[117] If a limited state and a responsible private sector would do the job, there was little need to mobilize and organize. Canada's labour movement was strengthened in the postwar era, but it was not as strong a pro-Keynesian factor as in some other countries.

These considerations regarding political discourse, the character of the governing party, and especially underlying ideological traditions and the balance of power among social interests, together resulted in a relatively weak political commitment to full employment and Keynesianism.

The Economic Structure of an Open Resource-Based Economy
Keynes's *General Theory* was written for a closed economy. The openness and structure of the Canadian economy resulted in further constraints on Canadian Keynesianism. A component of these constraints was the relationship between Canadian economic development and American capital after the Second World War. From this point onward in our narrative, the United States, rather than Britain, is the entity to which the Canadian economy and polity are primarily oriented. Canada's postwar 'social structure of accumulation' was constituted by three components. We are already familiar with Keynesian stabilization policy and free collective bargaining. Here the third element can be introduced, 'that American capital was to be the engine of economic growth.'[118] Direct American investment in resource industries and branch plants protected by the tariff was to drive the investment portion of the aggregate demand equation. But it put economic decision making outside the country.[119] American capital would object strenuously to any infringement of its decision-making autonomy. Even if Canada had an interest in a greater socialization of investment, its dependence on US capital seriously complicated that option. Of course, had Canada been attracted to a more radical economic model in the first place, it would not have allowed itself to become so reliant on American capital. But C.D. Howe and Mackenzie King did not have much interest in more aggressive Keynesian policy or in keeping American capital out of the country. On the contrary, they encouraged it to migrate.

Another consequence of openness was that domestic demand stimulation would 'leak out' of the country to the extent it was spent on the imports that weakened Canadian aggregate demand. Canada's dependence on American capital for investment and growth also led to substantial debt-servicing payments and remittances to home offices from Canada to the United States. Again, leakage could emerge from domestic stimulus, and Canada's balance of payments with the United States was an ongoing issue. Campbell identifies the tensions in Canada's commitment to an 'open international economy.' The balance of payments left Canadian aggregate demand dependent on unstable world commodity markets because Canada had to sell its raw materials to finance manufactured imports as well as service dividends and interest payments.[120] In addition, Canada's role in the continental economy was primarily to supply natural resources. Since those resources were a matter of geographic endowment at given technology levels, pressure for regional support emerged. Jane Jenson concludes: 'Because of permeability [the openness of the Canadian economy], state strategies to alter uneven regional development, to deal with long-term structural unemployment, and to keep capital flowing into the economy to replace that which was being repatriated all supplemented Keynesianism.'[121] Bretton Woods arrangements protected domestic policy autonomy. However, the structure of Canada's open economy was an important constraint on Keynesian demand management.

The Pursuit of Non-Keynesian Policies

As Jenson's comment indicates, stabilization policy became but one strategy among several. Regional, sectoral, and supply issues also acquired some pride of place. The resulting policies were not necessarily reducible to Keynesian precepts. One regional program Ottawa developed was the Equalization program in 1957, which provided revenues to 'have not' provinces so that comparable public services could be provided to citizens across Canada at comparable tax rates. Sectoral policy usually had a regional component as well because provincial economies were very different. The 1965 Auto Pact, for example, favoured Ontario. Regional variation was to some extent not amenable to amelioration by aggregative Keynesian procedures, which in any event were designed with a close eye on Ontario.[122] Liberal Finance Minister Walter Gordon cast his gaze on regional unemployment in 1964 and argued that general demand management policy could not deal with regional problems.[123] It was also true that Keynesian procedures could not, in themselves, solve sectoral issues.

Another cause and effect of Canadian regionalism was 'province building.' This started for nationalist and modernization reasons in Quebec with the Quiet Revolution of the 1960s, and for reasons of economic autonomy regarding resources in 1970s Alberta. A strong provincial state could mitigate dependence on, and protect from exploitation by, Ottawa. While provincial governments were not much of a factor with respect to demand management in the 1940s and 1950s, they became increasingly important afterward. Some commentators argued that provinces too should play a role in countercyclical demand management.[124] Certainly provinces became more active in economic policy.[125] This, over time, complicated the federal government's previously plenary capacity regarding fiscal stabilization. Large provincial governments could at least partially offset Ottawa's fiscal actions.

On the supply side, in 1955, the new Liberal Minister of Finance, Walter Harris, argued that fiscal policy was only one instrument to be directed to stabilization and expansion. Harris claimed that monetary, trade, resources, and incomes policy were also important.[126] From the second half of the 1950s onward, the federal government increasingly employed structural supply-side, in addition to Keynesian, policies. These included measures to narrow regional economic disparities, enhance labour force skills, rationalize industries, control foreign investment levels, encourage energy self-sufficiency, and improve Canada's capacity for technological innovation.[127] Prime Minister John Diefenbaker's Progressive Conservative government introduced a second 1960 budget that focused on issues not directly resolvable by Keynesian policy. The emphasis was on productivity, efficiency, and Canada's competitive position rather than aggregate demand management.[128] In 1961 Finance Minister Donald Fleming argued that budget policy alone was insufficient. A mix of broad and specific economic and fiscal policies was needed to deal fully with economic issues.[129] In 1962, Fleming claimed that recovery from the recent economic downturn was in part due to the fiscal stimulus from deficits that expanded short-run domestic demand.[130] At the same time, he argued that more than demand expansion was needed. Skills development, modernization and diversification, developing resources, and developing domestic capital markets were also required, he said, for better economic performance.[131] There was a commitment to Keynesianism and to deficit finance after the Second World War, but the commitment was diluted by the pursuit of other policies that might actually frustrate Keynesian approaches by determining expenditures and revenues through a lens other than stabilization. With the Pearson Liberals taking office in 1963, Finance Minister Walter Gordon's 'face the facts' budget continued this focus on the supply side. But Gordon also argued that deficits had a place in combating recessions and depressions.[132]

Implementing Countercyclical Demand Management
Keynesianism in the circumscribed form I have just described maintained itself until 1975. Due to the constraints on Keynesian policy, stabilization efforts tended to be implemented relatively ineffectively. Keynesian bureaucrats dominated the Department of Finance. Policy makers were moderate or 'technocratic' Keynesians. But the academic consensus, although there is dispute at the margins, is that countercyclical demand management did not manage demand very well. Often fiscal policy was neutral or procyclical

in its effect, rather than countercyclical.[133] As Campbell also points out, most budgets were passive and accepting of circumstance, rather than endeavouring to improve economic performance. Changes in budgetary stances were usually a very small proportion of GNP.[134] The weak political commitment to Keynesianism, the structure and openness of the Canadian economy, and the pursuit of non-Keynesian goals meant governments did not do as good a job at demand management as they might otherwise have.

Conclusion

Canada's Keynesianism was grafted onto a political economy that moulded the country's reception of these new ideas. That this Keynesianism was circumscribed, though, does not imply it was insignificant. In policy terms Canada operated on somewhat different norms from those that preceded the Keynesian era. Keynesian ideas were embodied in some policy, although very imperfectly. There was also a major change in the ways the government described its fiscal position. Responsible fiscal policy entailed budgeting for the business cycle.[135] While limits on the efficacy of deficit finance were sometimes described, never was the notion that deficits offset economic slowdowns challenged. This new justification for deficit finance recognized that deficits could be inflationary at high employment levels. But there was no suggestion that deficits were necessarily inflationary. Even if deficits emerged not from planning but from error, they were rationalized after the fact in Keynesian terms. On the whole, the public life of the winning ideas about deficit finance displayed important differences from those that dominated the interwar years. It also forged higher expectations regarding the state's capacity and responsibility for economic performance.

I want to measure subsequent change against these Keynesian conceptualizations of deficit finance and the concomitant policies. Persistent, rather than countercyclical, deficits emerged in Canada in the mid-1970s. The year 1975 is also often identified as the close of the Keynesian era. Certainly, the economic conditions on which the postwar order was built began to unravel in the 1970s. But did the Trudeau government's conceptualizations of deficit finance really change in 1975? Were persistent deficits unrelated to Keynesian countercyclical budgeting? And were the policy changes in 1975 that are said to mark the end of the Keynesian era categorically different? Or were they rather applications of Keynesian and embedded liberal notions in new and difficult circumstances? In other words, did the Keynesian era just stop in 1975, or did the ideas persist in discourse and continue to work their way into policy, just as classical norms persisted through the Keynesian era? The next two chapters confront these questions.

3
The Political Economy
of Economic Decline

> Inflation can be cured by having unemployment. However, with
> this cure no Keynesian can agree: the essence of the Keynesian
> system is that it cures unemployment. One can stop the increase
> in corporate prices and trade-union wages by direct action. (I've
> long thought such action inescapable.) This does not leave the
> market system intact as Keynes, the conservative, had intended.[1]
>
> – *John Kenneth Galbraith*

Pierre Trudeau's Liberals were in a difficult position by the mid-1970s. On
the one hand were the government's political commitments to a 'just society,'[2] the Keynesian welfare state, and a Keynesian mode of regulating the
economy that was associated with impressive rates of growth over the previous thirty years. On the other hand were expectations that this growth
would continue indefinitely and the as yet unrecognized reality that a secular decline in economic performance had begun. Macroeconomic policy
was conditioned by: the profundity of a new economic situation; the difficulty in the short run of identifying economic change as structural rather
than cyclical; the increasing viability of 'monetarist' ideas about economic
policy; and the continued impact of Keynesian ideas and political commitments on rhetoric and policy. Moderate Keynesian rhetoric, and to a
lesser extent policy, were among the mechanisms by which Trudeau navi-
gated the political waters. These tools were used to position the Liberals
in relation to the other federal parties. They were also designed to curry
favour with an electorate that had developed comparatively high expectations regarding the state's capacity to ensure strong economic performance, and that therefore conceived of the state as directly responsible for
such performance. This was so even as the Liberals sought to diminish
expectations regarding the economy's potential.

As we saw in the previous chapter, it is the academic conventional wisdom that Canada's Keynesianism was equivocal. Political economists and
political scientists are also generally of the view that what life Canadian
Keynesianism had was extinguished in 1975.[3] Three relevant policies –
wage and price controls, the Bank of Canada's 'monetary gradualism,' and
the restriction of growth in federal spending to no more than trend
growth in Gross National Product – were introduced in that year. Wage
and price controls marked the end of the Keynesian consensus to the

extent Keynesianism had been confined to the management of macroeconomic aggregates. With controls, the government was directly interfering with traditionally private micro-level decisions. Monetary gradualism was designed to gradually reduce the growth rates of Canada's money supply. Since growth rates would be lowered annually without regard to immediate economic conditions, gradualism was inconsistent with Keynesian countercyclical monetary policy. Limiting growth in spending to trend growth in the economy fettered the government's expenditure capacity to implement countercyclical fiscal policy. At a more general level, analysts present these three policies as instantiating changes in kind rather than degree. Commentators associate these policies with inflation taking pride of place over unemployment as the government's first object of concern.

These changes clearly marked an important disjuncture. They were the beginning of a long process that culminated in the retrenchment of the 1990s. These policies also need to be revisited in light of subsequent events. From the point of view of the 1970s and 1980s, the elements of change in the mid-1970s policies were of primary visibility. Analysts writing in the mid-1980s did not have the benefit of analyzing the 1975 policies through a lens coloured by more recent experiences. For example, the Bank of Canada's 'price stability' policy in the late 1980s was a far harsher approach to inflation control than anything introduced in 1975. Balancing the budget in the late 1990s entailed far deeper retrenchment than anything contemplated in 1975. Given that Canadian politics subsequently engaged in measures even further removed from Keynesianism, I am concerned with explaining what can now be understood as the relative moderation of what occurred in the mid-1970s. My enterprise is to complete our understanding of the mid-1970s changes by demonstrating that elements of the Keynesian paradigm persisted in precisely the mid-1970s policies that brought the Keynesian era to its formal end. Rather than making fighting inflation the priority over combating unemployment, Ottawa was trying to *avoid* choosing between these goals. The reports of the birth of Canadian Keynesianism were exaggerated; so were the reports of its death.

Economic Decline

The success of Keynesianism after the Second World War was premised in part on the postwar boom which resulted in impressive economic performance under the auspices of a Keynesian mode of regulating the economy. The economic conditions underpinning Keynesianism unravelled in the 1970s with the onset of an economic decline that left no major industrial country unscathed. The year of the first oil price shock, 1973, was a watershed in terms of economic performance.[4] The most conspicuous manifestation of worsening performance was 'stagflation.' This term refers to the coexistence of high inflation and high unemployment.[5] Other factors, sometimes less obvious but no less important, were causes and effects of stagflation. Chief among these were the two Organization of Petroleum Exporting Countries (OPEC) oil price shocks (1973 and 1979); a substantial rise in food prices; declining rates of productivity growth; high wage increases; a corporate profitability crisis; competition in some industries from newly industrializing economies; precipitous increases in interest rates in the late 1970s and early 1980s; expansionary macroeconomic policy in the late 1960s and early 1970s; and American decisions, particularly the 15 August 1971 'Nixon shock' which entailed the United States removing the greenback from the gold standard and instituting a 10 percent surcharge on imports into the United States, reflecting that country's declining relative position.[6] International economic decline normalized by the mid-1980s and, to some extent, eased. But many of its components, particularly historically high unemployment and low productivity growth, endured. The early 1970s to the mid-1980s constituted the most confounding circumstance in the international political economy for the major industrial countries since the Great Depression. The G-7 countries all suffered.[7] Some did better than others. Germany and Japan fared relatively well. Economic decline transcended Canada, but was expressed in Canada in particular ways.

The most obvious evidence of economic decline is found in the standard macroeconomic indicators. The G-7 countries, on average, experienced major setbacks in all important variables. Growth in real GNE/GDP in these countries averaged 5.4 percent from 1966 to 1973, but this fell to 2.7 percent from 1974 to 1978, and to 1.1 percent from 1979 to 1982. Canadian growth was very close to these averages. The mean unemployment rate across the G-7 during these time frames rose from 3.4 percent to 5.5 percent to 6.6 percent. Canada fared particularly poorly with respect to unemployment. Canada's unemployment rate exceeded these averages by 1.4 to 1.8 percent. In 1982, Canadian unemployment reached 11 percent. Consumer price inflation in the G-7 averaged 4.7 percent from 1966 to 1973, 9.5 percent from 1974 to 1978, and 9.6 percent from 1979 to 1982. Canada marginally outperformed these trends in the first two time periods, and did marginally worse in the third. Stagflation ruled the day. Finally, G-7 productivity growth fell from 3.9 percent to 1.5 percent to 0.9 percent during these time frames. Canada did worse in each period, with average productivity growth of 2.5 percent, 0.6 percent, and -1.1 percent, respectively.[8] Whether a worsening in absolute terms or a lowering of rates of growth, these broad variables are the numerical face of a secular decline in economic performance.

Unemployment that was very high by postwar standards was problem enough in the 1970s. High unemployment in concert with high inflation (added together, American presidential candidate Jimmy Carter called the sum the 'misery index' in 1976) made for confounding and increasingly unpleasant stagflationary economic conditions. Inflation worries in Canada increased in the late 1960s, a fact reflected in the creation of a Prices and Incomes Commission in 1969. But inflation obtained a new salience around 1973, and remained a central concern of policy makers for about a decade.

Policy Paradigms and Recognizing Economic Decline

Issue Identification and Competing Policy Paradigms
In themselves, the numbers that quantified economic decline and the 'reality' that it constituted did not generate policy conclusions or political outcomes. Canada's 7.2 percent average unemployment rate from 1974 to 1978 was portrayed as a major problem by the Liberal government of the day; when Canada's unemployment figure reached 6.9 percent in the fall of 1999, its lowest level in eighteen years, a different Liberal government shouted its triumph from every pulpit in the land. Economic decline acquired its meaning through a process of political interpretation.

My reading of the public documents Ottawa produced in the mid- and late 1970s is that symptoms of economic decline were very salient to the government. Both discrete and coordinated responses were issued. But these symptoms were not conceptualized as reflections of an underlying disease during the 1970s. The secular downshift in economic performance was not immediately recognized as such. It took time to understand that the world had changed. What was once bad performance was perhaps 'bad' only in light of now unrealistic expectations. One reason for the lag between changing circumstances and changing understandings is that it takes several years of consistent data to establish that a change is permanent.

Interviews with senior officials who worked in the Department of Finance in the 1970s confirm this reading. The two oil price shocks were identified by these officials as playing a crucial role in the interpretation of economic decline. Policy makers expected the second oil shock to be permanent.[9] Ottawa's response to the second shock, 1980's National Energy Program, was a structural answer to what was seen as an enduring change. However, the first oil price shock was viewed as temporary. It was thought within the department that oil prices would not hold because the OPEC cartel was expected to break.[10] Structural solutions therefore seemed inappropriate. Countercyclical answers still appeared sufficient. In addition, the first oil shock's impact was probably underestimated. The Organization for Economic Cooperation and Development (OECD) analyzed its impact primarily on the demand side, in the recollection of one former official. But supply consequences were also important.[11] To the extent the first shock's impact was underestimated, the depth of what would be viewed as appropriate policy responses was circumscribed. Finally, the first shock was so salient it either disguised, or was treated as the cause of, the other constituents of economic decline. The depth of the shock's impact may have been underestimated. But to the extent that economic under-performance was recognized, the shock was seen as the origin of most evil. If the shock was handled properly, things would be fine.[12]

What role could ideas about the economy and the state's role therein play in such circumstances as those found in the mid-1970s? Judith Gold-stein and Robert Keohane argue that ideas can determine outcomes in a number of situations. These circumstances include moments of uncer-tainty that allow ideas to serve as road maps. Ideas can also contribute to results in the absence of a unique equilibrium outcome and objective cri-teria on which to base choice. Finally, the embedding of ideas in institu-tions can permit ideas to specify policy without other innovation.[13] Each of these conditions obtained to some degree in 1970s Canada. The status of the economy was uncertain; there was neither a clearly attainable opti-mal outcome nor obvious 'objective' criteria on which to make decisions; and contradictory sets of ideas were informing the Department of Finance and the Liberal government. Though ideas can shape outcomes in these circumstances, it does not follow that only one set of ideas will matter. This is particularly so at a time of dislocation when multiple policy para-digms are in play. As Neil Bradford argues, from 1973 to 1980 'the govern-ing paradigm was in crisis, but no alternative had yet been formulated, much less embedded.'[14] The technocratic or optimistic Keynesianism of the postwar years still had some pride of place; but post-Keynesian[15] and monetarist[16] ideas were challenging this once dominant approach. The resulting ad hocery reflected the political inability of one paradigm to dominate the others. In this sense, while the mid-1970s mark a break from the Keynesian paradigm, that paradigm still offered some solace as a road map in the face of uncertainty, as an answer to objective situations that did not speak for themselves, and insofar as it remained embedded in the Department of Finance, the Prime Minister's Office, and the Privy Council Office. Other sets of ideas performed these functions as well. The mix was not coherent. This was in part precisely because Keynesian notions con-tinued to matter after the Keynesian era came to its formal end. Nowhere was the tension between simultaneously competing paradigms more evi-dent than in Ottawa's conceptualization of the relationships between infla-tion and unemployment, which informed the wage and price controls, the monetary gradualism, and the expenditure restraint said to mark the death of the Keynesian paradigm.

Inflation and Unemployment

Ottawa's conceptualization of the relationships between inflation and unemployment had economic, technical, and political components. In economic terms the federal government's view was an interesting hybrid. The Phillips Curve tradeoff associated with Keynesianism was presented as the short-run determinant of inflation and unemployment levels. The monetarist position that there is no tradeoff between inflation and unemployment in the long run was also accepted by Finance. Ottawa's effort to square the circle between Keynesian and monetarist economics goes a long way to explaining the 1975 policy changes. In technical terms, officials were relatively confident of their ability to manage macroeconomic aggregates in the short run. Finally, in political terms, to the extent the Liberal government conceptualized inflation and unemployment as a tradeoff, it was not willing to sacrifice employment on the altar of an attack on inflation. The Liberals were also concerned that inflation fires should not be further stoked, and this concern functioned to limit the aggression of Ottawa's demand-based employment measures. But the primary political commitment at least not to worsen unemployment gave the Liberals an anchor with the electorate and circumscribed the range of anti-inflation policies the government would consider viable.

Economic Theory

As we saw in the previous chapter, the Phillips Curve understanding of the relationships between unemployment and inflation is that the variables are inversely correlated. If the one is high, the other would be relatively low. In a 1978 paper that rationalized the policies of the immediately preceding years, the Department of Finance repudiated the view 'commonly' held in the 1960s that the tradeoff was permanent, but did accept that inflation and unemployment were tradeoffs in the short term.[17] This distinction between time frames meant that the short-run Phillips Curve tradeoff had to coexist with the department's acceptance of the monetarist position that in the long run inflation is exclusively a monetary phenomenon. The monetarist view, as Finance described it, is that in the long run lower inflation requires lower money growth. Real growth in the long run is independent of the money supply. Finance agreed that there is a Non-Accelerating Inflation Rate of Unemployment (the NAIRU).[18] At any rate of inflation, unemployment below the NAIRU level would cause inflation not only to rise but also to rise at accelerating rates. The use of monetary or fiscal policy to force inflation below the NAIRU would, over time, accelerate inflation without any real (that is, employment and growth) benefits.[19]

The NAIRU had won the public mind of Finance where the long run was concerned. The Phillips Curve approach was read down to apply only to shorter time frames. This meant that the Phillips Curve tradeoff was not permanent. In the long haul, argued Finance, inflation depended on the money supply and concomitant inflation expectations. Therefore, the levels at which inflation and unemployment were traded off could change over time. Put differently, the Phillips Curve could shift up or down the Y axis (see Figure 1, p. 35). If it shifted up, the tradeoff would take place at higher levels of inflation for each level of unemployment. If it shifted down, the tradeoff would take place at lower inflation rates. Finance was of the view that the tradeoff had shifted upward since the mid-1960s.[20] At each unemployment rate, a higher level of inflation was expected than in happier times. The tradeoff was neither unique nor stable because inflation expectations were a shift parameter of the Phillips Curve. Finance argued that inflation expectations were an important theory refinement because expectations explained wage and salary demands, which in turn had a lot to do with inflation rates. If workers expected inflation to rise, they would demand more money to maintain their real wages. If firms expected price increases, they could cover the inflated wages and salaries.[21] The implication of it all was that if the government could lower inflation expectations, *inflation would fall without any employment costs.* The Phillips Curve could be shifted downward so inflation would be lower for any given level of unemployment. Since inflation was not presented as related to unemployment in the long run, low inflation with low unemployment was not a chimera. The zero-sum game between inflation and unemployment did not have to be played. This is the long-run monetarist pot of gold.

But because Finance had not jettisoned the view that there was a tradeoff in the short run, it was still thought that contractionary efforts to lower inflation and inflation expectations would increase unemployment. The monetarist pot of gold was at the end of a murky Keynesian rainbow. Demand contraction would have both nominal and real effects in the short run. The precise share of the demand pie that would be eaten by each of inflation reduction and unemployment was an empirical question over which economists disagreed,[22] and which depended on the shape of the Phillips Curve and the economy's position along it.[23] The Finance position – that in the short run demand management could have both nominal and real effects – implied that deficit finance still had a role under certain conditions. Fiscal stimulus could increase short-run employment to the extent it had a real impact. Similarly, fiscal contraction could reduce short-run employment.

To understand the policy changes of the mid-1970s, it is crucial to understand the development in economic theory of inflation expectations and the concomitant 'expectations adjusted' or 'augmented' or 'extended' Phillips Curves, for they provided the economic logic behind policy design.[24] The way the government would see itself out of its conundrum was not to try to lower inflation through contractionary policy. Such a policy would also lower growth and increase unemployment by shifting the economy's position along a given Phillips Curve. This was deemed unacceptable. Instead, Ottawa would try, through wage and price controls, monetary gradualism, and spending restraint, to reduce inflation expectations in a more gentle fashion. It was thought that reducing inflation expectations would shift down the Phillips Curve, resulting in lower inflation for a given level of unemployment.

Technical Capacity

Short-term policy mattered more in the 1970s than it did in the 1990s. In addition to the continuing basis in economic theory for concern about the short run, another reason aggregate demand management still seemed feasible in the 1970s was that it was believed to be technically possible. Short-term manipulation makes economic sense only if policy makers have both reliable forecasts and proper measures of the lags between policy actions and their effects. There were few 'literal fine tuners' among practical policy advisers in the 1960s. Developments in the 1970s and 1980s raised further concerns regarding practical constraints on the role of fiscal policy.[25] Nonetheless (as we saw in the previous chapter), in the late 1960s and early 1970s finance ministers defended their capacity to fine-tune the economy. In addition, impressive postwar economic results created high expectations regarding the possibilities for economic management. In the end, this optimism would be destroyed by perceptions of ineffective economic policy.[26] But in the 1970s government economists were still relatively confident about these issues.[27] Their sense of technical competence implied that policy makers believed changes in inflation and unemployment could be controlled in the short run.

Political Commitments

The short term also continued to matter in the 1970s because of the Liberal government's political commitment not to ignore the real short-term consequences of economic policy. By 1974 growth was strong but elements of economic decline were seeping into the Canadian economy. The salience of inflation in both the government's rhetoric and policy focus increased. But the existence of inflation was not taken to justify highly contractionary policy that would increase unemployment. The major aim of the first 1974 budget was inflation reduction. Yet Finance Minister John Turner insisted that he would not use severe monetary and fiscal policies to combat inflation. The result, he said, would be stagnation and unemployment. The cure would be worse than the disease.[28] This budget was designed by a minority government that sought its own defeat for better fortunes in a forthcoming election. The NDP held the balance of power, and criticized the government for doing nothing to help people with low incomes.[29] The Progressive Conservatives hammered the Liberals for being too timid in battling inflation because they would not introduce wage and price controls.[30] The Liberals were content to triangulate themselves between parties that would have the government fund potentially inflationary enrichments to social assistance, or control private decisions, respectively. They also wanted to be able to argue that the other parties were voting against taxes on fat-cat oil companies.[31] Aided by the NDP's attack on Stanfield's proposed controls, Trudeau was re-elected with a majority government.

In the midst of a recession in 1975, in his final budget, Turner argued that he had to strike a delicate balance. Dealing with inflation, unemployment, and energy was problematic because solving one problem could exacerbate the others. Parroting the Phillips Curve tradeoff, Turner said that expansionary policy risked creating inflation, but that contraction risked unemployment.[32] Handling the inflation problem without hurting immediate employment prospects was, Turner said, at the heart of his budget.[33] The Liberals' political stance with respect to short-run employment was more than a function of seeking to protect their immediate electoral flanks. It was manifest in an early budget of a majority government. As in 1974, Turner rejected 'categorically' the deliberate creation, through severe monetary and fiscal restraint, of whatever level of unemployment was required to arrest inflation.[34] The costs, said Turner, would be too high. He argued that in social terms, Canadian society's hard won sense of security would be replaced by fear and anxiety. In economic terms the cost in lost output and declining living standards would be unacceptable; in human terms, such a policy would be 'unthinkable.'[35] A former senior official confirms that within the department it was thought that severe restraint not only would be too harsh but also could inflict considerable harm on the economic process.[36] Turner settled instead on using the government's powers over taxation and spending in an effort to create a climate and set an example by which the country could meet the interrelated challenges it faced. Turner claimed it was essential that the government restrain its own spending. Business and labour, he said, had told the Liberals that if Ottawa wanted restraint from the country it would have to restrain itself.[37] He said 'by giving a lead to others in the exercise of restraint, this strategy will help to break inflation expectations and get inflation under control.'[38]

Turner's budgets were viewed at the time, and properly so, as primarily focused on inflation. Less noticed was the refusal, based on Keynesian political commitments and the Phillips Curve, to let inflation concerns excuse higher unemployment in the short run. Technical virtuosity, political commitment, and economic theory together meant that recession would not be a tool of economic policy. These factors, along with intractable inflation, would also drive the Liberals to introduce wage and price controls.

Three Policies

Recall from Chapter 1 Peter Hall's concept of orders of policy change. This concept holds that first-order policy change entails changing the settings of policy instruments, second-order policy change alters the instruments themselves, and third-order policy change embodies the overthrow of the hierarchy of goals behind policy. Hall associates third-order change away from a Keynesian to a monetarist 'policy paradigm' with the replacement of employment by inflation as the overriding goal of policy because Keynesianism's basic normative commitment is to employment rather than inflation. Understanding the mid-1970s policies said to mark the end of the Keynesian era in Canada through this concept will help to elucidate further the claim that these policies were not simply a break from, but were also informed by, the persistence of the Keynesian paradigm.

My argument is that both wage and price controls and expenditure restraint were in the nature of second-order policy change. Monetary gradualism participated to a greater degree in the kinds of changes associated with third-order change than the other two policies. Yet it was insufficient both in its internal construction and its impact on other policy fields to amount to an overthrow of priorities. Certainly, these new non-Keynesian policy instruments were introduced to cope with a newly intractable inflation problem. There was some encroachment on the priority of employment over inflation. Due to its inflation worries, the government made perhaps even less effort than in the postwar era to decrease unemployment. But inflation worries certainly did not simply trump the paradigmatic Keynesian concern with short-run employment, and the choice of instruments reflected the endurance of the commitment to protect short-term employment levels. The new focus on inflation reflected change in circumstance under a given paradigm as much as change in the paradigm itself. The government did not take the view that, in principle, inflation should be fought above all else. Rather, the position was that inflation had become a major problem that had to be confronted, but confronted in terms amenable to extant employment commitments.

The adoption of the monetarist position on inflation in the long run marked the beginning of the end of the Keynesian paradigm in Canada. The 1975 policies were not Keynesian policies in any strict sense. But the persistence of the government's employment commitments in light of the short-run Phillips Curve tradeoff indicates that the Keynesian paradigm was not simply overthrown in the mid-1970s. The essence of the Canadian turn to fiscal restraint is captured by the relative hold that views regarding inflation and employment, the long run and the short run, and the supply side and the demand side have had on the government of Canada. In the mid-1970s, the Keynesian paradigm was not the only paradigm that mattered, but it did still matter.

Wage and Price Controls

In his June 1975 budget John Turner rejected wage and price controls, although he claimed to have seriously considered the option. Turner argued that controls would be worth the problems they would cause if the result was lower inflation without higher unemployment. But he also claimed to be of the view that controls would work only if there was widespread public support. This, in turn, would require widespread conviction that such action was necessary. Turner stated that the country was not yet at that point.[39] Nonetheless, following Pierre Trudeau's television and radio address the night before, a new finance minister, Donald Macdonald, introduced wage and price controls under the auspices of an Anti-Inflation Program (AIP) on 14 October 1975. Macdonald's announcement of controls located the AIP with rhetoric that was foursquare in the Keynesian tradition. His language was redolent of the 1945 White Paper which set out the structure of Canada's postwar Keynesianism. Macdonald stated at the outset that the goal of price stability was to be seen as part and parcel of the government's *continuing* commitment to high and stable levels of employment and real incomes.[40] He also reminded Canadians that the government had rejected severe monetary and fiscal restraint as instruments in an anti-inflation policy due to the heavy immediate costs in unemployment and output.[41] The finance minister identified the inflation problem as one of expectations: current inflation was leading to expectations of further inflation and defensive self-protective responses. Self-protection only ensured that the feared inflation would emerge.[42] The solution to the problem was wage and price controls. The Liberals turned to controls because they held out the promise of lowering inflation expectations and therefore inflation for a given level of unemployment. This was not a Keynesian policy instrument, but it was deeply informed by Keynesian commitments. Controls were *post*-Keynesian because, in setting growth rates for wages and prices, the policy broke the postwar consensus that Ottawa would confine itself to the management of macroeconomic aggregates and defer to private decision making. But in their concern for protecting short-run employment levels, controls displayed continuity with Turner's 1974 and 1975 budgets, and with traditional Keynesian commitments. Incomes policies were the definitive policy recommendation of post-*Keynesianism*.[43]

The politics and economics of controls were distinct but related issues. The idea of controls had been propounded by the expatriate Canadian economist John Kenneth Galbraith in his noted 1973 book *Economics and the Public Purpose*.[44] The book influenced Pierre Trudeau, although the AIP fell well short of the kind of state planning Galbraith envisioned.[45] Turner, in fact, thought of his job as finance minister to consist partially of trying to 'de-Galbraith' the prime minister.[46] The wage and price control scheme actually emerged more from Trudeau's offices than the Department of Finance. Macdonald was able to introduce the policy shortly after taking on his new job because the program was not ministerially driven. Rather, 'much of the anti-inflation initiatives ... came from Mr. Trudeau's closest advisors in the Prime Minister's Office and the Privy Council Office.'[47] In addition, most of the details of the AIP were worked out by Finance officials without ministerial guidance.[48] Turner's objection to controls was that he did not believe in economic policy imposed by state fiat. Being the man to introduce a program so invasive to private decisions probably also seemed unwise to somebody with eyes on 24 Sussex. Certainly, there was fallout from the AIP. Even though the program was planned to end automatically at the end of 1978,[49] its politicization of the economic sphere was the immediate impetus behind the formation of the Business Council on National Issues.[50] Labour vociferously opposed the program. But the policy was more than a Liberal flight of fancy.

The idea of political control of inflation was not controversial by 1968; both the Tories and NDP then favoured either guidelines or controls.[51] The toothless Prices and Incomes Commission was formed in 1969 to encourage voluntary restraint. The Commission was mocked by Progressive Conservative leader Robert Stanfield, who claimed that its creation was 'ridiculously inadequate' to deal with inflation.[52] Trudeau used Stanfield's advocacy of hard controls to great effect in the 1974 election. Trudeau's critique of controls, distilled into his famous line 'zap, you're frozen,' contributed to the Liberal victory.[53] Trudeau's cynical appropriation of Stanfield's idea, and Stanfield's claim that he felt vindicated by the introduction of the AIP,[54] indicated, however, that controls were a mainstream notion. In light of tremendous public concern regarding inflation, public support for wage and price controls was actually quite high in 1974-5 and 1975-6. Along with expenditure restraint it was the most popular anti-inflation strategy.[55] The *Globe and Mail* critique of the AIP was based on the view it might not go far enough![56] Provinces were generally supportive, although Trudeau would use the AIP to try to expand federal powers. He referred the AIP legislation to the Supreme Court of Canada for a decision on its constitutionality six months after it came into force.[57] The Court upheld the legislation in part under the emergency doctrine. This was one more indication of how deep inflation worries had become.

Nonetheless, the acceptance of a controls approach also reflected the short-term commitment to protect employment levels. Campbell writes that the Keynesian synthesis weakened the economic discipline of the market by extending into the latter democratic politics. 'That [the claims of the working class] weakened [the ingredients and ideology of capitalism] has been evident, as the post-war years were marked by growing economic aspirations, the implications of which were that any significant costs to the working class (economic and social insecurity) in the continued existence of capitalism were simply unacceptable, while increasing benefits were in order.'[58] As Campbell argues, controls were, in part, designed to restrain these working class demands, which had an inflationary bias.[59] However, controls also permitted the exercise of this discipline in such a way that if everybody was restrained, the real value of working class wages would not decline. Controls required restraint of prices and wages; but not of the expectations for living standards that Keynesianism legitimated, even in the short run. In the end, though, controls were more effective in restraining wages than prices.[60] Distributional concerns made such programs even less appealing to labour.

Why did the Liberals introduce wage and price controls when the policy entailed such cumbersome and nontraditional bureaucratic mechanisms? In political terms, controls must be understood in the context of the Trudeau Liberals' refusal to worsen short-term employment levels to attain lower rates of inflation, even given the intractability and increasing salience of the inflation issue. The postwar Keynesian commitment to high levels of employment and income, which entailed protecting against short-run (cyclical) downturns, held at least to the extent that the government continued through controls to resist decline in incomes and employment. In economic terms controls have to be understood as a way of getting around the pitfalls of the perceived short-term tradeoff between inflation and unemployment. Controls were designed to lower inflation while protecting short-run employment by reducing inflation expectations. As one former senior official argues, there was an internal logic that made sense of the policy.[61] Controls were an effort to shift the Phillips Curve downward. For a given level of unemployment, it was hoped inflation would be lower. Another former senior official says that the AIP was seen as taking the 'high road' against inflation. Tightening the fiscal screws would have been to take the 'low road.'[62] Recession was viewed as a supine instrument for fighting inflation. That the AIP was preferred to drastic spending cuts and deficit reduction indicates how controls were seen as compatible with the mostly passive recessionary deficit in 1975, which was intended, if not to promote employment, at least to prevent it from falling further.

This is not the conventional conclusion in Canadian political science and political economy. Those who emphasize the very real disjuncture between postwar Keynesianism and the world of controls focus on the 'post' rather than the 'Keynesian' aspect of controls. But much of the political commitments and economic visions regarding controls and deficit finance were the same. To complete our understanding of the AIP, we must account for not only the changes but also the continuities that informed its adoption. It is true that the federal government's traditional refusal to intervene in micro-level decisions fell by the wayside. This is precisely because the Keynesian priority of maintaining short-term employment did not erode even in a context of seemingly runaway inflation. Ottawa would not use recession as a way to reduce inflation. Since the only way the government could see itself out of the problem was by lowering inflation expectations through a system of controls, the 'post' price of 'Keynesian' commitments was a price that Ottawa was willing to pay. Peter Hall describes the adoption of incomes policies in Britain in 1972-3 and 1975-7 as part of the process that 'ate away' the authority of the government and the Keynesian paradigm.[63] Such was the case in Canada as well.

But Hall's characterization implies that incomes policy had at least some relationship to the Keynesian paradigm. Authors writing about these issues in 1970s Britain and the United States have noted not only the inconsistency of controls with the Keynesian formula but also the linkage between controls and the Keynesian paradigm. The Galbraith epigraph with which this chapter begins is one example, but there are others.[64] The linkage between Keynesian approaches and controls has not been adequately captured in Canadian political science scholarship regarding controls. Wage and price controls constituted a second-order change. They were not a Keynesian policy instrument. But controls did not embody third-order policy change because prioritizing inflation over unemployment was antithetical to the very reasons controls were introduced. At most, it can be argued that since controls did not seek to promote employment (but rather protected against further unemployment), there was some erosion of these Keynesian allegiances. But that falls short of inflation overthrowing unemployment in the pantheon of the government's concerns.

Interestingly, two days after the AIP was introduced, it was reported that a Montreal lawyer named Brian Mulroney would contest the Progressive Conservative leadership Robert Stanfield was vacating.[65]

Spending Restraint
Another policy said to mark the end of the Keynesian era was the expenditure restraint attached to the AIP. John Turner had called for reductions in planned expenditures of about $1 billion in his 1975 budget.[66] In announcing the AIP, Macdonald stated, 'The federal government shares the view that the trend of total spending by all governments in Canada

should not rise more quickly than the trend of the gross national product.'[67] In 1976 he recommitted the government to this goal.[68] Of course, Macdonald could not directly enforce this goal for provinces or municipalities, but Ottawa could bind itself. The argument that this policy was another nail in the Keynesian coffin resides in the limitations formal spending restraint imposed on Ottawa's autonomy to run countercyclical deficits. But this reading is too simple.

Ottawa did basically meet this spending target through to 1982. All the while, it was running (structural) deficits. The policy was explicitly justified as compatible with fiscal stabilization measures. Macdonald said that the goal of keeping the trend in federal spending beneath the trend in GNP allowed for spending increases in excess of actual GNP growth in a down economic year.[69] When the economy underperformed, GNP growth would be beneath the trend. Spending could go as high as trend growth in GNP, and therefore exceed actual GNP growth in that year. The extent to which spending could be employed as a stimulative measure was certainly circumscribed, but this function of federal spending was by no means eliminated. Expenditure restraint implied changes in expenditure settings, and so entailed first-order change. It was arguably a second-order change as well. Expenditure restraint altered the character of the expenditure instrument by placing rule-based bounds on its settings. But it did not rise to the level of third-order change because it did not embody a simple reversal of government priorities.

It also has to be pointed out that none of this restraint restricted the use of tax reductions as a countercyclical stimulative measure. In fact, tax expenditures were the primary means in the late 1970s by which the government pumped money into the economy, although, as we will discuss in the next chapter, these tax expenditures were for the most part not countercyclical in character. Spending restraint over time did not extinguish the fiscal dimension of Keynesianism. The deficit instrument was not removed from Ottawa's policy tool kit; rather, it was defended. This conclusion is buttressed by Macdonald's statement that 'the primary means of reducing unemployment due to periods of slow growth lies in the maintenance of adequate overall demand.'[70]

Monetary Gradualism

Not only were wage and price controls introduced in October 1975 – the Bank of Canada announced a new policy of 'monetary gradualism' that same month. The policy was designed to gradually lower the growth rates of the money supply as measured by the monetary aggregate 'M1' (currency plus demand deposits). The policy was premised on the monetarist precept that in the long run all inflation is a monetary phenomenon. Over time, as growth in the money supply fell, so too should inflation rates. In principle, monetarism and Keynesianism are sworn enemies. Certainly Keynesianism has less in common with monetarism than it does with post-Keynesianism, in part because post-Keynesians support countercyclical demand management and cognate monetary policy.[71] Some Keynesian and post-Keynesian economists were much more comfortable with wage and price controls than with monetary gradualism.[72] They were very critical of the bank's policy, arguing that it resulted in excessive domestic interest rates and an overvalued Canadian dollar, which in turn decreased growth and employment.[73] They saw it as harsh rather than gradual.[74] In retrospect, though, the policy and rhetorical boundaries between monetary gradualism and persisting Keynesian commitments are not quite so clear. Like the AIP, monetary gradualism did mark a break from postwar Keynesianism. But those who emphasize the difference focus on the 'monetary' rather than the 'gradualism' part of the policy. Harsh it may have been in recent historical perspective, but subsequent events would show that monetary policy could be much less gradual. In its 'gradualism,' the policy shared more with Ottawa's Keynesian and post-Keynesian rhetoric and policy than is generally recognized. In part, monetary gradualism was a long-term complement to wage and price controls.

The conventional wisdom is that the bank's move to gradualism marked a disjuncture from Keynesianism not only because it interpreted inflation as strictly monetary. Since money growth would slowly decline regardless of economic conditions, the federal government's ability to fine-tune the economy was circumscribed. No longer could discretionary monetary policy accommodate immediate growth and employment concerns. Further, the policy emerged from the Bank of Canada. Finance did not have control of all the macroeconomic policy tools.[75] Finally, monetary gradualism was an early instance of the move to neo-liberalism. According to André Drainville, it was an effort 'to establish the credibility of its policy discourse and to discipline social relations. Thus, in the gradualist period, the meaningful control of monetary aggregates was less central to the policy of the Bank of Canada than the credibility of its public gestures, which were meant to signify that the Keynesian underwriting of private credit extension was over.'[76] These arguments are true as far as they go. I have no quarrel with the point that discretionary countercyclical monetary policy was at least in principle no longer available, nor with the view that gradualism participated in early efforts at neo-liberal discipline. However, more needs to be said.

With respect to institutional coordination, interviews indicate that there was not much of a schism between the Bank of Canada and the Department of Finance. Although memories are not always firm on this question, finance officials, who were on balance comfortable with both Keynesian demand management and post-Keynesian controls, do not appear to have been troubled by the bank's policy. They were very concerned with inflation, and gradualism was not seen as a harsh contraction. It was viewed as an intermediate road to inflation control consistent with other fiscal goals, including maintaining employment. To the extent there were doubts, they were mitigated by the 'pretty impressive' research and evidence that the bank marshalled for the policy.[77] Gradualism was also firmly supported by Finance Minister Donald Macdonald in his 1976 budget speech.[78]

Finance and the bank spoke with one voice, and it continued to be the voice of a fight on inflation that would protect employment. Gerald Bouey, the bank's governor, explicitly defended a gradual as opposed to a sharp contraction in money growth in 1975. He argued that the latter approach would seriously harm the economy in terms of output and jobs.[79] That is, the Phillips Curve and its accompanying commitments circumscribed the depth of monetary restraint. Instead, he sought to reduce inflation expectations, which would shift the Phillips Curve down.[80] Reflective of the bounds that gradualist commitments imposed on monetarism, in 1980 Bouey spoke of his retrospective regret that the slowing of money supply growth had been too gradual to have a greater impact on inflation.[81] Monetary policy lost its gradualist elements in 1979 and 1980, and a deep recession ensued. Even if the bank's critics were right that monetary gradualism weakened the real economy, without the policy's gradualism things could have been, and did become, a lot worse. Indeed, a cross-national study characterizes Canadian monetary policy from 1974 to 1979 as moderately expansionary in view of high unemployment.[82] In part, this was a result not of design but of the fact gradualism did not work. New financial instruments shifted money out of M1, which made it a less relevant measure of money in circulation.[83] But the moderate character of Canada's monetary restraint also had to do with how gradual a decline in M1 growth rates was planned. Even at its most ambitious level (set in 1981), the commitment, sometimes described as 'drastic,' was to reduce M1 growth from 10 to 15 percent in 1975 to 4 to 8 percent in 1982.[84] This was a reduction of about 1 percent annually, and the reduction was not to be absolute, but rather in rates of growth. In 1975, Bouey also argued that moderation in fiscal and monetary policy was appropriately supplemented by effective price and income restraints.[85] Monetary gradualism was presented as consistent with the orientation of the Department of Finance, with controls, and with the government's overall program and goals. All of these approaches were directed at reducing inflation without doing harm to employment and growth, particularly in the short run.

Monetary gradualism was at its core a monetarist rather than a Keynesian policy instrument. But insofar as it was gradualist, the policy was still informed by Keynesian norms and values. Having as they did in common the aim of protecting against economic dislocation, the norms of embedded liberalism informed not only controls but also gradualism. André Drainville is one analyst who argues that monetary gradualism was part of a movement toward globally defined monetary discipline. He also notes that global monetarism proscribed a world-wide monetarist 'shock treatment' that could threaten the stability of the world economy. This, argues Drainville, 'astutely recognized the boundaries of political possibilities.'[86] To my thinking, such recognition confirms what I have been arguing. Persisting Keynesian and embedded liberal norms circumscribed the depth of monetarist monetary policy directed against inflation. These notions informed politics and were operative in the policies that marked the nominal end of the Keynesian era. Third-order change in the paradigm was far from complete.

The break from monetary policy at least somewhat informed by Keynesian commitments really came in the late 1970s. Gradualism was not formally abandoned until 1982. But through higher interest rates and in violation of monetarist principle,[87] monetary policy became more severe in 1978 to support the Canadian dollar. It became harsher still after the American Federal Reserve's October 1979 'cold bath' monetary contraction, led by the Reserve's Chairman, Paul Volcker.[88] Other countries, including Canada, judged themselves compelled to follow suit. Canadian interest rates accompanied those in the United States in shooting skyward. Had they not, the fear was that the interest rate differential would have resulted in capital outflows to the United States. The Canadian dollar would have suffered what was deemed an unacceptable depreciation relative to the greenback.[89] The bank argued that a currency depreciation would result in even higher inflation.[90]

While monetary policy during the late 1970s and early 1980s was in no sense Keynesian, neither was it particularly monetarist or gradualist. The Bank of Canada was abruptly responding to short-run interest rate, exchange rate, and balance of payment concerns. These moves made a mockery of targeting money supply growth. Policy was directed not at long-term growth rates of the money supply, but toward American interest rates which were out of line with any economic fundamentals.[91] These rates strongly contributed to, although did not fully explain, the Bank of Canada's stance.[92] The budgetary concern with higher interest rates was that they increased debt-servicing payments and undermined fiscal control.[93] Indeed, Rudiger Dornbusch and Mario Draghi argue there are three reasons almost all countries had higher debt-to-GDP ratios at the end of the 1980s than at the beginning. In addition to low economic growth compared with previous decades and time lags before governments ran operating surpluses to cover debt interest payments, they identify higher real interest rates flowing from tight American monetary policy, which generated similarly tight policies elsewhere.[94] High interest rates were a very hot political issue at the time. There were always political points to be made by criticizing the Bank of Canada. Nonetheless, in 1980 Finance Minister Allan MacEachen endorsed the bank's policy for not accommo-dating inflation.[95] In 1981 he said high interest rates were a symptom of high inflation, so to get interest rates down the bank's inflation-fighting stance was essential.[96] MacEachen added that the inflation problem was more severe than originally anticipated, and argued that it must be given priority to sustain and improve growth, financial stability, and social progress.[97] There was not even a hint of the Keynesian paradigm or em-bedded liberalism in Canadian monetary policy from 1979 through to the early 1980s. There was very little public concern expressed by Ottawa for short-run employment levels when the government considered mone-tary policy during this period. Little was said in 1980 or 1981 in defence of countercyclical fiscal policy either.

This period is the outlier with respect to my overall account of the ori-entations and policies of the Trudeau government, particularly regarding monetary and fiscal policy. No country went unaffected by the Federal Reserve's actions. Canadian monetary policy in this period dropped its remaining Keynesianism and embedded liberalism due to seemingly intractable inflation and the overpowering force of the United States.

Conclusion

As Campbell argues, the image of a beleaguered government battling a suspicious but demanding public was universal for much of the Trudeau era.[98] Restraint was directed primarily at inflation, not Keynesian policy or deficit finance per se, in the mid-1970s. Inflation was confronted on the micro (wage and price controls), monetary (gradualism), and fiscal (spend-ing restraint) fronts. Deficits might, in the traditional analysis, raise infla-tion rates by changing Canada's position along the Phillips Curve. But this was not where Ottawa's inflation fight was primarily being waged. Rather than shift Canada's position along a given Phillips Curve, the government was trying to shift the Curve down by lowering inflation expectations. The mid-1970s policies surely marked a different way of doing economic pol-icy. Efforts to reduce inflation expectations certainly suggested the begin-nings of neo-liberal efforts to discipline social demands. But these policies were not a simple repudiation of Canadian Keynesianism because they were deeply informed by the persisting Keynesian paradigm. Ideas, once selected, can take on a life of their own and at least partially explain pol-icy outcomes. Keynesian ideas and embedded liberal ideology persisted beyond the expiration of the interested and material circumstances that supported their adoption in the first place. The refusal to use recession as a tool of inflation control indicated that Keynesian concerns with short-run employment levels were still politically operative, even with the onset of stagflation. So, too, were embedded liberal norms regarding the protection of society and economy from economic dislocation. In trying to have both high employment and low inflation, the Liberals did not replace unemployment with inflation as the fundamental goal of policy; they were trying to escape this unpleasant choice. The extant hierarchy of goals behind policy was not conquered.

These findings provide Canadian evidence for John Ruggie's argument that embedded liberalism did not die off with the early 1970s events and trends that unravelled the postwar order. In addition to economic decline, Ruggie identifies the 'decline' of American hegemony, the end both of the convertibility of the American dollar to gold and of fixed exchange rates, and the emergence of the 'new protectionism' as important features of the transition to new arrangements.[99] Ruggie's position is that these changes did not reflect a basic discontinuity with the embedded liberal compromise. On balance, they were responses to new circumstances and the contradictions of the Bretton Woods arrangements governed by the norms of embedded liberalism. Such was also the case with Canada's domestic policy. Keynesian approaches in Canada were one way in which embedded liberalism manifested itself. The new policies were responses to new circumstances governed at least in part by the extant conceptualization that the state was supposed to protect both society and economy from economic dislocations.

It is in these terms that deficit finance under the Trudeau Liberals must be understood. The fight against inflation was even less a repudiation of countercyclical deficit finance, which maintained its place in Ottawa's rhetoric as, in principle, sound fiscal policy. To the extent that countercyclical deficits were a central tenet of postwar Keynesianism, Keynesian ideas endured past 1975. Keynesian notions also informed the persistent, rather than the countercyclical, deficits that Ottawa ran after 1975. Chapter 4 will demonstrate that deficit finance was consistently vindicated as responsible fiscal policy in the circumstance.

4
Persisting Keynesian Conceptualizations of Deficit Finance, 1975-84

> Even my most politically inclined advisers weren't interested in
> throwing money around just to get votes. They did, however,
> have the traditional liberal view that the problem of finding jobs
> for the people should be solved without worrying about the
> deficit. That was our priority, to build a just society, and we
> assumed that the money we spent would be paid down with the
> swing of the cycle in a few years ... But, after 1974, with inflation
> growing at a dangerous rate and everyone competing for a larger
> share of a smaller pie, Canada was technically a poorer country
> with an unrealistic psychological inclination to want to be as
> rich as we were before.[1]
>
> – *Pierre Elliott Trudeau*

We can now turn to the federal government's articulations of deficit
finance in the era of economic decline. In general, the evidence indicates
that Ottawa's rhetorical commitment to countercyclical fiscal policy did
not erode during the 1970s or early 1980s. 1980 and 1981 did see some
weakening of these allegiances, but by 1983 the argument had increased
in sophistication and strength. In part this was due to the party in power.
The biggest exception to the trend was the budget of Joe Clark's minority
Progressive Conservative government in 1979. The rhetoric was also a
function of ownership – these were Liberal deficits so the Liberals needed
to justify Ottawa's fiscal position. But it was due as well to what had come
to be seen as responsibility in fiscal policy. The Liberals consistently
argued that in the economic circumstances, responsible fiscal policy required deficits. The opposition parties often agreed. A mass public seeking
protection from the economic dislocation of the 1970s, and not yet subject to strong neo-liberal discipline, showed little sign of dissent. The policies discussed in the previous chapter were designed to shift the Phillips
Curve down by reducing inflation expectations. The continuing commitment to Keynesian deficit finance entailed efforts to avoid further movement along a given Phillips Curve to a lower inflation rate at the expense
of higher unemployment. It also resulted in minor discretionary stimulative actions to increase employment levels.

Structural versus Countercyclical Deficits

The structural deficit is the deficit (if any) at average levels of economic activity with existing spending and revenue structures in place.[2] The structural deficit can also be calculated relative to levels of economic activity associated with high or full employment. In the late 1970s and early 1980s, the federal government calculated the structural deficit by estimating average levels of economic activity.[3] The cyclical deficit is the actual deficit less the structural deficit. The persistent and growing deficits in the second half of the 1970s were structural in character; they were not of a countercyclical Keynesian nature. Does this mean Keynesian political commitments and Keynesian ideas regarding countercyclical budgeting had no relation to these deficits?

Federal spending growth was kept in line with GNP growth in the second half of the 1970s, and even declined relative to GNP. By far the largest portion of annual deficits from 1975 to 1979 resided in revenue erosion relative to the size of the economy.[4] This revenue erosion resulted from a wide range of tax measures that began in 1971. Irwin Gillespie divides these measures into three categories: corporate taxes, personal taxes, and the Manufacturers' Sales Tax (the MST). In his view, corporate tax changes were introduced to keep Canada's tax rates competitive with those established in the United States on President Richard Nixon's initiative in 1971. Personal tax reductions were an antidote to the 1971 base-broadening reforms that followed partially on the recommendations of the Carter Commission. The MST was reduced both to help Canadian business's competitive position and to stimulate the economy.[5] In the late 1970s, Gillespie argues, further revenue erosion resulted from a number of sources. These included responding to foreign tax incentives and value added taxes; domestic demand for tax expenditures;[6] and 'a perceived need to stimulate the economy and reduce unemployment.'[7]

David Wolfe, by contrast, takes a more cynical view. According to his argument, most of these tax changes were efforts by a centrist Liberal government to restore its credibility with a business sector angered by the tax reform debate of the late 1960s and early 1970s. The corporate tax reductions, says Wolfe, went far beyond what was necessary to compete with American tax levels.[8] In addition, in Wolfe's argument, because these discretionary measures accounted for a lot of the structural deficit by the mid-1980s, deficits were not of a Keynesian countercyclical character.[9] For Robert Campbell, the tax moves in the early 1970s were the result of John Turner's 'supply-side,' rather than Keynesian efforts to reduce inflation by expanding the supply of goods through an expansion of productive capacity via tax incentives. In other words, contrary to the Keynesian view, taxes were reduced to combat inflation.[10] Consistent with Campbell's view, Doug Purvis and Constance Smith argue that tax cuts were preferred over spending increases 'partly because tax cuts have desirable supply-side effects and exert a downward impact on prices, and partly to limit the size of federal government expenditures.'[11]

Because there is merit in each of these positions, my ambition is modest. I wish to argue only, first, that the countercyclical Keynesian conceptualization of deficit finance rationalized the deficits that emerged in part from tax expenditures; second, that the perceived stimulative value of the resulting deficits was a factor in the introduction of at least some of these measures in the first place and a reason the deficits were permitted to exist; and third, that structural deficits were not recognized as such, so policy makers largely interpreted deficits as Keynesian in character.

This chapter will demonstrate that Ottawa's fiscal rhetoric usually described deficits as countercyclical responses to economic underperformance. Interviews reveal it was also thought within Finance that there was a sound countercyclical basis for deficits. The deficits were understood to have emerged through automatic stabilizers and discretionary actions. Since it was feared new spending could be inflationary, tax reductions were viewed as the best way to stimulate the economy.[12] It was also thought appropriate to spread the impact of the first oil price shock across a number of years.[13] Deficits would mitigate the shock's effects in the short term. It was a self-conscious intention of policy makers that tax moves serve some stimulative function.

Nonetheless, the deficits in the second half of the 1970s were, in fact, primarily structural.[14] But this conclusion can be drawn only with the knowledge after the fact that there was a secular decline in economic performance.[15] Recall that the structural deficit as calculated by the federal government in the late 1970s and early 1980s was the deficit (if any) at average levels of economic activity with existing spending and revenue structures in place. The cyclical deficit is the actual deficit less the structural deficit. If, as in the 1970s, average levels of economic activity are thought to be relatively high, the identified structural portion of the actual deficit will be relatively low. The cyclical portion of the actual deficit will be viewed as correspondingly larger. If, after a few years, the structural deficit in preceding years is recalculated by plugging lower levels of average economic activity into the equation, the structural portion of earlier deficits will appear to be that much larger. David Dodge, a long-time Finance official, argues that there was great confusion in the 1970s and early 1980s regarding underlying issues in budget planning. 'Expansionary fiscal policy was used to "cushion" the first oil price shock and to "stabilize" the economy. Expansionary fiscal policy was used during this period as a *substitute* for appropriate structural measures.'[16] The underlying economy, in addition to the tax moves, was a factor causative of the persistent deficits that propped up economic activity.[17] Tax expenditures (as well as

indexing both the personal income tax system and many spending programs effective in 1974)[18] or not, fiscal shortfalls would not have been
nearly as severe without the combination of the deteriorating economy
and the views that this deterioration was both temporary and at least
partly amenable to Keynesian fiscal remedy. Extant expectations about economic performance and persisting Keynesian ideas were the filters through
which Ottawa conceptualized its deficits. Keynesian deficit finance was
not being practised well, but it was being thought and talked.

The Rhetoric and Policy of Deficit Function and Dysfunction
The major preoccupations of finance ministers from 1975 to 1984 were
unemployment, inflation, and energy policy. Deficits and debt were generally far less salient, and relevant mostly with respect to their relationship
with these central preoccupations.

Between Oil Price Shocks and under the
Anti-Inflation Program, 1975-8
Countercyclical budgeting was accepted as sound policy in both government rhetoric and by the balance of expert opinion in the Department of
Finance, particularly through 1978. Interviews indicate that public documents represent the department's thinking reasonably accurately. There
was some internal debate, but the consensus was consistently in favour of
larger deficits, given economic conditions. Deficits were planned, although
they usually came in larger than anticipated.[19] There did not seem to
be many alternatives to deficit financing. As one former senior official
put the matter, 'It seemed the logical course.'[20] The ministers themselves,
although perhaps more by virtue of prior commitment than ongoing
thinking, tended as well to Keynesian views. Of course, the Liberals were
wedded to deficits in that shortfalls had emerged on their watch. Political
reasons for the deficit, which ministers may have brought to the table,
were often supported by department professionals on economic grounds.[21]
Smart economics and smart politics were commonly one. This fusion provided an incentive to use Keynesian rhetoric to justify the deficits the Liberals wore politically. As one former senior official saw it, finance ministers
in the 1970s would say almost anything to prove they were stimulating
the economy.[22] Given that the opposition parties generally favoured more
stimulation than the Trudeau government proposed, the political risk was
as much from making insufficient use of the deficit instrument as from
going deeper into debt.[23]

Deficits As Friends in Bad Times: Turner and Macdonald
To turn to the budgets of a freshly minted majority Liberal government,
in John Turner's 1975 effort he argued that Canada was performing

comparatively well despite a deep world recession.[24] One of the reasons he provided for this relative success was both partisan and Keynesian. In no small part, Turner claimed, Canada was outperforming its competitors, especially the United States, due to the expansionary policies previous Liberal governments had put in place.[25] A projected deficit of $5 billion for the 1975-6 fiscal year would, he said, provide just the right amount of stimulus. Any less would mean too little aggregate demand. Any more would cause inflation.[26] This was in essence a passive, rather than discretionary, deficit.[27] In 1976, Donald Macdonald followed Turner in noting Canada's relatively good economic performance, particularly in comparison with the United States. As did Turner, Macdonald acknowledged that high commodity prices were not all bad news for Canada: 'But undoubtedly the major factor was concerted and far reaching action by both federal and provincial governments to sustain output, employment and real incomes in the face of severe recession and inflation abroad.'[28] By this Macdonald specifically meant that countercyclical policies had maintained domestic demand. He argued that in 1974 monetary and fiscal policy became more expansionary. Provincial action reinforced federal measures.[29] Without these actions, Macdonald claimed, the recession would have been much worse.[30] Officials in the Department of Finance at the time agreed that deficit finance, among other things, had played a role in moderating the recession in Canada, particularly since Canada was thought to have a larger and more deliberate countercyclical apparatus than the United States.[31] Macdonald also said that the resulting record deficits were entirely appropriate. But, like a good countercyclical Keynesian, he added it was equally appropriate that deficits should recede with the recovery.[32] In 1977 Macdonald reiterated the position that, as slack in the economy was taken up, the deficit would be reduced. He did state, 'We will be urged to spend our way out of our problems, to provide even greater stimulus, to provide protection against the realities of international competition and to withdraw controls before their job is done. These temptations must be resisted.'[33] This was hardly deficit finance without limits. But Macdonald would not cut the deficit too soon, he said, because doing so would threaten the economy. With unemployment still high, he argued that stimulus was still needed.[34]

An important interpretive issue arises with respect to Macdonald's 1976 budget and the persistence of Keynesian rhetoric. David Wolfe argues that in this budget Macdonald 'proclaimed that the fiscal stimulation applied in late 1974 had intensified the inflationary spiral and worsened the balance of payments position. The Keynesian formulae, which had guided post-war economic policy, were no longer regarded as valid.'[35] I strongly disagree with this characterization because it is decontextualized from the minister's statements about fiscal stimulation which I just canvassed.

Macdonald located comparatively strong economic performance in expansionary fiscal policy. He added that this strong performance intensified some problems. Canadian salaries, wages, and prices were all accelerating at rates faster than those in the United States. The wage-price spiral, Macdonald said, posed a serious threat to Canadian competitiveness. He also observed that higher demand for goods and services in Canada than elsewhere had led to a strong deterioration in Canada's current accounts deficit. Finally, he argued, Canadian interest rates exceeded those in other countries due to different economic conditions. Macdonald stated that higher interest rates were caused by inflation, strong credit demand, and the Bank of Canada's moderation of money supply growth.[36] Nowhere was deficit finance singled out as a culprit. Wolfe's argument is not sustainable in direct terms because good economic performance, rather than fiscal stimulus, was identified as the primary cause of these problems. Only in the sense that fiscal stimulation was credited with the good economic performance that caused these difficulties can it be argued that deficits were presented as the problem. But to make this case is to ignore Macdonald's explicit defence of deficit finance precisely on the grounds it had resulted in a comparatively strong economy and mitigated the recession. Macdonald's defence suggests that these economic problems were conceptualized as the problems of success rather than of failure, that they were the kinds of problems the government preferred to face. Implementing the Keynesian formula was becoming more complex but, at least with respect to the fiscal stimulation provided by deficit finance, it was still conceptualized as valid. Without it, Macdonald's argument implied, the problems confronting Canada would have been much worse.

A Future Prime Minister?

Macdonald's budgets were rather blasé affairs, in no small part because the government seemed to be waiting for the Anti-Inflation Program to do its work. The budgets of his successor were more controversial, but not due to any major changes in Ottawa's fiscal stance. Although Jean Chrétien would, as prime minister, preside over the elimination of the federal deficit, in an earlier life, he was one of a succession of Trudeau's finance ministers who ran deficits. Chrétien was also Canada's first French Canadian finance minister. He supplied justifications for fiscal shortfalls that were consistent with the rhetoric of Macdonald and Turner. However, Chrétien's budgets also probably put a bit more emphasis on the fiscal constraints under which he said Ottawa operated. In his 1977 Economic and Fiscal Statement, Chrétien argued that deficits, both in the public accounts and the balance of payments, limited the government's room to manoeuvre.[37] But he also stated that Ottawa could do more to stimulate the economy. He lowered personal income taxes and increased direct job creation.[38] In identifying three major barriers to growth – weak world markets, high domestic costs, and a loss of 'confidence' – Chrétien made no mention of deficits.[39]

In his April 1978 budget, Chrétien argued that Canadians had come to expect too much from the economy after the high growth of the late 1960s and early 1970s. The result was inflationary demands on the economy that did not consider implications for efficiency and competitiveness.[40] He did not turn this view into an argument for retrenchment. Rather, he said there had been progress in the last few years. The AIP, control of federal spending and the money supply, lower wage increases, and better inflation trends augured well.[41] But unemployment was still at 'unacceptable' levels. Chrétien asked, given that the economy was in a gradual recovery, if it should get a further push from policy? He answered in the affirmative.[42] Now not only a downturn but also an upturn, in which unemployment remained high by postwar standards, was presented as sufficient reason for discretionary stimulative policy.

The stimulative measure Chrétien selected was a reduction in the retail sales tax. Since these were provincial taxes, the plan actually involved Ottawa persuading provinces to temporarily reduce their sales taxes in exchange for partial federal compensation. This seemed to be in keeping with John Turner's 1973 emphasis on provincial responsibility for stabilization and the concomitant need to coordinate stabilization policy.[43] The proposal also clearly implied that policy coordination should be led by Ottawa. Chrétien announced that provincial consent for the plan had been obtained. There was criticism from western provinces about federal intrusion,[44] although all provinces other than Quebec and Alberta (which does not have a sales tax) agreed to participate. But jurisdictional dissent reached new heights in Quebec. With the rhetorical moderation for which the Parti Québécois is renowned, Premier René Lévesque described Ottawa's proposed sales tax reduction as 'rape' for intruding upon provincial jurisdiction. He also argued that the idea for the plan came from Ontario, which he claimed would benefit more.[45] Quebec finance minister Jacques Parizeau either backed out of the deal or was never a party to it – the public record is unclear. He eliminated the provincial sales tax on all clothing, textiles, shoes, and furniture. These were products in which Quebec, not coincidentally, had a dominant market position. Ottawa eventually compensated Quebeckers directly, rather than the provincial government. These events demonstrated that federal-provincial fiscal cooperation was far from fully realized.[46] The incident was a political disaster for Chrétien, especially in Quebec. Combined with the subsequent 'Guns of August' episode, in which Trudeau announced $2 billion in spending cuts on national television without bothering to inform his finance minister, 1978 was a rough year for Chrétien.[47]

The Guns of August cuts were described at the time as 'drastic.'[48] Yet the eventual $2.5 billion in 'cuts,' an amount greater than the $2 billion Trudeau initially announced, were reductions only in planned expenditures. Spending was still expected to grow by 8.9 percent in the 1979-80 fiscal year, although this would reduce spending relative to GNP, which to that point was projected to increase by 11 percent.[49] For somebody writing after the mid-1990s, the term 'drastic' seems exaggerated. But this is an indication of how far the parameters of discussion have shifted. What was drastic in the 1970s would be tepid in the mid-1990s.

Chrétien's second 1978 budget did introduce restraint. But Trudeau's talk of retrenchment notwithstanding, deficit finance went relatively unscathed. Chrétien rejected what he described as calls for massive stimulative tax cuts, which the Progressive Conservatives, the NDP, and the Economic Council of Canada were pushing.[50] Chrétien argued that such action would overstimulate the economy and that Ottawa's cash requirements were already too high. The Canadian Chamber of Commerce and the Canadian Manufacturers' Association had warned against borrowing to fund tax cuts, preferring offsetting spending reductions.[51] Nonetheless, Chrétien argued that the spending reductions created some fiscal room: 'I think we should share these savings with the public.'[52] Chrétien cut taxes. The most important move was a 3 percent reduction in the Manufacturers' Sales Tax, which was a major reason this was described as a 'business budget.'[53] In the end, the budget was generally supported by business, but alienated the 'left' of the Liberal Party.[54] That 'the Trudeau government's willingness to continue with spending cuts waned as the 1979 general election approached' indicated that the political business cycle was still no friend of fiscal restraint.[55]

Turner,[56] Macdonald,[57] and Chrétien[58] all had real progressive social commitments. They were also fiscal conservatives by temperament. They were criticized for paying insufficient attention to unemployment and need. They were criticized for mismanagement and profligacy. Such is the dilemma of the Liberal finance minister. But the middle path walked by Ottawa in the second half of the 1970s was consistent with the Keynesian view that the government is responsible for evening out the business cycle through fiscal policy. The problem was they did not realize that the business cycle now functioned at substantially lower 'normal' levels of economic activity. These finance ministers were neither profligate nor bleeding hearts. They were Keynesians in the sense that Canada had been Keynesian since 1945. To have eliminated the deficit in the second half of the 1970s would have been a major political error. In the economic conditions of the time, as understood, there was a strong argument to be made for continuing deficits, given that Keynesian commitments still had weight. Even the Progressive Conservatives argued for more fiscal stimulus. To have greatly accelerated the deficit also probably would have been a political mistake. Classical budgeting norms acted as a check on Keynesian procedures. Part of why business tolerated these deficits in practice while opposing them in principle was that the Liberals were courting the corporate community with tax measures while constraining spending. These sorts of upward limits on fiscal expansion were entirely consistent with postwar norms. Writing in 1980, no less astute an analyst than Donald Smiley went so far as to include in his definition of an economic nation governments accepting their Keynesian responsibility to manage aggregate demand to attain the objectives of relatively full employment and relatively stable prices.[59] While the results were disappointing, I see little evidence on the fiscal side that the Liberal government fell afoul of this characterization in the latter half of the 1970s to any greater extent than did federal governments from 1945 to 1975.

Raising Revenue Followed by Recession and Recovery, 1980-4

The Liberals lost their birthright – national office – to Joe Clark's Progressive Conservatives in the 1979 election. But fortune smiled again and Pierre Elliott Trudeau was prime minister once more by early 1980. In addition to proposals for an industrial strategy, more intervention regarding the auto industry and foreign investment, and energy self-sufficiency,[60] deficit reduction was a 'significant' part of the Liberals' 1980 platform.[61] With a new mandate but little representation from the West, and in the wake of a referendum victory in Quebec, the Liberal agenda was one of federal assertion with respect to the provinces.[62] On the constitutional front, Trudeau began his effort to patriate the constitution with a domestic amending formula and a Charter of Rights. Most provinces were initially opposed, but eventually Trudeau was able to bring the constitution home. (His failure to get Quebec's signature on the document would haunt the federation in subsequent years.) On the energy front, the National Energy Program had fiscal, regional, international, and federal-provincial implications. It also greatly expanded Ottawa's role in the economy. One of the fiscal components of the NEP was Ottawa's attempt to right a fiscal imbalance between the federal government and resource-rich provinces. Reaping resource royalties, these provinces (British Columbia and Alberta) were running surpluses. Yet these royalties came about in part due to the huge tax incentives Ottawa had provided for energy exploration and development, incentives that increased the federal deficit.[63] This strategy of federal assertion had as a component a revenue grab, and this was related to a diminution in Ottawa's public enthusiasm for deficit finance.

Deficit Finance and the National Energy Program

Trudeau's new finance minister, Allan MacEachen, had a stormy couple of years at the head of Canada's fiscal ship. His budgets were less prone than those of his Liberal predecessors to wax poetic about the salutary effects of deficit finance. In 1980 MacEachen argued that poor economic performance justified deferring deficit reduction. He anticipated that growth would be slow and that the deficit should decline only as growth improved.[64] Pending better economic conditions, the deficit was projected to increase by $3 billion from 1979-90 to 1980-1.[65] But he also insisted that bringing Ottawa's 'very large deficits' into more manageable proportions was important. MacEachen took the position that Ottawa's persistent deficits and rising debt risked higher inflation.[66] Since deficit reduction was to await better economic times, however, this position was apparently consistent with the countercyclical Keynesian view.

The real focus of the 1980 budget was the National Energy Program, which did relate to the deficit question insofar as the NEP was designed to reap for Ottawa a substantial revenue windfall, although the policy was not primarily driven by deficit concerns.[67] New energy tax measures, above all a petroleum and gas revenue tax, along with a natural gas and liquids tax, were anticipated to generate $2.9 billion in new revenues in the 1981-2 fiscal year, $4.7 billion in 1982-3, and $6 billion in 1983-4.[68] In part, these measures were designed to fund federal efforts to move Canada toward energy self-sufficiency.[69] However, because by 1983-4 the energy expenditure envelope was expected to be about $2 billion below the value of the new revenue initiatives, if things had gone as planned, the NEP would have been a substantial net source of funds for Ottawa.[70]

But the implications of the NEP went well beyond the fiscal picture. Canada adopted a National Oil Policy in 1961. In 1973 and 1974, following the first oil price shock, Canada's oil policy was revamped by federal fiat and federal-provincial negotiations. The country set oil prices through the rest of the 1970s.[71] Then the Clark government, in 1979, introduced its own comprehensive energy policy. It was less offensive to Alberta than the NEP, but was still very interventionist (a matter to which we will return). The NEP was the final step in this escalating dance between oil interests, the provinces, and the federal government. The NEP set oil prices, used the tax system to distribute the benefits of high oil prices more widely, encouraged exploration (especially on government of Canada land) through incentives, and moved to ensure Canadian control of the Canadian oil industry.[72] The NEP did not originate in Finance. It was the inspiration of Marc Lalonde and mandarins in Energy, Mines, and Resources. Finance officials were coordinated into the process, and made important contributions through a grouping of high-level Energy and Finance bureaucrats called EnFin. Since the NEP involved so many tax changes,

Deputy Minister of Finance Ian Stewart agreed to make it the centrepiece of MacEachen's first budget.[73]

The NEP was a political earthquake in Canada. Its shockwaves are still felt over twenty years later. Beyond profits, there were two fundamental sources of domestic objection to the NEP: regional and ideological. Setting prices, redistributing benefits, and Canadian control were, from the point of view of the West generally and Alberta specifically, an especially brutal exemplification of the metropolitan-hinterland dynamics of Canadian politics. On this thesis, a federal government controlled by central Canada makes policy and propounds cultural values for the benefit of Ontario and Quebec at the expense of the West. With the NEP, Alberta's entitlement to its oil receipts was viewed as a lamb sacrificed to central Canada's appetite for comparatively cheap energy. That Trudeau held 74 of 75 seats in Quebec, but won no seats west of Manitoba in the 1980 election, made the case particularly plausible. The scars still remain in western Canada.

The energy conflicts transcended party. The Clark energy policy was similar to Trudeau's, although it was less aggressive about taking revenues out of the West, probably because Clark owed a lot more to western provinces and Alberta premier Peter Lougheed than did Trudeau. Richard Simeon and Ian Robinson argue that the Clark government's inability to ameliorate these regional tensions indicates that the energy conflicts were largely independent of any one government: 'If any federal government was to find compromise, it should have been this one.'[74] Rather, these disputes revealed the structure of regional economic interests. Western oil interests objected strenuously and systematically to the NEP.[75] Provincial governments, particularly the Peter Lougheed's Alberta Progressive Conservatives and Bill Davis's Ontario Progressive Conservatives, were powerful actors who vociferously articulated their cases to Ottawa. That Davis, as on constitutional matters, was effectively allied with the Liberal Trudeau against his western Tory brethren indicates the structural basis of the problem. With the NEP, the central Canadian position won the day. But in the long run, Alberta's orientation to the federal government was further radicalized.

In ideological terms, the NEP did not make Canadian business any more comfortable with the federal government or Trudeau's Liberal Party. The Anti-Inflation Program had set growth rates for wages and prices; the NEP indicated this was no fluke. Trudeau's Foreign Investment Review Agency, established in 1973 when the NDP held the balance of power in a minority Parliament, continued to cast a suspicious supervisory eye on the free flow of (foreign) capital and also interfered with business decision making. Any one of these policies might not have caused too much ideological unrest, but together they were perceived as a substantial threat to private capital. The NEP was certainly not a Keynesian policy. It was structural and supply-side in orientation. Yet it did contain elements of embedded liberal ideology. Its goals included protecting consumers from a precipitous rise in prices by setting prices that would gradually increase, and protecting consuming industries from having to adjust too quickly to the second oil shock. The resistance to the NEP was not so much on the grounds that Trudeau was violating the 'embedded' part of the embedded liberal compromise. Rather, his economic liberalism became suspect. The price mechanism is supposed to be the signal by which markets function. Usurping it with technocratic, bureaucratic, state-led management violated a central tenet of Anglo-American economic liberalism. Central Canadian business might have liked the relatively low oil prices, but it sensed a deeper risk. As Clarkson and McCall put it, 'not since the industrial mobilization of the Second World War had such an all encompassing governmental economic intervention been tried.'[76]

These regional and ideological tensions had another structural element to them. The West may be the hinterland of central Canada. But Canada, once the hinterland of Britain, now in part fulfils that role for the United States. The Americans were not pleased by Canada's interference with the access of American capital to Canadian oil. Recently, American writers have argued that 'investment flows to Canada turned negative in 1981-2 due to that country's adoption of restrictive policies such as the National Energy Program, which prompted US companies to sell their existing assets in the politically charged petroleum and mining sectors.'[77] Nor, with the Reagan administration taking office, were derogations from liberal economic arrangements viewed kindly. When the Reaganites noticed that the FIRA and NEP existed, they were outraged.[78] Over time the incentives for Canada to adopt more liberal arrangements increased.

Deficit Finance and Tax Reform

In this political and economic storm, and revenue elements of the NEP notwithstanding, deficit finance was not that big a deal. It is clear that MacEachen's deputy minister, Ian Stewart, supported deficits in the context.[79] But, in 1981, the government said little positive about deficits, other than to note in background documents that tax reductions and deficits were intended to stimulate the economy, as well as that they insulated Canada to some degree from the 1974-5 recession and strengthened the recovery through 1978-9.[80] Rather, in 1981 MacEachen was focused on tax reform. His reform was directed at both the structure of the tax system and the government's fiscal position. On the fiscal side, MacEachen argued, the deficit and the financial requirements had to be substantially reduced to take pressure off credit markets, ease interest rates, and create room for needy borrowers. This was part and parcel of a broad direction of 'restraint' in the name of fighting inflation.[81] He proposed to reduce the deficit by increasing revenues to control inflation. Fiscal restraint, MacEachen argued, had to support the Bank of Canada's monetary restraint.[82] MacEachen tabled a paper that demonstrated how the major share of deficit increases since 1974 resulted from tax expenditures.[83] The purpose of this demonstration was clearly to provide a fiscal rationale for increasing tax yields. The total budgetary impact of tax reform was expected to be net revenue increases of about $1.4 billion in 1982-3, about $2.1 billion in 1983-4, and about $1.2 billion in 1984-5.[84]

The MacEachen tax reform proposals also entailed revising the structure of Canada's tax system. Efficiency and equity were as important as restraint in motivating reform.[85] Numerous loopholes for the affluent and corporations, who were already gaining a disproportionate benefit from tax expenditures, were to be closed. While the government would make money on the deal, lower personal tax rates would partially offset these burdens. Privileged groups who would be disadvantaged by the elimination of preferences lobbied hard in opposition.[86] As happened with the 1971 tax reform, the Liberals found themselves backing down and modifying their tax measures a number of times. The measures eventually implemented were less ambitious than the original proposals. It is generally thought that MacEachen miscalculated the concerted business and high-income opposition he would face.[87]

The NEP and tax reform had in common the aspiration of increasing Ottawa's revenue capacity in light of the tax expenditures of the 1970s. Yet part of the controversy regarding the 1981 tax reform was that it would mean an insufficiently expansionary budget in the face of an imminent recession.[88] In 1982, with the recession in full swing and Ottawa's fiscal position deteriorating further, MacEachen and the Liberals embraced again the countercyclical rationale for deficit finance.

Deficit Finance and the 6 and 5 Program

MacEachen was in the uncomfortable position in 1982 of having to cope with a deep recession and very high inflation. To combat inflation, he introduced the '6 and 5' Program. MacEachen urged all Canadians to limit their income demands to an increase of 6 percent through to June 1983, and of 5 percent in the following year. He also urged business to limit price increases to covering costs. But, argued MacEachen, the private sector could not be expected to participate in restraint unless the public sector restrained itself. He held over 500,000 federal employees to these limits, and imposed other restraints on the public sector as well.[89] MacEachen claimed this policy would move Canada from the recessionary world of 12 percent inflation to the 6 percent world of recovery.[90] Six and five, like wage and price controls, was designed to lower inflation expectations. But while the underlying thinking was similar, the program was also a product of the tensions created by wage and price controls, and perhaps the NEP as well. MacEachen rejected broad and mandatory income controls because, as he noted, they were opposed almost unanimously by business and labour.[91] Nobody wanted another AIP. The 6 and 5 program was also more favourable to business. Restraint was legislated for the public sector; the private sector was subject only to moral suasion. The program was directed solely at wages, the price of labour. General prices were not directly targeted. David Langille notes that the 6 and 5 program came on the heels of the Business Council on National Issues recommendation that government wage and salary increases be held below 7 percent.[92]

This effort to lower inflation expectations was an indication that Ottawa still sought to beat inflation without creating unemployment, although partial deindexation of the tax system meant the federal government had a temporary revenue interest in inflation above 6 and then 5 percent (full indexing was planned to resume in 1985). That said, as discussed in the previous chapter, monetary policy was 'solving' inflation precisely by creating unemployment. The result was a jump in the federal deficit. MacEachen, however, located the recession not in policy, but in developments in the international political economy beyond Canadian control.[93] MacEachen argued, in his 1982 budget speech, that the increase in the projected deficit from $10.5 billion to $19.6 billion mainly reflected the automatic responses of the tax and expenditure system to the recession. He added that the automatic stabilizers had to be permitted to function. Otherwise the recession would get worse. MacEachen said this was not the time to slash Unemployment Insurance or cut spending that gave Canadians income.[94] But he would not do more to offset the recession, because printing money or increasing the deficit would only, according to the minister's argument, increase inflation, unemployment, and interest rates.[95] The budget was no vindication of fiscal profligacy, and did not support the use of discretionary stabilization measures. Indeed, one former official states that the 1981-2 deficit run-up was viewed within the department as excessive. Nevertheless, he argues that it is difficult to see how budgeting could have been more restrictive given a recession.[96]

Of course, budgeting could have been more restrictive if the fiscal structure were less sensitive to economic conditions, and if the government had been politically willing to cut more. Instead, the Liberals drew on Keynesian notions of automatic stabilization to justify the large deficit. Even if the Liberals had started to move away from their 1970s support for deficit finance in 1980 and 1981, the recession returned to deficits much of the respectability they may have lost. The countercyclical Keynesian approach to budgeting had not been challenged by the Trudeau Liberals. They had never said that in a recession a deficit would be a mistake. The automatic stabilization built into the system was still largely intact. When the recession arrived, Ottawa's de facto policy and traditional conceptual-izations re-emerged. Part of this was making a virtue out of necessity. The government had a large deficit and had pretty consistently argued the virtues of deficits, so it made good political sense to justify the shortfall as sound policy. That the structure of political justification meant good poli-tics entailed arguing a limited case in favour of the deficit indicates where the Liberals calculated public sentiment lay during a recession, relative to what their fiscal record allowed the government to credibly propound.

Reinvigorating Keynesian Deficit Finance
Marc Lalonde, perhaps Trudeau's finest minister, replaced MacEachen in 1982. He was also perhaps Canada's most Keynesian finance minister. At the same time, he would work to restore the confidence of the business community in the Department of Finance and the Liberal government. In his 1982 economic and fiscal statement, Lalonde had to explain why the projected deficit for the 1982-3 fiscal year had now reached $23.5 bil-lion. His statement retrieved the twin supports of deficit finance: good economics and social justice. On the social side, Lalonde stated that the government would not tighten the screws on the economy, cut billions from government spending, or seek to eliminate inflation by brute force. Rather, it would continue to ensure that the strong and affluent helped the weak and vulnerable.[97] Lalonde had prime ministerial support for his posi-tion; he twice mentioned Trudeau's statement of one week earlier that social programs were safe and that the federal government would not abandon people in a time of need.[98] Since Lalonde did not expect any trouble meeting borrowing requirements, when the economic factor was added to the social, the government was of the 'view that in current cir-cumstances the federal deficit provides appropriate support to economic activity and individual Canadians suffering from the recession.'[99] But like MacEachen, Lalonde expressed an unwillingness to add to the deficit through discretionary policy. Reallocated funding and automatic stabil-ization would have to suffice. 'While I am prepared to accept the larger deficits resulting from our weak economic performance, the principle of fiscal responsibility prevents consideration of massive new spending programs.'[100] Indeed, consistent with the emphasis on spending restraint that had characterized Liberal budgeting over the previous several years, Lalonde gave a spirited defence of the government's expenditure manage-ment. He noted that program spending had fallen continuously as a per-centage of GNP since 1975-6: 'Those who assert that federal expenditures are "out of control" should check the record of the past seven years.'[101]

Lalonde's 1983 budget was the most Keynesian in Canadian history. The deficit was projected to increase by about $6 billion over the previous year. The government's explicit goals were the provision of employment and reinvigorating private investment. Lalonde introduced a $4.6 billion Special Recovery Program to improve the recovery and restore the economy's capacity for job creation. Of this, $2.2 billion would be spent over the next four years under the rubric of the Special Recovery Capital Project. Over four years, the other $2.4 billion would be the cost of tax incentives for private investment projects. The idea was to spur the recovery and increase Canada's competitiveness by improving its capital stock. Of this money $700 million would come from accelerating previously planned spending projects. The remaining $3.9 billion was in new funds. The money would be recouped by a Special Recovery Tax levied from 1 October 1984 to 31 December 1988.[102]

This was portrayed in at least some press as a business budget,[103] and was received favourably by the business community in spite of reservations about the deficit.[104] The most controversial part of the budget was a 'breach' of budget secrecy in which a cameraman got a shot of its content a day in advance. Lalonde increased his spending and the deficit by $200 million over two years so that the leaked information would not be valid. He justified this seat-of-the-pants approach to fiscal policy by saying the event led him to follow his instincts and err on the side of more jobs.[105] Lalonde vindicated his budget in the usual countercyclical terms. He argued it was stimulative of recovery. Somewhat less conventionally, he also made the claim that deficit spending could improve growth trends by increasing capital formation. But given the size of the deficit, Lalonde sought to portray Liberal policy as fiscally prudent. In addition to his primary argument that the government was taking strong action, Lalonde also claimed that only $1.8 billion of the projected deficit resulted from discretionary measures.[106] He took credit for $4.6 billion in action but only $1.8 billion of the deficit's rise. This feat was possible in part because the Special Recovery Program was spread over four years.

But Lalonde did much more with respect to articulating the Liberal approach to deficits. He tabled the first major federal government document devoted to vindicating countercyclical deficit finance since the 1945 White Paper. Lalonde presented his interpretation of the federal government's fiscal record over the previous decade or so. He justified the record in the Keynesian terms that characterized the rhetoric of the postwar era. He also went further than previous finance ministers. The detailed treatment of the federal deficit provided a more sophisticated articulation of both Keynesian theory and practice than had recently been offered. The 1983 budget, along with this supporting document, is the high-water mark of rhetoric and policy regarding Keynesian deficit finance in Canada.

To summarize briefly *The Federal Deficit in Perspective*, Lalonde argued correctly, as he had in 1982, that the deficit was not primarily a result of increased spending. Spending had grown sharply relative to GNP in 1982, but on the whole revenue declines relative to GNP were presented as the culprit.[107] Cyclically adjusted federal spending was on a clear downward track from 1975 to 1979 and 'virtually' constant thereafter.[108] Lalonde also argued, as we have already discussed, that it was difficult to recognize in the 1970s the structural decline in economic growth rates that was evident by 1983.[109]

Lalonde's characterization of the resulting deficits consistently diminished any inimical implication that might attach to fiscal shortfalls. His most important claims related to inflation. Lalonde argued that inflation lessened the real value of the debt stock owed by the federal government. He also stated that debt interest payments included a nominal component designed to protect lenders against inflation, so the real value of debt charges was also not as large as it might appear.[110] In addition, Lalonde argued that because on the whole the provinces, as well as the Canada and Quebec Pension Plans, were expected to be in a surplus position,[111] and because with weak economic activity there was little risk of government 'crowding out' private investment,[112] the fiscal position was not dire. Lalonde also went further than any postwar finance minister. He argued that structural deficits could be of value in certain circumstances. If private investment was low and savings were high, a structural deficit could, he claimed, stimulate aggregate demand and employment. In an inflationary context, a balanced budget might be too restrictive or too expansionary (i.e., if inflation were eroding the real value of government spending, a deficit might be required just to create a neutral fiscal stance). And if the government was spending a lot on investment, and if it was desirable to spread these costs over future as well as present generations, a structural deficit could be appropriate.[113] Lalonde said that the government would reduce the deficit over the medium term to guard against a structural deficit problem. But in this regard, he exceeded the rhetorical bounds of the postwar Keynesian consensus, which had accepted only countercyclical deficits. Conceptualizing structural deficits as potentially sound policy suggested a modest move toward the 'left Keynesian' socialization of investment that Canada rejected when it adopted Keynesian procedures.

Lalonde's implication, unsurprisingly, was that the Liberals had managed the nation's finances responsibly. He concluded that deficits should not be perceived in a one-dimensional way. The 'common view' was, he said, no longer that the federal government should balance the budget every year; rather, the budget should be balanced after adjusting for cyclical effects.[114] That is, the cyclical portion of federal deficits was intrinsically justified for the Liberals. And in some circumstances, according to Lalonde's argument, even a structural deficit could have its place.

Lalonde's 1984 budget, the last of the Trudeau era, was entirely consistent with the 1983 exegesis. The recovery was underway, although the budget estimated unemployment to have been 11.9 percent in 1983, and projected it at 10.9 percent for 1984.[115] Lalonde argued that the deficit had provided much support to the welfare of individual Canadians and to the promotion of economic activity during the recession and the first year of the recovery. But deficits, he said, had to fall as investment recovered and the economy expanded.[116] The 6 and 5 Program was phased out, and Lalonde announced that full indexation would be restored to the tax system in 1985.[117] Perhaps the most relevant statements regarding this budget were those of the freshly minted leader of the Progressive Conservatives, Brian Mulroney. 'There is nothing in this budget that deals with the fundamentals, namely: an overwhelming deficit that is going to inhibit economic recovery [and] a degree of profligacy in public spending that is without precedent in any western industrialized nation.'[118] These and other comments warned of a coming change in the macroeconomic orientation of the federal government.

Keynesian Ideas and Changing Interests
Keynesian ideas regarding deficit finance endured from 1975 to 1984 roughly to the extent they had a hold from 1945 to 1974. Nor was the Keynesian paradigm overthrown. The persistence of concerns regarding short-term employment loss from deficit reduction or elimination meant that third-order policy change did not occur on the fiscal front. Inflation reduction did not trump employment concerns in the design of fiscal policy. Nor, in fact, was there a second-order change. The deficit instrument remained on the table.

The key differences under the 1975-84 Trudeau Liberals from fiscal policy during the postwar era were that deficits became structural, that deficits became persistent, and that the political demands for deficit succour may have increased in an embedded liberal ideological context with the onset of economic decline. Keynesian ideas persisted on top of the structural economic changes that were reshaping the economic interests of many actors. The politico-economic basis of the Keynesian paradigm and Keynesian deficit finance was eroding even as Keynesian notions received vociferous rhetorical support and some policy implementation. The application of both moderate Keynesian fiscal policy and the general Keynesian paradigm in a worsened economic environment brought disappointing results. The frustration of expectations was a key factor in motivating actors to reconceptualize their economic interests and to support different ideas so that those interests might be realized through different policies. It would, though, take time and political mobilization for new ideas to capture Ottawa.

The exception to the Liberal approach was the budget of the short-lived Clark government.

The Clark Interregnum

Ottawa's stance with respect to stabilization policy varied in the 1970s, 1980s, and 1990s in part with circumstance but primarily with changes in government. The Trudeau Liberals were defeated in the 1979 election by Joe Clark's Progressive Conservatives. Clark won the election almost without support in Quebec. He formed a strong minority government. Clark campaigned in part on a stimulative deficit and a $2 billion tax cut.[119] But soon after the election, his ministers began arguing that the Liberals had left too great a fiscal problem to implement the tax reduction.[120] Instead, Finance Minister John Crosbie's budget delivered tax increases and deficit reduction. Although the government fell when the budget did not obtain the confidence of the House, it would go too far to attribute the defeat to Crosbie's anti-deficit rhetoric and plans. The primary objection to the budget was an 18 cent per gallon increase (to 25 cents) in the excise tax on gas, diesel, and other fuels. In addition, central Canada was as upset about Crosbie's oil policy as Alberta was pleased.

But it is fair to say that the country was underprepared for Crosbie's vociferous fiscal rhetoric. He spoke of taking strong and necessary measures, even if they were not immediately popular. According to the minister, the government was elected because Canadians desired a new and realistic economic approach. In the long run, Crosbie claimed, good economics is good sense and therefore good politics.[121] But in the long run, alas, as Keynes pointed out, we are also all dead. In the short run, so was the Clark government, which fell two nights later.

In his autobiography, Crosbie claims that his major concern in the budget was inflation.[122] A former senior official, however, recalled that inflation was only a background issue in the budget process.[123] Nor does the public record support Crosbie's recollection. His major public preoccupations were, first, energy policy and then the deficit. Crosbie argued that to reach its potential Canada had to face realistically the problems caused by energy costs and shortages and by 'the huge and swelling budget deficit which we inherited from our Liberal predecessors.' In contrast to the Liberals, Crosbie said that to deal with the deficit issue would require more emphasis on the medium and long terms, and less focus on fine-tuning and immediate political 'subterfuges.'[124] Crosbie further asserted that recent experience showed that printing money, increasing government spending, and burgeoning deficits did not help the economy. In fact, they made things worse.[125] However, Crosbie's position was a position only. He provided little supporting argument for these claims. A reasoned articulation of the stance that persistent deficits and accumulating debt could be a serious economic problem was only just beginning to take shape. One former senior official argued that the budget's stance represented both an inchoate argument and an instinctive professional worry within the finance department about where deficits were leading. But it was not an understood critique, nor was it a radical policy change.[126] The same fiscal concerns were reflected in MacEachen's 1980 and 1981 budgets as well. MacEachen, though, was not nearly so vociferous in his rhetoric about the virtues of pain. Indeed, it is possible that part of the political problem with the budget was that Crosbie's anti-deficit rhetoric unnecessarily out-stripped the measures he proposed.

Broadly speaking, Crosbie chose three substantive responses to deficits. One was to institutionalize fiscal control. He fulfilled an election promise by tabling detailed fiscal projections through to 1983-4.[127] Allan Mac-Eachen would continue this practice. Crosbie also released a paper outlining the economic assumptions on which the projections were based.[128] But the most significant institutional innovation was the introduction of the Policy and Expenditure Management System (PEMS). While not developed to reduce deficits, the PEMS was to be used by Cabinet to determine resource allocations, and to bring accountability and restraint to fiscal planning. The system was adopted out of widespread concern within government regarding the continuing growth of the expenditure base due to increased spending on statutory programs, which was taking money away from new initiatives.[129] It was to work by forcing Cabinet committees to face the fiscal consequences of their policy decisions by giving them a finite spending envelope that would require them to prioritize.[130] Allan MacEachen would adopt this system as the Liberals' own in 1980, lauding it for facilitating priority setting and limiting spending.[131] It would be only speculative to comment on how the PEMS would have worked with regard to budgeting generally, or deficits specifically, under Joe Clark's leadership. But it clearly did not result in deficit reduction under Pierre Trudeau.

Crosbie's second measure against the deficit was spending restraint. For the Liberals in the latter half of the 1970s, spending limits had been aimed primarily at inflation control rather than deficit reduction. Crosbie characterized 'severe' restraint in the growth of federal spending as the most important action he was taking against the deficit. By severe restraint he meant that federal spending, including debt-servicing charges, would rise 10 percent annually over the next four years. There would be no real growth in spending.[132] Recall that the Liberal position had been to permit real spending growth, just not growth in excess of trend GNP growth. Depending on the accounting framework, and based on Crosbie's own numbers, spending increases under the Liberals in the two previous fiscal years were either a little under or a little over 10 percent annually.[133] In this respect, Crosbie's efforts were hardly a radical change of course from the Liberal path.

The third aspect of Crosbie's plan was tax increases. Crosbie said he did not anticipate tax increases beyond the measures in this budget. Tax moves were necessary for immediate fiscal purposes, but he argued that spending restraint would do the job in subsequent years. The most conspicuous tax move to fight the deficit was a special 5 percent corporate surtax for the specific purpose of deficit reduction.[134] The measure was to be terminated at the end of 1981. Crosbie also tabled a paper that defined tax expenditures and itemized their costs to the Consolidated Revenue Fund.[135] I mentioned earlier that MacEachen included with the 1981 budget a document outlining tax expenditures. This was another measure he appropriated from Crosbie.

The Clark Progressive Conservatives' position on deficit financing, as a government, differed significantly from that of their Liberal predecessors. Pierre Trudeau, as leader of the opposition, criticized the Tories in Keynesian terms. They 'are unduly obsessed with the size of the deficit ... In normal non-Tory budgeting in times such as these the budget wouldn't restrain the economy but encourage higher growth. In Liberal views, a deficit is an instrument. It is not something you necessarily want or necessarily steer away from. It is something you use to direct the economy when you want jobs.'[136] As opposition parties, both the Liberals and the Tories advocated greater deficit stimulation than the government offered. In Crosbie's retrospective view, his budget was well received by the business and financial communities, as well as by the media. But the general public, primarily because of the excise tax increase on transportation fuels, was far more negative.[137] Crosbie's budget was an outlier from the dominant trends of the Trudeau era, but it was significant for a number of reasons. The budget offered a glimpse of what was to come with Brian Mulroney in 1984 and after. It was received as bitter fiscal medicine, yet its measures were quite moderate compared with those Paul Martin would take with surprisingly little complaint sixteen years later. The failure to rally political support for the budget indicated the prematurity of these conceptualizations on the road to fiscal politics.

The Role of the State in the Economy

Compared with governments both before and after, the Trudeau Liberals had a generous vision of the appropriate role of the federal state in the economy. This vision had multiple origins. It was part of Trudeau's assertion of Ottawa with respect to provinces, particularly Quebec and Alberta, and had its legal parallel in the patriation of the constitution. The vision also flowed from Trudeau's commitment to 'rational planning' in government and the concomitant extension of bureaucracy and its processes.[138] And it was a result of the persistence of the Keynesian paradigm within an ideological framework of embedded liberalism in the face of economic decline. State protection from economic dislocation expanded the federal state's presence in economic life. But the Trudeau policies became fertile ground for the Mulroney seed that would reframe and circumscribe Ottawa's legitimacy as an economic actor. With the perceived failures of many of the Trudeau Liberals' policies to combat economic decline, it became increasingly implausible that direct intervention worked. The political friction created by some of these policies mobilized political resistance against the Keynesian paradigm. Economic failure and interested political energy generated conditions under which the more market-friendly Mulroney team could have public appeal.

That countercyclical deficit finance was conceptualized as a good thing during the Trudeau era ensured that the fiscal constraint did not limit state expansion and public expenditure to anything approaching the same degree it would in the 1990s. The view that the government's fiscal position was relatively unproblematic because countercyclical fiscal shortfalls were seen as good for the economy was part and parcel of the winning conceptualization of Ottawa's economic role. The view that the state had the capacity for effective short-term economic intervention to ameliorate unemployment meant the state was presented as directly responsible for economic performance. If the state could generate an effect, it was also a cause and therefore accountable for these immediate outcomes. The Keynesian paradigm judged deficit finance useful in this regard and condemned the use of unemployment to cure inflation. These short-term responsibilities and commitments deeply informed the policy choices and rhetoric of the day.

Given their ideational constructs and political commitments, the Liberals could not just let markets sort things out for themselves. The international political economy was consistently presented as an important determinant of Canadian economic life and problems. Although to some degree its imperatives were accepted, it was also taken as basic that sometimes the state could and should resist when external forces were seen as inimical to Canadian quality of life. In part this was due to the Trudeau administration's ambivalence toward the United States. This resistance was primarily a function of the state's accepted economic role. The government located comparatively good economic performance in the mid-1970s in federal policies, especially demand management, which were designed to mitigate the harsher consequences of the global economy. The fact that energy prices rose did not mean Canadians had to pay them all at once. If inflation was following the American lead, Canada could try to break from that course (at least until 1979).[139] Rather than give up in frustration, and rather than applaud what global forces would enjoin, the Liberal government regularly pursued what it saw as better paths. Protecting society and the economy from global dislocations was in keeping with the embedded liberalism of which Keynesianism was a component. In this context deficits were part of the government's policy tool kit for insulating from the worst effects of global change.

The legacy left by economic decline and Trudeau's economic policies is crucial to understanding subsequent change. The NEP further radicalized the West and did not work because the high international oil prices on which it was based collapsed. With this failure, the (central) Canadian nationalism on which the NEP was premised suffered lasting damage. Resistance to continentalism was diminished. This would provide Brian Mulroney with support for his dismantling of the Foreign Investment Review Agency and introduction of the Canada-United States Free Trade Agreement. The Anti-Inflation Program at best held some inflation off, but a year after it ended inflation increased again.[140] Inflation did come down with the 6 and 5 Program, but soaring interest rates and the resulting recession of 1981-2 were the primary cause and substantial price of inflation reduction. Deficit financing increased the national debt but unemployment crept stubbornly higher from traditional postwar levels.

The breakdown of Canada's Keynesian consensus came not simply from the failures of Keynesian and other policies but also from the invasiveness of the post-Keynesian solutions by which Robert Campbell and David Wolfe mark the end of the Keynesian era. The policies that interfered with private decisions were a source of tremendous tension precisely because they departed from the deference to the private sector by which Canadian Keynesianism had generally abided. The ideological conundrum that arose from post-Keynesian policy relates to the embedded liberalism of which Keynesianism was a component. Post-Keynesian policy emphasized the 'embedded' aspect of embedded liberalism. It was constructed to prevent society and economy from the dislocations an all-out war on inflation would engender. But the measures employed violated the 'liberalism' by which embedded liberalism was also constituted. At least in the Anglo-American tradition, a liberal economy meant a basic deference to the freedom of private actors to organize the details of their economic affairs. The postwar order was designed to save liberal capitalism, not to supplant it. In emphasizing the embedded, the Trudeau Liberals lost sight of what, in Canada, counted as liberal capitalism. Herein lie the negative origins of the neo-liberal counter-revolution. Neo-liberalism would protect and entrench anew – hence the 'neo' – the liberal economic tradition.

The introduction of the controversial policies that interfered with private decision making indicated there was considerable political room for state intervention in the economy in the latter half of the 1970s. But the tensions these policies created had the ironic effect of problematizing, in the future, actions of a similar genealogy. The political reaction against policies that asserted an immediate and direct state role was not a logical necessity. The problem with these programs might not have been that they overextended the state, but rather that they did not go far enough. The countries in the 1970s and early 1980s with the best inflation and unemployment performance were those with corporatist institutions.[141] Corporatism at the macro level entails tripartite cooperation between the state and authoritative peak business and labour organizations. This cooperation is designed to ensure competitive labour costs, continuing production, and a strong social safety net. Perhaps if Canada had moved in corporatist directions its policies would have been more efficacious. However, for two related reasons, government-led corporatist moves were not feasible in Canada. First, Canada did not, and does not, have the institutions in state or society capable of supporting corporatist arrangements on the Western European model.[142] Canada did not have a robust institution-building experience after the Second World War. Such an experience would have been antithetical to the Anglo-American capitalism Keynesianism was supposed to save, and there was no pressure in this direction from pre-Quiet Revolution Quebec. Canada has a comparatively weak federal state. Canada's labour and producer associations are comparatively disaggregated and are generally unable to bargain at a national level. There is no institutional legacy of legitimate state involvement in microeconomic decisions, and this is not easy to forge.[143] Indeed, this lack of legitimacy was a key source of the political reaction against the AIP and NEP.

Second, going further would have been treacherous indeed because the policies that were adopted, over time, generated costs of great political consequence. Interference with the autonomy of private decision making led to strong opposition from Canadian business. The business community has long held a privileged position in the Canadian industrial system, and concerted business opposition is difficult to ignore.[144] Peter Gourevitch argues that the resources actors can marshal for political disputes, along with the importance of the functions the actors perform in the economy, together generate the weight of threats to withdraw the actor's contributions. These factors are, for Gourevitch, important determinants of political outcomes.[145] In a capitalist economy primarily dependent on the private sector to perform economic functions, threats of capital withdrawal and employment loss carry great weight. Such was the case with resistance to the AIP, the NEP, the FIRA, and the like. With some provincial governments serving as both origins and transmission belts for this opposition, the institutional basis for resistance was further strengthened. After the stresses the Trudeau administrations experienced, and the political success Brian Mulroney would realize, in part through promises to defer to business decisions and provincial jurisdiction, a subsequent return to more interventionist policy became increasingly improbable.

The Liberals clearly knew, politically, that they had gone too far. The prestige and credibility of the Department of Finance had been eroded by John Turner's resignation, the problems with the AIP, the NEP, tax reform, and Trudeau's institutional downgrading of the department.[146] Lalonde's appointment as finance minister was meant to restore confidence in Finance. Lalonde's budgets were designed, even with their deficits, to restore the confidence of business. When Trudeau resigned in 1984, the Liberals chose John Turner to lead them in the next election. Turner was selected because he looked like a winner. This appearance consisted in no small part in his 1975 resignation and his following decade on Bay Street. Turner was disassociated from the unpopularity of Trudeau's economics and was on the 'right' side of wage and price controls. His main opponent, Jean Chrétien, was far too identified with these dead weights. One of Turner's few acts in his brief time at 24 Sussex was to eliminate the Ministry of State for Economic and Regional Development and the Ministry of State for Social Development. These, Trudeau's coordinating agencies, represented the planning and bureaucratization that were increasingly viewed as excessive. Mulroney trounced Turner in 1984, so Liberal aspirations were dashed, but the candidates of the two main parties were an indication that the economics of the 'just society' were increasingly out of fashion and the economics of Bay Street rather more in vogue.

Taking seriously the ideas a government propounds does not mean taking a government at its word. It means investigating the political, economic, institutional, and ideological factors that determine why a government speaks and acts as it does. The various Trudeau governments were much criticized for their intractability and combativeness. Some of this critique is well placed. But it underestimates the irreducibility of the Liberals' political attachment to the basic commitments and ideas that informed their economic and fiscal policy. Neither willing to cheerfully capitulate to the putative imperatives of the international economy, nor willing (for the most part) to cure stagflation by creating unemployment, the Trudeau Liberals tried many gambits to resolve Canada's economic problems. It is far too simple and cynical to describe, as John Richards does, this era as one of 'opportunistic Keynesianism,' that is, ignoring the other half of Keynesianism – the 'politically painful' half that would have governments run surpluses on the upside of the business cycle.[147] The Keynesian paradigm remained partially embedded in the policy process and in the expectations of voters. The Trudeau governments were politically committed to a vision in which the state had immediate capacities and responsibilities in the domestic economy, and sought to realize the aspirations this vision entailed.

5
Restructuring Power Relations

> Free trade is part of a whole that includes the GST, deregulation, privatization, and a concerted effort to reduce deficits, inflation, and interest rates, resulting in a more competitive, more prosperous Canadian economy.[1]
>
> – *Brian Mulroney*

In the previous chapter the negative reasons for Canada's move toward neo-liberalism were identified. These included restoring the liberal tradition that Trudeau's nontraditional emphasis on the embedding of liberalism had threatened, and preventing a return to Trudeau-style economic policy. There was also a positive agenda on which Mulroney's neo-liberalism was built, compatible with Canadian institutions and holding out the promise of a better economic future. His platform of decentralizing federal power to provinces and to markets, although initially vague, appealed to a number of overlapping constituencies. Decentralization to provinces was the basis of Mulroney's political coalition of Quebec and the West. Quebec's appetite for greater autonomy was to be part of how Mulroney would gain its signature on Trudeau's incomplete constitution 'with honour and enthusiasm.' Decentralization of the federation would also allow western provinces to emancipate themselves from what was viewed as a central Canadian parliament responsible for official bilingualism and the National Energy Program; western provinces could pursue their own paths more free of federal influence. Decentralization to markets would give Canadian business more control over its own destiny and remove the national shackles that lessened its ability to occupy a continental market. Mulroney's cry was for 'Jobs! Jobs! Jobs!' but jobs provided by the private sector rather than government.[2]

Mulroney's 1984 platform also promised to reduce the deficit. But it contained spending commitments that seemed to undermine the fiscal pledge.[3] It was too soon to get elected on fiscal restraint. Nonetheless, giving political expression to these repressed but emergent understandings of political and economic interests, along with John Turner's terrible campaign, helped Mulroney to realize a huge majority government in 1984. The force of these interests gave political life to the neo-liberal economic vision by which they were rationalized. This vision would gradually become autonomous as it became entrenched in institutions, policy, and politics, supplanting the embedded liberalism that had been the dominant strand during the previous forty years. Just as embedded liberal norms were a causal factor in some policy outcomes in the 1970s and early 1980s, neo-liberal commitments would be an important causal link in policy results for the rest of the 1980s and especially in the 1990s. The political system would eventually converge around neo-liberalism, and its precepts would become relatively less contested.

I do not use the term 'neo-liberal' in a judgmental sense. Rather, it is employed as a description of a set of policies; of the norms, values, and ideas embodied in those policies; and of the orientation of governments and other actors who propound these ideas and policies. In discussing the factors that favoured neo-liberalism, it is important to keep three things in mind. First, the processes of this broad change are ongoing. The processes have intensified over time, but have been in play since at least the 1960s. Second, states are key actors in precipitating and facilitating neo-liberalism. Finally, at least as important as the reality of these processes of change is the credibility of deploying them as tools in domestic political debate. For example, globalization may be real, but what also matters is the ability to persuade people that it is real so they will be susceptible to an argument framed in globalization's terms. Policies that facilitate globalization will, therefore, structure subsequent debate.

The argument in this chapter is that a number of related factors combined to substantially increase the appeal of the neo-liberal ideological and policy framework. Economic decline did not occur in a vacuum. It informed, and was informed by, other changes that also led down the road from embedded liberalism to neo-liberalism. Developments in economic theory cast doubt on the efficacy of state's demand-side efforts to stimulate growth. While these developments captured most of the economics profession, including practitioners working in finance ministries, these economic ideas required political sponsorship to attain hegemonic status. This sponsorship was much more likely to come from a political party ideologically predisposed to limiting direct state intervention in the economy. The Reagan and Thatcher examples demonstrated that winning coalitions could be built in part on neo-liberal economic restructuring. Mulroney's first electoral victory was somewhat ambiguous in these terms because his campaign was not very specific about economic reforms, and he held that social programs were a 'sacred trust.' But on taking office his government pursued an ambitious, pro-market reform agenda. The Progressive Conservatives located this agenda in the imperatives of 'international competition.' The credibility of their competitiveness argument resided in the economic dislocations of the 1970s and early 1980s, the failures of Trudeau's interventionist measures and the invasive responsibilities those measures imposed on institutions, and the increasing 'globalization' of the international political economy. Globalization tilted the domestic political playing field in favour of neo-liberal reform because it increased the leverage in political debate of policy that favoured capital. The threat of capital's exit, the increased power of financial capital as debt mounted, and capital's heightened distrust of inflation skewed perceptions of the state's policy autonomy and argued for pro-market reforms.

These factors all augmented neo-liberalism's viability. The state's embrace of neo-liberal policy crystallized with the Mulroney government's advocacy of 'free' trade with the United States, on which the Progressive Conservatives campaigned in 1988. The energy for this embrace came from concerted advocacy of such a deal by Canadian business as a strategy for emancipating itself from its profitability crisis. Corporate Canada reconceptualized its economic interests as continental rather than national, and the idea of a free trade agreement got its political life from this reconceptualization. The national interest was successfully presented as posited on allowing business to better compete, for the economic welfare of the country was largely dependent on the private sector. Free trade was also a mechanism by which Mulroney judged, correctly, that he could get re-elected. With the support of business, the West, and Quebec, Mulroney built a winning coalition, albeit one that received a plurality rather than a majority of the votes. The forces that were so manifest in the free trade debate also dwelt within other elements of Mulroney's program for renewal. Among these were deficit reduction and debt control. The Mulroney position on deficit finance can be understood only in terms of its relationship to the interested vision of the state role in the economy that directed his government.

International Ideological Change

Economic Theory about Economic Policy
Perhaps the watershed document signalling that economic policy should reorient itself to greater respect market integrity was the OECD's 1977 McCracken Report.[4] This document was particularly important in the realm of ideas because of its authoritative source.[5] It helped return to greater respectability policy designed to support rather than mitigate the outcomes of self-regulating markets. The report did not oppose demand management in itself, and so evinced little remarked vestiges of Keynesian thought. But it did argue that fiscal and monetary policy should be restrained along a 'narrow path' in view of inflation.[6] The report also largely located inflation and the deterioration of the conditions supporting growth in the expansion of the public sector associated with the Keynesian welfare state.[7]

The McCracken Report, though, was not very important in Canada. The

Canadian government had already undertaken a number of initiatives with respect to public expenditure that McCracken recommended. These included setting guidelines for public expenditure, indexing the tax system, and (at least nominally) reviewing priorities and improving the efficiency and effectiveness of public programs.[8] Indeed, a former senior official recollected that the McCracken Report received only a 'casual glance' in Canada's Department of Finance.[9] But what is (in retrospect) remarkable about the report is the extent to which at least the Anglo industrial countries now embody what Robert Keohane described as its 'disciplinary' rather than 'pluralistic Keynesian' state.[10] The McCracken Report argued that the former was necessary to generate the economic and political restraint required for growth.

Much of the McCracken Report centred on the scourge of inflation. The inflation issue was also being redescribed elsewhere. Contrary to the Phillips Curve notion that higher inflation could buy lower unemployment, inflation was increasingly viewed by economists as without purpose in a properly functioning economy. The theoretical justification for this view was captured in the concept called the 'natural rate of unemployment,' introduced by Milton Friedman in 1967.[11] (We became acquainted with this concept, also called the 'Non-Accelerating Inflation Rate of Unemployment,' [the NAIRU], in Chapter 3.) It already had some hold in Canada's Department of Finance by the mid- to late 1970s. Recall that the 'natural' level of unemployment according to this view is the one at which the rate of inflation is stable. Creating inflation to bring unemployment below its natural rate destabilizes and accelerates the inflation rate because inflationary measures work only so long as people are fooled into believing that inflationary growth has a real rather than a nominal basis. Printing money or excessive demand stimulation will be translated into higher wages, prices, and interest rates when actors recognize the inflationary basis of such demand and act to protect themselves from inflationary erosion of their real incomes. Not only will demand expansion fail to increase employment for very long; inflation will accelerate precisely because of these efforts to protect against the new inflation resulting from demand expansion. Since interest rates may also have increased, unemployment could now even exceed its natural rate. The harder government tries to accelerate growth by inflationary demand expansion, the more rapidly will markets anticipate inflation and raise interest rates. In this argument, the Phillips Curve tends toward vertical. Demand stimulation has only inflationary effects.

The implication, famously identified by Friedman in 1967, is that there is no long-run tradeoff between inflation and unemployment. According to Friedman, inflation is in the long run exclusively a monetary phenomenon. It is to be controlled by monetary policy (which allows money supply

growth equivalent to growth in the economy's real capacity and population increases). In the long run, supply-side policies designed to lessen
labour market rigidities, such as lowering the minimum wage or reducing
unemployment insurance benefits, will reduce the NAIRU. Neither demand management nor deficit finance has a place in reducing unemployment below its natural rate.

During the 1970s, Friedman's argument was extended by the 'rational expectations' theory developed by Robert Lucas and his disciples.[12] Rational
expectations theory differs from the NAIRU primarily in that the latter
sees inflation expectations as informed by past policy actions, while the
former goes further and presumes that market actors anticipate predictable
policy actions in advance. The rational expectations school argues, therefore, that discretionary policy *must* be destabilizing because rational economic actors will immediately understand any predicable macroeconomic
policy. Their recognition of inflationary demand expansion will be immediately built into prices. The state cannot create growth through macroeconomic management because stimulative measures will automatically
be translated into nominal rather than real outcomes. The only way to
fool rational actors would be to employ a random macroeconomic policy.
Since this would by definition make output more rather than less unstable, macroeconomic policy cannot serve a stabilizing function.[13]

The Friedman-Lucas attack on the Phillips Curve gained credence in
light of the coexistence of high unemployment and high inflation in the
1970s. The Phillips Curve view of the world could not easily make sense of
this circumstance, but the new economic theories could. Labour market
rigidities were presented as the cause of high unemployment; demand
expansion led to high and accelerating inflation. That the new theories
could offer low unemployment and low inflation made them all the more
attractive. Of course, the NAIRU was not a critique of demand stimulation
designed to reduce an unemployment rate that exceeded the NAIRU
toward its 'natural' level. And since inflation was presented as a monetary
phenomenon only in the long run, the short run was more complicated.
The NAIRU and associated ideas were adopted in varying degrees by
finance ministries across nations in the 1970s and 1980s. John Sargent, a
long-time official in Canada's Department of Finance, argues that the
NAIRU has gained almost universal acceptance among practitioners, although rational expectations theory is less unanimously adopted.[14] By the
mid-1980s, the NAIRU had clearly attained hegemonic status in Canada. It
ruled not only the Macdonald Commission Report but also the public
utterances from the Department of Finance. It increasingly directed conceptualizations of economic and social policy. These ideas could acquire
political sponsorship because they offered an economic rationale for limiting the state role in managing the economy. As Keynes's biographer,

Robert Skidelsky, notes, 'Politicians rarely look to economists to tell them what to do: mainly to give them arguments for doing things they want to do, or for not doing things they don't want to do.'[15] The NAIRU and cognate ideas could help rationalize and operationalize the neo-liberalism that, for political and ideological reasons, opposes short-run succour in favour of anti-inflationary discipline.[16]

Reagan and Thatcher

Developments in economic theory brought Keynesian notions of sound macroeconomic policy under increasing challenge across industrialized nations, including Canada. The acceptance of these theoretical changes in bureaucracies often required political sponsorship to be fully expressed. Conservative Margaret Thatcher attained power in England in 1979; Republican Ronald Reagan did the same in the United States in 1980. Each espoused an economic neo-liberalism and sought to circumscribe the state role in the economy. Neither Reagan's nor Thatcher's state was weak; strong action was required to enact and enforce both market-oriented reforms and neo-liberal discipline. However, in principle at least, the grasp of the strong state was limited.[17] It was not to interfere with market functions. Not only did Reagan and Thatcher provide examples for Mulroney and his disciples – their presence and power also made fending off the neo-liberal turn in Canada more difficult.[18]

Some components of the Reagan and Thatcher agendas never had strong analogues at the national level in Canada. For example, both Reagan and Thatcher espoused a social conservatism distinctly absent from Mulroney's agenda. The Mulroney government was also the least dogmatic of the three, in both rhetoric and practice. In addition, given the status of England and the United States at the time as, respectively, a faded and a fading superpower, the theme of restoration in the three countries had a more militaristic and nationalistic bent across the Atlantic ocean and to Canada's south. Reagan's 'military Keynesianism' (in which tax cuts combined with huge outlays for national defence created large budget deficits financed by foreign capital) distorted markets and intensified the Cold War. Mulroney's nationalism was both less aggressive and more derivative. Canada, obviously, could not take on an independent military role in the Cold War, although Mulroney did have plans for the Canadian military that were eventually sacrificed on the fiscal altar.

In economic terms, Canadian neo-liberalism also differed from neo-liberalism elsewhere. As John Shields and Stephen McBride argue, the traditional role of the Canadian state in economic development is a complicating factor for the development of Canadian neo-liberalism.[19] Reagan, Thatcher, and Mulroney did have in common that none fully succeeded in implementing their desired reforms.[20] But the broad direction in which they took their respective countries is also clear. The cross-national emergence of neo-liberal governments cannot be explained solely by reference to domestic or demonstration effects. We must look to change in the international political economy, and to related change in understandings of how corporate interests would best be realized, to grasp the appeal of the neo-liberal approach's promise of restoring industrialized nations generally, and Canada specifically, from economic decline.

Globalization and Neo-Liberalism

The Character of Globalization

The ongoing process of change in the international political economy, characterized by the increasing interconnectedness and interdependence of national economies, is now commonly known as globalization. 'Globalization is primarily a technological and economic process driven by the revolution in telecommunications and computers, massive increases in the movement of capital around the world, greatly expanded capacities for flexible world-wide production sourcing by firms, especially multinational corporations, and growing ecological interdependence and environmental spillovers.'[21] In this narrow sense, 'globalization' describes continuing changes integrating economic life. It also has normative dimensions, not only in the economic but also in other spheres: 'Put even more broadly, globalization embraces an expanding web of interlocking markets around the world, universal norms and standards that form common global reference points, communications that are virtually instantaneous, and the common social and economic practices brought about through computerization ... "Globalization" is really about "westernization," but it denotes none the less a world increasingly interconnected by economics, communications, and culture.'[22] I would add that this increasingly interconnected world is driven by forces more specific than those of the 'west.' Certainly after the Cold War, but also before, globalization is primarily about Americanization. Its political energy and economic rules originate in Washington; much of its finance is located in New York; its technological innovation emerges from Silicon Valley; and its cultural norms come from Hollywood. Certainly, the causal chain works in two directions. The world influences the United States, not least through immigration, but the relationship is asymmetrical, and skewed in favour of American norms and values.

The term globalization exploded into popular discourse in the 1990s. Indeed, the cheap ploy of putting 'globalization' in the title of university courses became a marketing tool for political science departments. The Mulroney government did not typically employ the word. Instead, 'international competitiveness' was its concern. Although this phrase did capture a number of the economic challenges of globalization, many of the features of globalization that we now take as basic, particularly the Internet, were not on the radar screen in the 1980s. The Mulroney government took office at an earlier stage of a process it would facilitate.

Globalization is not a simple fact; it is intertwined with a specific ideology. The rise of global capitalism in the mid-nineteenth century went hand in hand with the rise of classical economic liberalism.[23] Globalization in the 1980s and 1990s went hand-in-hand with neo-liberalism, a form of liberalism fitting to a new age of capital. Neo-liberalism is the dominant modern ideology and it is central to the 'global' political economy.[24] Neo-liberalism justifies the removal of barriers to the free play of market forces because doing so is understood to provide the highest level of general welfare. The state role is to supply public goods, but it is otherwise not to interfere with an individual's pursuit of her definition of her material interest.[25] Much of the symbiotic relationship between neo-liberalism and globalization resides in the capacity of the latter to leverage the removal of barriers to market forces which neo-liberalism applauds in any event: 'Of course, many nations still try to inhibit the flow of knowledge and money across their borders. But such inhibitions are proving increasingly futile, partly because modern technologies have made it so difficult for nations to control these flows ... Much of the knowledge and money, and many of the products and services, that people in different nations wish to exchange with one another are now easily transformed into electronic blips that move through the atmosphere at the speed of light.'[26] Globalization provides neo-liberalism with a material base; neo-liberalism makes capitalist globalization normative.

This globalized neo-liberalism is not the liberalism of free competition found in neo-classical economics. It is intimately intertwined with power. The global economy is oligopolistic in character. The international system is dominated by institutional investors and transnational firms.[27] In addition, the global economy did not emerge autonomously. It has been well supported by states, particularly the United States. In this regard it is very difficult to separate the economic from the political.[28] One could even argue that the sense of globalization's inexorability is tightly linked to the extent the American executive is committed to internationalism, liberalizing world trade, and managing protectionism in Congress. The technological change underpinning the global economy has been supported by military research;[29] the globalization of financial markets is inextricably linked to state activity;[30] and increasing world trade, while often restricted by states, has on the whole emerged from state participation in multilateral institutions like the GATT and the WTO, in addition to bilateral and unilateral efforts to force trade liberalization.[31] The state has not disappeared – it has become internationalized.[32] Effective international cooperation and the international labour movement, which seem forever around the corner, may again place boundaries on capital, in the manner of embedded liberalism. But when capital can both escape domestic regulation and turn contemporary supranational governance structures to its own ends, economic liberalism is not embedded. It is disciplinary upon states and societies.

State participation in globalization and neo-liberalism raises the question of the place of nationalism in a globalizing world. Ideologies that countervail hegemonic neo-liberalism do proliferate. These include fundamentalism and protective nationalisms.[33] But to the extent that this sort of nationalism is attributable to the rootlessness and uncertainty accompanying globalization, it is oppositional and reactionary. Yet nationalism can also be sustaining of, rather than in tension with, the global neo-liberal forces other nationalisms oppose. Such a nationalism arises through a redefinition of the 'national interest.' State-led nationalism can become pro-global and neo-liberal when decision makers in states judge that the costs of anti-global responses are prohibitive and that facilitating participation in the global system will best realize the country's economic and political goals.

The Mulroney government bought into this sort of nationalism wholeheartedly, going so far as to define national sovereignty as coextensive with international competitiveness after the Berlin Wall fell, on the grounds that to the extent the country was competitive, it was free. Canada, argued Finance Minister Michael Wilson, was a major trading nation and so could not turn inward. Rather, it had to work hard to realize the benefits of trade. But sovereignty, which he defined as the ability of a people to determine its own future, was in Wilson's view being eroded by inflation and growing debt.[34] Wilson also argued (before the end of the Cold War) that the Canada-United States Free Trade Agreement symbolized Canada's maturity as a sovereign and independent nation, for it demonstrated the country's ability to compete with products from around the world, both inside and outside Canada's borders.[35] To the extent globalization is an American-led phenomenon, however, this form of nationalism ironically brought Canada closer to the United States. An alternative approach to globalization would have been to treat it as a continuation of the complex relationship Canada has long shared with the United States, and long sought to manage. Instead, Mulroney's neo-liberal Canadian nationalism amounted to the continentalism about which governments had been less sanguine since Laurier's Liberals went down to defeat on the reciprocity issue in 1911.

Characterizations of Globalization

Globalization has profound implications for the state role in the economy. The range of ideas about the state's role that can be domestically viable is shaped by globalization. It is in terms of the neo-liberalism inherent in capital-based globalization that stances to the global political economy tend to be informed. To the extent the neo-liberal view is held, globalization will typically be applauded; to the extent neo-liberalism is opposed, so too will globalization be opposed, or at least globalization organized in capital's favour. In addition, the empirical reality and significance of globalization can be contested. It is in these terms that Keith Banting identifies three stances toward globalization.

The 'globalists' see integration as a fundamental change that governments should accept and support. Global competitive pressure is a good thing because it eliminates inefficient industry. The nation-state has lost a significant portion of its effective sovereignty. Divergent social policy that attempts to offset or delay adjustment only imposes longer-term economic costs. But if social policy facilitates change, Canadians will be properly equipped to face the future.[36] Beyond doubt, the globalist view was the Mulroney government's position on international competition and the state's role therein.

The 'anti-globalists,' by contrast, agree that globalization constitutes an important transformation. Rather than viewing it as an opportunity, the anti-globalists see globalization as a serious threat to equality, social justice, and democratic life. They concur that state sovereignty is eroded by economic integration, and view this erosion as a limit on the ability of democratically elected governments to carry out their citizens' wishes. As such, the anti-globalists recommend that governments resist unrestricted integration and make trade contingent on its compatibility with social and democratic ideals.[37] Anti-globalists also try to turn globalization in their favour by building cross-national political linkages among labour, social, and environmental groups.

Banting calls his third group the 'global skeptics.' On its face, their position is more empirical than ideological. Global skeptics doubt that the world is being so suddenly transformed. They argue that the late twentieth century was not characterized by greater change than earlier eras. Further, even if change is occurring its meaning is not obvious. Social policy across nations need not converge so long as programs reduce real incomes rather than increase production costs.[38]

The Mulroney government got on the globalization bus relatively early, and certainly before 'globalization' became a matter of everyday speech. If globalization has a meaningful existence, it has only increased since 1984. It is certainly true that there has been remarkable technological change since the birth of the computer after the Second World War. Any person in the West who was self-aware before the advent of the Internet knows that technology is remaking things, and maybe people.[39] These changes have political ramifications. New virtual communities are created at the same time as face-to-face contact is diminished. Different kinds of business emerge with different corporate cultures and different political agendas. These and other changes are only beginning to be recognized, much less understood. So from this point of view, the Mulroney government's early adoption of the globalist stance, in the form of international competitiveness, seems prescient. The anti-globalists may not approve of the response, but they have to agree with the diagnosis.

However, the global skeptics make some very serious points.[40] The world economy was more global before the First World War than it was in the 1980s or 1990s. Great Britain's pre-First World War economy was probably the most open economy in history. Its capital exports alone are mind boggling by today's standards.[41] Recall, after all, that Canada financed its railroads with British capital. The global market may work in something closer to real time now, but it is not as interconnected as was once the case. Globalization has also not yet led to the degree of policy harmonization that some of its critics anticipated. Tax rates still vary widely across the OECD nations, for example.[42] Domestic institutions and cultural norms also show substantial persistence. Even multinational corporations display distinctive national patterns in their creation, control, and use of technology. These patterns are based on national history and culture, and are not forcing deep convergence on national economies.[43] National governments continue to be the institutions through which global and continental forums are organized. John Helliwell argues that even after free trade the depth of economic linkages within Canada far outstrip Canada's economic linkages with the United States.[44] From this point of view, the Mulroney government's early adoption of the globalist stance seems ideological and ungrounded.[45]

Skepticism notwithstanding, some form of the globalist view has been propounded by the Canadian government since 1984. Insofar as neo-liberal norms are linked to this view, it entails by default the position that regulatory and welfare functions should be viewed as suspect. The anti-globalists have been losing because their position is relatively powerless when faced with the ascendant disciplinary power of capital backed by states. WTO protests in the streets of Seattle, or opposition to the Free Trade Agreement of the Americas in Quebec City, may over the long term shift power relations away from capital toward democratization. But in the 1980s and '90s, the structural *political* and *economic* power of capital clearly provided it with the upper hand.

Structural Power and Globalization
The success of neo-liberal globalization has been supported by a number of developments in the international political economy. Robert Cox identifies three key elements generating greater responsiveness to the perceived exigencies of global competition.[46] The first is the structural power

of capital. In a global environment, the weapons of investment strikes and capital flight, along with the threat of their deployment, exert discipline on unions and government spending. Capital once viewed inflation as relatively benign. But after the 1970s experience of high inflation and tight profits, capital punishes states that do not keep inflation low. The second element is the structuring of production. The emphasis is less on economies of scale attained by more production, and more on the economies of 'flexibility' that stem from producing in peripheral countries. Flexibility includes the option of moving production sites, which weakens the leverage of labour relative to capital. Workers, especially those outside of professional elites, are much less mobile than capital. Third, there is the role of debt. Corporations and governments became highly reliant on debt to finance their operations. As the percentage of revenues these entities dedicate to debt-servicing payments rises, they become relatively more accountable to bondholders and less accountable to shareholders and citizens. The options available to governments on the exchange rate, fiscal policy, and trade policy fronts are constrained by the implicit loan conditions set by global financial markets. Cox argues that productive corporations are similarly constrained. With financial and productive capital decoupled, financial capital driven by short-term returns is the real autocrat in the system.

Among the most important causes and consequences of globalization, then, has been the increasing mobility and quantity of international capital flows: 'Private capital movements began to return in the 1960s, grew rapidly in the 1970s, and then grew even faster in the 1980s (though global capital largely bypassed the developing countries mired in that decade's debt crisis). The worldwide trend of financial opening in the 1990s has restored a degree of international capital mobility not seen since this century's beginning.'[47] In principle, although not always in practice, financial capital can go where it wishes, punishing those who displease it and rewarding those who pay proper homage.[48] Computerization and the interlinking of financial markets have facilitated these dynamics. In this context, government budget deficits and mounting debt have become increasingly costly propositions. Debts and deficits are viewed by financial markets as inflationary. All things equal, which they are not, capital will either exit or not enter a high-inflation country unless a premium in the interest rate is offered to offset the higher risk of investment. Higher interest rates, though, both increase public debt to financial capital and suppress investment. To the extent the state is dependent on private capital to drive growth, financial globalization has certainly heightened limitations on state tolerance of debt and inflation.[49] As the next chapter will demonstrate, the Mulroney critique of deficit finance was very much located in financial market perceptions of connections between debt and inflation.

Increasing capital mobility has led states to adopt strategies of 'competitive deregulation' to entice capital to stay in or come to a country by domestic liberalization and deregulation. Competitive deregulation has made policy autonomy in the context of globalization more problematic. Without deregulation, the argument goes, a country and its firms will be less able to compete because regulatory requirements will keep cost structures too high to attract footloose capital.[50] This argument is applied not only to financial matters – excessive labour regulation is said to result in compensation too high to be competitive. If trade is not liberalized, domestic production is expected by deregulation proponents to be inefficient, costly, and uncompetitive. Capital, supposedly, will not be much interested in investing in such circumstances. These arguments are overdrawn because they put too much emphasis on only one of many factors that influence investment decisions. But both as economic policy and political program, deregulation, justified by international competition and capital mobility, has been both result and cause of capital's ascendancy in the last twenty years. This has also been perceived as a particular challenge for Canada, which has lost its status as a home for foreign direct investment: 'In 1967 Canada held over 18 per cent of the global stock of FDI. During the 1970s and early 1980s Canada's share fell dramatically to 10 per cent by 1980 and 6.6 per cent by 1990, as Europe and the United States became magnets for new FDI. This change came to be interpreted as a measure of the declining attractiveness of Canada as an investment location.'[51] Dramatic increases in Canadian direct investment abroad in the late 1970s and early 1980s were also presented by the Mulroney government as evidence that capital was fleeing because of Canada's declining attractiveness as a host for investment.[52]

Mulroney's domestic political project in part entailed competitive deregulation justified by increasing international competition and capital mobility. The Canada-United States Free Trade Agreement, the prioritization of deficit and inflation reduction over employment concerns, tax reform, the abolition of the Foreign Investment Review Agency, and privatization and deregulation were all part of a neo-liberal agenda.[53] But they were also pro-competitive policy responses to economic decline. Neo-liberal policies were backed by a big stick: the putative consequences of not respecting the power of capital.

So understood, globalization has structured policy debates to strongly favour neo-liberal outcomes. And of course, in the realm of politics, globalization is used as a tool by those of neo-liberal stock to realize policy outcomes they would support in any event. The credible deployment of international competition and globalization as a technique of persuasion is as important as any reality it may describe. One reason this technique has met with political success in Canada is that it has been used in a context of economic decline which seemed in part external in origin and also unresponsive to historically very interventionist domestic policy. Oil price shocks happened to Canada; the National Energy Program solved nothing. But in addition, the relative weakness of the Canadian state and economy, particularly in comparison with the American state and economy, has increased the leverage of the neo-liberal pro-competitive case. With respect to trade negotiations, Maxwell Cameron and Brian Tomlin argue that 'negotiators in weak ... states tend to be more responsive to the demands of the more powerful states than to domestic constituents. This proposition also implies a corollary: that international negotiators in weak states can more credibly use their vulnerability to international pressures to impose painful or costly domestic reforms.'[54] This is so not only in international negotiations, such as those leading to the Canada-United States Free Trade Agreement, but also for relatively weak states negotiating the politics of domestic budgeting and restructuring. In its budgets, the Mulroney government repeatedly argued that Canada had no choice but to adapt to increasing competition.[55] The rhetoric became more pronounced around 1989-90, but had been employed from the beginning.[56] The argument had credibility because Canada is mostly a 'price-taker' in the international economy. Using global competition as a reason for change, and improving competitiveness as the solution given that state intervention appeared counterproductive, worked well in this context.

Yet a question remains: Why did Canada avail itself of neo-liberal/ globalist responses when other options may have been available? The increasing structural power of capital loaded the debate in favour of globalism, but it does not logically follow that the neo-liberal turn would be embraced. There are two parts to the answer. The first involves Mulroney's political interests; he could get elected, after Trudeau, on decentralizing federal power to markets and provinces. The second is that not only did structural power tilt the field in favour of neo-liberal globalism; the latter also served the specific evolving profitability interests of increasingly politicized Canadian capital. Political and economic interests, supported by structural power, gave the neo-liberal train the power to move down its preferred track. Globalist ideas pointed the neo-liberal train in this specific direction. Policies embodying ideas about liberalizing the economy were selected for their utility in realizing interests so defined. Canadian capital's efforts to reconstitute itself in the face of economic decline expressed the symbiotic relationship between neo-liberal globalization and the power of capital. Neo-liberalism rationalized new understandings of how capital could best retain its status and achieve its interests. But once entrenched in policy and politics, neo-liberal reform reshaped the context in which subsequent decisions would be made. Indeed, Stephen Gill argues that hegmonic neo-liberalism does more than legitimate neo-liberal orderings; he sees neo-liberalism as a concrete form of structural and behavioural power that serves to discipline behaviour to conform it to neo-liberal imperatives.[57]

Shifting Corporate Interests

There is in modern liberal-capitalist democracies a rough consensus that economic growth is in everybody's interest. Governments depend primarily on private actors to generate growth, employment, revenue, and the like. Voters value a well-functioning economy and the maintenance of their material circumstance. Many depend on the private sector for employment. As such, there are important limits, although much national variation, on the actions governments can take when policies are seen as inimical to business interests.[58] However, neither the precise balance of power among social groups nor the specific understandings of these interests are immutable. Nor is the power of business to compel policy that will maintain its 'confidence' plenary. There has been change in the ways Canada's corporate community has understood and articulated its interests. These changes have been informed by change in the context in which business has operated. Together these alterations have provided powerful support over the last twenty-five years to the neo-liberal policies we have been discussing. Direct pressure was one way that business asserted itself. More important, these changes have altered conceptualizations of how the material interests of the nation are best pursued.

The support of Canadian business for the Keynesian consensus was never robust. Canadian business acquiesced to Keynesian policy and high wages rather than embracing them. The acquiescence resided in postwar rates of growth and productivity which maintained profits at levels sufficiently high that there was enough to spread around.[59] In this context, high wages were not a problem and small deficits were not a very salient issue. But only during war and transition to peace did Canadian business really endorse deficit financing. With the advent of economic decline, in which profits and productivity started to take a beating, the traditional pre-Second World War business opposition to deficit finance re-emerged. Harold Chorney argued in 1989 that business opposition to deficits had been more or less a fixed condition since 1975.[60] The volume of the opposition varied from budget to budget but the song was the same. This was also true in the 1990s.

Since the federal deficit was not eliminated until the 1998-9 fiscal year, it follows that business preferences do not automatically become policy outcomes. My concern here is to map out changes in the position of Canadian business and its behaviour, as well as the origins of these changes. The beginning point of the analysis is the 'corporate profitability crisis.' The 'crisis' in profits originated in factors definitive of economic decline. As David Wolfe argues, with increasing European and Japanese competition displacing American firms in the 1960s and 1970s, 'the existence of ever greater degrees of surplus capacity in key secondary manufacturing industries, combined with increasing degrees of international competitiveness and radically different rates of productivity, put increasing pressure on the rates of profitability of capitalist enterprises.'[61] In addition, tight labour markets and high wages also squeezed profits.[62] Reflecting the alternatives available from incipient globalization, firms in advanced capitalist countries began to relocate and restructure to resuscitate their profit levels. The relocation was to areas with substantially lower wage costs: the American Sunbelt and southern and Eastern Europe in the early 1970s, and the newly industrializing countries in the late 1970s and afterward. Restructuring included turning to mechanization instead of labour in the production process, and technological change provided this flexibility.[63] Indeed, Canadian corporate profits suffered greatly in the 1970s and 1980s. Measured as total profit to the stock of fixed capital, Canadian corporate profits generally declined from 1953 to 1972. Profits worsened substantially with the recession of the mid-1970s. There was a brief recovery in the late 1970s, but profits plummeted again in the early 1980s. Other measures of profitability mirrored these trends.[64]

The profitability crisis generated corporate response strategies. No longer was the corporate world obviously well served by national boundaries. A national economy and national regulation, including Keynesian stabilization, seemed increasingly to work against business by confining it instead of offering support. Companies were faced with new external competition, to which GATT tariff reductions contributed, and their wage structures were increasingly uncompetitive. Broadly speaking, business had two options: turn to the state for subsidies and protection, or enhance its ability to win the competition.

Canadian business embraced both of these options, but there was a relative shift in favour of competition. Canadian capital judged itself increasingly unable to stay competitive if it was confined to Canada, because of the country's small domestic market and high real wages. It started to look outward at opportunities for freer trade and investment. Free trade would allow the market access required for economies of scale, while free investment would allow setting up shop in low cost areas. Indeed, by the early to mid-1970s, 'the direction of continental capital flows had reversed: U.S. capital was less interested in setting up behind Canada's declining tariff wall, whereas Canadian entrepreneurs were starting to buy out U.S. branch plants and to expand their operations to the south.'[65] In addition, one American response to its competitive decline was protection from foreign competition. This, in combination with the desire of Canadian firms for access to the American market, also served as a strong Canadian impetus for the Canada-United States Free Trade Agreement.

The expansion of Canadian foreign investment reflected another important factor in the shift to continentalism: the maturation of Canadian business in the 1960s and 1970s. As Stephen Clarkson argues, some sectors of the Canadian economy, such as automobiles, had long been continental in orientation. Banks, real estate developers, the Canadian media, and the Canadian defence industry were all eager for the opportunity they saw to the south. Companies in sectors with relatively less tariff protection were already establishing branch operations in the United States to obviate its protectionism. Infant industry had grown up, and wanted the Canadian state in its role as parent to allow its children to flourish by opening the continental market.[66] In this regard, cleavages within the business community were overcome:

> Whatever interests divided the various fractions of Canadian capital, the cumulative effect of their deep-felt hatred of Pierre Trudeau's government, of their realization that further trade liberalization was unavoidable, of their concern about getting better access to the American market had built up an extraordinary consensus that crossed previously insuperable barriers to political co-operation. The less competitive manufacturing sector was ready to practice survival of the fittest. Branch plants threatened by the end of tariffs were told by their head offices to toe the line of continentalism. The more aggressive resource exporters wanted reduced US tariff barriers to hurdle. Canadian finance capital hoped for exemption from US protectionist restraints. Small business dreamed of competing in the big league by expanding operations across the border.[67]

Canadian business and its mouthpieces exerted substantial pressure in favour of liberalized trade. The 'staples fraction' of Canadian capital was represented by the Business Council on National Issues (BCNI, now the Canadian Council of Chief Executives). The BCNI was formed in 1976 out of concern the Keynesian welfare state was encroaching too much on the private sector. This engendered fears, which the Trudeau government aggravated, that capital was losing its authority with respect to the state. Composed of the chief executive officers of 150 leading Canadian corporations,[68] its membership included the resource staples sector, the financial sector, the manufacturing sector with links to staples production (i.e., steel, construction, pulp and paper), and the American-owned manufacturing sector producing consumer goods.[69] The organization, of course, puts its positions in terms of the public interest. But as David Langille argued in 1987, because the BCNI's members operate under the imperatives of international capitalism, its primary concern has really been to represent multinational capital in influencing the Canadian state to provide access to an integrated American market.[70]

The branch plant manufacturing fraction, by contrast, consisted primarily of American branch plant manufacturers oriented to the Canadian market. Its primary representative was the Canadian Manufacturers' Association.[71] This group was not a likely supporter of 'free' trade, and indeed had opposed it for over a century. However, CMA members felt the 1982 recession more deeply than did their BCNI counterparts. Over fourteen months, more than 30,000 employees of CMA firms were laid off. In addition, falling tariffs and changing trade patterns gradually increased the significance of trade to CMA members. Over the decade from the early 1970s, the proportion of association members exporting and importing rose from 15 percent to 40 percent.[72] These hard facts meant CMA members had to become more 'competitive,' and access to the US market was seen as the magic elixir. Those CMA member branch plants that had considerable autonomy from their parent corporations also established links with the BCNI.[73] Reflecting its evolution toward international trade, in the 1990s the CMA merged with the Canadian Exporters' Association to form the Canadian Manufacturers and Exporters (CME).

The Macdonald Commission

The BCNI, the CMA, and their members pushed hard for free trade with the United States. This push was central to the general business agenda of improving its profitability via competitiveness, and it became the agenda of the Mulroney government as well. Business advocated this agenda before the 'Macdonald Commission.' This Royal Commission was mandated by Pierre Trudeau in 1982 with the hope that, in the context of constitutional and economic upheaval, it would provide justification for enhancing federal powers relative to provinces in light of encroaching global interdependence.[74] It was chaired by Donald Macdonald, the former Trudeau finance minister who had introduced wage and price controls. Things did not end up as the Liberals might have hoped, and some of the same forces that propelled Mulroney to power also resulted in the commission's recommendation that Canada pursue a free trade agreement with the United States. There was nothing inevitable about the commission's recommendations or Canada's signing an agreement (which turned out to be very different from the kind of deal the commission suggested). But a concerted corporate effort in light of redefined interests, which were structurally supported by increasing competition and globalization, encouraged the selection of a new vision of how the national interest would best be realized.

The Macdonald Commission received submissions that reflected a polarization of views within Canada. On the one side were labour and social interests which pushed an 'interventionist nationalist' agenda. On the other side were 'liberal continentalist' business views.[75] The CMA ensured that it would be the first group the commission heard.[76] Broadly speaking, in recommending free trade the commission supported the liberal continentalist position. There is debate about the mechanism by which the 'business' view won. Richard Simeon argues that the commission's thinking was contextualized by economic conditions. Economic matters were of primary concern due to a sense of urgency borne of the recent recession, and a sense of threat to Canada in light of an increasingly competitive world. Since the problem was perceived as economic in nature, the commission's answers had to deal with productivity, competitiveness, and adaptability. The neo-classical economists tasked with the commission's economic research met this need.[77] The commission did not necessarily support free trade for the same reasons as the economists. The former saw it as a strategy for managing American protectionism, the latter as an unambiguous good. The social justice agenda, argues Simeon, might have won the day in more affluent times. But it failed because it did not deal in credible ways with questions of growth and efficiency, especially given the context informing the commission's thinking. The social justice approach failed, as it was not pro-growth, it presumed Canada was independent of the world, and it offered a critique of existing policy rather than a precise alternative.[78]

Duncan Cameron and Daniel Drache dispute Simeon's reading. They argue that the popular approach was realistic. Neil Bradford calls it a 'progressive competitiveness' agenda, although in his assessment it was not a viable alternative.[79] It was grounded in making full employment a priority as an impetus to growth. Drache and Cameron argue that in privileging the viewpoint of economists, the commission relied on an empiricism based on formal models that converged with the business agenda.[80] The social sciences are political because they are used in political debate. To describe a research program as coming out of a context is a pretence.[81]

In my view Simeon has the better of this argument precisely because Drache and Cameron are right about the appropriation of ideas by power. Drache and Cameron are correct that academic scholarship is used by political actors. But Simeon's account is not divorced from politics. His reference to the 'context' of the commission's research and mandate makes sense only if that context is understood as political. The context was one shaped by decline, failed intervention, and profitability challenges in the face of increasingly global competition. This is precisely the set of politico-economic factors that I have been arguing favoured disciplinary neo-liberal responses. Part of the progressive school's political weakness resided in the weight that corporate actors brought to the other side, not just in presentations to the commission but also in the structuring of power relations in Canadian politics. So long as capitalist liberal democracy is dependent on private capital to generate growth, the general interests of the country and its population cannot substantially diverge from those of the business community for too long. With politics shaped by economic decline, failed intervention, and global competition, concerns for national and social well-being became characterized not so much as ancillary to, but rather as posited on, neo-liberal economic arrangements supporting the competitive capacity of the business community. These politics did not determine policy recommendations in every detail. As Simeon notes, while the Macdonald Commission's point of view was primarily market enhancing, its recommendations regarding adjustment assistance, equalization, and regional development significantly mitigated this stance.[82] But these politics did establish the broad directions of the recommendations. Yes, business was using social sciences and pursuing its interests. That it was able to do so is part of the context and part of why the corporate view triumphed. It is no perfidy to explain these dynamics; it is good social science. The selection of ideas was not neutral. That is exactly my, and I believe Simeon's, point.

The Free Trade Election

The 1988 election was won not on fiscal restraint, but primarily by polarizing the country around the free trade issue. Corporate, regional, and political interests coalesced into a winning coalition built on a liberalized trade deal with the United States. The Macdonald Commission certainly handed Mulroney a gift. The Progressive Conservatives had been criticized for lacking focus and vision. When the commission's report was released in September 1985, in addition to giving free trade bipartisan and intellectual legitimacy, it provided Mulroney with a new issue on which he could campaign. The political advantages of the Macdonald Report and its recommendations were not lost on Mulroney, and with the report bilateral trade initiatives acquired a much higher priority.[83] Nonetheless, while the Tories did not campaign on free trade in 1984, and while trade officials were still exploring a range of trade options,[84] the initiative was not a radical departure from the Progressive Conservative program. The Department of Finance's *Agenda for Renewal* document in 1984 specifically listed bilateral trade negotiations with the United States as an item the government would investigate.[85]

The free trade initiative had substantial political advantages for the Tories. As Doern and Tomlin argue, 'Mulroney and his advisors wanted to differentiate themselves from the centralizing and state-led policies of the Trudeau government. They were also determined to build a strong Tory base in Quebec and to practise national reconciliation, especially regarding western Canada. Finally, the Conservatives wanted to build a closer and more co-operative relationship with the United States. Free trade offered the means to accomplish all four goals simultaneously.'[86] Differentiation from Trudeau in part entailed entrenching neo-liberal over embedded liberal norms. Free trade would increase Canada's integration into the United States. The CUFTA was popular in the West because it would undo the tariff and the National Policy, which were viewed as inherently discriminatory in central Canada's favour. Further, in 1985 the Tories had signed the 'Western Accord,' which killed the National Energy Program in favour of deregulating the oil and gas industries.[87] The CUFTA would cement the deal by making another NEP unlawful. Quebec supported the CUFTA not only because its maturing business class was onside but also for nationalist reasons. Particularly when the Parti Québécois was still in power, but even after Robert Bourassa's Liberals took over in 1985, the dominant vision was one in which tying Quebec to the United States would diminish the province's dependence on the rest of Canada and increase its autonomy from Ottawa.[88]

The federal-provincial dimensions of the CUFTA, then, were very significant. The deal was an assertion of federal power in that the initiative was clearly driven and negotiated by Ottawa. Strong federal action was required to tie Ottawa's own hands, and to persuade provinces to comply with the treaty in areas where they would be responsible for implementation.[89] But free trade would also decentralize power from Ottawa to markets by disciplining the federal government's domestic policy autonomy. So too would federal power within the federation be constrained. Mulroney built his coalition around Quebec and the West. The Macdonald Commission also thought free trade would mitigate regional tensions by undoing the National Policy and outlawing future national energy programs. In reference to the National Policy, the commission argued:

> It is probable that the most significant and long-term effect of free trade would be the strengthening of national unity and the removal of one of the most persistent and corrosive sources of regional alienation in Canada's political history ... It is difficult to think of any other act of Canadian public policy that would have so comparably healing an effect. This act could be expected, in time, to contribute enormously to our national sense of Canada as a single community and could regenerate our previous store of general good will. It would correspondingly reduce the level of federal-provincial conflict and increase our capacity to work together for common purposes.[90]

Over a decade of experience provides little evidence to support this view. At best, it can be argued that free trade kept regionalism from becoming even more exaggerated than was the case in the 1990s. Ontario governments radicalized toward Ottawa while governed by successive Liberal, NDP, and Conservative administrations.[91] Quebec came within a whisker of voting for independence in 1995 and gave the separatist Bloc Québécois the majority of its seats in Parliament in the 1993, 1997, and 2000 federal elections. Increased western distrust of central Canada was reflected and paced by the emergence of the regionally based Reform Party. Indeed, the failure of the other central plank of Mulroney's 1988 platform, the Meech Lake Accord, revealed the incoherence of Mulroney's Quebec-West coalition. These two parts of Canada could be united around liberalized North-South trade, which made them less relevant to each other, but their visions of Canadian nationhood were radically different.[92]

Of course, free trade was not the only issue by which Canadians determined their vote in 1988. But most Canadian elections are not so focused around one concrete issue. Certainly the business community had a clear understanding of what the election was about. Business contributions went overwhelmingly to the Progressive Conservatives in support of corporate Canada's pet project.[93] If the election was not 'bought,' it was certainly paid for. John Turner's Liberals won Atlantic Canada and Ontario, but the Progressive Conservatives took Quebec and the West. Overall, Mulroney won 58 percent of the seats with 43 percent of the vote. This sufficed as a mandate to the extent Canadian elections produce such things.[94] Nonetheless, free trade specifically, and neo-liberalism generally, were clearly not getting majority support in the 1988 election. To win on even a soft-edged neo-liberal platform was a matter of coalition building, political craftsmanship, and the complicity of the first-past-the-post electoral system. Business was solid in its support but the mass public was not fully onside. Regional wedges had to be built into a strategy for electoral support of the government's agenda. Indeed, the strategic and political value of free trade is demonstrated in Mulroney's selectivity regarding the Macdonald Commission's recommendations. The Macdonald Report recommended adjustment assistance and a guaranteed annual income, among many other things. But recommendations beyond free trade were of less political advantage to Mulroney, so he either ignored them or disposed of them when the time was right. The Macdonald Report was Mulroney's servant, not his master.[95]

Conclusion

The business mobilization to restore profitability and Mulroney's desire for re-election constituted the interests underlying Canada's embrace of reciprocity. The idea of liberalizing the economy was selected by the state because of its utility in realizing these interests. An expertly executed regional political strategy made it so. Over time, these interests for the most part overcame the continued hold of Keynesian ideas on Ottawa. As we saw in the preceding chapters, Keynesian ideas persisted past the interested circumstances that supported their initial selection. But these ideas, much less grounded from the mid-1970s onward, could not hold their position indefinitely when challenged by ideas grounded in structurally powerful mobilized interests. Free trade was the most conspicuous element of Mulroney's economic renewal. In removing policy levers from the federal state, free trade decentralized power to markets by disciplining both the Canadian government and those who would make demands on it. The neo-liberal corporate triumph was also manifest in Mulroney's policies of deregulation, privatization, tax reform, and his government's hostility to the federal deficit.

And yet, the Mulroney government never eliminated the deficit. In fact, fiscal shortfalls reached record levels by the time he left office. Indeed, Langille noted in 1987 that the BCNI was still frustrated in its efforts to persuade Ottawa to reduce the deficit.[96] In 1989 Michael Ornstein argued that the BCNI, its successes notwithstanding, had been ineffective in changing social programs, government spending, or the deficit.[97] It was apparently easier, or more accurately a higher priority, to restructure the economy than to get at federal finances. I will argue in the next chapter that these structural changes were incompatible with short- and medium-term deficit reduction. But they also laid down the groundwork for fiscal retrenchment. As Mulroney's economic renewal became embodied in policy, the country became increasingly subject to competitive pressure. This heightened the urgency of reducing a deficit argued to be inimical to the competitive position of Canadian business. Over time, Mulroney's fundamental economic reforms also shifted the interests of the Canadian mass public to the extent that citizens generally could be persuaded of the merits of fiscal restraint. Alas, the Progressive Conservatives were out of office before they could avail themselves of the opportunity for what would be, remarkably, popular and legitimate fiscal restraint. (I will elaborate on this claim in Chapter 7.) In bringing more fully the mass public into my account of a long process of reconfiguring interests, I will complete the political economy of fiscal politics.

6
The Priority of Structural Reform, 1984-93

> I still won fifteen or twenty seats more than Mr. Trudeau did at
> the height of his popularity. So I've had my share of popularity.
> The unpopularity comes when you have to do important things.
> And I guess you have to decide whether you'll be popular, or
> whether you want to make to affect [sic] important structural
> change.
>
> I believe that what should be done, we should be conducting our-
> selves not for easy headlines in ten days but for a better Canada
> in ten years.
>
> If you're asking me ... whether I think we, we did everything
> right, the answer's no, we didn't, if you're asking whether I think
> we made mistakes, I think we had obviously. If you're asking me
> whether I think we did the right thing for Canada, whether we
> believed we were doing the right thing, with these important
> structural changes the answer is yes because what we were trying
> to do was to deliver the kind of Canada we have today, with
> one exception [the failure to get Quebec's signature on the
> constitution].[1]
>
> – Brian Mulroney

A substantial reorientation of fiscal and economic policy is a long process
punctuated by key events.[2] Among these events can be new, authoritative
conceptualizations of fiscal and economic policy. The 1984 election of
Brian Mulroney's Progressive Conservative government marks the breaking
point from the postwar and Trudeau-era presentations of deficit finance.
Finance Minister Michael Wilson's first economic statement re-evaluated
the role Ottawa's fiscal position played in the economy. Broadly speaking,
Wilson did three things. First, he raised the importance of persistent deficits and accumulating debt in the pantheon of challenges facing the federal
government. Second, instead of applauding it, he problematized Ottawa's
fiscal situation. Third, he located this problematization within a vision
different from the Trudeau Liberal articulation of a properly functioning
economy and state. The Tory attack on deficits was at its core part of
a wider neo-liberal position regarding the state role in the economy. In
rhetorical terms, Wilson offered what Peter Hall describes as third-order

change. Over time, policy would in substantial measure also embody third-order shifts from the Trudeau-era in the fundamental goals and orientations of the federal government.

Indeed, it was the Progressive Conservatives' deep commitment to their program of neo-liberal economic renewal that primarily accounts for the yawning chasm between their anti-deficit rhetoric and their abject failure to attain their fiscal goals. The economic model under which the government operated impugned deficits, but it also mandated a number of other important structural reforms. The government's commitment to realizing economic renewal, above all else through the Canada-United States Free Trade Agreement and the Bank of Canada's price stability policy, were in the short and medium terms incompatible with Tory deficit objectives. In addition, Michael Wilson's argument against deficit finance was based on its inimical impact on Canada's competitive position. But thanks to the implementation of Mulroney's policy agenda, Canada was much more subject to the competitive pressures that would justify fiscal retrenchment after the Progressive Conservatives left office than in 1984. Another factor was that before fiscal politics became entrenched, the mass public was not politically prepared to support explicit retrenchment. The opposition parties, while happy to criticize the government for ongoing deficits, continued to oppose retrenchment and often advocated greater stimulation of the economy. Finally the fiscal objectives were frustrated by a little-remarked and surprising finding: a latent Keynesian discourse dwelt on the edges of the government's dominant fiscal conceptualizations.

From Economic Decline to Economic Renewal

The Progressive Conservatives' dominant conceptualization of deficit finance was always located within a wider economic model and program. Transforming this model into policy was presented as a recipe for economic renewal. The foundational document that Finance Minister Michael Wilson tabled in 1984 dovetailed nicely with the preferences the Tories expressed in opposition and in the 1984 election campaign. But it also indicated that the Department of Finance sought to reorient economic and fiscal policy. Wilson's program for renewal was adopted from transition documents prepared by the department.[3] The briefing books were very similar to what became the official government documents.[4] Finance had begun preparing these materials in May 1984, under the Liberals.[5] These documents were also designed to allow Finance to seize the initiative with a new government and heighten the department's stature, which had declined over the previous decade.[6]

According to Wilson's argument, only if Canada's economy became more productive, more efficient, and above all more competitive could Canadian living standards continue to rise. The world economy was changing, and this meant the Canadian economy must not be cosseted by the state. Instead, it must be on the competitive cutting edge. The major rationale Wilson presented for deficit reduction was his position that the deficit and debt caused underperformance in higher order economic variables such as growth, employment, inflation, and investment. Deficit reduction was of value mostly insofar as it would enhance competitiveness, ameliorate underperformance, and assist in the renewal of Canada's economy. Rarely did Tory rhetoric about the importance of international competition ease. This presentation, in my view, was the basis for the position that the deficit problem was a matter of 'reality' rather than 'ideology.'[7] The need for deficit reduction was premised on the reality of international competitive pressure. If international competition was a real challenge, and if the causal link between the deficit and weak competitiveness was real, then there really was a deficit problem. But there were also other competitiveness problems that the Progressive Conservatives identified. Presenting deficit reduction as one method of attaining higher order goals, rather than as prior to these goals, left deficit reduction subject to economic renewal. When the pursuit of other structural reforms also deemed necessary to enhancing competitiveness was inconsistent with deficit reduction, fiscal control took a back seat.

The Economic Question
Michael Wilson interpreted the 1984 election as Canadians' judgment on policy, process, and the recent past. He argued that deficits, unemployment, intrusive government, and sluggish growth were all parts of the problem. Canadians, he said, knew the economic world had changed, but government had not kept pace.[8] It was true, Wilson argued, that change in the international economy created difficulties, but it also offered opportunities of which Canada had not taken advantage. Policy had treated symptoms rather than causes, resulting in a worsened fiscal situation and the substitution of the judgment of markets by that of regulators. Regulation was sapping creativity while the inefficient were being protected. Indwelling economic dynamism, claimed Wilson, was vitiated by policies that compensated the less productive at the expense of risk-takers.[9] The government's stated objective was to provide a policy framework that would release the 'creative energies' of Canadians. This, in turn, would put Canadians back to work so all could have a better life.[10] To move away from protection, of course, was to begin disembedding liberalism.

The government identified four challenges facing Canada. First, the fiscal house had to be put in order. Second, the government's role had to be redefined to provide a better framework for growth and job creation, and fewer obstacles to change and innovation. Third, policies fostering higher investment, innovation, international competitiveness, and a better climate for the birth and growth of new enterprises were necessary. Fourth, all this had to be done in a fair and open manner consistent with the basic sense of fairness, compassion, tolerance, and justice in Canadian society.[11] Moving to provide a better framework for growth and job creation would, even though this framework entailed market liberalization, require strong state action to bring about the transition. This agenda also provided for a substantial state role in the third challenge, that of promoting economic activity. It was not an agenda of tax cuts to cure all ills. And the rhetoric of compassion did not describe a proudly antiwelfare neo-liberalism. At the provincial level, at least, Canada has since seen much worse.

That said, Wilson's construction of the interests pursued and ends sought by Canadians was a rather sparse account. To vindicate putting a liberalized economy first, Wilson posited an 'economic person.' Because state policy was presented as repressing intrinsic 'creative energies' to produce and innovate, policy should therefore be changed to release this animating force. So framing the issue allowed the government to present its agenda as original with the citizen. To deny the expression of economic energy was to deny Canadians access to their authentic selves. This fell by some measure short of an Aristotelian account of the soul. But the universalistic language did hide the preferences immanent in the model that Wilson's state would shape. In restructuring economic policy the government would clearly be helping some (the 'innovative') and harming others (the 'protected'). Not everybody voted Tory in 1984 (50 percent did, which in Canada is a lot) and not everybody would be better off under the Conservatives. Wilson's naturalization of his construction disguised the forces animating, and preferred by, the program for renewal.[12]

The Problematization of Deficits

If there was a shift from embedded to neo-liberal norms with the change in governments, it is also to be expected that the commitment to Keynesian fiscal policy, which was one mode of making embedded liberalism operational, would fall by the wayside. This is essentially what occurred. Since the need for renewal was located primarily in enhancing Canada's competitive position in the global economy, and since deficit reduction was a component of renewal, the perceived need for deficit reduction was conceptualized as a function of Canada's perceived international economic position. Michael Wilson described deficits as a problem rather than a solution not, in his own view, because to do so was popular. Rather, Wilson argued Canadians had to be educated about problems with Canada's fiscal position.[13] Economic dynamism may have been original with the citizen, but apparently consciousness raising was still necessary. Wilson thought Canadians were unpersuaded that there really was a deficit problem, so he purposefully and repeatedly made speeches, did talk shows and open-line shows, and spoke to editorial boards to convince Canadians otherwise.[14] Political scientists refer to the process of making voters more susceptible to a certain view of an issue as 'priming.'[15] This is usually done during election campaigns. But priming Canadians for deficit reduction would take ten years. Wilson deserves some credit for the eventual turn of the mass public in favour of budgetary balance. It is clear that Wilson believed what he was saying about the deficit on taking office. This accounts in part for the public life of the winning ideas about deficit finance from 1984 to 1991.

In 1984 Wilson argued that Canada's fiscal future was bleak unless the government took immediate steps. He stated that the 1984-5 deficit was likely to come in at $34.5 billion, or $5 billion more than Wilson's Liberal predecessor, Marc Lalonde, had predicted. Wilson added that it would probably be between $34 and $38 billion annually over the rest of the decade without government action.[16] The deficit, argued Wilson, would not decline naturally because growth was weaker than in the postwar era, interest rates were higher, and accounting changes would increase the official measure of the deficit.[17] Fiscal shortfalls were no longer a countercyclical response to moderate recessions, he stated correctly, but now remained through expansions.[18] Wilson argued that the problem would probably get worse because the government's fiscal position was very vulnerable to high real interest rates. If the real rate of interest exceeded the real rate of growth, revenue increases from increased growth would be insufficient to pay off increased debt-servicing charges. As each new deficit added to the principle on which interest was paid, growth would have to accelerate even more just to stay even. Wilson concluded that prudence dictated the debt should be prevented from growing faster than the economy as soon as possible.[19]

Comparing Problematizations

In November 1985, Michael Wilson released *Reducing the Deficit and Controlling the National Debt*. It confirmed and refined the government's position on deficits and debt as described in the 1984 Economic and Fiscal Statement and the 1985 budget. *Reducing the Deficit* was written by bureaucrats.[20] That this document was produced by the Department of Finance just two and a half years after Marc Lalonde's 1983 *The Federal Deficit in Perspective,* and that the two documents were largely incompatible, suggests that political rather than institutional factors drove their publication. In fact, both political and bureaucratic determinants were in play. The department was becoming concerned regarding continued deficits and accumulating debt in the early 1980s. Officials were not comfortable with the fiscal position in 1982 and 1983, although both they and Lalonde accepted the deficit and added to it in the circumstance.[21] That Finance began crafting, as I noted earlier, transition documents that would form the basis of the Tory economic plan when the Liberals were still in office indicates the department was, by the mid-1980s, more comfortable with an approach to fiscal policy built around the NAIRU than Keynesian stabilization. In interviews, two senior officials stated that the 1984 transition documents would have been the same regardless of which party won the election. From the inside, officials deny that the change in views was politically influenced. What seems to be a public disjuncture was a more smooth transition within the Department.[22] In the absence of political sponsorship, though, the ideas would have gone nowhere. In 1983, the department was on the whole not entirely comfortable with the government's approach to fiscal policy; the department and the minister were on the same page in 1985, although it is not clear that Cabinet as a whole shared this view of the fiscal situation.[23]

The Lalonde and Wilson documents had in common the view that persistent deficits from the mid-1970s onward resulted from an imbalance between spending and revenue. Recall from Chapter 4 that Lalonde's paper did not treat spending increases as an important component of these deficits. To the extent there were real spending increases, Lalonde couched them in terms of cyclical factors and diminished their tendency to persist.[24] Wilson did acknowledge that spending rose in a countercyclical fashion during the 1981-2 recession. But he argued that spending increases were a significant contributor to chronic deficits.[25] There were also other disagreements. On the crowding out of private investment and the fiscal positions of other governments, the ministers diverged substantially. But more important was their basic difference regarding the relationships between fiscal shortfalls and inflation. And yet, there was also a surprising similarity. Wilson's position displayed more vestiges of Keynesian conceptualizations than is commonly recognized.

Inflation and the Fiscal Position
The starkest contrast was with respect to inflation. Recall that for Lalonde, inflation was an ally in fiscal control. It eroded the real value of the stock of debt and of annual deficits. For Wilson, inflation caused higher deficits that were in turn inflationary. He argued that since the Second World War there had been unanticipated bouts of Canadian inflation. These price increases resulted in low real interest rates and eroded the value of the debt.[26] But, said Wilson, for three reasons this was not likely to continue. First, bondholders had learned from harsh experience and were more likely to anticipate inflation than in the past. When contemporary lenders foresaw inflation, they would demand a higher rate of interest to maintain real returns on investments. Inflation would no longer erode the cost of borrowing, and for Wilson this change in the character of financial markets

shifted the range of policy options available to the government. Second, the higher interest rates would increase debt-servicing charges. Third, higher interest rates would slow growth by depressing interest-sensitive spending. This, in turn, would increase the deficit because lower growth meant more spending and less revenue.[27]

Not only did inflation and inflation expectations increase fiscal shortfalls and their burdens but Wilson emphasized his view, previously articulated in the 1984 Economic Statement, that fiscal shortfalls caused inflation expectations. As the debt-to-GNP ratio rose, so would expectations that the government would 'print money' to inflate its way out of the problem. For Wilson, these fiscally induced inflation expectations would lead to demands for larger interest rate premiums to protect the value of loans to the government. Higher interest rates would reduce growth, investment, and employment, and increase the deficit. They would also raise debt interest charges. The now larger debt and deficit would breed another round of fears about printing money and the cycle would begin again.[28] Wilson's position on the relationship of inflation to the deficit and debt was an important moment in the entrenching of fiscal politics. The new caution of financial markets that Wilson identified had its genesis in the stagflationary experience of the 1970s and early 1980s. The ideational nexus between inflation and fiscal shortfalls lay in the NAIRU and perhaps also rational expectations notions that inflation expectations would prevent fiscal stimulus from having a positive and lasting real, as opposed to nominal, impact. To the extent inflation became the dominant macroeconomic concern even in the short run (this would occur officially in 1987), the problematization of deficits would only become more urgent. The break with Keynesian fiscal thinking was confirmed. Deficits did not support growth; instead, they were inflationary and undermined employment and investment.

The Remedy
Wilson concluded that not to attack the deficit in 1985 would only force much larger spending reductions and tax increases later.[29] Wilson's 1985 fiscal targets for the next several years were actually somewhat less ambitious than Lalonde's 1984 projections. Wilson projected greater spending and lower revenues than his predecessor.[30] But the normative stance and underlying rationales were markedly different. For example, Wilson did not speculate, contrary to Lalonde, about the salutary effects of structural deficits. Given that Wilson presented the deficit as a structural imbalance between spending and revenues, he was of the view that looser monetary policy would not solve the problem,[31] although from 1983 to 1987 the Bank of Canada did ensure that there was enough money in the system to allow recovery toward capacity.[32] The real answer, said Wilson, was to

cut spending and raise taxes in a ratio of three to one so that the deficit would decrease enough to stabilize the debt-to-GNP ratio by the early 1990s.[33] Wilson's goal in 1984 was to reduce spending by $10 to $15 billion from its projected levels by the end of the decade.[34] And in 1985, the ambition was greater. He desired a reduction of $15 billion in net expenditures.[35] At the time, these proposed reductions were generally interpreted as very deep. In retrospect, the 'cuts' (really reductions in planned spending growth) look quite modest. Indeed, they presupposed that a permanent structural deficit would remain, for the goal was to stabilize the debt-to-GNP ratio, not to balance the budget. Deficits would be tolerable so long as they did not increase the debt by a proportion greater than GNP growth.

Keynesian Stabilization

The position that debt and deficits were inimical to, rather than creative of, employment meant that Keynesian policies for jobs and growth were in principle out of the question. In his 1985 budget speech, Wilson stated that his greatest preoccupation was with creating good and durable jobs. He argued that trying to create jobs through higher deficits and rising debt had not worked in the past and would not work now.[36] Lalonde emphasized jobs in his 1983 budget but saw Keynesian policy as a partial solution.

The conclusion that the Mulroney government was essentially not Keynesian in orientation will come as no surprise. Less expected is my conclusion that Keynesian concerns persisted in Tory rhetoric and policy in a subordinate but measurable fashion. The Keynesian notion that there is a positive relationship between deficit finance and economic activity, at least in the short term, can be clearly identified in their public documents. In *Reducing the Deficit,* Wilson felt compelled to explain why he did not take deeper fiscal action, presumably because according to his primary argument deficit reduction should actually help the economy. The minister asserted that if the deficit-fighting measures went any deeper they could jeopardize the recovery.[37] In the 1985 budget speech, Wilson stated: 'I believe that larger reductions at this time would not be prudent in light of current economic conditions. Instead, I am proposing actions which control the deficit now while ensuring that significant reduction will occur over the balance of the decade.'[38] In other words, the Phillips Curve was not vertical after all, at least in the short run, and unemployment stemming from further retrenchment was still unacceptable.

Persisting Keynesian notions were also visible in the 1984 statement in which Wilson spoke of 'fiscal flexibility' and how deficits limited the government's room to manoeuvre.[39] This referred in part to the need to set spending priorities under conditions of limited resources.[40] But the fiscal situation, said Wilson, also imposed a fiscal policy 'straitjacket' that limited 'traditional,' which is to say Keynesian, stimulus of the economy.[41] Wilson also expressed concern that the government's approach to deficit reduction be even-handed in its ongoing commitment to social justice and the social safety net.[42] These references to maintaining the fiscal flexibility to stimulate the economy, and to maintaining social programs, represented the justification for deficit reduction from the point of view of the Keynesian welfare state.

This 'Keynesian touch' was not the most important element of the Mulroney approach to fiscal policy, but it mattered. Persisting Keynesian conceptualizations accompanied Wilson and Mulroney through two governments. It was not full-blown Keynesianism in either rhetoric or policy, but rather an ancillary set of operating ideas that had an uneasy coexistence with the government's hegemonic economic model. Mulroney does mark the primary disjuncture from the Keynesian paradigm but he did not fully extinguish Keynesian ideas regarding deficit finance.

The persistence of latent Keynesianism in rhetoric and policy was both a reflection and a cause of the Tory failure to eliminate the deficit. It reflected the government's lack of political will to make bold and explicit spending reductions in the name of fiscal balance. Mulroney was not elected on deficit elimination, although in the campaign he did criticize the Liberals for the deficit.[43] Canadians were still very attached to social programs and Mulroney would not risk reducing the welfare net and government spending too directly or explicitly. In the 1984 election campaign, Mulroney called the universality of social programs a 'sacred trust,' and argued the deficit could not be drastically reduced until employment was restored.[44] In the debate on the first Tory speech from the Throne, in his first question period as prime minister, Mulroney agreed with NDP leader Ed Broadbent that drastic cuts would impair the economy.[45] The rhetoric of the Keynesian touch, which Mulroney himself was speaking, provided an economic rationale for failing to do what the dominant model would applaud. I argued in Chapter 4 that John Richards's characterization of government's refusal to do the politically difficult work of running surpluses in boom times as 'opportunistic Keynesianism' does not adequately capture Trudeau.[46] It is appropriate to Mulroney, whose political commitments in the mid-1980s meant that a Keynesian touch had instrumental value to his government in spite of its repudiation of the Keynesian model.

The Keynesian touch also contributed in its own right to Mulroney's failure to get at the deficit. It left the government vulnerable in its own language to criticism that deeper cuts would cause unemployment, hurt the economy, and inflict pain. It was a weak political strategy if deficit reduction was the real goal. My case that the Keynesian touch had a substantive impact is buttressed by the fact that Mulroney and Wilson did not, through the 1980s, aim to balance the budget. They were content to reduce the deficit only so far as was required to stabilize the debt-to-GNP ratio. If the deficit served no economic or political function, why not go all the way? The Keynesian touch was embodied in policy as a constraint on retrenchment. In Peter Hall's terms, on the fiscal front there was not even a second-order change. The deficit instrument was not eliminated. Change was of the first-order variety. The setting of the deficit would be altered.

The character of the opposition in the House further demonstrates that Keynesian notions were still a relevant part of the political process, and this had an impact on the government's selection of ideas. John Turner's Liberals were not very credible on deficit reduction. The Liberals had, after all, run up the deficit in the first place, although Turner himself was not fully complicit. The Liberals also maintained some of their attachment to the virtues of deficit finance. In his reply to the first Tory Speech from the Throne, Turner recognized fiscal constraints. Having one's cake and eating it too being the privilege of opposition, he also attacked the Tories for wilfully reneging on election spending commitments and for not taking direct action on job creation. He stated 'that I will not stand by, nor will my colleagues, and watch the social programs built up by successive Liberal governments being dismantled in the name of economic expediency.'[47] The NDP also supported these social programs, which appeared to depend on continuing deficits, and as we just saw, expressed concern about deficit reduction on economic grounds. Indeed, Ed Broadbent, in his reply to the first Mulroney Throne Speech, explicitly disagreed with the view, which he attributed to the Tories and Liberals both, that dealing with the deficit was an urgent priority. He argued the deficit was a symptom of weak growth rather than the underlying disease.[48] The Progressive Conservatives were at political risk less from having a deficit than from trying to reduce the fiscal shortfall.

Analysts examining the Tory approach at the time either would not have noticed, or would have dismissed, persisting Keynesian rhetoric. To the extent it was identified, commentators would, correctly, have seen Keynesian strands as minor in relation to the dominant and profound (third-order) change in priorities the Progressive Conservatives were pushing, and the (second-order) instrument change accompanying this agenda. The tension between a dominant classical approach to budgeting that fundamentally distrusted debt and deficits and a Keynesian touch that was recessive but operating was a continuing element of Progressive Conservative fiscal policy.

The First Term

Taxation
Through 1986, Michael Wilson's fiscal rhetoric against deficits was strong. He consistently claimed that debt and deficits were problematic and used

this characterization to justify deficit reduction and stabilizing the debt-to-GNP ratio. In the first Tory mandate, most of the spending 'cuts' and tax increases occurred in 1984, 1985, and 1986. Wilson's clear ideological preference was for lower taxes and deficit control. Given the limits in how far the government was willing to cut on the spending side, however, it was difficult to avoid increasing the tax burden. In 1986, Wilson formally backed off his earlier pledge to focus the deficit fight on spending. Tax increases, he claimed, were required given the magnitude of the deficit problem.[49] As had previous finance ministers, he vindicated tax increases by reference to recent tax policy. Federal revenue, he said, had fallen from 18.3 percent of GNP in 1974-5 to 15.1 percent in 1983-4. The Tory plan was to normalize this level at 16.9 percent of GNP by 1987-8 and maintain it to the end of the decade.[50]

In 1985 Wilson said tax increases were his last choice.[51] Yet in his first full budget he partially deindexed the personal income tax system. Taxpayers would, starting in 1986, be protected from inflation increases only above 3 percent. This partially reintroduced the 'bracket creep' John Turner eliminated effective in 1974. Among other moves, Wilson also introduced a higher income surtax on basic federal tax, to last eighteen months commencing 1 July 1985, to reduce the deficit. Corporations were hit by a twelve-month 5 percent surtax. Sales taxes were increased and applied to a wider range of items. Tax expenditures, including the Registered Home Ownership Savings Plan, were axed.[52] In keeping, though, with the government's goal of spurring investment, a $500,000 lifetime capital gains exemption was introduced, to take effect over six years.[53] (The exemption never actually exceeded $100,000. Wilson would back off for fiscal and political reasons.) The next year, 1986, saw more of the same. In a budget that again hit the middle class hardest, a 3 percent surtax on federal tax was introduced. The federal sales tax was increased by 1 percent. And sin taxes rose.[54] Measures in this budget were designed in part to ensure the deficit would come in at under $30 billion. Business was grumbling about a perceived lack of fiscal progress. The fall in the dollar to below US$0.70 at around budget time provided Wilson with some ammunition for these measures.[55]

The tax-raising deluge stopped with tax reform in 1987 and the 1988 election. Introduced in two stages, personal income tax reform reduced the overall personal tax burden in advance of the 1988 election while delaying the introduction of what would become the very unpopular Goods and Services Tax (GST) until 1991. Tax reform was designed to keep Canadian tax rates and structures competitive with those in the United States, which were reduced and altered in 1986.[56] It was also designed to lessen the influence of the tax system on economic decisions, to simplify the tax system, and to improve fairness.[57] Allan Maslove argues that the tax increases of the first Mulroney government, plus those carried over from the Liberals, increased aggregate taxes between 1984 and 1988 by $6.5 billion (in 1984 dollars). As a result of tax reform, this figure declined to $3.4 billion. Tax reform reduced aggregate taxes by $3.1 billion, but the tax burden was still higher than when the Progressive Conservatives took office.[58] The GST, when finally introduced, taxed consumption of final products. It replaced the Manufacturers Sales Tax. The MST taxed domestic manufacturers only, and discriminated in favour of foreign firms. Eliminating it was good public policy.[59] The revenue from the GST was to offset that lost from eliminating the MST and the rate reductions of tax reform. Michael Wilson eventually succeeded in restoring the revenue stream.

Spending

While the Progressive Conservatives were increasing the tax burden, they also sought to control spending. Particularly in the early years of their two mandates, the Mulroney government was able to make some reductions and encroach on spending growth. But in 1984, for example, reductions in assistance for the employed were to be offset by $1 billion for job creation and training programs.[60] The strange dialectic between spending control and spending initiatives had its origins in both politics and the government's economic model.

Recall that one aspect of economic renewal was proactive. Policies to facilitate innovation and adjustment were part of the strategy. The emphasis on using social policy as a bridge to employment rather than as a protection against unemployment was a more neo-liberal approach to social policy, but it still entailed programs that cost money. Labour adjustment, under the rubric of the Canada Jobs Strategy, was an expensive proposition. It, along with enhanced employment initiatives for social assistance recipients, was budgeted to cost $1.8 billion in 1987-8.[61] Research and development spending was dear as well. By 1986-7 it cost, exclusive of individual tax assistance, $4 billion annually in direct science and technology support.[62] Regional economic development programs also increased substantially toward the end of the government's first term. The field was ripe for political opportunism, and the opposition criticized the government for ignoring both the West and the East.[63] As Donald Savoie points out, in June 1987 the government gave $1.05 billion in new money to establish the Atlantic Canada Opportunities Agency. A few months later, it announced an additional $1.2 billion for the Western Diversification Office. The next year, Ottawa agreed to share a $1 billion special regional development project with Quebec.[64] This spending was political, especially the regional development money, insofar as it was designed to curry favour with targeted groups. The spending was principled insofar as it was animated by the proactive government role the Tories had set out in their foundational documents. The deficit limited the resources available for these projects.[65] But to the extent priority was given to proactive state action in economic renewal, that portion of economic renewal devoted to deficit reduction suffered. Perceived competitive pressures may have been the origin of the need for deficit control but they were also a reason it was frustrated.

The government was attached not only to substantial spending commitments. From the beginning, spending reduction was a very complicated business. Wilson moved fairly aggressively to limit spending early in the first mandate. After a couple of years and several rounds of cuts, Wilson's always modest power to limiting spending growth declined considerably. Other ministers became both weary of the process and better able to defend their turf.[66] 'In fact, it became increasingly clear after Wilson's 1986 budget that spenders were beginning to turn the tide and win some major battles with the guardians.'[67] Wilson was not a strong figure in Cabinet.[68] Fiscal and economic progress weakened his leverage, and Mulroney's political instincts were not going to let fiscal rectitude interfere with re-election. The Nielsen Task Force on public sector reform also proved relatively ineffectual.[69] In 1989, having been re-elected, Mulroney changed the Cabinet structure. He eliminated the 'Policy and Expenditure Management System' which John Crosbie had introduced and Allan MacEachen had adopted, and replaced it in part with an 'Expenditure Review Committee' chaired by the prime minister. The ERC was to review spending and identify room for cuts. But as at the beginning of the first mandate, there was an initial wave of enthusiasm followed by business as usual.[70]

A number of public incidents demonstrated how tricky spending reduction, especially regarding social programs, could be. In its emphasis on targeting support to those most in need, Wilson's 1984 *Agenda for Renewal* strongly suggested that a review of the universality of social programs was in the offing.[71] Mulroney used the fiscal situation to justify backtracking on the election promise that universal social programs were a sacred trust, exempting only health care from the review.[72] Yet the government would back down in turn from its review of universality due to political pressure. The government's resolve was also weakened when the finance minister backed off his proposal in the 1985 budget to partially deindex Old Age Security. Wilson had thin Cabinet support for the initiative anyway.[73] After a fiery senior citizen named Solange Denis gave Mulroney a piece of her mind on camera at Parliament Hill, the proposal was embarrassingly withdrawn.[74] The government also decided against implementing the majority recommendations of the Forget Report regarding Unemployment Insurance reform, and instituted a review of the Canada Assistance Plan that confirmed its vital role.[75]

There is an argument that fiscal goals were frustrated because of the prime minister's approach to leadership. Peter Aucoin describes Mulroney's management style as a 'paradigm of brokerage politics.' The system, committees notwithstanding, functioned in no small part on the basis of the prime minister's frequent transactional interventions into major policy areas. Ministers could also go directly to the PM to gain support for their priorities.[76] As long as Mulroney's objectives corresponded with Wilson's, Wilson could press his fiscal agenda. But Mulroney did not trust Wilson's political instincts, and political factors at least partially trumped whatever spirit animated Mulroney to retrench the state when he took office.[77]

I would argue, though, that it was not Mulroney's style in itself that frustrated spending control and deficit reduction. Rather, it was his sense of the political wind. Mulroney's assessment was clearly that re-election was not compatible with deeper retrenchment. Being the consummate politician, if he believed that deficit reduction had further cachet, and given that the government was in principle committed to fiscal control, he would have intervened to ensure the cuts were deeper. The management style could go both ways but the content of politics tilted the style toward largesse rather than retrenchment. Not until the mass public came around to the business position on the deficit could wide political support be found for deficit reduction. Not until fiscal politics were entrenched would deficit elimination be a viable election strategy. In the 1980s the mass public still lagged behind business and government on the issue. And Mulroney was attuned to these realities.

This analysis of the politics of retrenchment is buttressed by how Mulroney did get at the social safety net. Social groups were not so marginalized in the 1980s that governments could attack them head on. Instead, the Tories chopped by 'stealth.' Restraint by stealth refers to the use of arcane technical amendments to taxes and transfers. It confuses the electorate and insulates the government from criticism. Deindexation of family allowances, the Children's Tax Exemption, the refundable tax credit, and the personal income tax system allowed the Progressive Conservatives to raise revenue and reduce benefits in a murky way. The universality of social programs, including Old Age Security, was eventually ended indirectly by clawing back benefits paid out to higher income earners. Changes to the formula for transfers to provinces limited the growth of these payments.[78] The Tories also began, after 1988, to attack social programs more directly. The 1992 budget eliminated the universal family allowance, replacing it with benefits targeted to lower and middle income families.[79] One day later, the government announced it was abandoning the national daycare program it had been promising to institute since 1984.[80] Of course, this was rescinding a promise rather than an actual cut. The 'stealth' argument has allowed us to see that in spite of the public difficulties with retrenchment, the social net was weakened. But that this stealth was necessary presupposes that the fiscal position was not an intrinsic justification for cuts with the public. Social policy by stealth was a mechanism by which fiscal and structural objectives could be furthered in spite of the mass public's apparent objection to retrenchment. Program spending under Mulroney did decrease as a percentage of GDP. Absolute spending cuts cannot occur without people noticing the chop, but reducing relative rates of expenditure growth is consistent with overall spending increases and therefore much less conspicuous. Because the public face of politics limited spending restraint, technical changes were a partial way around public objection.

The burden of the argument in this chapter is to explain both the retrospectively moderate extent of the Tories' fiscal goals and why not even these goals were attained. As such, I have emphasized factors that resulted in relatively less retrenchment than might otherwise have been expected. None of this should be taken to mean that retrenchment did not take place or that no progress on the deficit front was made. The Progressive Conservatives' main fiscal achievement was not insignificant. By the late 1980s, the operating, or program, budget was in surplus.[81] The government was taking in more money than it was spending on programs, although it did fall back into a small operating deficit in the early 1990s. Without debt-servicing charges the budget would have been in surplus. This achievement fell short of Mulroney's fiscal ambitions, but it indicated the fiscal problem was no longer one of excessive spending relative to revenue; rather, the legacy of earlier deficits and high real interest rates was now the challenge.

Moving toward a Second Term

In 1987 and 1988, the constituency building and urgency around deficit reduction eased. The most important reason for easing off rhetorically on the deficit, and for new spending, was the 1988 election. The 'political business cycle' was kicking in. The notion here is that as elections approach, governments tend to increase net spending by bribing voters with their own money. Don Mazankowksi, Mulroney's right-hand man, persuaded Wilson to go against his instincts and Bay Street, and announce new spending programs, primarily for the West, prior to the 1988 election.[82] In the 1988 budget, Wilson announced or confirmed new 'priority' spending, and also spending in response to 'unexpected' developments. These items included a national childcare strategy (which as we just saw, was abandoned in 1992), regional development agencies (already discussed), science and technology investments, resources to modernize Canada's national defence, and agriculture and energy support in view of falling prices.[83] Personal income tax reductions from tax reform had also already been announced. Yet, while spending control was being eased, the opposition parties both chortled that the budget had surprisingly few inducements to voters.[84] The pressure on the Progressive Conservatives, as usual, was for more rather than less spending. These spending items allowed the Tories to position themselves as socially and regionally responsive, thereby offering some protection to their left flank.

The Policy Mix of Neo-Liberal Renewal and Fiscal Control

Two important changes occurred over the course of two mandates. One was the transition of the economic model from a set of principles to a more or less actualized program. To a significant extent, over time the government's agenda was embodied in policy. This changed the political and economic context in which the model was applied. The other change was the increased salience of inflation in the Progressive Conservative competitiveness vision. This made concrete what Hall calls 'third-order' change of goals. The heightened focus on inflation skewed the implementation of the agenda and had profound fiscal implications. In the remainder of this chapter I will discuss the Mulroney government's fiscal rhetoric and position in view of their relationship to the implementation of the competitiveness agenda.

Mulroney's second term was rather less felicitous than the first. On the constitutional front, the Meech Lake Accord's failure was a national unity disaster. The Charlottetown Accord, crafted to undo the damage, was also rejected. On the economic front, Mulroney's Canada-United States Free Trade Agreement (CUFTA) notwithstanding, a deteriorating economy and the government's worsening fiscal position made life miserable for Canadians and the finance minister both. The depth of the economic malaise was primarily a result of policy; the worsening fiscal situation had the same origin. Ottawa's dogged pursuit of its economic renewal made realizing the fiscal elements of renewal chimerical. The ironic rhetorical consequence was that, precisely as the Progressive Conservatives were making fiscal control more difficult, they amplified and made more urgent their fiscal discourse. The government's fiscal credibility evaporated as it consistently set and missed ever more ambitious fiscal targets. The CUFTA was probably a short-term cause of economic underperformance, but the main culprit was the Bank of Canada's price stability policy.

Inflation

Preoccupations with inflation descended on Ottawa with a vengeance in the late 1980s. Low inflation was always conceptualized as an important part of Mulroney's economic renewal, but the government's definition of low inflation changed. During the first Mulroney administration, an inflation rate of 4 to 5 percent was presented as unproblematic. Certainly, compared to the 1970s and early 1980s, inflation was relatively low. In 1985, Michael Wilson stated that inflation was expected to stay 'subdued' beyond that year, 'subdued' meaning 1984's 4.4 percent rate.[85] In 1988 he took pride, and credit, in announcing that one of the agenda for renewal's successes was an average inflation rate of just over 4 percent in the previous three years.[86] He also said further progress was necessary. But it is inescapably the case that, in the first Tory term, inflation in the 4 to 5 percent range was considered appropriate. Inflation was just not that salient in relation to other components of economic renewal, including fiscal rebalance. All this changed for the minister of finance, at least explicitly, with the 1989 budget.

Wilson argued in 1989, while fighting off the embarrassment of his budget being leaked to a reporter, that inflation pressures were putting economic progress at risk. In response, he stated that short-term interest rates had been raised to much higher levels than anticipated just a few months earlier.[87] Even though the inflation rate was not much higher than in previous years, Wilson argued that underlying inflation pressures would soon reveal themselves and vitiate economic progress. This, he said, distinguished the inflation situation from earlier years, when the pressures beneath the inflation rate were far weaker.[88] To make sense of Wilson's position, two things need to be examined: economic conditions and policy in Ontario; and the Bank of Canada's adoption of its 'price stability' policy.

Ontario

If there were inflation pressures in Canada in 1989, they were in (southern) Ontario. The view in Ottawa was that, to at least some degree, Ontario inflation was driven by the unsound policies of David Peterson's Liberal government. Part of this assessment resided in partisan and policy competition between Ottawa and Ontario. The two governments were at loggerheads on economic policy. Disagreements were most conspicuous in the Peterson government's opposition to the free trade deal. In addition, the benefits of Mulroney's 1987 tax reform were not realized in Ontario because the province occupied most of the tax room Ottawa vacated by increasing its personal income tax rate from 50 percent to 52 percent of basic federal tax and by increasing the high income surcharge. This frustrated Mulroney's goal of keeping tax rates relatively competitive with those in the United States, and amounted to a tax transfer from Ottawa to Ontario.[89] In addition, Ottawa was not pleased that when Ontario eliminated employee health insurance premiums in its 1989 budget, the Ontario Employer Health Tax added about $700 million to Ottawa's spending because of its responsibilities as an Ontario employer.[90] Above all, the province was seen by federal officials in both Finance and the Bank of Canada to be encouraging inflation by spending its fiscal rewards from a booming provincial economy and by raising tax rates to fund large spending increases when Ottawa was keeping its program spending growth to 3.5 percent.[91] The Ontario budget was in balance or a small deficit position in the late 1980s, but only because the Ontario economy was overperforming. In other words, the Ontario budget was cyclically balanced but structurally in deficit. It is difficult to overemphasize the extent to which both bank and finance officials were troubled and frustrated by Ontario policy in the late 1980s, although public sector spending in a number of provinces was a concern.[92] David Dodge, a long-time Finance official, writes that 'problems in this period were exacerbated by totally inappropriate fiscal policies in many provinces, especially in Ontario where very strong revenue growth resulting from the economic expansion from 1987 to 1990 was more than matched by large structural increases in spending.'[93] The Ontario government was seen to be fuelling inflation precisely when the Bank of Canada was upping the ante against inflation through its price stability policy.

The Bank of Canada, the Department of Finance, and the Price Stability Policy

The Bank of Canada's responsibilities, as set out in the preamble to the Bank of Canada Act, are quite general.[94] They ring of Keynesian stabilization because they include mitigating fluctuations in levels of production, trade, prices, and employment, in addition to promoting the economic and financial welfare of the country. When John Crow became Governor of the Bank of Canada in 1987, he redefined its role. In his first major speech, Crow argued that the primary objective to which the bank should direct itself is 'price stability.'[95] William Coleman writes that 'since 1987, price stability or zero inflation has been elevated to a special place in Canadian monetary policy: it is presented as a necessary condition if other economic goals are to be achieved.'[96] The adoption of the price stability policy was perhaps the key formulation of 'third-order' policy change. There was movement in the direction of prioritizing inflation control in 1975 with the Anti-Inflation Program and monetary gradualism. Monetary policy in the late 1970s and early 1980s was highly restrictive. But announcing the price stability policy formalized a new order of commitment. Since high employment was presented as dependent on price stability, concerns with employment levels would in principle be irrelevant on the road to the prior inflation objective.

To understand policy change it is sometimes necessary to disaggregate the state. Policies can emanate from state institutions relatively autonomously. Price stability, a third-order change, was one such policy. But Wilson's rhetoric about inflation pressures notwithstanding, these pressures were not the reason the policy was adopted. A senior bank official indicated not only that the policy emerged from the bank rather than the

Department of Finance, but that the bank would have introduced it even without these inflation pressures. This official also revealed, however, that the forcefulness of the policy would not have been so great without the existence of inflation pressures.[97]

But could the Bank of Canada really determine macroeconomic policy? Nominally, Bank of Canada policy is subject to the finance minister's approval. This issue was formally settled in the aftermath of the disputes between then Bank of Canada Governor James Coyne and the Diefenbaker government in the late 1950s and early 1960s. The minister can now issue a directive compelling the governor to take a certain course of action. In fact, however, the bank has obtained substantial autonomy from the government. It has been argued that the 'spectacle' of the Coyne affair paradoxically resulted in a strengthening of the autonomy of the bank's governor from political interference.[98] The increased power of financial markets, and their concerns with inflation, have also structurally upgraded the bank's institutional position. Financial markets can punish governments more easily for what is viewed as 'inflationary' behaviour. As politicians are seen to have incentives to inflate the economy, ensuring that monetary policy is insulated from political influence is in itself taken to be an anti-inflationary stance.

Interviews indicate that there were important institutional differences between the Bank of Canada and the Department of Finance regarding the price stability policy. A senior bank official describes a game of 'chicken' between fiscal and monetary policy. The fiscal authorities blinked late, which meant that monetary contraction came first.[99] Senior bank officials report that initially suggestions of monetary contraction by the bank were typically resisted by Finance officials because the latter did not see economic performance as strong enough to justify tight money, although by the late 1980s Finance was more onside.[100] The 1986 partial deindexation of the tax system was also viewed within the bank as giving Finance an institutional interest in 3 percent inflation. But John Crow would not accept 3 percent as price stability.[101] It is clear the finance department did agree that inflation pressures were developing and that contractionary macroeconomic policy was warranted in the late 1980s.[102] A senior bank official reports that Michael Wilson himself was quickly persuaded of the merits of the price stability policy.[103] A former senior Finance official has a slightly different account, arguing that Wilson was hawkish on inflation but, like the department generally, was not persuaded regarding the merits of the price stability policy per se.[104] Regardless of any differences, Wilson made the policy politically his own in the 1989 budget, although it was technically the government's policy from the day it was announced. Wilson made it clear that his government supported both the principles and depth of the price stability policy.

The Fiscal Consequences

Ontario may have been behaving irresponsibly, but the Bank of Canada's outrageously high price stability interest rates and the overvalued dollar that resulted were even more harmful.[105] High interest rates caused all manner of fiscal problems in 1989, and were the cause of the shocking depth of the 1990-1 recession in Canada. The fiscal upshot of price stability enforced by extremely high short-term interest rates was a combination of increasing upward pressure on the deficit and more forceful fiscal rhetoric to justify further measures to keep the deficit down. Arguing that economic problems were a result of the deficit distracted audiences from the real causes of underperformance for which the government might be called to account. The Tories (and the bank) took the position that high interest rates were a reflection rather than a cause of economic difficulties. Interest rates were said to be a function of inflation expectations rather than policy.[106] It is difficult to believe that this position was strictly true, as 'monetary policy is implemented mainly through changes in short-term interest rates, specifically the Bank Rate, which is the rate of interest that the Bank of Canada charges on overnight loans to financial institutions.'[107] If short-term interest rates were simply a function of inflation expectations rather than policy, how was the bank implementing the price stability policy?

In his 1989 budget Michael Wilson announced that debt-servicing charges would be $6 billion higher than estimated the previous year due to interest rates 4 percent above the levels projected in the 1988 budget.[108] Wilson argued that the way to reduce interest rates was to reduce inflation pressures. This, he said, could be done by reducing the deficit and the stock of debt.[109] But if in fact provincial fiscal policy and Ottawa's monetary responses were the problem, this vilification of the deficit was nonsense. The 1989 budget referenced nearly everything in terms of the government's fiscal position. Wilson had to find $6 billion just to keep the deficit stable. He introduced substantial further revenue measures. Wilson introduced the tax clawbacks on family allowances and Old Age Security that eroded the welfare net's universality by stealth. The minister increased the 'temporary' 3 percent surtax to 5 percent, and added another 3 percent surtax on high income taxpayers. Surtaxes had the added benefit of being excluded from the calculation of Basic Federal Tax (BFT), so these increases did not automatically benefit provinces, whose tax rates were applied to BFT. Wilson also brought in a tax on the capital of large corporations and raised the 3 percent corporate surtax to 5 percent. On the spending side, Wilson completely withdrew Ottawa from financing Unemployment Insurance, effective 1 January 1990, with an anticipated deficit reduction of $1.9 billion in the first year. He scuttled a $6 billion plan to buy submarines, and chopped another $2.7 billion off planned defence spending over the next five years. He also knocked $4 billion over seven years off the

Tory promise of a $6.4 billion daycare program. And he cut growth in Established Program Financing transfers to provinces by 1 percent.[110] The opposition attacked the budget fiercely as a betrayal of election promises, an attack on universality, and a failure in terms of deficit control. The Liberal Finance critic, Roy MacLaren, argued that the government's earlier failure to control spending meant it could not fulfil election promises, nor, taking the Keynesian view, stimulate the economy in the event of a slowdown. Mulroney acknowledged, 'with regret,' that the fiscal position prevented moving ahead with a national daycare program.[111] This budget was the beginning of the economic and fiscal end for the Progressive Conservatives.

Things would get a lot worse before they would get better. The government's commitment to economic renewal, redefined by a new focus on inflation, undermined the economy. The Keynesian touch in Wilson's conceptualizations became a component of Ottawa's fiscal and economic struggles. In 1990 Wilson still expressed the view that inflation pressures were too high. He offered two main solutions. One, of course, was to decrease the deficit and lower the debt burden. But Wilson's other strategy was to dampen demand in the domestic economy. Wilson claimed that the economy was expected to slow down in 1990, and that since Canada had experienced seven consecutive years of growth, this was neither surprising nor to be avoided.[112] But then he went further. The 'natural' economic slowdown was not enough, he said. Further policy action to weaken growth was also necessary. Wilson argued that firm monetary policy would help ease the demand-creating inflation pressures, and that his restrictive budgetary measures would reinforce monetary policy in this regard.[113] Wilson stated that it would be a tough year for the Canadian economy.[114]

These last remarks could, in abstraction, have been those of a Keynesian at the top of the business cycle. If unemployment was as low as possible, and more demand would only result in inflation, then stepping on the brakes would make Keynesian sense. But the use of policy to reduce demand in this circumstance was in Keynesian terms backward because, as Wilson himself acknowledged, it was to exacerbate rather than stabilize the economy's own contraction. Wilson's budget papers flirted with recession (two consecutive quarters of negative growth). He predicted the first quarter of 1990 would entail zero growth, and possibly negative growth. Wilson also claimed that in both the preceding and following quarters growth would be very weak.[115] In the 1970s the Liberals had explicitly refused to contract fiscal policy to weaken growth and create unemployment as a means of fighting inflation. In 1990, Wilson self-consciously used fiscal policy to encourage an economic slowdown that would become the worst since the Great Depression. There were no new taxes, although the GST would take effect in January 1991. Wilson hit provinces hard by freezing Established Program Financing transfers and putting a 5 percent cap on

Canada Assistance Plan transfer growth to Ontario, Alberta, and British Columbia.[116] This last move was very difficult to cope with in a recession, as provincial welfare rolls (particularly in Ontario) grew. Wilson could only have described himself as slowing growth to the extent that a Keynesian model operated in which fiscal policy can influence demand, and demand management has predictable real effects. Wilson probably spoke this way to find one more justification for deeper fiscal retrenchment. The NAIRU expectations approach to inflation was dominant. Still, before 1990 the Keynesian touch had served to limit how much demand Ottawa was willing to take out of the economy. In 1990, in concert with a greater commitment to anti-inflation precepts, the Keynesian touch was made a procyclical, or in Keynesian terms perverse, instrument in the fight against inflation. It was the deployment of a Keynesian idea without Keynesian norms or values.

The government got more than it wished for. With economic activity grinding to a halt, a year later the economy was in dire straits. An interview with a senior Bank of Canada official indicates that it was close to the consensus position in the bank that with the inflation pressures of the late 1980s, it made sense to err on the side of too much, rather than too little, contraction. Had the bank foreseen the depths of the recession, though, it would not have made money so tight.[117] There is debate among economists regarding the extent to which the recession was a result of monetary policy. Pierre Fortin locates the recession, and indeed underperformance through the 1990s, almost exclusively in monetary policy, and then the fiscal contraction he argues monetary policy induced.[118] Bank of Canada economists argue the recession is better explained by multiple factors, including lower than expected American growth and sharper than expected declines in raw material prices.[119] Weaker American growth does not, though, explain why the slump was relatively mild in the United States but deep in Canada. Nor does it explain how the recession started in Canada first, reversing the usual order.[120] There are cognate differences over the extent the government's fiscal position weakened due to monetary policy. Fortin attributes most of the increase in the debt-to-GDP ratio from 1981 to 1994 to monetary policy that depressed economic activity and increased the amount by which the real rate of interest exceeded real growth.[121] Bank economists argue that although high interest rates contributed to the fiscal problem, the problem was really structural because deficits persisted throughout the business cycle. As such, it was not a result of cyclical underperformance.[122]

I am not an economist, but in my view Fortin has the better of the debate.[123] The deficits, because of debt-servicing charges, were primarily structural. Monetary policy in the late 1980s and early 1990s was still deeply unsound. Indeed, many predicted its consequences.[124] Monetary policy is the only reasonable explanation for the depth and timing of the recession in Canada. The variable over which the bank has the most control, very short-term interest rates, was exceptionally high. In consequence, the ratio between real interest rates and real growth was extremely unfavourable in fiscal terms. It is no coincidence that with precipitous declines in interest rates budgetary balance was quickly achieved in the latter half of the 1990s. In fiscal terms, the question is not whether monetary policy was generally sound, but rather whether it was compatible with the Mulroney fiscal agenda. In fact, inflation control through monetary policy was prior to, and in tension with, the government's fiscal goals in the short and medium terms. As Douglas Curtis concludes, 'the goal of lower or zero inflation may be defensible, but the timing of the policy initiative was inconsistent with the continued pursuit of deficit control.'[125]

Another factor that may have worsened economic performance on its own account, and that certainly combined with the price stability policy to unfortunate effect, was the CUFTA. It took effect on 1 January 1989. The free trade and price stability policies were the two most important tools by which the Progressive Conservatives sought to implement their competitiveness agenda. Free trade was to generate efficient firms, price stability was to ensure low costs. The evidence regarding the CUFTA's impact on employment is ambiguous. The balance of opinion is that it probably caused some transitional job loss. The best study is Daniel Trefler's. He argues that restructuring driven by tariff cuts may have been responsible for as many as one in four lost manufacturing jobs.[126] John McCallum agrees that 'it is very likely that there were at least transitional job losses as tariffs fell, in some cases from more than 20 percent to zero in the short space of a decade.'[127] To the extent the CUFTA contributed to job loss on its own account, and even if these jobs were replaced by the end of the 1990s, it weakened Ottawa's fiscal position at the beginning of the decade by reducing tax revenues and increasing social spending. And while tariff revenues were no longer a major source of federal funds, this income stream was also reduced. Ottawa repeatedly acknowledged that tariff revenue reductions due to the implementation of the CUFTA would reduce its yield from the sales and excise taxes/duties revenue category.[128] Indicative of the government's political and economic priorities in the program for renewal, it never did suggest that the CUFTA's weakening of the fiscal position should be relevant to free trade's implementation.

In addition to the effects they generated independently, the dynamic interaction of the CUFTA with the price stability policy also left the economy worse off. The main problem was that as the CUFTA was opening Canada's border, high short-term interest rates, particularly the large spread by which Canada's interest rate exceeded the American, raised the value of the Canadian dollar to an excessive US$0.89. This substantially worsened the country's terms of trade while Canada was turning more fully to trade. David Dodge, a long-time finance official who became governor of the Bank of Canada in 2001, acknowledges that 'the rise in interest rates and the exchange rate made the adjustment to free trade more difficult.'[129] Tom Courchene argued in 1992 that tight money was altering exchange rates and increasing Canada's unit labour costs: 'The unit labour cost gap [with the United States] is forcing a brutal restructuring of our economy.' In consequence, he said, the resource sector could not be used to buffer the Canadian economy from the manufacturing adjustments instigated by the CUFTA.[130] The Macdonald Commission Report had argued that Canada needed an adjustment policy to facilitate the transition to the CUFTA.[131] The commission went so far as to argue that Canada's flexible exchange rate should act as a brake against a rapid influx of imports.[132] In these terms, monetary policy was perverse and Canada would have been better off had the exchange rate been fixed before price stability was introduced. The price stability policy was a maladjustment policy.[133] Instead of smoothing restructuring, it made change harsher still, and further compromised the fight against the deficit. Not only were fiscal and monetary policy ill coordinated but neither fit well with trade policy either. The irony is that while the Mulroney government was arguing that international competitive pressure enjoined its policy responses, the Bank of Canada was running an independent monetary policy. According to the Mundell-Fleming theorem, also called the 'open economy trilemma,' where capital movements are uncontrolled a country can control its monetary policy or its exchange rate but not both.[134] The bank controlled monetary policy while letting the exchange rate rise beyond its fundamental value, but it did not have to be thus.[135]

This combination of errors ruined the Mulroney government's fiscal and economic credibility even as the agenda for renewal was being locked into place. The pursuit of economic renewal compromised deficit reduction. Recession led to demands for government action to offset its worst effects. Wilson brought down the 1991 budget, his last, just as the Gulf War was ending. The war on the deficit was going less smoothly. Wilson walked a fine line between spending and restraint. The Liberal and NDP opposition argued in advance of the budget that the government should fight the recession by stimulating the economy, rather than make deficit reduction a priority.[136] The budget offered $7.5 billion in new spending, rather a lot if deficit reduction was the goal. This included $3 billion for Unemployment Insurance benefits, $1.6 billion for the elderly, and $1.3 billion to farmers in difficulty.[137] Program spending was planned to increase by 6.9 percent, a development sharply criticized by business. Nor was business pleased by the 24 percent hike on employer Unemployment Insurance premiums, effective 1 July, which was designed to offset the new UI outlays.[138] Between UI premium increases and cigarette taxes, Wilson attempted to raise $3.4 billion through tax increases to partially pay for new spending.

Wilson argued that in spite of short-term spending, the budget was a tough one that did not compromise medium-term fiscal goals.[139] Unfortunately, this argument was not very credible. The government had been deferring deficit reduction for at least three years (and longer in some eyes). The short run had bled into the medium term. The inevitable deferral of fiscal control, while predicting substantial deficit reduction a few years further into the fiscal plan – predictions that never came close to being met, undermined the Progressive Conservatives' fiscal credibility.

The continuities between Wilson's last budget and those of his successor, Don Mazankowski, suggest that the government's approach to inflation and underperformance was sourced in much more than personal idiosyncrasy. In 1992 Mazankowski reduced taxes with the explicit goals of bolstering the recovery, spurring investment, initiative, and jobs, and providing a 'social dividend.'[140] This time, though, such assistance was supposed to be entirely offset by reduced spending.[141] Optimistically promising 600,000 new jobs by the end of 1993, Mazankowski focused on deficit and tax reductions while attacking spending.[142] Some commentators argued that the budget, oriented as it was to cutting taxes and the deficit, was a response to the emerging Reform Party and the threat it posed to the Conservatives, particularly in the West.[143] Recall that in this budget the government ended the Family Allowance, which it had started to claw back in 1989, and that the next day it abandoned its commitment to a national daycare program. As things turned out, to the surprise of nobody, the fiscal predictions did not come in quite as planned. Revenue declines were not nearly matched by spending reductions. Spending, in fact, increased. The 1992-3 deficit came in a remarkable $13 billion higher than predicted. In 1993, with a Tory leadership campaign underway and the Mulroney era coming to a close, Mazankowski's budget was a stand-pat affair without major initiatives. In 1992 the government projected a financial requirements (although not a public accounts) surplus for 1995-6.[144] In keeping with typical Tory forecasting, the 1993 budget pushed back the arrival of a financial requirements surplus to 1997-8.[145]

Revisionist History

While the primary culprit in failing to attain deficit reduction goals was the mix of neo-liberal policies, I have also argued that a Keynesian touch was an ancillary factor. That Keynes still preyed on the government's conscience and consciousness was evident in some remarks offered by Michael Wilson in supporting documents to the 1991 budget. He tried to justify the price stability policy by recourse to Keynes, who some might have thought would have opposed such a program.[146] Wilson quoted from Keynes's brilliant *Economic Consequences of the Peace* on the perniciousness of a debauched currency. Such erosion in value, according to Keynes, puts economics on the side of destruction and most cannot even understand why.[147] Not only did reference to Keynes indicate that Maynard dogged the government; it also showed that the government had lost perspective. The inability to distinguish between the kind of inflation that would plague interwar Germany, about which Keynes was obviously and explicitly writing, and inflation in Canada in the late 1980s and early 1990s, did not speak well of Ottawa's understanding of the issue. Wilson was right, though, to agree with Keynes that economic conditions can breed reactionary politics. But runaway inflation is not the only cause of a bad economy. Runaway anti-inflation policies can also damage economies and create conditions for political reaction. I will argue in the next chapter that the 1990-1 recession and its concomitant economic orderings are tightly linked to the radicalization 'rightward' of the mass public and Canadian parties in the middle and late 1990s.

The Role of the State in the Economy
Brian Mulroney swept to power in 1984 on a platform of national reconciliation and economic renewal. Upon taking office, and consistently over the next nine years, the Progressive Conservatives would justify most of economic renewal's important features in terms of their utility to enhancing Canada's ability to compete in an increasingly competitive world economy. There was certainly objective foundation for the position that the global economy was becoming more integrated and competitive. But the solution the Mulroney government offered did not logically follow; nor was it inevitably determined by global imperatives. The American economist Paul Krugman has argued that the focus governments have developed regarding 'competitiveness' in the 1980s and 1990s is dangerous and misleads policy. Firms compete with each other, but due to the principles of comparative advantage, countries do not. Countries will always produce something.[148] Economic logic can point in a variety of directions. The Mulroney government's model of the state role in the economy rested on the corporate and regional interests that provided the Tories with their electoral support and political leverage. These interests were shaped and politically strengthened by international developments. Yet without these domestic interests and the concomitant political leadership, the energy required to mobilize Canadian politics to adopt a policy framework so sensitive to the so-called imperatives of the international political economy would not have existed. The success of Mulroney's approach was ultimately a matter of domestic politics.

The relationship of international competition and economic integration to domestic politics and policy was threefold. First, competition and integration altered the economic and political costs and benefits of policy alternatives, and thereby made some options more palatable than others. Second, coming out of economic decline and the accompanying failures of Trudeau's politically overembedded liberal interventionism, the idea of international competition could be deployed as a tool to persuade people of neo-liberal policy's virtues. It did not seem that statist responses would work in the face of seemingly irresistible external forces. Finally, these two developments tilted the field on which the game of domestic politics is played. By giving ideational and structural support to some interests and weakening others, ideational and structural change in the international political economy altered power relations in Canada. In baseball, the teams with the greatest resources do not always win, but on average they do a lot better than 'small market' clubs. So too with politics. Global competition, economic decline, and corporate support provided Mulroney with many resources to realize his political interests and to further corporate economic interests. But the game still had to be played, and Mulroney played it expertly.

A reasonable argument for deficit reduction was constructed in terms of the dominant economic theories, the functioning of financial markets, and the spectre of deficit-induced inflation. The deficit, understood in terms of the model Mulroney propounded, reflected bad management, impeded economic success, and had to be rectified to permit Canada to become a highly competitive producer. Opposition to the deficit, however, was also based on what the deficit symbolized for the role of the state in the economy: an overextended state that had to be retrenched. Rather than, as with Trudeau, the deficit serving as a tool to minimize negative consequences flowing from international economic change, under Mulroney *deficit reduction* was a means by which Canada should manage the international economy.

Indeed, what is particularly interesting about the Mulroney government's policy responses is that they were designed to enhance the very pressures thought to necessitate change in the first place. This point can be illuminated by reference to the political theorist Niccolò Machiavelli and the economic historian Karl Polanyi. For Machiavelli, while Fortune may govern half of what happens to us, the rest is more or less within our control:

> And I compare her [Fortune] to one of those ruinous rivers that, when they become enraged, flood the plains, tear down the trees and buildings, taking up earth from one spot and placing it upon another; everyone flees from them, everyone yields to their onslaught, unable to oppose them in any way. And although they are of such a nature, it does not follow that when the weather is calm we cannot take precautions with embankments and dikes, so that when they rise up again either the waters will be channelled off or their impetus will not be either so disastrous or so damaging.

The same things happen where Fortune is concerned: she shows her force where there is no organized strength to resist her; and she directs her impact there where she knows that dikes and embankments are not constructed to hold her.[149]

To extend this analogy to the modern international political economy, the torrential rivers of Fortune would be ineluctable forces of globalizing international competition. The statecraft used to manage the upheaval generated by these forces would be the equivalent to dikes and embankments. Adjustment policy, capital controls, tariffs, and countercyclical stabilization would all be ways of channelling the competitive floods. In these terms, the peculiarity of Tory policy was that while it was to some extent designed to channel economic pressures, it also sought to release them. Not only was the flood let in, especially by the CUFTA; the land was also intentionally flooded by procompetitive reforms such as deregulation, privatization, and as the government presented it, the price stability policy. In this regard, embedded liberalism was not easily found. Embedded liberalism treats the tyranny of economic circumstance as resistible. Indeed, this is a premise of Keynesian stabilization. Mulroney's 1850s-style response to economic circumstance was to exacerbate circumstance's tyranny.

The great economic historian Karl Polanyi argued precisely for resistance to economic circumstance. His most important book, *The Great Transformation,* was largely about the rise and fall of the first modern global economy, which was destroyed by and between the world wars. Polanyi posited that while economic change might be inevitable, the process of change is of crucial importance. Time can allow people to adapt to change without destroying their ways of life. 'The rate of change is often of no less importance than the direction of the change itself; but while the latter frequently does not depend upon our volition, it is the rate at which we allow change to take place which well may depend upon us.'[150] It is for the lack of concern with the pace of change that the Mulroney government deserves particular opprobrium. There was some early discussion about the appropriate rate of change.[151] The quick and large rise in interest rates, the CUFTA's implementation without the adjustment assistance recommended by the Macdonald Commission, and the all-at-once introduction of the GST are examples of the Progressive Conservatives' emphasis on renewal rather than measured adjustment. There was nothing 'conservative' in the Burkean sense about this approach. It also reflected the diminution of the short run, which was such a traditional Keynesian concern.

So understood, the Tories' neo-liberal approach to the state role in the economy ruled the day, although the Keynesian touch I have identified was operative and subordinate to the dominant ideological strand. Neo-liberalism and latent Keynesianism were inconsistent and in tension. Ancillary but real Keynesian norms and ideas in state and society prevented the government from taking stronger spending and deficit reduction measures in its first term. In the second mandate, the Keynesian touch was piggybacked on the government's price stability agenda and perversely used to encourage recession. For the most part, though, latent Keynesianism restricted the government in the pursuit of its fiscal goals by constraining the extent of retrenchment. From the neo-liberal point of view, extinguishing the last vestiges of Keynesianism from state and society would have emancipated the government from these shackles.

Policies to enhance Canada's international competitiveness and free business from regulatory shackles reoriented Canada's policy horizons and created subsequent path dependencies. The price stability policy, liberalized trade, tax reform, deregulation, privatization, reform of the regulation of financial institutions, and the 1986 Competition Act all altered the Canadian political economy and generated a host of reactions. They also reshaped the boundaries of the politically possible. Whether one applauds or condemns it, the Mulroney legacy with respect to Canadian economic orderings continues to be the most important and defining feature of Canadian politics. Mulroney's economic policies, certainly more than Trudeau's, and perhaps more than any prime minister since Sir John A. Macdonald and his National Policy, profoundly shaped the country. This was not always a result of good planning or design, as the terrible interaction between monetary, fiscal, and trade policy in the late 1980s and early 1990s indicates. But this makes it no less a legacy. Mulroney is a transitional figure in the move to fiscal politics. With respect to economic reform, he is seminal.

The Mulroney government never achieved its fiscal goals for four major, and related, reasons: deficit reduction was subject to economic renewal, not its content; the subjection to competition upon which the argument for deficit reduction was premised was much more complete in 1993 than in 1984; the political conditions for deficit reduction were present in neither the mass public nor the party system; and the Keynesian touch constrained the extent to which the Tories pursued fiscal restraint. These factors are the basis for my argument that the transition to fiscal politics was set deeply in motion, but not entrenched, in the Mulroney era. However, once economic renewal was otherwise in place, fiscal politics could ascend to dominate the policy agenda and define the hegemonic set of ideas. Under Jean Chrétien, the political pressure in the party system was for stronger rather than weaker action on the deficit, and deficit elimination was popular; economic policy was made subject to perceived fiscal requirements; Canadians experienced themselves as sufficiently subject to competitive pressures that the argument for fiscal balance was persuasive;

and the last vestiges of a Keynesian touch were extinguished. From the triumphs and tragedies of Mulroney's economic renewal would come the relative victory of fiscal politics over even a strictly economic agenda. Economic concerns would remain of the highest import. But no longer would economic or social goals trump fiscal imperatives. Balancing the budget, in turn, would become an exceptionally effective tool in further redefining the role of the state in the economy.

7
Economic Insecurity and the Political Conditions for Deficit Elimination

Jean Chrétien's Liberal Party won a majority government in the 1993 election with strong support in Ontario, solid support in Atlantic Canada, and some support in Quebec and the West. Brian Mulroney's coalition of western Canada and Quebec exploded in the wake of the recession, the Goods and Services Tax, and the failed Meech Lake and Charlottetown constitutional accords. The Tory void in these regions was filled not by a national party, but by the Reform Party and the Bloc Québécois, respectively. In part, the Progressive Conservatives were decimated because of the inept and naive campaign run by Mulroney's successor, Kim Campbell; it is impossible to imagine Mulroney, however reviled, winning only two seats. But the structural reason for the Tory collapse was the political incoherence of the Mulroney coalition. It could be united around trade for instrumental reasons. On the national question, though, the West and Quebec were apparently at irresolvable loggerheads. Ontario, while never the key to Mulroney's power, did not fare well under Tory rule, and became a Liberal stronghold in the 1990s.

The victorious Liberals ran on a broad platform outlined in the party's 'Red Book.' The Red Book was designed in part to allay voter cynicism by setting out a specific program that provided a standard against which a Liberal government could be held to account. This approach fit well with the Liberal theme of restoring trust in government and its operations after the perceived corruption of the Mulroney years.[1] Major economic and fiscal promises included the elimination of the GST, the renegotiation of the CUFTA and the pending North American Free Trade Agreement, a program for building infrastructure in cooperation with provinces and municipalities, and the reduction of the deficit to no more than 3 percent of GDP by 1996-7.[2] This last target was less ambitious than the 1.6 percent of GDP goal for 1996-7 listed in the 1993 Progressive Conservative budget.[3] Promises were also made regarding other issues, including the environment, health care, crime, cultural identity, and Aboriginal peoples.[4] The campaign was not, then, fought by the Liberals in defence of Mulroney's economic restructuring. The Liberals, in 1996, would give themselves a rather high grade (78 percent) on meeting their Red Book promises.[5]

The Red Book, though, was not reflective of the Liberals' real policy orientation on taking office. Their neo-liberalism would put them in some opposition to the social constituencies to which the Red Book was designed in part to appeal. Particularly remarkable about the first two Chrétien administrations was the degree to which the government's rhetoric and action focused on deficit elimination and securing Ottawa's fiscal position. This focus imbued all policy fields to the extent that even nonfiscal issues were framed primarily through a fiscal lens. The core Red Book promise, which the Liberals not only kept but exceeded, turned out to be its deficit-to-GDP target. The government met and improved upon every fiscal target it set. It cut spending in areas the Progressive Conservatives were not willing to touch. This stands in stark contrast to the Mulroney fiscal legacy of missed targets, growing debt and deficits, and perceptions of managerial incompetence.

But in a more fundamental sense, the Liberal fiscal record was an extension of the work the Progressive Conservatives started. In its first year in office, the Liberal government clearly adopted the most important aspects of their predecessor's economic agenda. The GST was not scrapped and the NAFTA was signed with merely cosmetic changes. The price stability policy remained in place. Debt control and deficit reduction were the major elements of the Tory program for renewal that had not been implemented. Fiscal concerns finally took pride of place as the content of economic renewal. In part, this was possible because the Liberals were the party that largely built the postwar Keynesian welfare state. They were also the party of Trudeau's 'just society.' This gave them some credibility on social issues, and allowed them some space to cut social programs, space that Mulroney had been denied. Just as 'only Nixon could go to China,' perhaps only the Liberals could explicitly retrench the welfare state. The irony is that Chrétien completed Mulroney's work.

More important were changes in the mass public, parliamentary representation, and the party system – the issues with which this chapter is primarily concerned. With the emergence of the Reform Party as the most significant English-speaking opposition, the political pressure and risk for the government resided in fiscal restraint that was too mild rather than too aggressive. The emergence of Reform, and the fall of the NDP, both reflected and led newly dominant visions of the role of the state in the economy. And in this resided the sufficient condition for elimination of the federal deficit. The mass public had come around to the business position, although for somewhat different reasons, and supported balancing the budget. Fiscal politics became firmly entrenched in the 1990s because deficit elimination and the concomitant retrenchment finally became popular. Like castor oil, nobody really liked it, but Canadians thought it was good for them. Extinguishing the deficit, in turn, furthered neo-liberal reform. A focus on Ottawa's fiscal position meant looking carefully at the structure of revenues and expenditures and entailed further examination of the state role in the economy.

In the 1970s the Canadian public demanded much of the state, insisting on at least some protection from economic dislocation. In the 1980s Canadians were still sufficiently attached to the state's welfare functions that retrenchment had to be done by 'stealth.' But in the 1990s, Canadians no longer identified their interests with the Keynesian welfare state. The state was viewed as extractive rather than as a source of succour, and as the economic problem rather than as part of the solution. With the economic interests of society decoupled from the state, for the mass public the intertwined ideas of deficit elimination and state retrenchment had instrumental value in realizing those interests.

Alteration of the mass public position on deficits in the 1990s resulted from dislocating economic experiences in a political context that increasingly problematized the Keynesian welfare state and the deficits that supported social programs. The genesis of these politics resided first in the economic decline associated with Trudeau's overembedding of liberalism, and then in the corporate and state restructuring accompanying Mulroney's neo-liberal globalism. But the 1990-1 recession, and the glacial recovery from it, was the cudgel that broke the camel's back. No external political pressure explains the price stability policy as it was implemented; an autonomous policy decision by the state profoundly shaped Canadian politics. Without the recession's depth, the fiscal problem would not have been as extreme in either mathematical or political terms. Coming as the recession did out of the long history we have specified, the accompanying insecurity and hardship expressed themselves through a reactionary politics that identified the source of economic suffering as an overextended and ineffective state. Rather than turn to the state for assistance in a time of need, the increasingly resonant position was one of turning inward for self-protection. This inward turn was made possible by political activity organized to reduce the extractive capacity of the state to interfere with individual accumulation. Deficit elimination would limit the ability of the state to extend its tentacles, and also eventually permit tax reduction.[6] The argument I will present comes down to the following propositions: experiencing deep economic insecurity, people felt their economic situations to be precarious; people conceptualized the state, and particularly its welfare functions, as the problem; and people supported parties that promised to restore control over their economic lives by eliminating the deficit and retrenching the state.

As liberalism became disembedded, economic insecurity climbed. The concomitant politics were manifest in government budgets and the party system, which gave form to this insecurity. Popular Liberal budgets represented the concerns of the mass public by framing them in terms of economic anxiety and by justifying deficit elimination through a specific conceptualization of the general rather than special interest. The Liberals shifted politically to the right, both of their own accord and to protect their 'right' flank from the Reform Party. Reform, above all other federal parties, articulated the reactionary populism of the 'general' over the 'special' interest that permeated Canadian politics in the 1990s. It is no coincidence that Reform was also hawkish on the deficit. Of course, not everybody changed their views or their voting preferences. But both the mass public and political parties shifted sufficiently that many once-controversial neo-liberal polices were no longer matters of great dispute. A new political 'consensus' established itself that was more supportive of neo-liberal orderings than were the politics of the 1980s. Indeed, not until the fiscal politics of the 1990s entrenched itself was the Keynesian conceptualization of deficits fully laid to rest and a neo-liberal approach to the state role in the economy secured.

A note of caution should be added here. It is important to be clear about what can and cannot be 'proved' regarding the economic experiences of the mass public, much less the relationships between these experiences and political preferences. It is one thing to identify changes in labour market structures and real income patterns. It is something else entirely to determine the meaning of these changes. Gordon Betcherman argued in 1995 that available data could neither measure 'insecurity' nor control for change in the hardship of economic experiences over time.[7] Efforts to quantify insecurity have been made in recent years, which in itself suggests that researchers believe insecurity may have become more politically relevant. These efforts are based on both 'objective' measures of insecurity and public opinion data. For example, as part of an impressive effort to measure overall economic well-being, Lars Osberg and Andrew Sharpe argue that economic security posted the largest decline among the components of 1990s economic well-being in their index.[8] Frank Graves argues that Canadian public opinion was very bleak in the early 1990s (although his data appears to begin in March 1993, and cannot be compared with earlier years). Two out of three Canadians agreed with the proposition they had lost control of their economic future. This despair continued even as the economy and fiscal position started to improve in the mid-1990s, although it moderated toward the end of the decade.[9] Others certainly agree that insecurity and vulnerability have increased.[10] To the extent there are measures of insecurity, they support my argument that insecurity in the 1990s increased. However, these measures are not, in themselves, enough to make the argument. As always, we must take the path of interpretation[11] to glean the political meaning of economic trends and events.[12]

The Recession and After

Although the origins and fiscal impact of the 1990-1 recession were discussed in the previous chapter, the following points about the recession and the recovery bear mention. The recession was deeper in Canada than in the United States by a factor of three. While the recovery was just beginning in Canada in 1994, it was almost complete in the United States.[13] This stands in stark contrast to the downturn of 1981-2, which was of similar magnitude in both countries, although the Canadian recovery was more sluggish.[14] Divergence from the United States is notable because over the two preceding decades the two countries had the same average unemployment ratio.[15] The cumulative employment loss in Canada from 1990 to 1996 was double that from 1982 to 1986.[16] The Canadian recession was very deep in wider comparative terms as well. From 1990 to 1995 Canadian unemployment above the estimated NAIRU exceeded that in Japan and the European Union in addition to the United States.[17] In terms of growth, the recession was much deeper in Canada than in the other G-7 countries. This raised relative Canadian unemployment substantially.[18]

Such poor economic performance put Canada on a path that, while not isolated from the directions in other countries, contained particularly profound turns. The public sector debt-to-GDP ratio in the United States and Canada was very similar at the end of the 1980s – 38 percent in the United States and 40 percent in Canada. From 1990 to 1996, American net public debt rose only to 48 percent of GDP, whereas in Canada, net public debt hit 70 percent of GDP.[19] Since American fiscal policy did not tighten more than Canadian fiscal policy during this period, the only explanations for this increasing debt burden gap were much higher Canadian real interest rates and much weaker Canadian economic growth.[20] The depth of the recession itself was policy driven, and policy constraints made it difficult to begin recovery as quickly as elsewhere. Bank of Canada economists argue, no doubt rightly, that monetary conditions in the first half of the 1990s would not have been so tight but for nervous financial markets concerned with Canada's fiscal position, Quebec's status, and international developments such as the Mexican peso crisis. In these circumstances, the bank's freedom to lower short-run interest rates was constrained.[21] It seems clear that the high stock of public debt in Canada in the mid-1990s, although in no small part a function of monetary policy, was a source of continuing restrictive monetary conditions. Fiscal contraction, reaching its heights with the 1995 budget, was another source of continuing economic underperformance. As Pierre Fortin argues, 'through standard multiplier effects on aggregate demand and output, the sharp fiscal restraint had a further delaying impact on the recovery of domestic demand.'[22] After 1995, the scope for Canadian interest rates to fall widened considerably. Setting the deficit on a clear downward track and diminished political uncertainty in Quebec were surely factors. Canadian overnight interest rates fell more than 2 percent below American rates by the end of 1996. Longer-term interest rates (up to ten years) also went below American levels.[23] Economic performance picked up considerably by the middle of 1997, and unemployment rates finally started to fall.

But the damage was done, in both economic and political terms. Canada had the worst economic performance in the G-7 in the first half of the 1990s. From 1992 to 1999 Canada's total government sector also experienced the most dramatic fiscal turnaround and the sharpest reduction in program spending in the G-7.[24] This was no coincidence. Indeed, Roderick Hill argues that the impact of deflationary policy on subjective well-being may not even be fully captured by conventional economic analysis.[25] Economic and fiscal conditions in the first half of the 1990s limited policy flexibility and radicalized the mass public.

The Structure of Economic Insecurity

Ken Battle and Sherri Torjman argued in 1993 that Canada needed comprehensive long-term social and economic policies to combat the roots of insecurity and poverty, which they correctly identified as deeply embedded in a changing society and changing labour markets.[26] But ironically, this very insecurity made state-led solutions less likely, because the forms it took and the history out of which it emerged further weakened what remained of embedded liberalism in Canada. Self-protection in the 1990s involved primarily an atomistic and inward response. The economic insecurities flowing from declining real incomes, high unemployment, labour market segmentation, and tax burdens made it politically much more difficult to persuade citizens to support the social safety net.

Declining Real Incomes

No matter how measured, Canadian real incomes did terribly in the 1990s. In the immediate postwar era, the real incomes of Canadian individuals and families consistently increased. With this promise of middle class comfort came certain expectations for the material well-being of oneself and one's progeny. But real income stagnation became a characteristic of Canadian economic life, and was associated with the failures of the postwar growth model. Real private disposable income (after taxes and transfers) grew by 3.2 percent annually between 1970 and 1979. It grew by 1.8 percent annually between 1979 and 1989, although income growth during the 1981-2 recession was negative. In the 1990s, ending in 1998, real personal disposable income was *in total* a paltry 0.5 percent above its 1989 peak.[27] Aggregating over these years disguised a substantial real disposable income drop in the early 1990s.[28] In addition, the near absence of inflation meant that nominal wage increases were not creating the illusion of higher incomes. Canada's real income performance was also terrible in comparative perspective. This is so not only when contrasted with the United States, although Canada did do a bit better when public disposable income (basically, government spending) is added to the equation. Compared with countries like Ireland, Portugal, Norway, the Netherlands, and Spain, Canada did even worse.[29]

Employment, Unemployment, and a Shrinking Labour Force

The unemployment rate in 1981 was 7.4 percent. In 1986 it hit 10.3 percent. Unemployment fell in the late 1980s, although with substantial regional variation. But it was 10.2 percent in 1991 and 10.1 percent in 1996, a time by which Canada was supposed to be several years into a recovery.[30] Even worse, these unemployment figures disguised a drop in the labour participation rate of over 4 percent from 1989 to 1996. Canadians who in better times would be looking for work had given up. In the 1980s, Canadian employment growth relative to population kept pace with that in the United States, even as Canadian unemployment exceeded American levels. In the 1990s, while Canadian unemployment did not much exceed 1980s averages, employment and labour force participation declined sharply.[31] Long-term unemployment also rose, although not to European levels.[32]

The employment rate in Canada picked up again after 1996, but still fell well short of its 1989 peak. It was also consistently well below the American employment rate from the early 1990s onward.[33] Pierre Fortin argues that decline in the employment rate – more than worsening terms of trade, weak productivity growth, and the private rate of retention of income after government transfers and taxation – accounts for the largest proportion of declining personal disposable income per adult relative to the United States in the 1990s.[34] American average incomes have outperformed those in Canada not because the United States is a lower inflation country. Canadian inflation has been lower than that in the United States. Only to a small extent has superior American productivity been the explanation, and so too with the tax burden and government spending. The United States boomed while Canada stood still in the 1990s because US employment expanded. Lower employment levels undermined average real income levels. The continuing threat to future incomes was kept in high relief by the spectre of unemployment and labour force exit. It was difficult indeed to trust that income streams were secure from 1990 through at least 1996.

Nonstandard Work

Real income decline and fear of job loss were exacerbated by the very restructuring of work that contributed to the restoration of corporate profitability. Nonstandard work, meaning temporary employment, part-time employment, and independent contracting (defined as self-employment without any employees) built insecurity into the structure of labour markets. Insecurity was the flipside of the 'flexibility' that companies insisted was necessary for their profitability. The figures are difficult to pin down, but Gordon Betcherman argues nonstandard work in Canada probably rose from less than 24 percent of total employment in 1975 to over 29 percent in 1993.[35] 'Much of this employment (although not all) is relatively poorly paid, provides few benefits, rarely includes training or advancement opportunities, and the jobs themselves are, by their very nature, insecure.'[36] Harvey Krahn provides slightly different figures. He argues that part-time work increased from 11 percent to 17 percent of employees between 1976 and 1994, but that since many people worked more than one part-time job, by 1994 23 percent of jobs were part time. Self-employment rose from 7 percent of workers in 1989 to 9 percent in 1994, making over 1 million Canadians their 'own boss.' Temporary employment increased from 8 percent of total employees in 1989 to 9 percent in 1994.[37] These changes were largely involuntary from the point of view of workers.[38] Restructuring of the labour market created an increasingly large segment of the labour force that was underemployed and underprotected. As long as people were working, they were not getting much obvious help from the state. But they were paying taxes.

Nor were those who owned a small business in an easy circumstance. Small business owners often do quite well, and small business gets a stunning array of tax breaks. But such enterprises are very vulnerable to changes in market conditions. This is indicated by the high proportion of both job loss and job gain in the small business (i.e., fewer than twenty employees) sector.[39] The recession made this vulnerability all the more acute. Small business owners had to deal with a lot of red tape, and often worked very hard. The self-employed – whether owners of small businesses or independent contractors – were increasing in number while, indeed because, the economy was stagnant. They were structurally prone to economic dislocation. Both overwork and underwork, then, emerged from the threat and reality of economic marginalization.[40] Declining present real incomes and insecure future incomes made state-mandated income drains highly conspicuous.

Taxation

The state was represented as the culprit in economic struggles for a number of reasons. One was that Canadians were objectively overtaxed. I mean this in the sense that a large imbalance between taxes collected and services provided arose because of the large proportion of government revenues that were devoted to debt-servicing charges.[41] Ottawa had the largest debt relative to the economy of Canada's governments. At its worst, the federal government was paying 36 cents of every dollar collected in debt-servicing charges. Only 64 cents of each federal tax dollar could be seen as returning benefits to Canadians. Even if every dime in debt-service charges went to Canadians, these payments were not benefits to citizens; they were obligatory charges paid on loans. Nobody, including the state, gets moral credit for fulfilling legal obligations. The state was not providing benefits proportionate to what it was extracting.

Recession and slow recovery made these conditions all the more salient. Support for a robust state role in the economy became more precarious under the circumstances, even though total government taxation increases (when netted against total government spending increases) bore almost no responsibility for real income declines from 1990 to 1998. Market incomes were the culprit.[42] The stagnation, and in the 1990s steep decline followed by glacial restoration, of Canadian real incomes made support for the unemployed and others who were treated as disadvantaged an increasingly burdensome proposition for those with taxable incomes. No longer was the tax bite being taken as a proportion of a growing income. With taxes rising to fight the deficit, the tax yield was taking an increasing bite out of a declining income. Acquiescence to taxation is not a 'post-material' phenomenon.[43] It depends on a specific material circumstance which, in this case, was being vitiated.

It is against the backdrop of Canadians not getting a proportional return in spending for their tax dollars, and of their tax dollars taking up an ever-increasing portion of their incomes, that public reaction against the Goods and Services Tax must be understood. It was introduced on 1 January 1991, in the midst of the recession. While designed to be revenue neutral, the Manufacturers' Sales Tax it replaced was applied on production rather than consumption and therefore hidden from consumers. In addition to Mulroney's unpopularity, the contempt in which the GST was held had rather more to do with its apparent contribution to state extraction from Canadians than its soundness as public policy. The Department of Finance argued internally that the public reaction against the GST was evidence Canada was on the verge of a 'tax revolt.'[44] Opposition to taxation became manifest throughout Canadian politics. The Harris Conservatives in Ontario were particularly explicit in their concern with 'taxpayers' rather than 'citizens.' Justice so conceived was to be delivered by political power that recognized radicalizing and growing segments of the population who felt at best ignored and often victimized by the state. Economic insecurity created deep resentments toward individuals and groups that appeared cosseted by the state. The resentful were those who believed that they, in their economic isolation, bore the burdens of protecting the 'privileged.' Parties that did not pander to these reactionary politics, such as the federal Liberals, could not ignore the discontent political rivals were expressing. Electoral prospects by the mid-1990s depended not just on credibility regarding balancing the budget; voters also had to trust that a party would not raise taxes, and that it would reduce taxes either sooner or later.

The State and Income Polarization

Economic and political conditions in the 1990s favoured an atomistic vision of self-interest in which an 'other' was conceptualized as rewarded, through state redistribution, by 'my' hard efforts. Market functions, left to themselves, would have increased income polarization over time. Taxation and government spending kept total income differentials among quintiles roughly constant between 1965 and 1995.[45] Market differences were particularly acute during recessions, at which point compensating redistributions became even more pronounced. In addition, over time there was an upward drift in the percentage of total income received by the bottom quintile from the state. In 1971, 43.4 percent of the bottom quintile's total income came from the state. By 1992 the figure exceeded 60 percent. For the second lowest quintile these numbers went from 10.3 percent to 26.8 percent. The state contribution to the other quintiles increased as well, although the percentages were lower and grew much more slowly. From 1989 to 1995, the market incomes of the top two quintiles increased while those of the bottom three quintiles declined, increasing the market gap. But in total incomes, which include state redistributions, the gap stayed relatively constant. In fact, the gap between the top two and the bottom three quintiles narrowed slightly from the early 1970s to 1995.[46]

The top two income quintiles, then, had an objective economic interest in decreased state income redistribution. This interest intensified in the 1990s. Objective economic interests were increasingly the reverse of this the further down the income scale a person resided. However, the general climate of economic insecurity alienated further from the state citizens whose marginal economic positions were experienced as undermined by taxes and redistributive transfers. Some of the middle class who distrusted the state actually benefited from its redistributive functions. Robert Cox properly argues that contemporary labour segmentation results in people with similar objective economic interests perceiving each other as enemies. Rather than understanding the problem in systemic terms, and without political cohesion and organization, people focus on personal survival rather than collective action.[47] It should come as no surprise that with deficit elimination and state retrenchment in the second half of the 1990s, the income gap between the top and bottom quintiles increased even after accounting for taxes and transfers. Indeed, it increased from 1995 to 1998 by almost as much as the increase in the differential between market incomes.[48] This was part of the point for the political energies motivating deficit reduction. As *The Economist* has noted, 'the greatest increases in income inequalities are found in the countries which have most zealously pursued free market policies.'[49] Increasing income inequality is a structural component of such policies.

The atomization of economic interests was perhaps most explicit in the increasing polarization of the labour market into 'good jobs' and 'bad jobs.' So-called knowledge workers had relatively scarce skills and relatively more opportunities, although the sands of these opportunities shifted quickly. Those without equivalent intellectual endowments, education, or training had fungible skills, were geographically relatively confined, and had far fewer economic options.[50] This structurally delinked the 'haves' from the 'have-nots,' especially insofar as the economic lives of the former had more to do with similarly situated individuals in other countries than with the have-nots in their own. The upshot, as Robert Reich argued in the American case, was a serious challenge to the notion of a domestic 'us.'[51] At the end of the 1990s, these questions became manifest in Canada as the so-called 'brain drain' became a matter of great public debate.[52] While the underlying reality of talent bleeding to the United States was suspect, the issue was a useful way of leveraging income distributions in favour of higher income earners. This was in spite of the fact that the complex web of factors informing migration decisions went well beyond relative tax rates.[53] To the extent the top two income quintiles had an objective economic interest in weakening state income redistributions downward, and also had a declining objective attachment to other Canadians beneath them in the economic hierarchy, the support of the 'haves' for the Keynesian welfare state was disposed to decline. The 'have-nots' were left extremely vulnerable. As Gordon Betcherman puts it, 'While workers with a high degree of skills or experience are not immune from insecurity, they are much more able than their less skilled or experienced counterparts to protect themselves.'[54]

The Politics of Economic Insecurity

The atomization of interests stemming from these economic experiences was politically mediated. To turn away from the state and look inward for self-protection required political organization that could weaken state efforts to extract benefits from some citizens for the succour of others. Developments in the federal party system gave political meaning to structural economic experiences. These changes were visible in the emergence of the Reform Party, the fall of the New Democrats, and the 'rightward' shift of the Liberals.

The NDP lost official party status in the 1993 election. Like the Progressive Conservatives, who were even more decimated in 1993, the NDP regained this standing in 1997, and barely retained it in 2000. The Reform Party broke through in 1993, winning almost all of its seats west of Ontario. It started as a western protest party, and in spite of herculean efforts, including its transformation into the Canadian Alliance in 2000, was unable to make material gains into central and eastern Canada. The regional concentration of its votes provided it with many more seats than the Tories, in spite of comparable overall vote totals in 1993 and 1997.[55] The Bloc Québécois (BQ) took the most seats in Quebec in 1993, 1997, and 2000, although it lost the popular vote in the province to the Liberals in the last of these elections.

The BQ was the official opposition in 1993; Reform won the honour in 1997. The BQ was not a significant influence on fiscal and economic policy because of its separatist raison d'être. It tended to offer a social democratic critique of government policy, but its positions regarding these policy areas were not representative of an identifiable socio-economic base. The BQ's fiscal and economic stances were grafted onto its independence objective, and Quebeckers voted BQ primarily on national rather than economic grounds.[56] As such, Reform was the opposition party whose fiscal and economic stances could claim some pride of place as representative of (English) Canadian views. The significance of Reform's consistent deficit reduction argument was that, in contrast to the dilemma Mulroney faced, the Chrétien Liberals' most relevant opposition was attacking them for being too soft on the deficit. No longer would the government have to worry much about political risk from the left for strong fiscal retrenchment. Neither the NDP nor the BQ had any real growth potential. But Reform threatened to spill into Ontario and undercut the Liberals' primary base of support.

Populism and the Reform Party

Unlike the BQ, Reform had a reasonably coherent socio-economic support base. Tom Flanagan is right when he claims that Reform's success in the 1993 election is best understood through its positioning itself first as 'the party of the West' and second as the 'party of the right.'[57] Reform's seats were in the West, and the party emerged out of perceived failures of federal institutions to represent that region adequately. That it was of the West, along with its social conservatism, is why Reform was unable to make inroads in Ontario. Regarding the state role in the economy, though, Reform spoke to a wider audience that the Liberals were always trying to prevent from bleeding to Reform. This audience was ready for the Reform message, if not always the messenger, precisely because of the developments in the international political economy, Canadian public policy, and domestic political strategies we have discussed at such length. As David Laycock wrote of the Reform Party in 1994:

This appeal has struck a responsive chord for many small business people, self-employed, retired people, unionized and non-unionized workers experiencing job insecurity and others who feel they lack institutional means to penetrate opaque and distant policy processes. Reform speaks to their sense of exclusion and alienation from political life. Low-income people have been joined by many previously secure middle class citizens in feeling threatened by emerging contenders for power and opportunity within provincial societies and the federal system.[58]

The feeling of being 'threatened by emerging contenders for power' explains the distaste in Reform for 'bureaucrats' and their 'special interest' constituencies.[59] Preston Manning himself argued that bureaucrats, politicians, and special interests exert a tyranny of the minority over the democratic majority.[60] And so too Reform's displeasure with deficits, which were presented as permitting extractive transfers from taxpayers to unjustly enriched, if vaguely defined, others.

The party system underwent tremendous change in the 1990s, but it also displayed certain continuities with longstanding Canadian traditions. The main institutional difference was that, contrary to the 1940s and 1950s, in the 1990s there was no second party (i.e., the Progressive Conservatives) obviously capable of winning the next election. This left the Chrétien government relatively unaccountable. But it is striking how similarly Liberal governments functioned in the immediate postwar era when the CCF was more viable, and in the 1990s when faced with the Reform Party. In each case, these 'third' parties represented political constituencies that were seen as a threat to the political base of the government. In each case, strong populist elements could be found in these parties. In each case, these parties represented the direction toward which Canadians as a whole were ideologically moving. And in each case, the Liberals understood that they had to be responsive to the directions these parties represented, but also that Reform in the 1990s, and the CCF in the 1940s and 1950s, were more extreme than were Canadians generally. This is suggested by the fact that the more moderate Liberals held office. As such, the Liberals in both eras poached on some of the policy directions propounded by these parties without going as far as these parties would have preferred. *Plus ça change, plus c'est la même chose* in Canadian politics. What could be more Canadian than a brokerage Liberal government using the ideas of an opposition party to co-opt the latter's support and maintain the former's power?[61] Just as the Liberals' could once describe the CCF as 'Liberals in a hurry,' the same could be said of Reform.

The form of this political manoeuvring was, upon reflection, hauntingly familiar. The content of these politics, however, was markedly different. While always within the broad confines of liberal democratic capitalism, politics after the Second World War were moved by the Liberals, the CCF, and the mass public modestly in the direction of resistance to market forces. This resistance included both countercyclical demand management and the construction of the Keynesian welfare state. In the 1990s, the Liberals, Reform, and the mass public moved in a direction that prioritized market forces over government intervention. This was manifested, in part, through an attack on deficits and the Keynesian welfare state. The Martin budgets, and Reform rhetoric, presented deficit finance as favouring the privileged over the common person. Interfering with markets had once been seen, from the populist point of view, as favouring the common person. Usurious (central Canadian) banks were presented as the problem and some form of state intervention as the solution. Now, interfering with markets was conceptualized as the state preferring privileged special interests and bureaucrats instead of allowing neutral meritocratic markets to function, and so was put in opposition to the general citizen.[62] Embedded liberalism – the protection of state and society from the excesses of unfettered market functions – lost some of its resonance in the society it was supposed to protect. The ideological content of populism changed.

There is debate about the nature of the Reform Party and its supporters. I have endorsed David Laycock's position, arguing that in addition to western alienation Reform's energy was based on economic insecurity and directed against state supported 'privileged' elites.[63] Tom Flanagan has argued that Laycock misunderstands Reform, at least at the level of leadership. Rather than seeing the country as divided into various groupings, Reform leader Preston Manning actually saw no real divisions at all. Canadians were all the 'people,' and Manning's appeals to the 'people' were appeals to everybody, not to specific groups.[64] Flanagan takes the point of view of an 'insider' gleaning the speaker's intent; Laycock takes the point of view of an 'outsider' interpreting the social meaning of political statements. Only the 'outsider's' view can divine the wider implications in which the statements publicly participate. Reform's support was too specific to be understood as transcending interests. Manning's appeals may have been genuinely inclusive, but they were clearly not heard in this way. The electoral success of the Reform Party resided not in its generic appeal but in its resonance with the particular experiences, resentments, and aspirations of the 'people.' Support for Reform was the most profound expression of these dynamics in federal politics, but the Liberals accommodated some of this political energy. Provincial politics also manifested these tendencies. Mike Harris's Ontario Conservatives were elected in 1995;[65] Ralph Klein became leader of Alberta's government party, the Progressive Conservatives, in 1993.[66] Each shared much with Reform. Indeed, members of both provincial Tory parties would be key figures in the fin de siècle effort to 'unite the right' under the post-Reform banner of the Canadian Alliance.

Politically, the Canadian parties that embodied and articulated populist conservatism in the 1990s were not, at least initially, speaking on behalf of Bay Street. The Reform Party, the Harris Conservatives in Ontario, and the Klein Conservatives in Alberta had their original roots and appeal on 'Main Street.' Preston Manning had no more time for subsidies engineered by the business lobby than he did for the benefits extracted by other interests he saw as minoritarian.[67] Reform supporters in the early to mid-1990s generally came from the employed or retired middle class. According to Flanagan, 'one meets few single mothers, welfare recipients, or unemployed people in the party; but one also meets few of the really well-to-do – executives of large corporations and professionals such as lawyers and doctors. People with very high incomes tend to prefer the Liberals and Conservatives.'[68] And the parties that more affluent Canadians were disposed to support, particularly the Liberals, were influenced by this fraction of their voter base toward neo-liberal policies that enhanced after-tax incomes.

The Liberals
These politics were not, at least with respect to visions of the state role in the economy, confined to radical fringes. That Ontario could elect both Mike Harris to Queen's Park and the Chrétien Liberals to Ottawa indicates that its doubts regarding Reform were about regional distrust and social conservatism, not economic and fiscal policy. And indeed, the move of the Liberal Party away from embedded liberalism and toward neo-liberalism was not merely a matter of pressure from the party system. It also resulted from an assessment of where the mass public's preferences were now located and from change within the party itself. The Aylmer conference in 1991 revealed ideological movement within the party and indicated that many important Liberals were prepared to move to the 'right.'[69] In fact, by this time the party was ahead of the caucus on fiscal responsibility (as well as law and order).[70] The Liberals of Jean Chrétien's 'Canadian way'[71] were not the Liberals of Pierre Trudeau's 'just society.' That Liberals held power in the 1970s and 1990s sometimes disguises that policy and politics were quite different in these decades. That the Liberals could hold power at both times was indicative not of the party's enduring commitments but of its adaptability to the preconditions of power.

Paul Martin located his 1996 budget in what he described as the unparalleled anxiety Canadians were experiencing.[72] Insecurity acquired its meaning, though, not from objective circumstance but from politics. During the Great Depression of the 1930s, economic failure was associated with laissez-faire economics and Gladstonian sound finance. This, along with the Second World War, created political conditions for a more robust state role and the use of deficits. The 1990s was the culmination of recurring underperformance associated with interventionism. The Mulroney government continuously argued that the state, and particularly the fiscal deficits that symbolized its alleged excesses, was the economic problem. Given that Trudeau-style interventionism had been politically delegitimated, the only viable explanation of continuing economic underperformance in the 1990s was that economic renewal had not gone far enough. Certainly the early 1990s recession, even though its depths were a function of neo-liberal policy, seemed to vindicate Mulroney's claim that Canada was subject to international competition, which demanded further domestic reform. The recession, contextualized in this way, created political conditions for circumscribing the state role, for fiscal retrenchment, and for less generous social programs. Recall from Chapter 1 Robert Reich's argument about how it is that questions, such as whether the deficit should be eliminated, catch on. He claims that the art of policy making lies in giving voice to half-articulated fears and hopes in convincing stories about their origins and normative dimensions.[73] Politicians who addressed the deficit in a convincing story about excesses of the state were rewarded. The story was convincing because it resonated with the dominant experience, politically constructed to be sure, of economic life that developed over the preceding years. It allowed citizens to regain a sense of control over the state and their economic lives in a fashion consistent with how their economic interests were now conceptualized.

To their credit, the Liberals did not typically try to exacerbate these resentments for political advantage. But no Canadian government could ignore the force of these pressures. Formerly, prebudget consultations were done one group at a time. The consultations therefore encouraged each group to ask for the moon.[74] By contrast, in 1994, Paul Martin opened up the prebudget consultations, providing interested participants with at least some sense of ownership over fiscal policy. One conference was held in each major region of the country to consider budgetary issues. As Evert Lindquist argues, prebudget consultations such as Martin organized at the federal level, but which were also held by provincial governments, functioned to channel traditional discussions with interest groups by forcing them to contend with other groups, experts, and citizens. Such arrangements cast deficit reduction as a strategy directed to furthering the common good and as thwarting interest group demands.[75] The fiscal principles Paul Martin set out in his 1995 budget spoke to concerns with the common good, but to a very specific conception of the common good. He argued that fiscal rebalance would be attained in keeping with the priorities of the 'people,' and that these priorities favoured spending cuts over tax increases. The people were defined as opposed to new spending and as strongly supportive of budgetary balance.[76] And indeed they were. From 1988 to 1992, only between 4 and 13 percent of respondents thought deficit reduction should be a federal priority. From the summer of 1993 through 1997 the range was usually between 20 and 30 percent, and peaked at 48 percent just before the budget of February 1995.[77] In historical terms, this was very high support for deficit reduction. The government's descriptions were consistent with contemporary populist conceptualizations of the 'people,' although they did not include the victimization that often accompanies populist rhetoric. The claim that the government had only the money the 'people' provided functioned to restore a sense of sovereignty over their economic lives.

Budget pronouncements manipulate. In part Martin was trying to manage down this populist wave. But budget rhetoric also responds, and the Liberals had to acknowledge the very potent political forces percolating in the country. Suggestive of the extent to which economic hardship had acted as the political impetus to reform, by the year 2000, Martin was vindicating the policies of the previous five years by arguing that progress was ultimately to be measured by the real income increases Canadians were only just beginning to realize.[78]

The Keynesian Welfare State

With the combination of high interest rates and low growth, debt-servicing charges in the first half of the 1990s were eating up an increasing share of the expenditure budget. Only if tax yields and/or deficits continued to rise could social support be maintained. Deficits, although not countercyclical, were supporting what remained of the Keynesian welfare state. The elimination of persistent deficits was the mechanism by which the Keynesian welfare state was redesigned and retrenched. The business community and its mouthpieces had been impugning the social support system and the deficit for a very long time. Only when economic circumstance, shaped by policy and constructed for political purposes, supported at the popular level an attack on the Keynesian welfare state could deficit reduction take centre stage as an instrument of retrenchment. Electoral feasibility overcame the power of institutionalized 'special' interests to maintain social programs and their supporting deficits. Fiscal politics emerged to retrench the state in the interest of the 'people,' for whom social programs and persistent deficits were conceptualized as drains on insecure incomes. Other government spending, of course, was also suspect. Fiscal politics took hold primarily because of its value in realizing these interests. But although deriving its original cachet from its instrumental value, upon entrenchment fiscal politics functioned autonomously. The ideas constituting the fiscalization of politics would provide an independent rationale for retrenchment and reform. In this respect, the emergence of fiscal politics was a moment in the unfolding of neo-liberalism in Canada.

To put the point in conventional terms, the citizenry had shifted to the 'right,' so electoral support and fiscal retrenchment were no longer incompatible. A 'left' case against fiscal shortfalls was available, but in this context the 'right' argument prevailed. Discretionary action to reduce deficits would be through spending decreases. Although it is too simple to use preferences for spending cuts over tax increases as definitive of 'right' rather than 'left' stances, this measure provides at least some guidance. A study by Ronald Kneebone and Kenneth McKenzie concludes that discretionary fiscal retrenchment across Canada from 1993 to 1996 was primarily on the expenditure side.[79] For example, Saskatchewan, governed by Roy Romanow's NDP, is often thought to have taken the revenue road to fiscal retrenchment in the 1990s, but Kneebone and McKenzie find otherwise. In fact, Saskatchewan took more discretionary action on the spending side to reduce the deficit, measured by year-over-year change in the ratio of program spending to GDP, than any other jurisdiction, including Ottawa.[80]

I argued in previous chapters that, in the 1980s, election of a neo-liberal federal government required strategy; by the second half of the 1990s, a neo-liberal administration could be assumed. The Liberals' ambivalent 1993 platform left this issue ambiguous. But in the 1997 and 2000 elections it was clear that the Liberals were a party of free trade, price stability, and balanced budgets. When the 39 to 41 percent of the vote the Liberals took was combined with the 19 to 26 percent to Reform/Alliance and the 12 to 19 percent going to the Progressive Conservatives, a good 70 to 75 percent of voters were supporting neo-liberal parties in federal elections. The proportion was much higher in Canada outside Quebec. There were differences among these parties, to be sure, but their shared neo-liberalism was evident. The NDP still ran candidates in every riding. Yet it was stuck with only 9 to 11 percent of the popular vote. While declining voter turnout suggested increasing alienation from the political process, the preferences of Canadian voters during the 1990s regarding the role of the state in the economy seem clear.

There is a caveat, however. The Liberals became, and I will demonstrate this point further, a neo-liberal party. The third-order policy change of the Mulroney era was continued and even deepened. But there were other reasons to support deficit elimination. As I argued at the beginning of this book, neo-liberalism and embedded liberalism are ideal types. Elements of both always exist. There was an embedded liberal aspect to Liberal justifications for deficit elimination.

Part of the basis for economic insecurity and a turn inward for self-protection was located not only in a felt personal inability to afford the

Keynesian welfare state but also in fears that the Keynesian welfare state would evaporate. These fears emerged from the precarious condition of Canada's finances, and from the emerging distaste in citizens and parties for the social safety net. Edward Greenspon and Anthony Wilson-Smith report that December 1995 was the lowest ebb Canadians reached, and that most of the malaise was related to economic insecurity. Ninety percent of Canadians expected Unemployment Insurance and welfare to be less generous or gone in five years, and that the young would find it harder to obtain meaningful employment. Eighty percent expected the end of the Canada Pension Plan and 60 percent foresaw the demise of Medicare. Only 2 percent expected the deficit to be eliminated. Consumer confidence in the last quarter of 1994 was at its lowest nonrecession level since the statistics were compiled. Sixty-eight percent thought the Liberals had done poorly in delivering on their jobs pledges. An amazing 80 percent of Canadians thought the 1990-1 recession never ended. Yet the Liberals were in the mid-50s in the polls.[81]

Another factor in insecurity was the status of Quebec. David Cameron argued in 1995 that 'for almost 30 years, Canadians, not just Québécois, have been forced to bear in mind the possibility that the country might not exist in the future, that its very existence was up for grabs.'[82] The province had come within a whisker of voting in favour of independence in the November 1995 referendum. One in three Canadians (one in two in Quebec) believed the country as they knew it would cease to exist by the end of the decade.[83] This facet of insecurity had an economic component. Who knew what would happen to the currency, the debt, the social safety net, and the economy were Quebec to leave? But the national question in Quebec obviously went well beyond economic and fiscal matters. It was not a primary factor in the generation of economic insecurity. However, it encouraged widespread doubts about not only the federal government's competence but also its continued existence. The uncertainties the separatist movement created for the Canadian state, which were particularly acute in the first half of the 1990s with the failures of the Meech Lake and Charlottetown Accords, and the near-miss in the 1995 referendum, contributed to the political concerns associated with economic insecurity.

The amazingly dispirited polling numbers suggested three things. First, the Liberals' popularity in the face of this startling pessimism indicated that Canadians accepted, or were at least resigned to, poor economic performance and erosion in the social tapestry. There was little expectation that the state could or should try to make things better through short- or medium-term measures. Second, the deficit itself was a factor in the creation of economic insecurity. It was a major reason the social safety net was not expected to survive. The deficit became a symbol of the inability of the Canadian state to manage itself and to protect its citizens. Third, since the welfare system was expected to shrivel, it did not make sense to rely on the state for protection from economic dislocation. Whether one supported the Keynesian welfare state or deplored it, little in the social, economic, fiscal, or political milieu suggested it would be there for those who needed it.

From this point of view, deficit elimination was not so much an exercise in state retrenchment as a strategic withdrawal that would allow the state to reassert itself at a later date. Martin spoke in the March 1996 budget, in light of the anxiety he said Canadians were feeling (and it is important to note that he subjected nearly everything he said and did in his budgets to extensive focus group testing),[84] of 'securing the future.'[85] The modest expansion of spending which came with the 1998 budget announcement that the books for 1997-8 were balanced was described as part of a process of building a secure society.[86] Programs were to be durable. This conceptualization was a defence of social programs from an embedded liberal, although not a Keynesian, perspective. The new programs were not vindicated in Keynesian terms. They were never justified on the grounds they provided support for demand in the economy. Nor were automatic stabilizers nearly so robust. The Canada Assistance Plan was changed from a shared cost transfer to a block grant by rolling it into the Canada Health and Social Transfer (CHST). Transfers through the CHST were fixed and therefore independent of economic conditions. The recently renamed Employment Insurance program was made considerably less generous.[87] And the federal Stabilization Program, designed to protect provincial revenues in an economic downturn, was made almost impossible to access.[88] But the new programs were consistent with the tenets of embedded liberalism to the extent that they were constructed to offer protection from economic change. The future could be secured, according to Paul Martin's argument, if the deficit was eliminated and debt-servicing charges declined as a percentage of federal spending. An ancillary embedded liberal element in the redesign of social programs was identifiable in an era of deficit elimination and retrenchment.

Conclusion

Economic decline and the violation of the Anglo-American liberal parameters of legitimate state intervention under Trudeau took some policy options off the table. Restructuring Ottawa's economic role so that it would conform to perceived imperatives of international competition under Mulroney resulted in the adoption of policies that made for terrible short- and medium-term economic performance, and a social security tapestry less capable of protecting society and economy from dislocation. The problems under Mulroney were interpreted as an indication his work needed to be completed. The Chrétien governments were able to pick up the fiscal torch and succeed where Mulroney failed because a radicalized mass public finally applauded the retrenchment that would go with deficit elimination. A populist vision anchored in a specific experience of economic insecurity defined the state as inimical to the 'people's' interests. The idea of deficit elimination was selected because of its instrumental value to realizing interests so defined by disciplining an extractive state. Balanced budgets represented the end of state incontinence and the retrieval of a sense of control over its activities. Tax reductions were the other policy that served this function. Even public opinion analysts who argued that Canadians were prepared to support an increased state role recognized that this support was conditional on fiscal discipline.[89] The public may have wanted better health care and education, but balanced budgets were the condition precedent to realizing these desires. In a context of deep economic insecurity for which an overextended state and its deficits were blamed, and with embedded liberal and Keynesian norms ever more remote from the socio-economic conditions that supported their reception in the first place, the deficit was eliminated not in spite of the unpopularity of such a move, but rather due to substantial public support.

8
Only Nixon Can Go to China, 1993-8

The Chrétien Liberals were essentially a neo-liberal administration that extended rather than opposed the Mulroney economic renewal. This conclusion is based on the Liberal approach to key Mulroney economic policies, and in continuities over the two governments regarding their conceptualizations of global competition. By the end of 1994, Liberal preferences were clear. Any doubts were erased by the 1995 and 1996 budgets, which took Ottawa down a road of fiscal retrenchment that Mulroney had been unable and unwilling to travel.

The Economic Model

The vision of the economy and the state role therein that the Liberals propounded in the Department of Finance's fall of 1994 'Purple Book' was updated from Tory days to reflect some new thinking on globalization and the 'information economy.' For the Liberals, the intensity and scope of global competition was being dramatically increased by three factors. First, they argued, globalization of transportation and communication had improved efficiency and speed. Round-the-clock global financial markets, the diffusion of management techniques, and the dominance of 'free market' philosophies after the Cold War, enhanced global integration.[1] Second, said the government, developing regions, particularly the Pacific Rim and Latin America, were very dynamic and could add one to two billion producers and consumers over the next thirty years.[2] Third, the Liberals claimed, the information economy was undermining traditional business and political forms. Falling computer costs enhanced the position of knowledge relative to energy and raw materials as the key source of economic value.[3] For the Liberals, these three factors taken together implied that financial capital, technology, and educated people could be combined and located almost anywhere. As such, the number of potential competitors was mushrooming.[4] The government argued that the root of economic decline was the failure of productivity to grow at old rates.

Productivity growth, it said, was the foundation of economic progress and had to be the primary focus of economic policy.[5]

The emphasis on productivity was important, and the approach was thoroughly contemporary. But it was also old wine in new bottles. At its core, the Liberal approach was essentially the globalist Tory vision of international economic change and competition requiring facilitative state responses. The modesty of the Liberal five-point plan to foster its economic and productivity vision indicated that much of the procompetitive work entailed by the vision had already been done. The government claimed it would help Canadians acquire skills, through facilitative rather than invasive methods.[6] It would encourage Canadians to adapt.[7] This was code for minimizing subsidies to both business and individuals, including through Unemployment Insurance.[8] The government stated that it would provide leadership in the economy by supplying public goods and facilitating the country's capacity for innovation.[9] The Liberals also aspired to 'get government right' by reviewing priorities and making targeted, rather than across-the-board, cuts that would help get better value for money. Hence the necessity of 'Program Review.'[10] Other than skills development, which would nonetheless be funded in part by reallocations, none of these four items threatened to cost much money. Indeed, some would provide substantial savings. It was really the government's fifth agenda item, the provision of a healthy monetary and fiscal climate, that defined its economic policy plan. Since a 'healthy' monetary climate was already in place, the fiscal side of the equation became the object of focus.

Tory Economic Policy in Liberal Dress

Not only was the economic model of the Mulroney era consistent with the Liberal problematization; the Liberals adopted Progressive Conservative policy regarding inflation, unemployment, and trade. On the core policies that were definitive of Mulroney's neo-liberalism, the Liberals did some minor window dressing to make the policies look more appealing, but accepted the disciplinary anti-inflation stance and trade rules. Liberal choices in these regards were not inevitable. However, the feasibility of the options before them was structured by path dependencies created by previous decisions. The 'neo' in neo-liberalism is about making it very difficult to turn back the clock. Classical economic liberalism is not to be undone again. Putting authority in independent banks, and in continental trade agreements that amount to an economic 'constitution,' erodes the direct sovereign capacity of elected national governments to 'politicize' and interfere with market functions.[11] By design, it takes an act of great political will to wrest this authority back. Such an exercise of sovereignty is particularly problematic when there is strong political support for alienating state authority. The CUFTA meant protection from Ottawa's incursions for both the West and Quebec;[12] price stability meant comfort for financial capital. It is difficult for a 'left' or 'social democratic' party to imagine, win office on, and implement alternatives to neo-liberal policy in such politico-economic settings. The Mitterrand Socialists in France in the early 1980s and the Rae NDP in Ontario in the early 1990s learned this the hard way. That a bourgeois party like the Liberals was in power in the first place also suggests something about the content of this politico-economic context. Finally, Bob Rae's remark about adjusting to 'the necessary discipline of political responsibility' has some weight here.[13] Rae meant this as a criticism of more radical elements in his own party and the labour movement. But federal Liberal opposition to Mulroney policies was also easy when the party did not face the pressures and responsibilities of governing. Given that the policies that increased the subjection to the competitive pressures said to generate the need for deficit reduction in the first place would not be dislodged, alternatives to the neo-liberal approach to the deficit were increasingly out of step with the rest of the policy framework.

Inflation

The Liberals were strongly critical of the Bank of Canada's price stability policy while in opposition. Upon taking office, the Liberals made two changes regarding the bank and monetary policy. They did not renew the term of the bank's impolitic governor, John Crow, when his tenure expired at the end of 1993. In addition, the Liberals renegotiated the bank's inflation target with the new governor, Gordon Thiessen. In 1991, Michael Wilson and John Crow had introduced inflation targets to clarify the goals of the price stability policy and to create lower inflation expectations. The targets were 5 percent for 1991, 3 percent for 1992, and 2 percent by the end of 1995. After 1995, inflation was to be below 2 percent. Since precision is difficult in such matters, a 1 percent leeway was permitted around each target. The 2 percent target in 1995 therefore implied an inflation band of 1 percent to 3 percent.[14] The Liberals backed off the commitment to a post-1995 target of less than 2 percent inflation. In 1994, Martin and Thiessen agreed that the Bank of Canada would aim at 2 percent inflation within a range of 1 percent to 3 percent though 1998.[15] This target has remained in place ever since. In the 2001 economic update, Paul Martin announced it would be extended for five years.[16] Changing the governor and changing the post-1995 target were related in that Governor Crow insisted on a target band of 0 to 2 percent.[17]

The changes were not irrelevant, but they were hardly a reversal of bank policy. The Liberals squared their stance as a government with their earlier opposition position by arguing that the costs of attaining the lowest inflation rate in the G-7 had been high. As such, the government should not squander the gains for which Canadians had paid such a price.[18] Forcing the Bank of Canada right off its policy also would have compromised the bank's perceived independence in the eyes of financial markets. Since the Liberals had not yet established their credibility with those markets, such action could have been especially costly. The Liberals were extremely worried about financial market reaction to the decision not to renew John Crow.[19] Under these circumstances, a substantive change in policy direction was improbable.

Unemployment

Given that it broadly accepted the Tory vision of inflation, the Liberal government was analytically compelled to the Progressive Conservative conceptualization of unemployment. If one believes in an expectations model of inflation, it is difficult not to believe in the Non-Accelerating Inflation Rate of Unemployment. The Department of Finance argued that 'core' unemployment (the NAIRU) had risen over time and by 1994 was probably about 8 percent. This was 3 percent higher, said the government, than in the 1960s.[20] Rather than emphasize demand management to get unemployment down even to its core level, the new Liberals, as did the Progressive Conservatives, emphasized reducing structural sources of a high core rate of unemployment. These included skill mismatches, disincentives (including Unemployment Insurance and regulation), payroll taxes, and severe recessions. In spite of an acknowledgment that there had been insufficient aggregate demand in the Canadian economy since 1990, there was no discussion of a Phillips Curve tradeoff between inflation and unemployment with this Liberal government.[21]

Trade

As with inflation, so too with trade. Under John Turner, the Liberal Party fought the 1988 election against the Canada-United States Free Trade Agreement. Under Jean Chrétien, there was clearly movement in the party toward greater comfort with liberalized trade generally and continental trade specifically. This became clear at the party's Aylmer conference in 1991. But, in their Red Book, the Liberals opposed the North American Free Trade Agreement as negotiated. They promised they would not ratify the deal without certain changes. Upon winning the election, Chrétien told the Americans what he needed to legitimate his signature. Minor changes were made and the NAFTA was signed.[22] In part, Liberal opposition to the NAFTA was a strategic element in the 1993 election campaign. It appears Chrétien's inner circle really supported the deal.[23] But on taking office, the Liberals' policy options were also structured by the sunk costs of transition to the CUFTA, by the economic and political difficulties of abrogating such an important treaty with the United States, and by the concomitant difficulties of insulating Canada from American-led expansion of its trading bloc. Once on this train, it was politically very difficult to get off.

It is plausible that the Liberals were not as enthusiastically neo-liberal as their Progressive Conservative predecessors. The Liberals nonetheless walked neo-liberal and talked neo-liberal. Under Chrétien, Canada became probably the most enthusiastic proponent in the Americas of free trade. Canada signed trade deals with Israel and Chile, and pushed the Free Trade Agreement of the Americas. It used police power to quell dissent at both the APEC meeting in Vancouver in 1997 and the FTAA meeting in Quebec City in 2001. This was the most visible manifestation of neo-liberal discipline. The Chrétien Liberals also attacked the deficit, both in rhetoric and practice, with a discipline and efficiency that put the Mulroney Progressive Conservatives to shame.

The Place of Deficit Finance

The Liberal commitment to deficit elimination, however, was not firmly in place until the 1995 budget, although the Grey and Purple Books the Department of Finance published in late 1994 indicated the direction the government would take. Paul Martin's first budget, in February 1994, did not give the deficit pride of place.

The 1994 Budget: Continued Fiscal Ambivalence

The 1994 budget identified the deficit as but one of three 'central challenges.' Restoring 'fiscal sanity' was presented as necessary to helping Canadians adjust to a world of challenge and change. But equally important, argued Paul Martin, was building a framework for economic renewal, and constructing affordable social programs which would act as bridges rather than barriers to employment.[24] Martin implied there were tensions between these objectives when he argued the government was taking a balanced approach to jobs and growth on the one hand, and deficit reduction on the other.[25] That there were seen to be tensions was also manifest in Martin's 'challenge' to critics. To those who wanted the government to spend more, Martin insisted they explain from where the money would come. For those who wanted deeper cuts, he demanded they tell of the extent to which jobs, growth, and the less fortunate would be harmed.[26] Martin's linkage between cuts and both social and economic harm indicated that a Keynesian touch remained. The government would not remove too much demand from the economy for fear of the consequences. Indeed, Martin stated that in addition to direct budgetary action, growth too was necessary for deficit reduction. Growth, he said, was central to the government's fiscal strategy.[27] This statement was quite the reverse of the basic Progressive Conservative position that deficit reduction was a precondition rather than a product of growth.

There was substantial spending restraint in the 1994 budget, particularly regarding unemployment insurance and defence. But fiscal politics was not entrenched in the state because budgetary balance was not presented as prior to reaching other objectives. Indeed, in his response to the pre-budget consultations, Martin stated that the government did not agree that an absolute cut in 1994-5 spending levels was appropriate, for it could, as some consultation participants argued, threaten the economic progress needed to sustain medium-term economic improvements.[28] Shortly after the budget, Jean Chrétien stated that no further reductions would be necessary.[29] So understood, Martin's 1994 claim that his first budget was part of a two-stage process for reordering the fiscal framework that would be completed with the 1995 budget does not hold up to scrutiny.[30] Persisting Keynesian rhetoric and insufficiently bold fiscal action continued to go hand in hand. The 1995 budget would implement absolute spending cuts, and, not coincidentally, kill the last vestiges of Keynesian rhetoric.

From Ambivalence to Voice

In fact, opinion both within and outside the Department of Finance accelerated between the 1994 and 1995 budgets. First, having just taken office, the Liberals had only about a hundred days to prepare the 1994 budget. This did not offer much opportunity to rethink the role of government.[31] Further, it is the consensus of politicians, officials, and journalists that elite opinion about the 1994 budget changed. It was initially well received, except by the *Globe and Mail*. Some around Paul Martin believe the newspaper's reaction is what turned him into an anti-deficit hawk. In any event, over the next few months the 'economic chattering classes' and bond traders came around to the position that the 1994 actions were inadequate.[32] But as a senior Cabinet minister also noted, opposition to the budget after its three months of popularity was not confined to elites. The public, if anything, was ahead of governments in terms of the desirability of deficit reduction, and opinion on this matter accelerated between the 1994 and 1995 budgets.[33] Indeed, by February 1995, for the first time deficit reduction had become the top priority of Canadians.[34] That the New Brunswick and Alberta governments had 'aggressively pursued restraint measures' without apparent loss of popularity also indicated that a deficit reduction agenda could be politically viable.[35] Finally, a January 1995 editorial in the *Wall Street Journal* suggesting Canada might have to call in the International Monetary Fund to stabilize the currency if it hit the debt wall had a 'major effect on those in the Cabinet still hesitant to accept the general expenditure stance advocated by Finance.'[36]

Political reasons, then, were a major explanation of the much firmer measures the government would take in 1995. Economic and fiscal factors were also in play. The Bank of Canada was having difficulty pushing down long-term interest rates. Canada's large public sector debt was seen as an important cause of this problem. After the 1995 budget, long-term interest rates did decline.[37] In addition, the Mexican peso crisis hit on 20 December 1994. The Canadian dollar fell about 1.5 cents relative to the American dollar in a month. Investors went to the comparatively safe haven of the greenback in the face of uncertainty. Canadian interest rates went up 157 basis points to protect the currency. The excess of the Canadian over the American short-term interest rate more than doubled, to nearly 2.5 percent.[38] These high interest rates threatened the country's fiscal position. Public debt charges for 1995-6 were projected to be $7.5 billion greater than forecast in the 1994 budget.[39] The Grey and Purple books, to which we will return shortly, were produced in advance of the peso crisis, so it is possible to overstate the latter's importance.[40] The greatest relevance of the peso crisis, an interviewee argued, was that it undermined the fiscal projections in the 1994 budget, which had held at least until the early fall. Deeper cuts were now required to stay on track, and the 1995 budget had to be reformulated. Certainly, Martin's leverage for cuts with Cabinet was strengthened.[41]

These factors provided positive impetus for an attack on the deficit. Finance also felt somewhat emancipated to cut because it was less concerned about the economic impact of contraction. As one former senior official put it, the Keynesian multiplier 'was kind of dead' in the department by the mid-1990s. In the mid-1980s, it was still thought in Finance that deficits could support economic activity through 'multiplier' effects.[42] Finance now had more serious doubts about the efficacy of deficits given Canada's high debt level. It was thought possible by officials that deficits could actually harm growth when financial market expectations were built into the equation. Any growth from deficit-induced demand could be more than offset by higher interest rate premiums demanded by financial actors for perceived risks in loaning to a high-debt borrower.[43] In fact, Finance did expect retrenchment would suppress growth for a year or two.[44] Nonetheless, the risks of contraction were understood to be relatively less than in previous years when the debt-to-GDP ratio was lower.

The thinking on the extent of the deficit problem and of the measures to combat it changed during the summer of 1994, for both Finance officials and the minister. Martin underwent an education process directed by Finance Department officials and other advisors, who were convinced that the inimical consequences of the debt and deficits demanded immediate attention.[45] But once persuaded, a former senior official reports, Martin was ahead of his officials on the matter. It was he who argued that cuts should mean, as in the private sector, absolute cuts rather than reductions in rates of spending growth. Officials had never before considered so drastic a measure as absolute spending reductions. Martin was also very aggressive in setting expenditure reduction targets for federal departments.[46] With department officials and a very strong finance minister onside, the other key figure was the prime minister. Jean Chrétien, and on this there is no debate, consistently supported the finance minister against 'spending ministers' and their efforts to make 'end runs' around Martin to the PM.[47] Some Cabinet ministers were more enthusiastic about deficit reduction than others. Roy MacLaren, Marcel Massé, Doug Young, John Manley, and of course Paul Martin are identified by Greenspon and Wilson-Smith as the hawks, at least relative to the rest of Cabinet.[48] One Cabinet minister argued, by contrast, that while Cabinet supported the general goal of deficit elimination, dissent was at the level of specifics.[49] Indeed, Industry Minister John Manley was an anti-deficit hawk, but his department was perhaps the most recalcitrant.[50] Hilariously, the deputy minister of finance strongly resisted the Clerk of the Privy Council's direction that Finance (along with the Privy Council Office and the Treasury Board) take a 15 percent staff and budget cut. In the end, Finance did acquiesce.[51] Even at the worst of times, not many individuals or institutions like being cut. But retrenchment can still be politically supportable. In a parliamentary system of prime ministerial government with strong party discipline, the commitment of the authoritative actors is enough. That Chrétien and Martin were on board, and that Finance and Privy Council Office officials were eager to implement the policy thrust, was all the necessary political artillery.

The New Vision
In the Purple Book, the government gave fiscal health, as it defined the term, a priority never before attained. Fiscal health was presented as a prerequisite of all the other elements in the government's economic strategy.[52]

The Problematization
While the priority was different, the winning Liberal problematization of the deficit, and particularly the debt, was very similar to that under Mulroney. Productivity improvements and job growth were presented as dependent on investment, entrepreneurial vigour, and consumer confidence. Each of these, the Liberals argued, was vitiated by the debt load, for the debt caused higher taxes, higher real interest rates, and diminished the capacity of the government to address other important issues of economic strategy for the future. Therefore, argued the Liberals, the fiscal deterioration had to be stopped and reversed. Unusually high real interest rates and an unstable dollar were said to be signs of the debt's unsustainability.[53]

The government identified some now familiar consequences of debt and deficits. The Liberal conceptualization of the impact of a rising debt-to-GDP ratio on economic growth was identical to the vicious-circle position of the Tories.[54] In addition, the Liberals also argued there were more specific consequences. Taxes, and expectations of future taxes, would rise. Higher real interest rates would result from financial market inflation expectations. Program spending would be crowded out by rising debt-servicing charges. Government borrowing would increase foreign indebtedness because domestic private savings were insufficient to finance both private and public sector borrowing. In the Department of Finance's own words, 'we have suffered a tangible loss of economic sovereignty' because of Canada's exposure to volatile global financial markets.[55] Finally, the Liberals argued that future generations would have to foot the bill.[56]

The Liberals also particularized the harms caused by the fiscal situation. The debt and deficit, argued the government, were often portrayed as of interest only to financial markets and ideologues. In fact, it claimed, those who suffered the most immediately from fiscal problems were the unemployed, the poorer regions, and 'average' young to middle-aged families with mortgages and other debts incurred to raise and educate their children. The discomfort of financial markets in the face of the debt spiral caused higher loan and mortgage payments. Compound interest eroded the ability of the state to provide for less-advantaged citizens and regions. The social consequences of debt, argued the government, were as grim as the economic ones.[57] Fiscal control was presented as a matter of middle-class security as much as of financial capital's imperatives.

The Fiscal Problematization's Priority

The basic fiscal problematization was very similar to that under Mulroney. The differences resided in the pride of place given to fiscal control, and the ambition of the fiscal goals. For the Liberals fiscal health was prior to realizing the other elements of the economic strategy set out in its Purple Book. On occasion the Tories had spoken in this way too, but in general fiscal reform was but one aspect of economic renewal. The Liberal government acknowledged that fiscal reform entailed the *completion* of economic renewal. It argued that if it acted firmly to put federal finances on the track to balance, 'the last fundamental obstacle standing in the way of sustained growth and job creation will have been eliminated.'[58] It is in terms of Mulroney's economic renewal that Chrétien's deficit elimination and debt control was vindicated. And because the rest of Mulroney's renewal was in place, Chrétien's project was possible both politically and as a matter of policy; its implementation did not threaten to throw the Liberals off their fiscal goals.

The Liberals' fiscal ambition also exceeded that of the Tories. The campaign promise of getting the deficit to 3 percent of GDP by 1996-7 remained in place. But the ultimate goal was to balance the budget and significantly reduce the debt-to-GDP ratio. In addition, fiscal discipline was to be ongoing so that the debt-to-GDP ratio would not surge when the inevitable next recession hit.[59]

The Death of the Keynesian Touch

Understood through Peter Hall's concept of orders of policy change, the Liberals in late 1994 were offering first-order policy change. The setting of the deficit policy instrument was to be zero. The second-order policy change would come with the 1996 budget, in which Paul Martin stated that deficit elimination would be permanent.[60] This commitment took the deficit instrument off the table. The Progressive Conservatives' initial goal, recall, had been to reduce the deficit sufficiently to stabilize the debt-to-GDP ratio, and never did they commit to balance the Public Accounts budget. Mulroney, then, promised less ambitious first-order change, and did not propose second-order removal of the deficit instrument. The Liberal fiscal approach did not entail third-order change because it accepted the underlying objectives and priorities of Mulroney's neo-liberalism. Setting the deficit instrument at zero and removing it from the government's policy tool kit brought fiscal policy into line with the third-order changes introduced by Mulroney. Hall identifies as a component of 'monetarist' third-order policy orientations an emphasis on balanced budgets and tax cuts rather than short-term employment. This is exactly the direction the Liberals took.[61] The Liberal position that deficit reduction should focus on reducing spending rather than increasing taxes was much closer to the 'business' than the 'labour' and 'social movement' views propounded in the prebudget consultations for the 1994 budget.[62] The Liberals did view deficit elimination as prior to tax reductions. Permanent fiscal recovery was presented by Martin in 1997 as the only road to permanent tax relief.[63] The Liberals did not introduce major tax relief until the 2000 budget and the 2000 pre-election economic and fiscal statement.[64] (In the latter, Martin claimed these measures together constituted the largest tax cut in Canadian history.)[65]

The government argued that failure on the fiscal front would prejudice job creation and growth in both the short and the long run.[66] No longer was the Keynesian notion that deficits enhanced performance, at least in the short term, presented as a constraint on the extent of retrenchment. This was sound strategy, for no longer would the government be assenting to the criticism that its measures would cause harm. Yet since it was still thought within the department that deficit reduction would depress growth for a couple of years, the rhetoric that eliminated Keynesian vestiges reflected, but cannot simply be explained in terms of, internal thinking. One senior official stated that once a decision is made, it is not smart to talk about the awkward parts.[67] Another argued that removing concerns about the economic impact of demand contraction from public speech was putting a brave face on the situation.[68] But Mulroney and Wilson never took these rhetorical steps; their not doing so was both cause and effect of their political weakness with respect to deficit reduction. The Liberal rhetoric was part of a strategy designed to realize the government's political, economic, and fiscal objectives. Such are the impure forces that determine the public selection of ideas by governments.

The Face of Fiscal Politics

In the mid-1990s, fiscalized Canadian politics were very different from any time in the postwar era. The focus on the deficit provided a normative framework that legitimated spending cuts on a scale the government had never before contemplated. The fiscal targets identified in late 1994 were presented as non-negotiable.[69] The 1995 budget put the rhetoric of the late 1994 Liberal documents to the test. The commitment to the fiscal agenda was demonstrated to be firm. Keynesian vestiges were purged. The rhetoric became action. The 1995 budget defined the Chrétien administrations. It was also very popular with the public and financial markets.[70]

Budget Measures

In the 1995 budget speech, Paul Martin announced that the predicted 1994-5 deficit of $39.7 billion would come in $4.4 billion below that level.[71] The 1995 budget would generate, he said, cumulative savings of $15.6 billion in 1995-6 and 1996-7. Spending cuts would account for $13.4 billion of this total. In 1997-8, the reforms from the 1995 budget would save an additional $13.3 billion, with $11.9 billion of that on the spending side. As such, Martin argued, over three years the 1995 budget would cumulatively save $29 billion – $25.3 billion of this would come from spending. Program spending in 1996-7 was projected to fall below $108 billion, down from $120 billion in 1993-4. Program spending would be lower relative to GDP than at any time since 1951, Martin announced with pride.[72] Martin projected that by 1996-7 financial requirements would fall to $13.7 billion, or 1.7 percent of GDP. This level, he claimed, would put the debt-to-GDP ratio on a permanent downward track.[73]

Martin did announce some minor tax measures, but the action was elsewhere.[74] Few stones were left unturned as Martin announced his spending reductions. Government departments had their funding reduced. Between the 1995-6 and the 1997-8 fiscal years, annual spending was projected to decline by $1.6 billion for defence, $550 million in international assistance, $1.4 billion in transport, $600 million in natural resources, $900 million in human resources, $200 million in fisheries, $900 million in industry, $550 million in the regional agencies, and $450 million in agriculture.[75] Any economic growth that was contemporaneous with these cuts would leave spending even lower relative to the economy than the numbers suggested on their face. But these were hardly the only measures. The federal public service would be cut by 45,000 positions, 20,000 of which would be gone by the summer of 1996. Business subsidies would be reduced from $3.8 billion in 1995-6 to $1.5 billion in 1997-8. Subsidies under the Western Grain Transportation Act would be eliminated, saving $2.6 billion over five years.[76] The Liberals were able to eliminate the progeny of the Crow Rate, which was first introduced in 1897 as a change in the terms of Sir John A. Macdonald's National Policy. Further still, employability policy would be put under the rubric of a Human Resources Investment Fund to yield permanent savings.[77]

Perhaps as important as any other measure was the introduction, effective in 1996-7, of the Canada Social Transfer, which was soon renamed the Canada Health and Social Transfer, or CHST. The Mulroney government had been willing only to reduce or freeze growth rates of transfers to provinces. The CHST rolled the Established Programs Financing block grant for health and post-secondary education and the Canada Assistance Plan (CAP) shared-cost grant for social assistance into one block grant.[78] The cash value of these transfers was reduced by over $6 billion over two years. The tradeoff was increased 'flexibility' for provinces because most of the conditions attached to the CAP were removed. Only the CAP condition that provinces not establish residency requirements for social assistance eligibility was retained. The others, including the requirement that assistance be available to anybody in need, were dropped. Canada Health Act conditions remained in place.[79] Shifting the CAP from a shared-cost to a block grant also vitiated its countercyclical quality. Under the CAP, the federal government paid 50 percent of a province's social assistance costs (except in the three 'have' provinces by virtue of the 1990 'cap on CAP'). Social assistance payments increase during economic downturns, so the CAP entailed automatic countercyclical federal contributions. Indeed, Finance officials have been described as 'obsessed' with restructuring spending patterns to protect the government's fiscal position in the next recession.[80] The CHST, which set cash transfers at planned fixed levels indifferent to economic conditions, was another element in taking the Keynes out of fiscal and social policy.

The Liberals also gave notice in the 1995 budget that they would review social policy for the elderly. The result, in 1996, was rolling the Guaranteed Income Supplement and Old Age Security into the 'Seniors Benefit.' This, it was argued, was a fairer system because benefits would relate to income, and 75 percent of seniors would be as well or better off than in the past. Higher income seniors would have their benefits reduced. As it turned out, Martin revoked the Seniors Benefit in the summer of 1998, before it came into effect.[81] It was withdrawn mainly because of the high marginal tax rate it would have imposed on middle and lower ranges of income.[82] Its clawbacks kicked in at low enough income levels that there were large disincentives for citizens to bother saving for retirement. The Liberals were also so far ahead of their fiscal targets that the Seniors Benefit was unnecessary for attaining their fiscal goals.

Fiscal Politics and Program Review

Martin claimed to introduce changes to the role and structure of government so that savings would be found every year, and to secure such change irrevocably.[83] Structural change was primarily facilitated by the Program Review process, which Martin announced in the 1994 budget would be chaired by Treasury Board president Marcel Massé. The Liberals' position was that across-the-board cuts were inappropriate because the priority and efficacy of existing programs varied.[84] The result of across-the-board cuts, claimed the government, was overhead costs without the capacity to deliver value for taxpayers' money. Priorities must be set, and the federal government should withdraw from activities better done by others. On the other hand, some things, such as securities regulation, were better done on a national basis. So, the Program Review was necessary to make these determinations.[85] Program Review took on much greater scope and significance than anybody anticipated, because the government became truly serious about not only eliminating the deficit but also doing most of this work on the spending side.[86]

Program Review functioned by Finance setting expenditure targets for other departments, and those departments determining where their cuts would be made. These determinations were to be made in light of tests, developed by the Privy Council Office, against which programs were to be measured.[87] To pass muster, programs had to meet the tests of the public interest, the role of government (filling a legitimate and necessary government role), federalism (being an appropriate federal role rather than a candidate for realignment with provinces), partnership (could or should the program be transferred in whole or part to the private or voluntary sector?), efficiency (if the program continues, how could its efficiency be improved?), and affordability (was the resulting package of programs and activities affordable with fiscal restraint? If not, which programs or activities should be abandoned?).[88] Finance officials were of the view that allowing departments to make their own determinations of what to cut had the advantage of forcing them to 'buy into' the process.[89] In the end, the Equalization program, spending on Aboriginals, and seniors' benefits were the only major spending items that escaped the knife.[90]

One result was public sector employment loss. According to the Treasury Board, under Program Review from March 1995 to March 1997, there was a 13.8 percent reduction in the size of the public service. Employment declined from 225,619 person-years to 194,396 person-years. Seventy-six percent of this reduction occurred in four departments. Transport Canada lost 8,234 person-years, or 61.9 percent of its workforce. The civilian side of Defence lost 8,242 person-years, or 28.5 percent of its personnel. Human Resources Development lost 3,824 person-years, which amounted to 14.3 percent of its workforce. And Public Works and Government Services lost 3,439 person-years, or 22.2 percent of its personnel.[91] This may or may not have amounted to a reinvention of government, but it was certainly a government that was leaner with respect to a number of functions. Unless 30,000 people were literally unproductive, some of the state's capacity to deliver programs and perform functions must have been diminished.[92] Martin did recognize the 'valuable service' rendered by public servants who would lose their jobs.[93] This was to his and the government's credit, and in pronounced contrast to the rhetoric of the Mulroney Tories (one thinks back to Mulroney's promise of 'pink slips and running shoes' for civil servants) and the Reform Party.

Some sort of program review may have occurred without the hegemony of fiscal concerns, but the fiscalization of budgetary politics gave the review its significance. According to Donald Savoie, most participants agree that Program Review was a success in terms of cutting the deficit and rethinking programs and priorities. However, he also notes that those involved in social policy review would agree that Program Review 'degenerated into an exercise in fiscal restraint,' and that for most officials what drove the process were the notional spending cut targets produced by Finance. In other words, the affordability test is what mattered. 'The other five questions were, by most accounts, of limited relevance.'[94] Neither the depth of the cuts nor the reassessment of priorities would have been possible in the absence of the fiscalization of politics within the government. Indeed, the rhetoric for the need to prioritize notwithstanding, the process by which cuts were determined was 'utterly unscientific.'[95] Ken Battle writes that 'without the success of the anti-deficit campaign, governments never would have embarked on what became such ambitious and far-reaching reforms to social policy.'[96] Finally, phase 2 of Program Review (leading to the 1996 budget) entailed across-the-board 3.5 percent cuts. Program Review was turned over to the Treasury Board Secretariat following the 1996 budget.[97] With a balanced budget on the horizon, the impetus for continuing 'reform' lost steam. To the extent it was reinvented, fiscal politics is what drove the reinvention of the Canadian government and the recasting of social policy.

The Rise of Fiscal Politics and the End of Social Policy by Stealth

The fiscal politics entrenched within Ottawa were manifest in the budget pronouncements that spoke to bond markets and the mass public. Cuts were justified by their utility in rehabilitating the fiscal position, but their political energy was located in distrust of the state. Martin trumpeted his cuts for all to hear. The spending reductions were not, Martin said quite accurately, 'phony' reductions in rates of spending growth. The cuts were real.[98] Not only did Martin boast that these were the largest budgetary actions since the Second World War demobilization; he also argued that they were without precedent in their content.[99] But, the minister warned, there was more to do. The government would not let up when the next election approached.[100]

That Martin was able to brag about not only deficit reduction but also absolute spending cuts indicated that Canadian politics had undergone substantial change that made explicit retrenchment and deficit elimination politically saleable. The political cachet in spending cuts and deficit reduction undermines in substantial measure the argument that the Liberals continued the Tory tradition of social policy by stealth.[101] Certainly, remaking social policy through the budget process did not entail robust democratic participation in its development.[102] The CHST, for example, was a Department of Finance creation that emerged essentially without consultation.[103] Partial deindexation of the tax system persisted until full indexation was restored in 2000, and the Liberals continued through the CHST to claim credit for twenty-year-old tax point transfers.[104] But for the most part the Liberals did not hide from their efforts to reduce spending. They took proud credit for what had once been understood as medicine too harsh to be administered. Such measures were now presented and widely accepted as definitive of responsive government. Nor was it easy for Ottawa to hide, what with provincial campaigns to explain that the cuts provinces were making had been forced on them by reductions in federal transfers. The stealth argument, once a key insight, now masks how Canadian politics changed in the 1990s.

Formalizing Fiscal Restraint

Paul Martin introduced three much-ballyhooed budgetary techniques to facilitate deficit elimination: prudence in planning assumptions, a contingency reserve, and two-year rolling fiscal projections.[105] Prudent assumptions were used as insulation against uncertainty. The government wanted to be confident that there was a 'high probability' of meeting its targets.[106] A former senior official reports that Paul Martin expected the forecasts would be off and did not want to take the political heat.[107] As such, the fiscal goals the government set were goals that would be outperformed unless everything went wrong. Prudence was also built into the new 'contingency reserve,' that Paul Martin introduced in 1994. The reserve was initially set at $2.4 billion.[108] It was a set-aside budgeted as a planned expenditure. The money in the reserve was to be spent only in case of an emergency, such as flooding in Manitoba. To the extent the reserve was not in fact spent, it would be applied to the deficit, and the government would outperform its targets. This approach to the contingency reserve differed from past use of reserves as a spending resource. The Department of Finance's new policy was that 'the contingency reserve is not a source of funding for potential new initiatives.'[109] Third, the government eliminated the five-year projections that John Crosbie introduced in 1979, and that the Mulroney governments had often employed. Instead, Martin employed rolling two-year targets. He was of the view that if a longer projection horizon was used, something like the Mexican peso crisis could be treated as a short-term blip and ignored in the name of longer-term deficit control.[110] A commitment to short-term fiscal targets required internalizing all events into the immediate planning process to avoid deferring fiscal progress. Certainly under Mulroney, as we saw in earlier chapters, deferral of short-term deficit reduction was often legitimated by forecasts of substantial declines in the fiscal shortfall further out in the planning horizon.

Martin's efforts to institutionalize fiscal control can be contrasted with those introduced by the Progressive Conservatives in the early 1990s: the Expenditure Control Plan (the ECP), the Spending Control Act, and the Debt Servicing and Reduction Fund. The ECP was introduced in 1990 and meant to last for two fiscal years. All areas of spending were reviewed and a wide range of programs were affected.[111] The reductions were deep in comparison with earlier retrenchment. But in spite of extending and deepening the ECP, its cuts were too limited in scope to reduce the deficit in the economic and political context of the early 1990s. The Spending Control Act was Canada's version of the American Balanced Budget and Emergency Deficit Control Act (better known as 'Gramm-Rudman-Hollings'), and worked just as well – Gramm-Rudman, enacted in 1985, was to eliminate the federal deficit in the United States by 1991. The 'Debt Servicing and Reduction Fund' was a specified purpose account into which any GST revenues above predicted levels would be credited, and then applied against debt-servicing charges. Other credits to the account included privatization proceeds, and most quaintly, gifts.[112] The grand futility of this measure was revealed in Don Mazankowski's proud 1992 announcement that individual Canadians had contributed $375,000 to the fund.[113] Charity has rarely been an adequate substitute for concerted state action, and this case was no exception.

Comparison allows us to distinguish not only the forms for fiscal control that were selected but also the levels of commitment to fiscal retrenchment of each government. If there was a theme uniting the plan, the act, and the fund, it was that the Tory government was trying to fetter itself to attain its fiscal goals. Like an alcoholic telling the clerk at the liquor store not to sell the poor sot any more booze, the government was trying to force itself to be free. Alas, there is always another liquor store just around the corner, and there is always another way to increase the deficit. Tory efforts to institutionalize fiscal control, which failed miserably, were not unlike those they made to institutionalize inflation control, which were wildly successful. Recall that in the 1991 budget Michael Wilson announced the government and the Bank of Canada had agreed to inflation targets. These targets were not, in form, unlike the fiscal control measures the Tories introduced at around the same time. Each was in part aimed at convincing private actors of the government's resolve on an important issue, and in principle each limited the government's discretion. The inflation targets succeeded and the fiscal ones failed for the same reason. That is, formalizing policies does not determine their success. What matters is the commitment of authoritative actors to the policy goals. The bank's and the government's firm commitment to the price stability policy clearly predated the 1991 formal agreement. Mulroney's fiscal institutionalizations reflected not determination, but rather its absence. In the result, the fiscal programs were of little substantive significance.

The Liberal fiscal techniques, by contrast, reflected a deeper commitment to deficit elimination. Unlike the Expenditure Control Plan, the Liberal techniques amounted to more than just slapping a name on what the government would have done in any event. Prudence and contingency reserves were internal to budget construction rather than attached as an afterthought. But the mechanisms, in themselves, still could have been subverted if the government had wished. The value of the contingency reserve could have been reduced. The finance minister could have reneged on his commitment and used the reserve for new spending. Given the indeterminacy of the concept of prudence, the economic and fiscal assumptions could have been made less 'prudent' than they were. Because no formal constraint could prevent any of these actions, fidelity to principles must be explained in political rather than technical terms. Whether the alcoholic was cured, or was just taking it one day at a time, there were no runs to other liquor stores.

The upshot was that the largest budget forecasting error in Canadian history was the 1997-8 projection of a $17 billion deficit when the budget wound up with a $3.5 billion Public Accounts surplus.[114] Buckets of money were hidden, but there was little complaint at the time.[115] Of course, if Ottawa had been this far off in the other direction, the government would have been eviscerated. Preferences regarding forecasting errors and the government's fiscal position were clear.

After the Earthquake
The fiscalization of politics was not confined to Ottawa. Here, we examine first its effects in provinces and on federalism, and then its impact on the electoral politics of budgeting.

Provinces, Fiscal Federalism, and Intergovernmental Relations

Ottawa's transfer payment cuts contributed substantially to provincial fiscal problems. Since provinces were actually responsible for delivering key priorities like health care and education, their room to cut was more circumscribed, and politically more treacherous, than Ottawa's. But fiscal politics became operative at the provincial level as well. While the Alberta and New Brunswick governments moved on their fiscal problems before the federal government, the actions in the provinces must all be understood in terms of Ottawa's pervasive fiscal critique since 1984. By 1995, fiscal politics could be found across the country, but this did not always mean that deficits were eliminated (although this was usually the case). It did mean that provincial politics were energized by, and organized and debated in terms of, the fiscal positions of provincial governments. It also meant that credibility regarding fiscal restraint was crucial to political prospects.

That everybody was playing the fiscal politics game did not mean that everybody played the game the same way. All the teams in the American League play baseball, but some win with power hitting, others with pitching and defence. So too with the fiscalization of politics. 'Left' and 'right' governments all had to establish their fiscal credibility to retain their electability. Governments in most jurisdictions attacked their deficits before reducing taxes. The Harris government in Ontario was vociferously opposed to the provincial deficit. Yet it cut taxes while reducing the deficit, a path that obviously delayed deficit elimination in the province by a couple of years. Artificially retaining the deficit justified continued restraint on the spending front. But because Harris's deficits were clearly moving the government toward the lessened capacity for expropriation that lay beneath the political energy for deficit elimination, he was cut more slack than was Bob Rae, his NDP predecessor. Failure to play the anti-deficit game was fatal, even in Atlantic provinces, whose citizens are chronically accused of clientistic relationships with the state. For example, in 1999, Nova Scotia's minority Liberal government presented a budget with a $200 million deficit dedicated to health care funding, nominally the top priority of citizens. The government sought its own defeat to run as defenders of health care. In the ensuing election campaign, the opposition parties argued the deficit meant not that the Liberals were defenders of health care, but that Liberal mismanagement left health funding unsustainable. The Liberals were crushed by the third party, John Hamm's Conservatives, for whom balancing the budget was prior to sustainable social policy. In its first Throne Speech, Hamm's government spoke of changing the relationship between government and its citizens.[116] The importance of seeming to have the fiscal situation under control may be what drove Glen Clark's NDP in British Columbia to fudge its pre-election 1996 books sufficiently that the government was taken to court. The Campbell Liberals in British Columbia implemented tax cuts that exacerbated, if not created, deficits in 2001. But like Harris, Campbell was given more room to manoeuvre because his actions seemed to offer immediate real income relief by reducing expropriation. Whether this would occur, given the spending reductions Campbell also introduced, and whether this was good policy, are different questions.

The fiscal crunch also affected federal-provincial relations. The ever-tightening federal fiscal position from the mid-1970s onward resulted in increasing provincial distrust of Ottawa. Relying on its discretion over the spending power, the federal government made repeated unilateral downward adjustments in the growth rates of its Established Programs Financing transfer to provinces. The cap on the Canada Assistance Plan in 1990 deeply offended Ontario, Alberta, and British Columbia. The introduction of the CHST, and the substantially reduced cash transfers that came with its promise of increased 'flexibility,' was the final straw that radicalized provinces against Ottawa. Although the federal government's capacity to cut presupposed substantial strength, Ottawa's weakness relative to provinces was probably unprecedented in the mid-1990s, due to both fiscal retrenchment and the equally grave pressures resulting from a separatist near miss in the 1995 Quebec referendum. Responding to the prime minister's promises in the dying days of the 1995 referendum,[117] in the 1996 Speech from the Throne, Ottawa committed to decentralize certain powers,[118] an approach that has been described as 'non-constitutional renewal.'[119]

While some of the decentralizing pledges were kept, Ottawa still managed to shift and in some respects expand its role relative to provinces. The most conspicuous result of provincial-territorial radicalization was the Social Union Framework Agreement (SUFA), signed by the prime minister and all premiers except Quebec's Lucien Bouchard in February 1999. Ottawa was able to use the SUFA to legitimate the spending power while managing down provincial discontent. There is little reason to believe that the Framework Agreement served the provincial purposes that provided its original energy.[120] Alain Noël describes the cooperation embodied in the SUFA as 'hegemonic cooperation.' It is not cooperation between equals, but between one party (Ottawa) that sets the rules and creates incentives for compliance (usually by offering money), and other parties who fail to comply at their own peril.[121] Even when Ottawa was losing some ground, at worst the federal government did an excellent job of minimizing its losses. Commentators began to expect that, less than three years after it was signed, the SUFA would drift toward oblivion.[122] Over time, provincial anger eased, but residual distrust of Ottawa was a product of federal retrenchment even as provinces also worked to balance their budgets.

Budgeting Continues

The 1995 budget was a profound shift, and subsequent budgets were consistent with its precepts.[123] We observed earlier that in the 1996 budget Martin put the coup de grace to Keynesian fiscal policy by stating that deficit elimination would be permanent. The major substantive actions in this budget were the specification of the CHST and the announcement of the (eventually cancelled) Seniors Benefit. There were a few new spending initiatives in 1996. There would be assistance for those in need, particularly children, provided primarily through the tax system. To ameliorate youth unemployment $480 million was announced over three years, through spending and tax incentives; $250 million would be spent by 1998-9 on technology partnerships; $50 million in equity support was provided to the Economic Development Corporation to encourage international trade.[124] This spending, while not irrelevant, was a far cry from, for example, the extra $7.5 billion the Mulroney government announced it would drop in the 1991 budget for the 1991-2 fiscal year. In the era of fiscal politics, new spending was not proscribed, but it gained salience from lowered spending expectations. Comparison is also useful when considering election budgets.

The 1997 budget was widely seen by commentators as a budget with a view to an election because it loosened the purse strings a little bit. What the punditocracy tended to miss, however, was that even a few years earlier the levels of generosity in the 1997 budget would have been interpreted as miserly. Expectations, and fiscal virtue, had been so greatly redefined that historically low levels of government spending in the face of an election could be taken as the same old bribing of voters with their own money. Indeed, at least one senior Cabinet minister was of the view that even if the government had been in the fiscal position to introduce substantial new spending, Canadians would not have stood for it and the government would have been punished.[125] The one major post-budget Liberal spending pledge during the election campaign, made by Chrétien, was that planned cuts to the CHST would not be fully implemented. Cash transfers would not fall below $12.5 billion annually, as opposed to the projected $11 billion.[126] This was not even really new spending – it was a cut to planned cuts. Still, literally the next day, Paul Martin promised that this would be the Liberals' sole big spending promise, because, he claimed, maintaining the budgetary targets was maintaining confidence in the economy.[127] Insofar as the government had built its credibility in terms of fiscal politics, that credibility could erode if the government violated the budgeting principles for which it so strenuously had argued the virtues. Electoral possibility resided in maintaining the government's new-found fiscal position.

Simply put, the reason the Liberals allowed even some new spending in the 1997 budget was that the government was so far ahead of its fiscal targets for the 1996-7 and 1997-8 fiscal years. The deficit target for 1996-7 was $24.3 billion, or the 3 percent of GDP the Liberal Red Book had promised. Martin stated in 1997 that while the final numbers were not in, the deficit would be no higher than $19 billion in 1996-7. In fact, it came in at $8.9 billion.[128] The reasons the government was so far ahead of the targets were the conservative nature of the planning assumptions and, as Martin acknowledged, a drop in short-term interest rates of 5.5 percent in the previous two years. Canadian rates were 2.25 percent below American rates, which on average Canadian rates had exceeded by 2 percent over the previous twenty years.[129]

In this context of meeting and exceeding fiscal targets, some new spending was permitted. Martin argued that the notion of infrastructure had to be broadened. On the measures in the 1996 and 1997 budgets, tax assistance to students would increase from $900 per year to $1,200 annually. The student loan grace period was extended, and the Registered Education Savings Plan limit doubled. The minister argued that investment in research and innovation had to increase, so he endowed a Canada Foundation for Innovation with $800 million. Martin stated that 25 percent of overshooting the deficit targets, after applying the contingency reserve, would go to infrastructure in major research institutions. The other 75 percent would go to deficit reduction.[130] This promise was marginally modified during the election campaign so that 50 percent of any surplus was to be dedicated to tax cuts and debt reduction, and the other 50 percent to increasing program spending.[131] The sum of $300 million over three years was put into responses to the National Forum on Health. In much celebrated cooperation with provinces, Ottawa provided tax assistance to children in low income families. There was also some action to help Canadians with disabilities.[132]

Let us contrast these measure with those in the election budgets of the Mulroney years. In 1988 the Progressive Conservatives developed spending categories of priority initiatives and of responding to unexpected developments. These included, although not all were implemented, a multi-billion dollar National Childcare Strategy, regional development strategies in every region except southern Ontario, science and technology investments, spending on national defence to reform the armed forces on the basis of White Paper recommendations, even more support for agriculture in light of falling grain prices, and wide-ranging support for the energy industry following the 1986 oil price collapse.[133] This was a far more ambitious spending program than anything the Liberals proposed in 1997, although recall that the opposition in 1988 found these initiatives to be shockingly insufficient.

It is not clear whether the 1992 or the 1993 budget was the next real Tory election budget. In 1992, before Mulroney resigned and probably in response to the emergence of the Reform Party, substantial tax reductions were introduced. In 1993, with a Progressive Conservative leadership race underway, Don Mazankowski emphasized the measures in the 1992 budget. In discretionary terms, it is difficult to make the case that the 1993 budget was a lot more lavish than that of 1997. Structurally, however, the differences were profound. The 1993 budget projected program spending at $120 billion in 1993-4.[134] The 1997 budget projected it at $105.8 billion for 1997-8.[135] The gap was greater still when calculated as a percentage of GDP. If the political business cycle still existed in 1997, it did so at measurably lower levels of both spending and promises of largesse. Recall also that Martin did not introduce across-the-board tax relief in 1997, arguing that permanent fiscal recovery was the only road to permanent tax relief. One poll found that 58 percent of respondents thought the 1997 budget put the government on the right track. Only 25 percent thought it misplaced.[136]

The Liberals suffered a seat reduction in the 1997 election that left them with a bare majority government. They were probably punished in Atlantic Canada for what were seen as cuts to Employment Insurance that unfairly harmed the region. But in general, the Liberal problem in the election was not fiscal retrenchment. Richard Nadeau and his colleagues argue that 'the Liberals chose to focus on their major economic accomplishment, deficit reduction, and to focus voters' attention on expectations about the economic future of the country, which ... were quite positive.'[137] They conclude that this was a reasonable strategy,[138] and note that optimism for the future was related in part to deficit elimination.[139] In my view, the Liberal problem resided in allowing the campaign to get away from their strongest card, that of the restored postwar Liberal position as the party of managerial competence.[140]

At the campaign's beginning, the Liberals appeared situated to expand their majority, and particularly to make inroads in the West. Paul Martin was extremely and, given his effectiveness, justifiably popular. However, upon announcing the country would go to the polls just three and a half years into his mandate, Prime Minister Chrétien was unable to articulate a reason for the election beyond the implicit position that he thought it was to the advantage of the Liberals. Without credible ammunition on the economic and fiscal fronts, the Reform Party played its familiar politics of 'otherness' by turning the election into a battle as much about the status of Quebec as anything else. Reform did this to stave off a Liberal sweep, and managed to attain official opposition status. The Liberals had a problem insofar as the campaign was *not* about the government's fiscal record. Nadeau and colleagues argue that perceptions of a poor record on unemployment cost the Liberals 3 percentage points in the popular vote.[141] Even if the Liberals suffered due to perceptions of unemployment, in my view this was better for them than the alternative of trying to reduce unemployment. It is not clear the mass public expected policy-driven unemployment reductions. Voters no longer saw the state as possessing the capacity to reduce unemployment in the short or medium terms; nor did they see such action as desirable, especially if it weakened the fiscal position. A post-election poll in October 1997 found that 47 percent of respondents favoured using surpluses to pay down the debt, 33 percent favoured cutting taxes, and only 13 percent thought increased spending should be the top priority.[142] If these were the priorities of a polity that favoured government measures to improve unemployment, the preferred approach was structural rather than direct intervention. But in any event, as Nadeau and others also note, the Liberals became the first government in recent Canadian history to be re-elected despite an unemployment rate close to 10 percent.[143] The real story was not that unemployment cost the Liberals but that expectations were sufficiently reduced, so that if it cost the Liberals, it cost them so little. How Canadian politics had changed over the previous two decades. Canadian politics had now become fiscalized.

In Paul Martin's first budget after re-election, he announced that the books were balanced for the 1997-8 fiscal year. He projected that the budget would also be balanced for 1998-9 and 1999-2000. Financial surpluses of $12, $6, and $9 billion were projected over these three fiscal years, respectively.[144] Persistent deficits had passed from the federal scene under the stewardship of the Liberal Party, which had presided over their emergence in the first place. This, as much as anything, indicated the transformation of Canadian politics, in not just budgetary and other policy, but in the party system and the mass public. A new 'politics of the surplus' emerged. It could be made sense of only in terms of the long history that led to the development and disappearance of the federal deficit. Those who thought it heralded a new age of old-style spending were profoundly mistaken. (I will return to this issue in the concluding chapter.)

The Role of the State in the Economy

Paul Martin was by far the most powerful minister in the Chrétien Cabinet, and without question the finest Canadian finance minister of the postwar era. Martin made communications central to Finance's work.[145] He was magnificent at articulating the government's policies and goals. Martin's ability to craft budgets that resonated with the population was a great asset. Winning the battle against the deficit was very much Martin's victory. But deficit elimination and the fiscalization of politics also went beyond any individual's contribution. This victory was the crowning moment of a deeper neo-liberal triumph. It pushed the front in the perennial war between embedded liberalism and neo-liberalism as far as in the neo-liberal army's favour as Canadian terrain could accept.

The entrenchment of fiscal politics was more than a result of the evolving state role in the economy. It also became a cause of that change through its instrumentality to the 'reinvention of government.' Martin claimed reform in the structure of government spending, which he took to mean the redefinition of government itself, as the main achievement of the 1995 budget.[146] Through the mediation of fiscal politics, the vision behind Mulroney's economic renewal realized some of its remaining imperatives with respect to the state. In particular, the redesign of social programs became possible. Neil Bradford points out that the Macdonald Commission's continental free trade recommendation was accompanied by cognate proposals to reformulate social policy by integrating labour market and income security programming. This could organize the neo-liberal Mulroney government's legislative agenda for many years. 'Moreover, the commission's adjustment discourse provided a much more politically attractive rationale for social policy reform than the unvarnished deficit reduction case made by the Finance bureaucrats.'[147] The CUFTA may have been the necessary condition of neo-liberal social policy complementary to continental free trade. But the entrenchment of fiscal politics was the sufficient condition for absolute reductions in spending and for the redesign of social programs so that they would serve as 'bridges' to employment rather than as protections against unemployment. As it turned out, the 'unvarnished' deficit reduction case was the compelling rationale for social policy reform. The ideas constituting fiscal politics, selected originally for interested reasons, took on a life of their own and were the proximate cause of further outcomes.

Only by locking in on the 'reality' of having to engage in fiscal retrenchment, in a context where neo-liberal rather than social democratic policy options were more viable, could the bureaucratic and social interests against cuts be overcome. Insofar as retrenchment is more likely to be supported at the level of principle than specifics, part of the political viability of deficit elimination depended on the government's success in framing the fiscal issue as one of the general over the particular interest. This presentation 'took' because the 'general interest,' as defined, in fact spoke to particular but widely shared and highly mobilizing interests. The Liberal approach participated in political developments regarding real income erosion and economic insecurity, and promised to restore to middle-class citizens a sense of control over their economic lives and the state. Martin stated in 1995 that the government's priorities would reflect those of the 'people,' and that this would be clear in how the government defined its role.[148] Institutional incentives within the state, institutionalized interest groups outside the state, and the ways ministers, the bureaucracy, and the interest groups reinforced each other had together usually trumped fiscal retrenchment. But through an entrenched fiscal politics, the institutional constraints paled before more 'general' populist and popular demands for the retrenchment of spending.

Indeed, one way of understanding the tectonic shifts in Canadian politics in the 1990s is to see them as constituting a minor form of Lockean revolution. Locke's liberalism was in part an effort to vindicate the protection of bourgeois property from the incursions of monarchical executive power. Locke saw the dissolution of government as justified when the prince or the legislative body goes beyond the bounds of the people's consent and acts contrary to their trust:

> The reason why men enter into society, is the preservation of their property; and the end why they chuse and authorize a legislative, is, that there may be laws made, and rules set, as guards and fences to the properties of all the members of the society, to limit the power, and moderate the dominion, of every part and member of the society: for since it can never be supposed to be the will of the society, that the legislative should have a power to destroy that which every one designs to secure, by entering into society, and for which the people submitted themselves to legislators of their own making; whenever the *legislators endeavour to take away, and destroy the property of the people,* ... they put themselves into a state of war with the people, who are thereupon absolved from any farther obedience,... Whensoever therefore the *legislative* shall transgress this fundamental rule of society; and either by ambition, fear, folly or corruption, *endeavour to grasp* themselves, *or put into the hands of any other, an absolute power* over the lives, liberties, and estates of the people; by this breach of trust they *forfeit the power* the people had put into their hands for quite contrary ends, and it devolves to the people, who have a right to resume their original liberty, and, by the establishment of a new legislative, (such as they shall think fit) provide for their own safety and security, which is the end for which they are in society.[149]

Canadian populism in the 1990s was motivated in no small part, as we saw in the previous chapter, by middle-class real income decline and economic insecurity interpreted as sourced in the state's extractive privileging of 'special interests' and 'bureaucrats.' Canadians withdrew their consent to be governed as they had been. Evidence of lost trust in representatives could be found in the Reform Party's emphasis on theories of representation that aspired to make legislators more directly accountable to constituents, as well as in its support for instruments of direct democracy (such as initiatives, referendums, and recall) which would allow electors to circumvent or trump their elected representatives. Diminished trust could also be seen in the concerns with accountability expressed by the Klein government in Alberta and the Harris government in Ontario, and the proliferation of taxpayer protection and balanced budget legislation in the provinces.[150] No longer trusted with the public purse, governments sought to present themselves as constrained in their capacity to expropriate by taxation and borrowing. The federal Liberals did not employ such legislation, but Paul Martin's budget rhetoric, which located the problem with government and the solution as responding in a fashion consistent with the priorities of the people, was another manifestation of efforts to restore the legitimacy of elected representatives. What happened in Canada in the 1990s was not revolutionary in any formal sense. It all occurred through the institutions of parliamentary government. But it was no coincidence that Mike Harris in Ontario claimed to be leading a 'common sense revolution.' It was a conservative revolution in the sense that Lockean revolution is conservative; it was an attempt to reconstitute government in a fashion consistent with the prior consent and trust of citizens who considered themselves entitled. In a different terminology, this was reactionary counter-revolution against what was perceived as the excessive Keynesian revolution. It was also no coincidence that citizens were not the normative unit for the Harris Conservatives; rather, the 'taxpayers' whose property earlier governments had violated were to be restored to the democratic throne. The federal Liberals were perhaps trying to stave off this revolution as much as foment it; but they could not hold power without accommodating these property-oriented democratic aspirations.

To put these dynamics into more contemporary language, we can turn to John Porter's notion of 'creative class politics.' For Porter, writing in the mid-1960s, ideological political parties organized around class were a good thing, in part because when the major 'left' party was in power, it would legislate reforms. When the 'right' party took office, it was politically unable to roll back these changes.[151] Porter properly argued that in Canada, at the federal level, unity rather than class was the defining cleavage.[152] As such, class issues and innovation, as we saw in the preceding chapter, have typically been introduced into federal politics by a third party. In the postwar era this party was the NDP. There was certainly a leftward 'drift' from the end of the Second World War through the early 1970s. Since then, while Canadians and federal Canadian parties continue to have a relatively low subjective experience of class membership, it is clear that political creativity has reversed itself. From the mid-1980s onward innovation has come from the right. Parties on the relative right of the political spectrum make the changes, and those on the relative left do not roll them back. 'Left' parties may even take these changes further. The Mulroney Progressive Conservatives introduced a new relationship between state and economy; the Chrétien Liberals continued this work.

The Reform Party encouraged this pattern of innovation in the 1990s. As I argued in the previous chapter, even if the forms of politics were similar, the content of politics had changed.

As such, Jean Chrétien's claim that his government represented a distinctive 'Canadian way' does not pass muster. Chrétien argued that the Canadian way was distinguishable from the politics of the Reagan, Thatcher, and Mulroney regimes. He clearly sought to locate himself in the emergent tradition of so-called 'third way' 1990s politicians.[153] The third way was supposed to embody an alternative to both excessive postwar statism and excessive 1980s laissez-faire ideology. England's Labour prime minister, Tony Blair, was perhaps the politician most concerned with presenting himself as embodying a third way. But the label was also applied to Bill Clinton in the United States, Gerhard Schroeder in Germany, and Canada's Chrétien.

The 'first way' was the embedded liberalism of the postwar era, which was often accompanied by a Keynesian policy orientation. The neo-liberalism of the 1980s was the 'second way,' operated, broadly speaking, by an approach to economic policy organized around the NAIRU. As we have seen, the move from embedded liberalism to neo-liberalism entailed third-order policy change in which the objectives and orientations of policy were fundamentally altered. For the third, or Canadian, way to be analytically distinguishable from the second way, it must embody a third-order category shift in the objectives and orientations of policy. I have argued that no such shift occurred in Canada. The Liberals of the 'third way' adopted and, on the fiscal front, extended the disciplinary policies of their neo-liberal predecessors. Chrétien's claim that his first two administrations participated in a third way provided a quasi-progressive legitimation of his approach, but was not supported by the facts. The Canadian way was second-way neo-liberalism implemented by a party that once propounded the first way. This perhaps disguised the continuing dominance of neo-liberalism, but made it no less real. Not only was it embedded within the state – it appeared in the second half of the 1990s that Canadians too wanted the state, along with 'special interests,' subjected to discipline.

9
Maynard Where Art Thou?

Political scientists are, for the most part, overinvested in change.[1] Alterations in policy and politics, conspicuous precisely because of their differences from what precedes them, tend to become the focus of study. Continuity is rarely as exciting or as interesting. Careful analysis of the evolution of the state's role in the economy requires not only that change be identified but also that continuity be understood. The Canadian turn to neo-liberal fiscal restraint clearly contained important elements of change. Yet substantial continuities shaped that change. For all the movement from embedded liberalism to neo-liberalism, liberalism of one form or another remained entrenched. Similarly, the emergent 'politics of the surplus,' which rose from the death of deficits, is deeply informed by continuities with the fiscalization of politics.

Ideas, Interests, and Institutions

The capture of the state by a set of ideas is an interested process. The ideas with which we are concerned, those regarding deficit finance specifically and the role of the state in the economy generally, are found at a macro or aggregate level. As such, to grasp the selection of these ideas, the interests by which they are animated cannot be usefully disaggregated into groupings such as, for example, textile workers or the pro-life movement. The corresponding interests must also be macro in nature. I have identified two aggregate interests that over time have together driven the state toward a neo-liberal role and balanced budgets. The broad corporate interest in the restoration of profitability and the broad populist interest in the restoration of economic security were the engines that powered the train of politics. Both interests entailed visions, sometimes explicit and sometimes inchoate, of appropriate state activity. I argued in Chapter 1 that interests and ideas are inseparable because an interest is politically meaningless without a conceptualization of what that interest is and how it will best be realized. I also argued that ideas are selected in the first instance for instrumental reasons, for their utility in rationalizing interests or as tools in political battles. The operating conceptualization of the corporate interest in the late 1970s and the 1980s was that profitability had to be restored. The conceptualization of how best to realize that interest was to enhance and secure access to a continental market. The idea selected for its instrumental value in rationalizing and promoting interests so defined was a Canada-US free trade agreement, and its cognate economic reforms. The operating conceptualization of the populist interest in the 1990s was that economic security had to be restored. The conceptualization of how best to realize that interest was to reduce the extractive power of the state. The idea selected for its instrumental value in rationalizing and promoting interests so defined was deficit elimination. In each case, the theme of restoration presupposed a sense of prior entitlement, and these interests were sufficiently powerful to push the state in specific directions.

I also argued in Chapter 1 that ideas, once selected by the state for instrumental reasons, can persist and at least partially explain political and policy outcomes long after the interested conditions that supported their selection in the first place expire. Stagflation and the corporate profitability crisis undermined the Keynesian consensus, but Keynesian notions informed the very policies said to constitute the end of the Keynesian era, and were propounded by Ottawa until the Liberals left office in 1984. Even after the dominant paradigm changed, latent Keynesian ideas continued to inform Tory budgeting. Not until the mid-1990s, twenty years past the nominal end of the Keynesian era, were Keynesian ideas fully extinguished. Once ideas supporting deficit elimination became entrenched via the fiscalization of politics, those ideas became a cause of subsequent outcomes and continued to endure. In the long run we may all be dead, but it may take a very long time to kill a powerful set of ideas. Distinguishing between the selection of ideas and the persistence of ideas once selected, which is to distinguish between ideas as dependent and independent (or at least intervening) variables, allows us to better understand the political roles of ideas.

This analysis implies that at any given moment (witness wage and price controls and the National Energy Program), the state may have substantial freedom from social forces to manoeuvre, especially if ideas from an earlier era continue to matter; but it also implies that the autonomy of the state from social forces is, over time and with respect to the state's economic role, limited (this does not mean the state is weak).[2] The state, though, remains the primary locus of public deliberation and consensus. Corporate and populist interests were able to push the state in their preferred direction because political leaders and parties could build winning political coalitions around these interests. And in this sense a third interest arises: the interest of politicians and parties in political power. Winning political office is usually a precondition of political efficacy for politicians and parties. Winning depends on identifying and articulating interests into forms through which political coalitions can be built. Insofar as a long process of change regarding the role of the state in the economy is concerned, underlying economic interests drive, but are mediated by, the political interests that implement change. Any one election or any one policy can be idiosyncratic. Patterns revealed over time tell us rather a lot about the content citizens attach to their interests, the positions politicians propound publicly, and the reasons certain ideas win out over others.

And as neo-institutionalists know, changes in socioeconomic variables and political contexts can result in changes in the roles, importance, and goals of existing institutions.[3] The position of Canada's Department of Finance in the federal bureaucracy has gone up and down over the years.[4] The department has never been more powerful than under Paul Martin in the 1990s. Robert Cox, speaking about nations generally, identifies an increase in the power of the centre of governments relative to more domestically oriented labour and industry departments. He locates this pre-eminence in finance ministries and other central agencies functioning as transmission belts for the world and continental economies.[5] The fiscal constraint in Canada further strengthened Finance. Keith Banting has argued that while the battles between Finance and social policy line departments are perennial, the fiscal and economic problems since the middle 1980s have enhanced Finance's position, and made it the dominant social policy department in the government: 'Increasingly, new policies have come from Finance and have been announced in the budget by the Minister of Finance rather than by the ministers of relevant social-policy departments.'[6] The fiscalization of bureaucratic politics was a key factor in Finance's hegemony in the 1990s. Finance's authority was derivative of the forces that it enthusiastically embraced.

Reconsidering Legitimacy
In the result, politics became fiscalized. Electoral success in the 1990s presupposed that a political party would be on the side of balanced budgets, and credibly so. This turn of events poses some challenges to the conventional wisdom in political science and political economy about politics, democracy, and legitimacy.

Most writing on politics assumes that spending money entails greater popularity and more legitimacy for governments and states; or, put differently, that good 'politics' always leans in favour of more spending and therefore the fiscal and monetary irresponsibility good 'economics' condemns. These assumptions are found not just in financial markets. They can also be identified in a number of seemingly disparate, but nonetheless related, theoretical concepts. For example, Neo-Marxists distinguish between two functions of the state: accumulation and legitimation. Accumulation functions are those activities the state undertakes to assist the capitalist process. Legitimation functions are the welfare measures the state introduces to make accumulation acceptable to the mass public.[7] In a related vein, students of international political economy associate legitimacy with the exercise of domestic policy autonomy, and locate challenges to that legitimacy in dislocations caused by transnational economic flows.[8] Another version of these assumptions is found in the idea of the political business cycle, which has been both discussed and challenged in this book. The notion is that to retain office governments will take steps to increase economic activity generally, and at least some people's incomes specifically, as elections approach. Similarly, public choice theorists argue that politicians have greater incentives to run deficits than surpluses.[9] Democratic theorists ask if retrenchment can occur in a manner consistent with democratic principles, a question that presupposes that expansion is consistent with such precepts.[10] And writers on federalism suggest that federalism is better suited to a context of increasing rather than declining fiscal resources.[11] Perhaps these presuppositions are summed up in the argument made by David Stockman, Ronald Reagan's budget advisor, who claimed that Reagan's failure to institute fiscal control was 'the triumph of politics.'[12]

These concepts, and the cognate assumptions, are not simply wrong. But they overstate both the intrinsic political value of social spending and the dichotomy between the accumulation function and legitimacy. The Canadian record demonstrates that legitimacy is not simply coextensive with the ongoing extension of welfare measures or the state. On the contrary, and building on the Lockean remarks I made in the conclusion to the previous chapter, legitimacy may require circumscribing the state's role and disciplining its expenditures. There is not always an opposition between 'hard choices' and 'democracy.'[13] That politics do not necessarily support ever-growing spending and welfare measures is particularly so when politics become fiscalized. Paul Pierson argues that 'welfare state expansion involved the enactment of *popular* policies in a relatively undeveloped interest-group environment. By contrast, welfare state retrenchment generally requires elected officials to pursue *unpopular* policies that must withstand the scrutiny of both voters and well-entrenched networks of interest groups.'[14] Framed in terms of fiscal probity, welfare state retrenchment in Canada in the 1990s was not unpopular.[15] It was conceptualized as restoring control of the state to 'average' citizens, and as wresting control of the state away from the entrenched interests Pierson properly identifies. Retrenchment was also accepted because it was viewed as necessary to attaining the deficit elimination that was presented as prior to every other goal. Balancing the budget and retrenching the welfare state *enhanced* the Canadian state's legitimacy. By eliminating the deficit Ottawa established that it could run itself 'responsibly' and continue to be an important actor. Retrenching the welfare state and eliminating the deficits seen to support it retrieved a sense of federal accountability to citizens. Of course, if the Liberals had cut too much, their popularity, and Ottawa's legitimacy, would have suffered. But the popularity of the federal Liberals, and the renewed legitimacy of the federal government, resided in these measures; it was not in spite of them.

In addition to these evidentiary challenges to the conventional wisdom regarding state legitimacy, there are analytical reasons that limit the typical view's utility. A commitment to Anglo-American liberalism places limits on the extent to which the state can legitimately intervene on behalf of economy or society. In addition, states cannot maintain their legitimacy unless they appear to perform the accumulation function well. The opposition between the accumulation and legitimation functions is too stark. Neo-Marxists argue that capitalist accumulation requires legitimation measures;[16] but the reverse is true as well. There cannot be liberal-democratic capitalist legitimacy without accumulation.[17] The Canadian case demonstrates that legitimacy presupposes an image of the state as effectively facilitating accumulation. There can be ebbs and flows in the balance between the kinds of measures seen to support the two functions, but they remain enmeshed. Arguments that, for example, capital mobility can disrupt long-standing patterns of life, and that few states directly address its unintended social consequences, are true. More contentious is the concomitant view that at the core of the 'problem of legitimacy' is resentment among those not benefited in the short term.[18] These effects can generate legitimacy issues. But restricting capital mobility can also undermine legitimacy. If a state's economic intervention is deemed excessive, either because it goes beyond the bounds of political consensus, or because it is viewed as undermining the economy it is designed to help, then the state's legitimacy can become suspect. This is the problem that vexed the Trudeau governments and provided the political conditions for Mulroney. As Keynes knew, the measure of capitalism's success or failure is the level of affluence it provides, so it had better be good at wealth creation.[19]

On the cusp of major retrenchment in the 1990s, Canadian political scientists had a very difficult time imagining a way through the fiscal impasse that would satisfy both fiscal imperatives and democratic concerns. Located in this challenge to conventional views of legitimacy, the Canadian turn to fiscal restraint allows political scientists to better comprehend the political viability of deficit elimination in Canada in the 1990s.

Ideology and the Role of the State in the Economy

Liberalism

The reception of Keynesianism in Canada, as Robert Campbell has well argued, cannot be understood outside of how Keynesianism rescued and even strengthened Canada's liberal democratic and capitalist traditions. I have argued, following John Ruggie, that Canada's postwar liberalism is best described as 'embedded liberalism.' The turn to neo-liberalism, in its own way, also rescued and strengthened Canadian capitalism and liberal democracy. Neo-liberal policy was a way to restore corporate profits. It disciplined the state so that, consistent with the basic tenets of Anglo-American liberalism, the state would not skew or interfere so much with 'private' affairs. And neo-liberalism had a democratizing element insofar as it was seen as a way of retrieving a captured state from the privileged interests that some perceived as controlling government.[20]

Whether taking a 'neo' or 'embedded' form, the underlying ideological continuity regarding the role of the state in Canada is hegemonic liberalism. When under threat, liberalism has reconstituted itself and maintained its place. The first preference of Canadians and their governments has almost always been a liberal-democratic state and a capitalist economy. Liberalism writ large is clearly consistent with different approaches to the state role in the economy. The differences between Keynesianism and the NAIRU, which have instantiated alternative forms of liberalism, make this clear. As such, there is a way in which the changes in Canada that so concern political scientists and political economists amount merely to a local debate. The only ideological formation that has won out is liberalism. During the Great Depression, and in the 1970s, liberalism came under substantial threat and ideological alternatives were able to obtain some relevant political expression. But in each case liberalism carried the day. In the absence of a truly profound crisis, perhaps on the environmental front, we should not expect liberalism to lose its hegemonic status in Canada. The power relations that support the ideology, and the extent to which liberal precepts are inculcated and held, make change away from an underlying liberalism highly improbable.

Neo-Liberalism

That said, the merely local debate between embedded liberalism and neo-liberalism is significant. Actors would not have fought so hard on one side or the other if they thought the battle unimportant. To specify change on the ideological front regarding the economic role of the state, we must look at the extent to which the basic premises of one form of liberalism have trumped those of the other. Substantial change in favour of neo-liberalism has occurred on the policy front. Locking Canada into trade pacts, particularly the Canada-US Free Trade Agreement, the North American Free Trade Agreement, and the World Trade Organization, proscribes the use of some policy instruments and imposes political constraints on the use of instruments that remain permissible. The price stability policy and continued adherence to an inflation target of 2 percent ensure that wage demands do not get too ambitious. Program spending in the late 1990s was at its lowest levels since the early postwar era when the Keynesian welfare state was only beginning to be constructed, and the government committed in 2000 to continuing to reduce program spending relative to the economy over the next five years (although it seems this commitment has been forgotten).[21] The pledge not to return to deficits prevents the state from expanding its spending beyond what its revenues allow. The balanced budget promise, in combination with commitments to substantial tax reductions over the next several years, further circumscribes Ottawa's expenditure budget. With the exception of expenditure restraint at much higher spending levels relative to the size of the economy, and a somewhat different approach to tax reductions, none of these policies were in place in the 1970s.

Change can also be identified in political discourse. Indeed, the old dogs that no longer bark, and the new ones that do, are as definitive of the alterations over the last quarter-century as anything else. Even with rapidly rising energy prices in 2000 and 2001, there was no serious talk of a new National Energy Program. If anything, its antithesis, a continental energy pact, seems more likely. On the other hand, Alberta instituted a flat tax in 2001, and a flat tax proposal for the federal government was supposed to be a centrepiece of the Canadian Alliance's electoral platform in 2000 (Stockwell Day rescinded the pledge). That some policies are now in principle off the table, and others have become respectable after much time on the fringes, indicates substantial political change.

Not only is neo-liberalism dominant, it is also stable. Successive Progressive Conservative and Liberal federal governments have embraced the new parameters. Officials in the federal bureaucracy appear to concur; Keynesian-minded bureaucrats have long been replaced, especially in Finance, by mandarins of neo-liberal inclination.[22] It was Canadian negotiators who proposed evolving the General Agreement on Tariffs and Trade into the more robust World Trade Organization.[23] There is evidence that between 1993 and 1997 the Canadian public moved ideologically in the same direction as the rhetoric and policies of political parties.[24] And Canadians vote en masse for parties that promise to continue along this path.

The Meaning of Neo-Liberalism

As William Watson points out, those on the 'left' regretfully see themselves as enduring a neo-conservative age (Watson uses the word 'conservative' because he is also concerned with the moral dimensions of social policy). Those on the 'right' wish that it were so.[25] In light of the previous analysis, my view is that the left is correct that this is a neo-liberal era. Wistful claims that neo-liberalism in Canada never took hold make sense only from the point of view of a very high standard for what counts as neo-liberalism, and a very ambitious attitude regarding the kind of change that is reasonably possible. Watson argues that a neo-conservative (or neo-liberal) revolution 'should have brought about a reduction in rent-seeking, yet there is little evidence of that. Lobbying continues apace; indeed, it gives every appearance of still being a growth industry. If globalization has stripped national governments of much of their power, as is so often claimed, no one seems to have told national politicians, who keep legislating frenetically. Trade agreements have caused tariff revenues to decline as a share of GDP, but companies show little disinclination to ask for special favours.'[26] This characterization is founded on a utopian wish for change. First, it entails a hope that interested behaviour will disappear. This is the ironically shared desire of utopian socialists and neo-liberals both. Utopian socialists want interested behaviour to vanish so that a collective good can be pursued. Neo-liberals seek an end to interested behaviour that might capture the state so that 'neutral' market outcomes can maximize individual and aggregate welfare. But vanquishing interested behaviour is a fantasy, especially for the neo-liberal, because the economic model of liberalism assumes rational self-interested actors. Neo-liberals have no problem with self-interest; but neo-liberals want people to be situational altruists by not trying to use the state to their advantage. Self-interest, however, does not confine itself so easily. Neo-liberals know, on some level, that self-interest cannot be extinguished. As such, the state can always be captured by the interested. Neo-liberalism's alternative strategy is not to have the state wither, but instead to turn the state to its advantage. The neo-liberal state was never meant to be irrelevant; it is strong but limited. A strong state is a precondition for bringing about the kinds of changes that Brian Mulroney introduced. Society and state cannot be disciplined if the state is not strong enough to do the disciplining. For a neo-liberal, or a neo-conservative, to decry rent seeking on the one hand and strong national governments on the other, is to try to have one's cake and eat it too.

Indeed, the aspiration at the heart of neo-liberalism that rent seeking cease and powerful national governments vanish is really an aspiration that politics die in the name of neutrality and an expanded private sphere. If neo-liberalism has failed, it is only because this underlying aspiration is in principle and practice unrealizable. With Aristotle, (hu)man is a political animal.[27] Neo-liberalism could never attain this objective because the extinction of politics is the extinction of the human condition. As we have seen, politics did not disappear in Canada under the weight of the fiscal issue; rather, politics became fiscalized. But if neo-liberalism is understood to be a more reasonable agenda, an agenda in which a strong state functions to discipline state and society in the name of restoring and strengthening liberal-democratic and capitalist traditions, then its success in the 1990s seems clear. The real question is how the strong state exercises its power. In the 1990s, this power was exercised to discipline demands in society and the state for protection, expenditures, and inflationary wage increases.

The flipside of this analysis is that the left's despair regarding the neoliberal hour, when compared with the postwar era, is a bit romantic. Because the postwar era was not a socialist utopia, but rather a different kind of liberalism, there are limits to how much 'better' it could have been. Writing in 1977 with respect to the Depression of the 1930s, Plumptre argued that 'the impact of unemployment on those thrown out of work was far more severe than it is today. There were no national or provincial arrangements for unemployment insurance, no family allowances and no Medicare; old age pensions, recently introduced, were subject to a strict means test.'[28] This basic claim remained true even in the mid-1990s when urban homelessness remained a national disgrace.[29] But however tattered, the welfare state in the 1990s was much more robust than the assistance available before the Second World War. Family allowances were gone, but children's tax benefits were developed. Universal health care, probably Canada's most progressive social program and a product of the 1950s and 1960s, remains in place. It was and is under considerable stress – efforts to rethink the system are under way – but it also was and is, in principle, widely supported by politicians and the mass public. Canadian neoliberalism exists in the context of a past that has not been fully eradicated. It is built on the embedded liberalism that in part created the conditions that made neo-liberalism viable.

I have repeatedly argued that embedded liberalism and neo-liberalism are ideal types, and that in modern liberal Canada elements of both can always be identified. That the other is always present always moderates the hegemonic form of liberalism. But one type of liberalism usually has the upper hand. In short, these issues about the dominant ideology reduce to the following question: Was Canadian neo-liberalism a change in kind or a change in degree? It depends on whether we analyze the question in terms of the noun or the adjective. Insofar as neo-liberalism was a matter of continuing liberalism in the context of a mature state, it was a change in degree. Insofar as it was a matter of disembedding liberalism and reorienting the state to be strong and disciplinary, but limited, neo-liberalism was a change in kind.

The Strength of the Neo-Liberal State

As the neo-liberal state is limited but strong, it is too simple to conclude that Canada's federal government is weakened by its neo-liberal turn. To divest itself of authority the Canadian state had to take strong action. And retrenchment entailed fights that Ottawa willingly joined. The federal government's post-1995 strength comes from three sources. These sources support federal autonomy from provincial governments and from social demands. Ironically, two of these wellsprings of strength originate in claims of weakness. First, Ottawa claims, with some justification, that its weakness relative to other states, particularly the United States federal government and the European Union, limits its capacity to intervene on behalf of some domestic interests.[30] This presentation has proved its worth in the federal government's remarkable resistance to angry and forceful claims for assistance by western farmers and provincial premiers in the face of the agricultural subsidies war between the United States and the EU. Second, Ottawa claims, with less justification, that it has lost monetary and fiscal sovereignty to global currency flows, which restricts its ability to spend or to inflate the economy. And there has been some loss of this sort of sovereignty. Nonetheless, Canada still has a lot of discretion on the fiscal and monetary fronts, among others, if it keeps within the pretty general 'rules' of the continental and global economies.[31] But the argument that sovereignty is lost has been very effective in insulating the state from social pressures. Peter Drucker writes that 'paradoxically, losing its fiscal and monetary sovereignty may make the nation-state stronger rather than weaker.'[32] Finally, the construction of a citizenry that will always seek particular favours from the state, but that distrusts political parties seen as pandering to special interests or as spending beyond their means, generates some autonomy from social demands for the state. In disaggregated form, discrete elements in society may seek rents; but aggregated and on election day, in normal circumstances Canadians will not vote for parties that are perceived as captured by interests or as irresponsible, especially on the expenditure side, with the public purse. Drucker also argues that governments will never practise self-discipline, and that only the sovereignty of global money can create fiscal responsibility.[33] I disagree. Governments will practise self-discipline if they calculate it is in their interests. Maintaining the value of the currency is one such interest. But a corporate sector and population that, for whatever reason, define good government as government built around balanced budgets, will also create powerful incentives for governments to keep themselves in check.

Neo-Liberalism, Fiscal Politics, and the Politics of the Surplus

Debt, Deficits, Taxation, and Spending

With the elimination of Ottawa's deficit in 1998, balanced budgets were planned for the next three years. But due to prudent planning and the contingency reserve, substantial surpluses were anticipated. And indeed they arrived. The fiscal question changed from 'how and when do we eliminate the deficit?' to 'how do we distribute the surplus?' Commentators generally assumed that without the deficit constraint, pressures for new spending would be overwhelming. Some also thought that the fiscal dividend would put the neo-liberal consensus under stress.[34] But the politics of the surplus comes out of, and is deeply informed by, the fiscalization of politics. Those who think, or fear, that the sluice gates will be opened ignore the history on which contemporary surpluses are built. The surpluses immediately following the Second World War were described in Keynesian terms and dealt with in a fashion consistent with unwinding the war economy. The surpluses at the turn of the twenty-first century are not vindicated in Keynesian terms, and will be distributed in a fashion consistent with the distrust of the state and the restoration of real incomes and real income growth that animated deficit elimination in the first place. We must remember a metaphor I introduced in Chapter 1, about entrenched ideas as rings on a tree, receding over time but still shaping the exterior that is the visible and immediate content of politics. Fiscal politics will slowly recede as surplus politics become the subject of explicit debate. But just as the inner rings of a tree give form to the visible exterior, fiscal politics inform debates about the distribution of the surplus.

First, deficit avoidance in Ottawa shows remarkable resilience. Both before, and indeed after, the 11 September 2001 terrorist attacks on the World Trade Centre and the Pentagon, there was no danger of deficits emerging in Ottawa in 2000-1 or 2001-2 in spite of the slowdown in the United States and weakened growth in Canada. Prudent planning assumptions and the contingency reserve continue to protect Ottawa against falling back into deficit even in light of an 'average' slowdown or recession.[35] Of course, the risk of deficits arising in a deep recession remains. But that risk can at best be minimized, not completely avoided. Tom Courchene posits that Paul Martin (before he was fired) could probably get away with running a post 9/11 deficit, but not with planning such a deficit.[36] With real income growth and increasing economic security, fiscal politics in Canada may have receded enough that one or two deficits could be politically sustainable. Provincial budgeting will provide a partial test of this hypothesis. Provinces have primary responsibility for health and education, for which spending demands are ever-growing; provincial post-retrenchment fiscal positions are not as secure as Ottawa's. With the slow-down, deficits appeared in some provinces in 2001-2, but it is premature to conclude that provincial deficits are respectable. Governments usually present these deficits as aberrations and the shortfalls are not typically justified by their stimulative effects. It is highly likely that opposition parties will campaign against these deficits on the grounds they demonstrate fiscal mismanagement. But it is also plausible that intermittent deficits are again not political poison in Canada.

That said, in Ottawa the issue is framed as one of distributing the surplus or the fiscal dividend. This presupposes that federal deficits are, at least in principle, out of the question; only the surplus is to be distributed. The Liberals have repeatedly committed to at least balancing the budget.[37] The surplus can be distributed through three avenues: debt reduction, tax reduction, and new program spending. Indicative of the hold the fiscal constraint continues to exert on Ottawa, the federal government has displayed pretty substantial early determination to reduce the debt, both in absolute terms and relative to the size of the economy. It was not entirely clear on the elimination of the deficit to what extent Ottawa would work to pay down the debt. First, Canada's appropriate debt-to-GDP ratio is not obvious.[38] Second, the depth of the government's political commitment to debt paydown was not evident. With net public debt reduction of $3.5 billion in the 1997-8 fiscal year, $2.9 billion in 1998-9, $12.3 billion in 1999-2000, and $17.1 billion in 2000-1, Ottawa's front-end dedication to debt reduction is clearly substantial.[39] New spending items and tax reductions are expected to eat into the surplus and limit the funds available for debt reduction in future years, but the continuing practices of the contingency reserve and prudent assumptions mean that budgets are structurally predisposed to deliver surpluses that automatically reduce the debt. The fiscalization of politics in Ottawa has extended to the debt as well as to deficits.

With respect to taxation, the Liberals offered $58 billion in tax relief in the 2000 budget. A substantial package of personal and corporate tax reduction was then promised immediately in advance of the 2000 election campaign. The government estimated these initiatives' combined worth at $100 billion over five years.[40] The political business cycle shows some sign of returning, but the biggest initiatives have been on the tax reduction rather than the spending increase front. Although offset to some degree by rising Canada Pension Plan premiums, tax reductions at least appear to help restore real income growth. These tax reductions are of sufficient scope that they impose limits on the funds available for new spending initiatives. They also probably mean that at least some government programs 'will remain in a more-or-less permanent state of financial crisis, even as the economy around us becomes ever-wealthier.'[41]

Beyond increasing health care funding, as the 2001 Throne Speech[42] and the February 2002 'Innovation Strategy'[43] suggest, if Ottawa is really interested in spending its money, it will probably be spent on developing an 'innovation economy' where indigenous research and development is quickly commercialized, and a flexible skilled labour force is encouraged. The federal government has already provided some pretty substantial tax assistance to students, but also seems, under the rubric of 'skills,' interested in getting back into the labour market training it had partially abandoned to provinces during the cuts of the 1990s. The Throne Speech also stated that children and families will continue to receive support. It continued the trend of anchoring education, health care, and training in their relevance to the provision of a flexible, skilled, and productive work force.[44] Social programs were once presented as sound economics because they helped stabilize demand; proactive social policy is also acquiring an economic anchor, that of supplying needed skills. Ottawa is again not conceptualizing a state without a role in the economy. But the efforts Ottawa claims it will make are not particularly invasive to the private sector. Rather, they are the efforts of a national government that, consistent with the Mulroney conceptualization put forward in 1984, will work to facilitate rather than supplant market functions.

I would describe the politics of the surplus in 2001, and I anticipate for the next several years, as balanced budget neo-liberalism under conditions of fiscal easing. Fiscal imperatives have proved to be the only force capable of leveraging retrenchment. The fiscal constraint no longer justifies retrenchment, so some expansion should be expected. Political attacks against spending increases are much weakened if budgets remain balanced. Expansion, though, will be under the rules imposed by the NAFTA, the WTO, price stability, and balanced budgets. Politics at the federal level all occurs within the parameters set by these policy choices.

The Future of the State and the State of the Future
I anticipate that just as the Keynesian 'consensus' weakened over time because it was insufficient for dealing with the complex problems that faced the country, so too will the neo-liberal formulation wear thin over the course of a couple of decades. Problems to which it cannot adequately speak, foreseeable and unforeseeable, will likely emerge. Both political and economic forces could present new challenges. On the economic front, anticipated labour shortages in professions and skilled trades will very probably substantially increase the leverage of at least some labour groups in wage negotiations with both government and private sector employers.

Greater bargaining power will weaken the disciplinary capacity of the neo-liberal state and impose significant fiscal demands. Provinces will probably bear a relatively greater burden in hiring doctors and nurses, among others, but all employers can expect this challenge. The increase in economic security and real incomes which will result from the power to strike more favourable wage bargains could also make social programs seem more affordable and therefore more politically supportable. On the other hand, the fiscal challenges in program delivery in the context of reduced tax rates could also result in an increasing privatization of functions, particularly in health care. Another potential economic challenge resides in linked concerns regarding energy and the environment. These could lead to major changes in economic structure in the twenty-first century. The impact of such changes on neo-liberal arrangements is not at all obvious.

On the political front, until Parliament and the party system provide some sort of imaginable alternative government to the Liberals, it will be difficult to hold the 'government party' to account. To the extent this leaves the Liberals relatively more autonomous from political or social forces, neo-liberalism's continued hold is relatively more a matter of contingency than structure, although if the Liberals go too far to the left, this would probably galvanize both voters and opposition parties. The corporate scandals identified with Enron, WorldCom, and the like could do to trust in the private sector what Watergate and Vietnam did to trust in the public sector. In addition, the issue of governance as states become increasingly internationalized will be another challenge in the twenty-first century. As the European Union moves to more extensive integration, so might Canada with the United States and Mexico. The relationships between integration and neo-liberalism are highly ambivalent, and their reciprocal impact could either strengthen or weaken the neo-liberal consensus.

Finally, as the events of 11 September 2001 demonstrate, there is always the possibility of everything being thrown off by a crisis. The attacks on the United States brought new factors into play, the implications of which are not obviously hospitable to neo-liberalism. First, and most obviously, states are the primary actors who respond to terrorist threats. Neo-liberal states often have strong militaries, but ongoing military action and both economic and political liberalism are typically in some tension. Second, issues that had been framed in terms of economic liberalism, including trade, finance, to some extent immigration, and even relations between states, will to some degree be increasingly reconceptualized in terms of security and military power. Neo-liberalism is supposed to discipline states; after foreign attack on its own soil, the American state will impose some discipline on economic flows and other states to enhance American security. Security also costs money. Third, I have argued in this book that globalization is very much Americanization. Any reformulation of globalization will be driven by the United States, and economic globalization may take a backseat to globalized security. George W. Bush's protectionism and unilateralism are also distinctly less hospitable to other countries than was Bill Clinton's globalization, and may generate backlashes. It is unlikely that 11 September in itself will undermine the neo-liberal consensus in Canada. History does demonstrate, though, that 'crises' can overturn orderings that had previously seemed secure.

But ideas, once entrenched, hold on for rather a long time after the conditions that supported their selection has expired. Such was the case with the Keynesian paradigm and embedded liberal ideology. So too with neoliberalism and the accompanying economics. Absent crisis, and perhaps a crisis bigger than the challenges introduced by 11 September, those who hope for the demise of the neo-liberal era will have to wait for at least a generation.

Maynard Where Art Thou?

The federal government completely ceased propounding Keynesian ideas regarding fiscal policy in late 1994, but this rhetoric did not fully reflect the status of Keynesian ideas in either theory or practice. Within the economics profession, 'new Keynesian economics' was part of the mainstream in the 1990s.[45] In addition, Keynes's biographer, Robert Skidelsky, has argued that 'most macroeconomic models are still based on the Keynesian aggregates and their interrelationships; but governments no longer seek to control these aggregates – prices, output, saving, investment – so directly or so persistently as in the heyday of Keynesian 'fine-tuning.' Monetary policy has supplanted fiscal policy as a short-term stabilizer. Budgets are to be balanced 'over the cycle,' with discretionary deficits for use only in emergencies.'[46] Where does this leave Keynes on his Canadian journey? Better, perhaps, than we might expect. With respect to monetary policy, the Bank of Canada is showing distinctly countercyclical tendencies. On the fiscal policy front, the 1990s were not kind to Keynes. But on the margins, Keynesian notions were seeping their way back into Ottawa's discourse by the year 2000. It is possible to see at least the beginnings of a movement toward the relegitimation of countercyclical stabilization.

Following the lead of Alan Greenspan and the United States Federal Reserve, the Bank of Canada is pursuing a monetary policy that displays substantial sensitivity to immediate economic conditions. During the so-called Asian flu, while the bank did intervene to support the Canadian dollar, the loonie was ultimately allowed to fall to record low levels. This clearly cushioned Canada from the effects of falling commodity prices and worldwide slowdown. With the US economy's weakness in late 2000 and through 2001, and a concomitant (although not as deep) slowdown in

Canada, the Bank of Canada reduced interest rates substantially in consideration of short-term economic performance. This could not be pure Keynesian monetary policy. It was and is still confined by the inflation target of 2 percent, within a band of 1 to 3 percent. As such, monetary discretion remains fettered. But within this constraint, the conduct of Canadian monetary policy looks very much like Keynesian countercyclical monetary policy. The Bank of Canada actually reduced interest rates in the summer of 2001, in spite of the news that the annualized inflation rate was almost 4 percent, which was outside the target band. This was permitted on the grounds that high energy prices were distorting the Consumer Price Index. Energy prices were expected to fall. It is hard to imagine such a thing happening on John Crow's watch. The bank has learned, perhaps, from both its own errors and the successes of the demi-god Greenspan. Canada's improved fiscal position also gives the bank more flexibility.

In fiscal terms, just as the inflation target limits monetary policy discretion, the commitment not to return to deficits constrains fiscal discretion. Still, federal officials and politicians are beginning to utter statements that ring of the Keynesian idea that the government's fiscal position can either stimulate or restrain the economy. When asked in 1999 if the federal government still has a role in economic stabilization, then Deputy Minister of Finance Scott Clark argued that automatic stabilizers are still in place (although I would add that due to program changes such as the elimination of the Canada Assistance Plan and the weakening of Employment Insurance, they are substantially less robust than in the past), that in a very deep recession there may be a role for discretionary fiscal policy, and that relative stimulation can occur even when there is no deficit if the government takes measures that reduce the surplus.[47] William Watson has made this last point as well, noting that the political consensus against deficits does not prevent active Keynesian fiscal policy 'from moving back and forth between bigger and lower surpluses.'[48]

More important, the Liberals' major tax reductions started to take effect in January 2001. Coincidentally, the economy started to slow. Paul Martin refused, as a matter of sound policy and principle, to allow the federal budget to fall back into a deficit.[49] Martin also stated that the cuts were not introduced as a stimulative measure. However, he repeatedly argued, the tax reductions were fortuitously very well timed because they stimulated the economy just when it was necessary.[50] Such rhetoric was explicitly after-the-fact rationalization. But these statements were the first pro-stabilization comments Martin had publicly uttered since before the Purple and Grey Books were released in 1994. He was using Keynesian notions to stave off demands that the government do more to fight the slowdown. Martin's interest in retrieving these ideas was clearly political. Ideas, as I have argued throughout this book, usually see the light of public day when they serve some instrumental purpose. Keynesian stabilization notions were extinguished by the Canadian government as part of its political strategy for deficit elimination. This did not mean the ideas were simply wrong. If circumstances emerge in which these ideas once again serve political ends, we can imagine the beginnings of a process by which Keynes might be gradually disinterred from his Canadian coffin.

Appendix: Fiscal Tables

Table A.1

Fiscal transactions

Year	Budgetary revenues ($mil)	Program spending ($mil)	Operating surplus or deficit (-) ($mil)	Public debt charges ($mil)	Budgetary surplus or deficit (-) ($mil)	Net public debt ($mil)	Non-budgetary transactions ($mil)	Financial requirements (-)/source (excluding foreign exchange) ($mil)
1946-7	3,034	2,135	899	469	430	12,592	-896	-466
1947-8	2,884	1,713	1,171	457	714	11,878		
1948-9	2,790	1,644	1,146	463	683	11,195		
1949-50	2,600	1,997	603	437	166	11,029		
1950-1	3,153	2,452	701	423	278	10,751		
1951-2	4,101	3,252	849	512	337	10,414	83	420
1952-3	4,628	4,563	65	442	-377	10,790		
1953-4	4,737	4,666	71	470	-399	11,189		
1954-5	4,440	4,555	-115	476	-591	11,780		
1955-6	4,748	4,299	449	489	-40	11,819		
1956-7	5,582	4,757	825	508	317	11,502	138	455
1957-8	5,456	5,114	342	543	-201	11,703	-145	-346

Year								
1958-9	5,159	5,399	-240	636	-876	12,580	-602	-1,478
1959-60	5,896	5,788	109	776	-668	13,247	184	-484
1960-1	6,322	6,118	204	788	-584	13,831	260	-324
1961-2	6,468	6,630	-162	832	-994	14,825	141	-853
1962-3	6,662	6,595	67	915	-848	15,673	-91	-939
1963-4	7,099	7,304	-205	993	-1,198	16,871	939	-259
1964-5	8,220	7,542	678	1,050	-372	17,243	456	84
1965-6	9,063	7,933	1,131	1,110	21	17,223	77	98
1966-7	9,860	9,164	696	1,182	-486	17,708	-176	-662
1967-8	10,745	19,501	244	1,286	-1,042	18,750	-340	-1,382
1968-9	12,047	11,250	798	1,464	-666	19,417	-151	-817
1969-70	14,399	12,566	1,833	1,694	139	19,277	91	230
1970-1	14,982	14,111	871	1,887	-1,016	20,293	-17	-1,033
1971-2	16,619	16,295	324	2,110	-1,786	22,079	413	-1,373
1972-3	19,205	18,807	399	2,300	-1,901	23,980	586	-1,315
1973-4	22,430	22,076	354	2,565	-2,211	26,191	686	-1,525
1974-5	29,251	28,238	1,013	3,238	-2,225	28,416	77	-2,148
1975-6	31,657	33,892	-2,235	3,970	-6,205	34,620	1,421	-4,784
1976-7	34,408	36,596	-2,188	4,708	-6,896	41,517	1,338	-5,558
1977-8	34,626	39,974	-5,348	5,531	-10,879	52,396	2,418	-8,461
1978-9	36,974	42,980	-6,005	7,024	-13,029	65,425	1,805	-11,224
1979-80	42,029	45,502	-3,473	8,494	-11,967	77,392	1,818	-10,149
1980-1	48,867	52,765	-3,898	10,658	-14,556	91,948	4,6339	-9,917
1981-2	60,307	60,867	-560	15,114	-15,674	107,622	6,410	-9,264
1982-3	60,662	72,808	-12,146	16,903	-29,049	136,671	5,230	-23,819
1983-4	64,168	78,968	-14,800	18,077	-32,877	169,549	7,658	-25,219
1984-5	71,056	87,100	-16,044	22,393	-38,437	207,986	8,613	-29,824

▲

▼ *Table A.1 continued*

Fiscal transactions

Year	Budgetary revenues ($mil)	Program spending ($mil)	Operating surplus or deficit (-) ($mil)	Public debt charges ($mil)	Budgetary surplus or deficit (-) ($mil)	Net public debt ($mil)	Non-budgetary transactions ($mil)	Financial requirements (-)/source (excluding foreign exchange) ($mil)
1985-6	76,933	86,106	-9,173	25,422	-34,595	242,581	4,085	-30,510
1986-7	85,931	90,005	-4,074	26,668	-30,742	273,323	7,824	-22,918
1987-8	97,612	96,453	1,159	28,953	-27,794	301,117	8,945	-18,849
1988-9	104,067	99,688	4,379	33,152	-28,773	329,890	6,349	-22,42
1989-90	113,707	103,848	9,859	38,789	-28,930	358,820	8,400	-20,530
1990-1	119,353	108,765	10,588	42,588	-32,000	390,820	7,462	-24,538
1991-2	122,032	115,215	6,817	41,174	-34,357	425,177	2,557	-31,800
1992-3	120,380	122,576	-2,196	38,825	-41,021	466,198	6,524	-34,497
1993-4	115,984	120,014	-4,030	37,982	-42,012	508,210	12,162	-29,850
1994-5	123,323	118,739	4,584	42,046	-37,462	545,672	11,620	-25,842
1995-6	130,301	112,013	18,288	46,905	-28,617	574,289	11,434	-17,183
1996-7	140,896	104,820	36,076	44,973	-8,897	583,186	10,162	1,265
1997-8	153,162	108,753	44,409	40,931	3,478	579,708	9,251	12,729
1998-9	155,671	111,393	44,278	41,394	2,884	576,824	8,607	11,491
1999-00	165,708	111,763	53,945	41,647	12,298	564,526	2,268	14,566
2000-1	178,590	119,348	59,242	42,094	17,148	547,378	1,843	18,991

Note: These numbers will not always be identical to numbers cited in text. The numbers in the text are typically taken from documents produced around the time in question, and were not necessarily calculated on the same accounting basis as the figures in this table. Figures in this tables are all calculated on the basis the federal government used to measure its fiscal position before the changes announced in the 2003 budget.

Source: Fiscal Reference Tables — September 2001, Department of Finance, Canada, 2001. Reproduced with the permission of the Minister of Public Works and Government Services, 2002.

Table A.2

Fiscal transactions

Year	Budgetary revenues (% GDP)	Program spending (% GDP)	Operating surplus or deficit (-) (% GDP)	Public debt charges (% GDP)	Budgetary surplus or deficit (-) (% GDP)	Net public debt (% GDP)	Non-budgetary transactions (% GDP)	Financial requirements (-)/source (excluding foreign exchange) (% GDP)
1946-7	24.9	17.5	7.4	3.9	3.5	103.5	-7.4	-3.8
1947-8	20.7	12.3	8.4	3.3	5.1	85.2		
1948-9	17.5	10.3	7.2	2.9	4.3	70.1		
1949-50	15.0	11.5	3.5	2.5	1.0	63.6		
1950-1	16.5	12.8	3.7	2.2	1.5	56.2		
1951-2	18.4	14.6	3.8	2.3	1.5	46.7	0.4	1.9
1952-3	18.4	18.1	0.3	1.8	-1.5	42.9		
1953-4	17.9	17.7	0.3	1.8	-1.5	42.4		
1954-5	16.7	17.2	-0.4	1.8	-2.2	44.4		
1955-6	16.2	14.7	1.5	1.7	-0.1	40.4		
1956-7	17.0	14.5	2.5	1.5	1.0	35.0	0.4	1.4
1957-8	15.8	14.8	1.0	1.6	-0.6	34.0	-0.4	-1.0
1958-9	14.5	15.1	-0.7	1.8	-2.5	35.2	-1.7	-4.1
1959-60	15.6	15.3	0.3	2.0	-1.8	35.0	0.5	-1.3
1960-1	16.0	15.5	0.5	2.0	-1.5	35.1	0.7	-0.8
1961-2	15.7	16.1	-0.4	2.0	-2.4	35.9	0.3	-2.1
1962-3	14.9	14.7	0.1	2.0	-1.9	35.0	-0.2	-2.1

▲

▼ *Table A.2 continued*

Fiscal transactions

Year	Budgetary revenues (% GDP)	Program spending (% GDP)	Operating surplus or deficit (-) (% GDP)	Public debt charges (% GDP)	Budgetary surplus or deficit (-) (% GDP)	Net public debt (% GDP)	Non-budgetary transactions (% GDP)	Financial requirements (-)/source (excluding foreign exchange) (% GDP)
1963-4	14.8	15.2	-0.4	2.1	-2.5	35.1	2.0	-0.5
1964-5	15.6	14.3	1.3	2.0	-0.7	32.7	0.9	0.2
1965-6	15.6	13.7	1.9	1.9	0.0	29.7	0.1	0.2
1966-7	15.2	14.1	1.1	1.8	-0.7	27.3	-0.3	-1.0
1967-8	15.4	15.0	0.3	1.8	-1.5	26.8	-0.5	-2.0
1968-9	15.8	14.7	1.0	1.9	-0.9	25.5	-0.2	-1.1
1969-70	17.1	15.0	2.2	2.0	0.2	22.9	0.1	0.3
1970-1	16.6	15.6	1.0	2.1	-1.1	22.5	0.0	-1.1
1971-2	16.9	16.5	0.3	2.1	-1.8	22.4	0.4	-1.4
1972-3	17.4	17.1	0.4	2.1	-1.7	21.8	0.5	-1.2
1973-4	17.4	17.1	0.3	2.0	-1.7	20.3	0.5	-1.2
1974-5	19.0	18.3	0.7	2.1	-1.4	18.4	0.0	-1.4
1975-6	18.2	19.5	-1.3	2.3	-3.6	19.9	0.8	-2.8
1976-7	17.2	18.3	-1.1	2.4	-3.4	20.7	0.7	-2.8
1977-8	15.6	18.1	-2.4	2.5	-4.9	23.7	1.1	-3.8
1978-9	15.1	17.5	-2.4	2.9	-5.3	26.6	0.7	-4.6
1979-80	15.0	16.2	-1.2	3.0	-4.3	27.6	0.6	-3.6
1980-1	15.5	16.7	-1.2	3.4	-4.6	29.2	1.5	-3.1

1981-2	16.7	16.9	-0.2	4.2	-4.3	29.9	1.8	-2.6
1982-3	16.0	19.2	-3.2	4.5	-7.6	36.0	1.4	-6.3
1983-4	15.6	19.2	-3.6	4.4	-8.0	41.2	1.9	-6.1
1984-5	15.8	19.4	-3.6	5.0	-8.6	46.3	1.9	-6.6
1985-6	15.9	17.7	-1.9	5.2	-7.1	50.0	0.8	-6.3
1986-7	16.8	17.6	-0.8	5.2	-6.0	53.4	1.5	-4.5
1987-8	17.4	17.2	0.2	5.2	-5.0	53.7	1.6	-3.4
1988-9	16.9	16.2	0.7	5.4	-4.7	53.7	1.0	-3.6
1989-90	17.2	15.8	1.5	5.9	-4.4	54.4	1.3	-3.1
1990-1	17.5	16.0	1.6	6.2	-4.7	57.3	1.1	-3.6
1991-2	17.8	16.8	1.0	6.0	-5.0	61.9	0.4	-4.6
1992-3	17.1	17.5	-0.3	5.5	-5.8	66.4	0.9	-4.9
1993-4	15.9	16.4	-0.6	5.2	-5.8	69.7	1.7	-4.1
1994-5	16.0	15.4	0.6	5.4	-4.8	70.6	1.5	-3.3
1995-6	16.0	13.8	2.3	5.8	-3.5	70.7	1.4	-2.1
1996-7	16.8	12.5	4.3	5.4	-1.1	69.5	1.2	0.2
1997-8	17.3	12.3	5.0	4.6	0.4	65.5	1.0	1.4
1998-9	17.0	12.2	4.8	4.5	0.3	63.0	0.9	1.3
1999-00	17.0	11.5	5.5	4.3	1.3	57.9	0.2	1.5
2000-1	16.9	11.3	5.6	4.0	1.6	51.8	0.2	1.8

Note: These numbers will not always be identical to numbers cited in text. The numbers in the text are typically taken from documents produced around the time in question, and were not necessarily calculated on the same accounting basis as the figures in this table. Figures in this table are all calculated on the basis the federal government used to measure its fiscal position before the changes announced in the 2003 budget.
Source: Fiscal Reference Tables – September 2001, Department of Finance, Canada, 2001. Reproduced with the permission of the Minister of Public Works and Government Services, 2002.

Notes

Chapter 1: Fiscal Politics

1 John Maynard Keynes, *The General Theory of Employment Interest and Money* (1936; reprint, New York: St. Martin's Press, 1957), 383-4.

2 See, for example, Jeffrey Simpson, 'Remorseless Arithmetic: The Citizen and the State in Canada,' *Queen's Quarterly* 101, 4 (1994): 781-99; Richard G. Harris, 'The Public Debt and the Social Policy Round,' in *Paying Our Way: The Welfare State in Hard Times,* ed. Richard G. Harris, John Richards, David M. Brown, John McCallum (Toronto: C.D. Howe Institute, 1994); Douglas G. Hartle, *The Federal Deficit,* Discussion Paper Series no. 93-30 (Kingston, ON: Queen's University, School of Policy Studies, 1993); William B.P. Robson and William M. Scarth, 'Debating Deficit Reduction: Economic Perspectives and Policy Choices,' in *Deficit Reduction: What Pain, What Gain?* Policy Study no. 23, ed. William B.P. Robson and William M. Scarth (Toronto: C.D. Howe Institute, 1994); Editorial, 'When the Deficit War Was Over,' *Globe and Mail,* 11 February 1997, A14.

3 See Michael Wilson, *A New Direction for Canada – An Agenda for Economic Renewal,* 8 November (Ottawa: Department of Finance, 1984), 19; Paul Martin, *The Budget Speech,* 27 February (Ottawa: Department of Finance, 1995), 2. For the view, characteristic of the leader of a government in the 1990s, that fiscal shortfalls are real and are what drove his government toward deficit reduction, see Bob Rae, *From Protest to Power: Personal Reflections on a Life in Politics* (Toronto: Viking, 1996), 198-203.

4 For a brief explanation of these methods of measurement, see Marc Lalonde, *The Federal Deficit in Perspective,* April (Ottawa: Department of Finance, 1983), 23-32. On the different deficit measures economists use to quantify the economic impact of deficits, see Neil Bruce and Douglas D. Purvis, 'Consequences of Government Budget Deficits,' and John Bossons, 'Issues in the Analysis of Government Deficits,' in *Fiscal and Monetary Policy,* research coordinator John Sargent, Collected Research Studies Series/Royal Commission on the Economic Union and Development Prospects for Canada, vol. 21. (Toronto: University of Toronto Press, 1986). On using separate current and capital expenditure accounts within the public accounts, see Jack M. Mintz and Ross S. Preston, *Capital Budgeting in the Public Sector,* Policy Forum Series no. 30 (Kingston, ON: Queen's University, John Deutsch Institute for the Study of Economic Policy, 1993).

5 John N. Turner, *Budget Speech,* 19 February (Ottawa: Department of Finance, 1973), 6, 23.

6 Louis Pauly, 'Capital Mobility, State Autonomy and Political Legitimacy,' *Journal of International Affairs* 48, 2 (1995): 383.

7 Ibid., 382.

8 Linda McQuaig, *Shooting the Hippo: Death by Deficit and Other Canadian Myths* (Toronto: Viking, 1995); Harold Chorney, *The Deficit and Debt Management: An Alternative to Monetarism* (Ottawa: Canadian Centre for Policy Alternatives, 1989); Harold Chorney, *The Deficit: Hysteria and the Current Economic Crisis* (Ottawa: Centre for Policy Alternatives, 1985); Fred Bienefeld, Duncan Cameron, Harold Chorney, et al., *'Bleeding the Patient:' The Debt/Deficit Hoax Exposed* (Ottawa: Canadian Centre for Policy Alternatives, 1993); Harold

Chorney, John Hotson, and Mario Seccareccia, *'The Deficit Made Me Do It!' The Myths about Government Debt,* ed. Ed Finn (Ottawa: Canadian Centre for Policy Alternatives, 1992). Andrew Jackson argues that the deficit was a real problem, but a problem caused by 'monetarist' rather than Keynesian economics. As such, alternative policies, including not only lower interest rates but also the re-regulation of finance, were required. Andrew Jackson, *Deficit, Debt and the Contradictions of Tory Economics* (Ottawa: Canadian Centre for Policy Alternatives, 1990). In the Alberta context, see Kevin Taft, *Shredding the Public Interest: Ralph Klein and 25 Years of One-Party Government* (Edmonton: University of Alberta Press, 1997).

9 For a subjectivist who understands the political hurdles facing the 'deficit-is-not-an-urgency-left' (my label, for lack of a better phrase), see Mel Watkins's comments in *Bleeding the Patient,* 16-17.

10 See, for example, Leo de Bever, 'International Impact of the Federal Budget,' in *The 1995 Federal Budget: Retrospect and Prospect,* ed. Thomas J. Courchene and Thomas A. Wilson, Policy Forum Series no. 33 (Kingston, ON: John Deutsch Institute for the Study of Economic Policy, 1995), especially p. 4.

11 Thom Workman makes the patriarchy argument, in his *Banking on Deception: The Discourse of Fiscal Crisis* (Halifax: Fernwood, 1996); and 'The Discourse of Fiscal Crisis,' *Studies in Political Economy* 59 (Summer 1999): 61-89. Barry Cooper, a rare deficit critic who does not see political success as a simple matter of objective necessity, makes a structurally similar argument. Speaking with respect to the province of Alberta, Cooper attributes the success of the Ralph Klein government in eliminating that province's deficit to leadership and appeals to the pride, self-respect, and virtue of the Albertan people. See Barry Cooper, *The Klein Achievement,* Monograph Series on Public Policy and Public Administration no. 1 (Toronto: University of Toronto, 1996). Keynesianism was once a matter of pride, self-respect, and virtue, so Cooper's position does not explain the politics of moving to eliminate deficits.

12 Donald Savoie, *Governing from the Centre: The Concentration of Power in Canadian Politics* (Toronto: University of Toronto Press, 1999); Edward Greenspon and Anthony Wilson-Smith, *Double Vision: The Inside Story of the Liberals in Power* (Toronto: Doubleday Canada, 1996).

13 Hugh Heclo, 'Ideas, Interests, Institutions,' in *The Dynamics of American Politics: Approaches and Interpretations,* ed. Lawrence C. Dodd and Calvin Jillson (Boulder, CO: Westview Press, 1994), 374-83.

14 Max Weber, 'The Social Psychology of World Religions,' in *From Max Weber: Essays in Sociology,* ed. H.H. Gerth and C. Wright Mills (London: Kegan Paul, Trench, Trubner, 1947), 280. See also Judith Goldstein and Robert O. Keohane, 'Ideas and Foreign Policy: An Analytical Framework,' in *Ideas and Foreign Policy: Beliefs, Institutions, and Political Change,* ed. Judith Goldstein and Robert O. Keohane (Ithaca, NY: Cornell University Press, 1993), 11-12.

15 Judith Goldstein, *Ideas, Interests, and American Trade Policy* (Ithaca, NY: Cornell University Press, 1993), 9.

16 See H.H. Gerth and C. Wright Mills, 'Introduction: The Man and His Work,' in *From Max Weber,* 61-5. But for Weber, ideas also could be in tension with interests and follow developments of their own.

17 Hugh Heclo, *Modern Social Politics in Britain and Sweden* (New Haven: Yale University Press, 1974), 305-6.

18 See Peter B. Evans, Dietrich Rueschemeyer, and Theda Skocpol, eds., *Bringing the State Back In* (New York: Cambridge University Press, 1985).

19 Kathleen Thelen and Sven Steinmo, 'Historical Institutionalism in Comparative Politics,' in *Structuring Politics: Historical Institutionalism in Comparative Analysis,* ed. Sven Steinmo, Kathleen Thelen, and Frank Longstreth (New York: Cambridge University Press, 1992), 14-15.

20 Ibid., 14.

21 See, e.g., Kenneth J. McKenzie, *A Tragedy of the House of Commons: Political Institutions and Fiscal Policy Outcomes from a Canadian Perspective,* Benefactors Lecture Series (Toronto: C.D. Howe Institute, 2001) for a rational choice or economic theory of politics approach

to the impact of political institutions on fiscal outcomes. As McKenzie is aware, such an account cannot, alone, explain both deficits and surpluses under unchanged institutions (8).

22 Peter A. Hall, 'Conclusion: The Politics of Keynesian Ideas,' in *The Political Power of Economic Ideas: Keynesianism across Nations*, ed. Peter A. Hall (Princeton, NJ: Princeton University Press, 1989), 371-4.

23 Peter A. Hall, 'Policy Paradigms, Social Learning, and the State: The Case of Economic Policymaking in Britain,' *Comparative Politics* 25, 3 (1993): 279-87.

24 Ibid., 279-81. See also Neil Bradford, 'The Policy Influence of Economic Ideas: Interests, Institutions and Innovation in Canada,' *Studies in Political Economy* 59 (Summer 1999): 24-5.

25 Robert B. Reich, Introduction to *The Power of Public Ideas*, ed. Robert B. Reich (Cambridge, MA: Ballinger, 1988), 5.

26 Paul Pierson states that politics in the United States became 'fiscalized' because politicians seeking change had first to deal with the deficit. See 'The Deficit and the Politics of Domestic Reform' in *The Social Divide: Political Parties and the Future of Activist Government*, ed. Margaret Weir (Washington, DC: Brookings Institution Press, 1998), 127.

27 Paul A. Sabatier, 'Policy Change over a Decade or More,' in *Policy Change and Learning: An Advocacy Coalition Approach*, ed. Paul A. Sabatier and Hank C. Jenkins-Smith (Boulder, CO: Westview Press, 1993), 33.

28 Pierre Elliott Trudeau, *Approaches to Politics* (Toronto: Oxford University Press, 1970), 88.

29 On the relationship between truth and power, see Michel Foucault, *Power/Knowledge: Selected Interviews and Other Writings*, ed. Colin Gordon (New York: Pantheon Books, 1980), 131.

30 This view implies that even in totalitarian systems that employ propaganda, power is not simply unidirectional. Propagandists must construct consent or obedience through not only force and terror but also the presentation of 'truth.' As Hannah Arendt argues, 'Where the rule of terror is brought to perfection, as in concentration camps, propaganda disappears entirely.' See Hannah Arendt, *The Origins of Totalitarianism* (New York: Harcourt Brace, 1973), 344, and Chapter 11 generally.

31 Liberal society counts something as true, in the public sense, insofar as it is the winning result of free and open encounters, freedom and openness being understood not as independent of power but as proscribing physical force. As Richard Rorty says, 'A liberal society is one which is content to call "true" whatever the upshot of such encounters turns out to be.' *Contingency, Irony, and Solidarity* (New York: Cambridge University Press, 1989), 52 (emphasis removed).

32 David A. Wolfe, 'The Politics of The Deficit,' in *The Politics of Economic Policy*, research coordinator G. Bruce Doern, Collected Research Studies Series/Royal Commission on the Economic Union and Development Prospects for Canada, vol. 40 (Toronto: University of Toronto Press, 1985), 133.

33 Stephen A. Clarkson and Timothy Lewis, 'The Contested State: Canada in the Post-Cold War, Post-Keynesian, Post-Fordist, Post-National Era,' in *How Ottawa Spends 1999-2000 – Shape Shifting: Canadian Governance toward the 21st Century*, ed. Leslie Pal (Toronto: Oxford University Press, 1999), 293-340.

Chapter 2: Deficit Finance in Historical Perspective

1 Glen Williams, *Not for Export: The International Competitiveness of Canadian Manufacturing*, 3rd ed. (Toronto: McClelland and Stewart, 1994), 39-46.

2 On this point, see William Watson, *Globalization and the Meaning of Canadian Life* (Toronto: University of Toronto Press, 1998), 24.

3 Michael J. Piva, *The Borrowing Process: Public Finance in the Province of Canada, 1840-1867* (Ottawa: University of Ottawa Press, 1992), 68-9.

4 Ibid., 31.

5 Ibid., xiii.

6 Ibid., 67.

7 Reg Whitaker, *A Sovereign Idea: Essays on Canada as a Democratic Community* (Montreal and Kingston: McGill-Queen's University Press, 1992), 19.

8 Michael Bliss, *Right Honourable Men: The Descent of Canadian Politics from Macdonald to Mulroney* (Toronto: HarperCollins, 1994), 21.
9 Bliss, *Right Honourable Men*, 18-19.
10 David A. Wolfe, "The Delicate Balance: The Changing Economic Role of the State in Canada," vol. 1 (PhD diss., University of Toronto, 1980), 119-34.
11 J. Harvey Perry, *Taxes, Tariffs, and Subsidies: A History of Canadian Fiscal Development*, vol. 1 (Toronto: University of Toronto Press, 1955), 38-9.
12 Ibid., 41-6.
13 Ibid., 16.
14 See Eric Hobsbawm, *The Age of Capital: 1848-1875* (London: Abacus, 1975), 107 and Chapter 5 generally.
15 Gordon Laxer, *Open for Business: The Roots of Foreign Ownership in Canada* (Toronto: Oxford University Press, 1989), 180-97.
16 See Daniel Drache, 'Introduction – Celebrating Innis: The Man, the Legacy, and Our Future,' in *Staples, Markets, and Cultural Change*, by Harold A. Innis (Montreal and Kingston: McGill-Queen's University Press, 1995), xxiv-xxvii.
17 Piva, *The Borrowing Process*, xii.
18 Bliss, *Right Honourable Men*, 47-53.
19 O.D. Skelton, as cited in Perry, *Taxes, Tariffs and Subsidies*, 1:104-5.
20 Perry, *Taxes, Tariffs and Subsidies*, 1:139.
21 Bliss, *Right Honourable Men*, 77.
22 See ibid., 82-5, for a brief account of this divisive issue.
23 J.J. Deutsch, 'War Finance and the Canadian Economy, 1914-1920,' *Canadian Journal of Economics and Political Science* 6, 4 (1940): 527.
24 Ibid.
25 Perry, *Taxes, Tariffs and Subsidies*, 1:141.
26 Ibid., 144-5.
27 Deutsch, 'War Finance' 527.
28 Ibid., 529.
29 Ibid., 532.
30 Perry, *Taxes, Tariffs and Subsidies*, 1:143-4.
31 J.L. Ilsley, *Budget Speech*, 12 September (Ottawa: King's Printer, 1939), 5; J.L. Ilsley, *Budget Speech*, 12 October (Ottawa: King's Printer, 1945), 1.
32 Ilsley, *Budget Speech* (1945), 143.
33 Deutsch, 'War Finance,' 537.
34 See Bliss, *Right Honourable Men*, 145-51, for an account of the conscription question in Canada during the Second World War.
35 Perry, *Taxes, Tariffs and Subsidies*, 2:329-30.
36 Ibid., 330-2.
37 David W. Slater, *War Finance and Reconstruction: The Role of Canada's Department of Finance, 1939-1946* (Ottawa: David W. Slater, 1995), 47-9.
38 Perry, *Taxes, Tariffs and Subsidies*, 2:332-3.
39 Ibid., 334-40; Ilsley, *Budget Speech* (1939), 5; Ilsley, *Budget Speech* (1945), 2.
40 Perry, *Taxes, Tariffs and Subsidies*, 2:328-9.
41 Slater, *War Finance and Reconstruction*, 11.
42 John Kenneth Galbraith, 'John Maynard Keynes,' in *A View from the Stands: Of People, Politics, Military Power, and the Arts* (Boston: Houghton Mifflin, 1986), 315.
43 See Donald E. Moggridge, *Keynes* (Toronto: University of Toronto Press, 1993), 1-12 on the presuppositions and morals of the Bloomsbury group
44 John Kenneth Galbraith, *The Age of Uncertainty* (Boston: Houghton Mifflin, 1977), 198-207.
45 John Maynard Keynes, *The Collected Writings of John Maynard Keynes*, vols. 5-6, *A Treatise on Money*, ed. Don Moggridge (1930; reprint, London: Macmillan, 1971).
46 John Maynard Keynes, *The Collected Writings*, vol. 2, *The Economic Consequences of the Peace*, ed. Donald Moggridge (1919; reprint, London: Macmillan, 1971). On Keynes's life and work generally, one cannot do better than Robert Skidelsky's magnificent three-volume biography, *John Maynard Keynes: Hopes Betrayed, 1883-1920* (Toronto: Penguin

Books, 1983); *John Maynard Keynes: The Economist As Saviour, 1920-1937* (London: Macmillan, 1992); and *John Maynard Keynes: Fighting for Britain, 1937-1946* (London: Macmillan, 2000).

47 John Maynard Keynes, *The General Theory of Employment Interest and Money* (1936; reprint, New York: St. Martin's Press, 1957).

48 See ibid., Chapter 2, for Keynes's basic critique of classical economics.

49 Galbraith, *The Age of Uncertainty,* 217.

50 David A. Wolfe, 'The Rise and Demise of the Keynesian Era in Canada, 1930-1982,' in *Readings in Canadian Social History,* vol. 5 (Toronto: McClelland and Stewart, 1984), 53-4.

51 Jukka Pekkarinen, 'Keynesianism and the Scandinavian Models of Economic Policy,' in *The Political Power of Economic Ideas: Keynesianism across Nations,* ed. Peter A. Hall (Princeton, NJ: Princeton University Press, 1989), 318; see also Galbraith, 'Gunnar and Alva Myrdal,' in *A View from the Stands,* 404-5.

52 Slater, *War Finance and Reconstruction,* 11.

53 Neil Bradford, 'The Policy Influence of Economic Ideas: Interests, Institutions and Innovation in Canada,' *Studies in Political Economy* 59 (Summer 1999): 29-31.

54 Walter S. Salant, 'The Spread of Keynesian Doctrines and Practices in the United States,' in *The Political Power of Economic Ideas,* ed. Hall, 27-36.

55 Indeed, David R. Cameron argues that the Second World War, in addition to unemployment levels and the openness of the economy, together account for almost all of the increases in government spending in Canada since the war. 'The Growth of Government Spending: The Canadian Experience in Comparative Perspective,' in *State and Society: Canada in Comparative Perspective,* co-ordinated by Keith G. Banting, Collected Research Studies Series/Royal Commission on the Economic Union and Development Prospects for Canada. vol. 31 (Toronto: University of Toronto Press, 1986), 43.

56 Slater, *War Finance and Reconstruction,* 4, 274.

57 Peter A. Hall, 'Conclusion: The Politics of Keynesian Ideas,' in *The Political Power of Economic Ideas,* ed. Hall, 387.

58 John Burton, 'Fifty Years On: Background and Foreground,' in *Keynes's General Theory: Fifty Years On – Its Relevance and Irrelevance to Modern Times* (London: Institute of Economic Affairs, 1986), 5.

59 See, for example, Cy Gonick, *The Great Economic Debate* (Toronto: James Lorimer, 1987), 73-102; Joan Robinson, 'What Has Become of the Keynesian Revolution?' in *Essays on John Maynard Keynes,* ed. Milo Keynes (London: Cambridge University Press, 1975), 123-31; Mario Seccareccia 'Keynesianism and Public Investment: A Left-Keynesian Perspective on the Role of Government Expenditures and Debt,' *Studies in Political Economy* 46 (Spring 1995): 43-78; Timothy Lewis, 'How Keynes Came to Canada: Keynesian Indeterminacy and the Canadian Interpretation of Keynesianism' (paper presented at the annual meeting of the Canadian Political Science Association, June 1996).

60 Galbraith, 'Keynes,' in *A View from the Stands,* 319.

61 Robinson, 'What Has Become of the Keynesian Revolution?' 127.

62 Robert M. Campbell, *Grand Illusions: The Politics of the Keynesian Experience in Canada, 1945-75* (Peterborough, ON: Broadview Press, 1987), 32; see also Campbell's wonderful article, 'From Keynesianism to Monetarism,' *Queen's Quarterly* 88, 4 (1981): 636-7.

63 Mitchell Sharp, *Budget Speech,* 29 March (Ottawa: Queen's Printer, 1966), 5; Mitchell Sharp, *Budget Speech,* 1 June (Ottawa: Queen's Printer, 1967), 4, 7-8; Edgar J. Benson, *Budget Speech,* 18 June (Ottawa: Department of Finance, 1971), 30, 33.

64 David A. Wolfe, 'The Rise and Demise of the Keynesian Era,' 48.

65 D.C. Abbott, *Budget Speech,* 28 March (Ottawa: Queen's Printer, 1950), 8; D.C. Abbott, *Budget Speech,* 10 April (Ottawa: Queen's Printer, 1951), 7.

66 James M. Buchanan and Richard E. Wagner, *Democracy in Deficit: The Political Legacy of Lord Keynes* (New York: Academic Press, 1977), 38-41. Keynes gave a hint of what discretionary countercyclical fiscal policy might entail in 'How to Pay for the War,' in *The Collected Writings of John Maynard Keynes,* vol. 9, *Essays in Persuasion,* ed. Donald Moggridge (1940; reprint, London: Macmillan, 1971), 367-439, especially pp. 404-7.

67 See J.C. Gilbert, *Keynes's Impact on Monetary Economics* (Toronto: Butterworth, 1982), chap. 14 for the evolution of Keynes's monetary thinking.

68 Wolfe, *The Delicate Balance*, 486.

69 Gilbert, *Keynes's Impact*, 242; Keynes, *General Theory*, 119-20.

70 Paul Krugman, *Peddling Prosperity: Economic Sense and Nonsense in the Age of Diminished Expectations* (New York: W.W. Norton, 1994), 30-2.

71 Gilbert, *Keynes's Impact*, 239; Keynes, *General Theory*, 164, 204.

72 Gilbert, *Keynes's Impact*, 238-9.

73 Ibid., 234.

74 Inflation is a repeated theme in the papers collected in Keynes's, *The Collected Writings*, vol. 9, *Essays in Persuasion*.

75 Keynes, *General Theory*, 118-19, 303-4.

76 A.W. Phillips, 'The Relation between Unemployment and the Rate of Change in Money Wage Rates in the United Kingdom, 1951-1957,' *Economica* 25 (November 1958): 283-99.

77 Krugman, *Peddling Prosperity*, 42.

78 See, for example, Paul A. Samuelson, 'Fiscal and Financial Policies for Growth,' in *The Collected Scientific Papers of Paul A. Samuelson*, vol. 2, ed. Joseph Stiglitz (Cambridge, MA: MIT Press, 1966), 1387-403. For a critical view of these recommendations, see Buchanan and Wagner, *Democracy in Deficit*, 84.

79 Abbott, *Budget Speech* (1951), 5.

80 Campbell, 'From Keynesianism to Monetarism,' 637-8.

81 Wolfe, 'Rise and Demise,' 47-8.

82 J.L. Ilsley, *Budget Speech*, 27 June (Ottawa: Queen's Printer, 1946), 9.

83 Benson, *Budget Speech* (1971), 30-1.

84 Edgar J. Benson, *Budget Speech*, 22 October (Ottawa: Queen's Printer, 1968), 15.

85 Keynes himself advocated the introduction of a family allowance in Britain. See 'How to Pay for the War,' 394-5.

86 Karl Polanyi, *The Great Transformation: The Political and Economic Origins of Our Time* (Boston: Beacon Press, 1944).

87 See John Gerard Ruggie, 'International Regimes, Transactions, and Change: Embedded Liberalism in the Postwar Economic Order,' in *International Regimes*, ed. Stephen D. Krasner (Ithaca, NY: Cornell University Press, 1983); 'Embedded Liberalism Revisited: Institutions and Progress in International Economic Relations,' in *Progress in Postwar International Relations*, ed. Emanuel Adler and Beverly Crawford (New York: Columbia University Press, 1991); and 'Trade, Protectionism and the Future of Welfare Capitalism,' *Journal of International Affairs* 48, 1 (Summer 1994): 1-11.

88 Ruggie, 'International Regimes, Transactions, and Change,' 209.

89 See Eric Helleiner, *States and the Reemergence of Global Finance: From Bretton Woods to the 1990s* (Ithaca, NY: Cornell University Press, 1994), chap. 2.

90 Ruggie, 'International Regimes, Transactions, and Change,' 213.

91 Ibid., 212.

92 Canada moved to a floating exchange rate in 1950, in violation of the Bretton Woods agreement, but was not penalized. Peter B. Kenen, *The International Economy*, 3rd ed. (New York: Cambridge University Press, 1994), 492. The Canadian dollar was pegged at 92.5 cents in American dollars in 1962.

93 William H. Beveridge, *Full Employment in a Free Society* (London: George Allen and Unwin, 1944), 219-25.

94 Sylvia Ostry, *The Post-Cold War Trading System: Who's on First?* (Chicago: University of Chicago Press, 1997), 57-67.

95 Ruggie, 'International Regimes, Transactions, and Change,' 210.

96 A.F.W. Plumptre, *Three Decades of Decision: Canada and the World Monetary System, 1944-1975* (Toronto: McClelland and Stewart, 1977), 28-9.

97 Ibid., 30-1.

98 See, for example, Campbell, *Grand Illusions*; Wolfe, 'The Rise and Demise.'

99 H. Scott Gordon, 'A Twenty Year Perspective: Some Reflections on the Keynesian Revolution

in Canada,' in *Canadian Economic Policy since the War,* ed. S.F. Kalisky (Montreal: Canadian Trade Committee, 1966), 26.

100 Clarence L. Barber and John C.P. McCallum, *Unemployment and Inflation: The Canadian Experience* (Toronto: Canadian Institute for Economic Policy, 1980), 92-3 and 154-5 n. 10. See also Gordon, 'A Twenty Year Perspective,' 27.

101 See Campbell, 'From Keynesianism to Monetarism,' 639-41, for an overview of the problems with Keynesianism in Canada. My account of the determinants of Canada's reception of Keynesianism draws on, but also tries to move beyond, the factors identified by Peter Hall in his cross-national study. See Hall, 'Conclusion: The Politics of Keynesian Ideas,' in *The Political Power of Economic Ideas,* ed. Hall, 375-89.

102 Canada, Department of Reconstruction, *Employment and Income with Special Reference to the Initial Period of Reconstruction* (Ottawa: Department of Reconstruction, 1945), especially p. 21; see also W.A. Mackintosh, 'The White Paper on Employment and Income in Its 1945 Setting,' in *Canadian Economic Policy since the War,* ed. S.F. Kalisky, 9-21.

103 On the American case, see Margaret Weir, 'Ideas and Politics: The Acceptance of Keynesianism in Britain and the United States,' in *The Political Power of Economic Ideas,* ed. Hall, 70-2; on the British case, see Burton, 'Fifty Years On,' 5.

104 Canada, 'Employment and Income,' 1.

105 Campbell, *Grand Illusions,* 39.

106 Canada, 'Employment and Income,' especially pp. 1, 2, 7, 16, 18.

107 Robert M. Campbell, *The Full-Employment Objective in Canada, 1945-85: Historical, Conceptual, and Comparative Perspectives,* Study prepared for the Economic Council of Canada (Ottawa: Supply and Services Canada, 1991), 2-5.

108 Campbell, *Grand Illusions,* 29.

109 See Gonick, *The Great Economic Debate,* 88; and Harold Chorney, *The Deficit and Debt Management: An Alternative to Monetarism* (Ottawa: Canadian Centre for Policy Alternatives, 1989), 7-24, for the 'sound finance' position that the business community in Canada fairly consistently took, especially in hard times, in opposition to the Keynesianism it nominally accepted.

110 See Co-operative Commonwealth Federation, 'The Regina Manifesto,' in *Canadian Political Thought,* ed. H.D. Forbes (Toronto: Oxford University Press, 1987), 241-50.

111 Gonick, *The Great Economic Debate,* 89.

112 David A. Wolfe, 'The Politics of the Deficit,' in *The Politics of Economic Policy,* research coordinator G. Bruce Doern, Collected Research Studies Series/Royal Commission on the Economic Union and Development Prospects for Canada, vol. 40 (Toronto: University of Toronto Press, 1985), 138-49, provides a very effective description of the Liberal balancing of business and social demands, as a centrist, rather than leftist, party.

113 Campbell, *Grand Illusions,* 55.

114 Michael Kalecki, 'Political Aspects of Full Employment,' in *Collected Works of Michal Kalecki,* ed. Jerzy Osiatynski, vol. 1, *Capitalism: Business Cycles and Full Employment* (Oxford: Clarendon Press, 1990), 351.

115 Whitaker, *A Sovereign Idea,* 62-6.

116 Jane Jenson, '"Different" but Not "Exceptional": Canada's Permeable Fordism,' *Canadian Review of Sociology and Anthropology* 26, 1 (1989): 78-9.

117 Stephen McBride, 'The Continuing Crisis of Social Democracy: Ontario's Social Contract in Perspective,' *Studies in Political Economy* 50 (Summer 1995): 71-2.

118 Frank Strain and Hugh Grant, 'The Social Structure of Accumulation in Canada, 1945-88,' *Journal of Canadian Studies* 26, 4 (1991-2): 78.

119 Campbell, *Grand Illusions,* 196.

120 Ibid., 196-7.

121 Jenson, 'Canada's Permeable Fordism,' 80.

122 Thomas J. Courchene with Colin R. Telmer, *From Heartland to North American Region State: The Social, Fiscal and Federal Evolution of Ontario – An Interpretive Essay,* Monograph Series on Public Policy and Public Administration no. 6 (Toronto: University of Toronto, Faculty of Management, 1998), 11.

123 Walter L. Gordon, *Budget Speech,* 16 March (Ottawa: Queen's Printer, 1964), 5-6.

124 Clarence L. Barber, *Theory of Fiscal Policy As Applied to a Province,* Study prepared for the Ontario Committee on Taxation (Toronto: Queen's Printer, 1966).
125 Donald V. Smiley, *Canada in Question: Federalism in the Eighties,* 3rd ed. (Toronto: McGraw-Hill Ryerson, 1980), 188.
126 Walter Harris, *Budget Speech,* 5 April (Ottawa: Queen's Printer, 1955), 10.
127 Smiley, *Canada in Question,* 188.
128 Donald M. Fleming, *Budget Speech,* 20 December (Ottawa: Queen's Printer, 1960), 4-8.
129 Donald M. Fleming, *Budget Speech,* 20 June (Ottawa: Queen's Printer, 1961), 6-9.
130 Donald M. Fleming, *Budget Speech,* 10 April (Ottawa: Queen's Printer, 1962), 5-6.
131 Ibid., 6-7.
132 Walter L. Gordon, *Budget Speech,* 13 June (Ottawa: Queen's Printer, 1963), 6.
133 Gordon, 'A Twenty Year Perspective,' in *Canadian Economic Policy,* ed. Kalisky; Irwin W. Gillespie, 'Postwar Canadian Fiscal Policy Revisited, 1945-1975,' *Canadian Tax Journal* 27, 3 (1979): 265-76. But see also, in partial disagreement with at least Gordon regarding the efficacy of Keynesian procedures, Robert M. Will, 'Canadian Fiscal Policy 1945-63,' Studies of the Royal Commission on Taxation no. 17 (Ottawa: Queen's Printer, 1967).
134 Campbell, *Grand Illusions,* 191-2.
135 Surpluses were justified by their role in helping fund deficits while avoiding long-term debt accumulation. See D.C. Abbott's budget speeches: (29 April 1947), 1; (18 May 1948), 4, 9-10; (22 March 1949), 9; and (8 April 1952), 4.

Chapter 3: The Political Economy of Economic Decline

1 John Kenneth Galbraith, *The Age of Uncertainty* (Boston: Houghton Mifflin, 1977), 226.
2 On Trudeau's 'just society,' see *Towards a Just Society: The Trudeau Years,* ed. Thomas S. Axworthy and Pierre Elliott Trudeau (Markham, ON: Viking, 1990).
3 Robert M. Campbell, *Grand Illusions: The Politics of the Keynesian Experience in Canada, 1945-75* (Peterborough, ON: Broadview Press, 1987), 6; Robert M. Campbell, 'From Keynesianism to Monetarism,' *Queen's Quarterly* 88, 4 (1981): 635-50; Robert M. Campbell, 'Post-Keynesian Politics and the Post-Schumpeterian World,' *Canadian Journal of Political and Social Theory* 8, 1-2 (1984): 72-91; David A. Wolfe, 'The Rise and Demise of the Keynesian Era in Canada, 1930-1982,' in *Readings in Canadian Social History,* vol. 5 (Toronto: McClelland and Stewart, 1984), 71-2. Richard French argues that oil price shocks, monetary gradualism, and wage and price controls were the demise of 'fine-tuning.' Richard French, *How Ottawa Decides: Planning and Industrial Policy Making, 1968-1984,* 2nd ed. (Toronto: James Lorimer, 1984), 67. Cy Gonick argues the Canadian government was swept up in a monetarist tide in 1975. He identifies monetary gradualism and the Anti-Inflation Program as components. Cy Gonick, *The Great Economic Debate* (Toronto: James Lorimer, 1987), 115, 184-5.
4 Michael Bruno and Jeffrey D. Sachs, *Economics of Worldwide Stagflation* (Oxford: Basil Blackwell, 1985), 1.
5 On stagflation in cross-national perspective, see ibid.
6 On the Nixon shock, see Sylvia Ostry, *The Post-Cold War Trading System: Who's on First* (Chicago: University of Chicago Press, 1997), 73-5.
7 The United States, Japan, Germany, France, England, Italy, and Canada.
8 All figures are from Marc Lalonde, *The Economic Outlook for Canada,* 19 April (Ottawa: Department of Finance, 1983), 4.
9 Confidential interview, 21 May 1998.
10 Confidential interview, 26 June 1998.
11 Confidential interview, 21 May 1998; Bruno and Sacks also argue that supply factors have been underestimated in demand-based models of stagflation. *Worldwide Stagflation,* 6-7.
12 Confidential interview, 21 May 1998.
13 Judith Goldstein and Robert O. Keohane, 'Ideas and Foreign Policy: An Analytical Framework,' in *Ideas and Foreign Policy: Beliefs, Institutions, and Political Change,* ed. Judith Goldstein and Robert O. Keohane (Ithaca, NY: Cornell University Press, 1993), 12-13.
14 Neil Bradford, 'The Policy Influence of Economic Ideas: Interests, Institutions and Innovation in Canada,' *Studies in Political Economy* 59 (Summer 1999): 35.

15 For a definition of post-Keynesianism, see Alfred S. Eichner, Introduction to *A Guide to Post-Keynesian Economics,* ed. Alfred S. Eichner (New York: M.E. Sharpe, 1978), 11-16.

16 On analytical differences between monetarists and post-Keynesians, see Arthur W. Donner and Douglas D. Peters, *The Monetarist Counter-Revolution: A Critique of Canadian Monetary Policy 1975-1979* (Toronto: James Lorimer, 1979), 10-12. See Chapter 5 for a more complete treatment of monetarism and its associated concepts.

17 Department of Finance, *Canada's Recent Inflation Experience, November 1978,* One of a Series of Papers on Medium and Long-Term Economic Issues (Ottawa: Department of Finance, 1978), 218.

18 Ibid., 19. See Chapter 5 for a more detailed exegesis of the Non-Accelerating Inflation Rate of Unemployment.

19 Ibid., 20.

20 Ibid., 2.

21 Ibid., 21-2.

22 Ibid., 24.

23 Ibid., 23.

24 See Canada, Royal Commission on the Economic Union and Development Prospects for Canada (The Macdonald Commission), *Report,* vol. 2 (Ottawa: Minister of Supply and Services, 1985), 273-7, for an exegesis of developments in economic theory regarding the Phillips Curve.

25 John Sargent, 'Comment: On Macro Public Finance,' in *Retrospectives on Public Finance,* ed. Lorraine Eden (Durham, NC: Duke University Press, 1991), 345.

26 Campbell, 'Post-Keynesian Politics,' 80-4.

27 Confidential interview, 21 May 1998.

28 John N. Turner, *Budget Speech,* 6 May (Ottawa: Department of Finance, 1974), 6.

29 William Johnson, 'Lewis Says Budget Is Cruel, Hypocritical, Can't Be Supported,' *Globe and Mail,* 8 May 1974, A1.

30 Terrance Wills, 'Lapel Daisies a Reply to PM,' *Globe and Mail,* 9 May 1974, A1.

31 Wayne Cheveldayoff, 'Stanfield Says Liberals Deserve "Honor" of Defeat over Budget,' *Globe and Mail,* 9 May 1974, A1.

32 John N. Turner, *Budget Speech,* 23 June (Ottawa: Department of Finance, 1975), 1.

33 Ibid., 2.

34 Ibid., 11.

35 Ibid.

36 Confidential interview, 26 June 1998.

37 Turner, *Budget Speech* (1975), 13-14.

38 Ibid., 21.

39 Turner, *Budget Speech* (1975), 12.

40 Donald S. Macdonald, *Attack on Inflation – A Program of National Action,* 14 October (Ottawa: Department of Finance, 1975), 1 (my emphasis).

41 Ibid., 4.

42 Ibid., 2.

43 Eichner, Introduction to *A Guide,* 16-18. See also John Shields and Stephen McBride, *Dismantling a Nation: The Transition to a Corporate Rule in Canada,* 2nd ed. (Halifax: Fernwood Press, 1997), 66.

44 John Kenneth Galbraith, *Economics and the Public Purpose* (Boston: Houghton Mifflin Company, 1973).

45 For Galbraith's impact on Pierre Trudeau's thinking, see Stephen Clarkson and Christina McCall, *Trudeau and Our Times,* vol. 2, *The Heroic Delusion* (Toronto: McClelland and Stewart, 1994), 124-7.

46 Confidential interview, 13 July 1998.

47 Donald Savoie, *The Politics of Public Spending in Canada* (Toronto: University of Toronto Press, 1990), 150.

48 Confidential interview, 26 June 1998.

49 Peter W. Hogg, *Constitutional Law of Canada, Student edition* (Toronto: Thomson Canada, 1999), 435.

50 David Langille, 'The Business Council on National Issues and the Canadian State,' *Studies in Political Economy* 24 (Autumn 1987): 47.
51 Campbell, *Grand Illusions,* 163.
52 Ibid., 186-7.
53 For an assessment of the election and the place of controls therein, see William P. Irvine, 'An Overview of the 1974 Federal Election in Canada,' in *Canada at the Polls: The General Election of 1974,* ed. Howard R. Penniman (Washington, DC: American Enterprise Institute for Public Policy Research, 1975), 39-55.
54 Canadian Press, 'Program Goes beyond PC '74 Plan, Stanfield Says,' *Globe and Mail,* 15 October 1975, B4.
55 Lawrence Leduc and J. Alex Murray, 'Survey Shows More Public Support of Curbs,' *Globe and Mail,* 25 May 1976, B1.
56 Editorial, 'A Patchwork War,' *Globe and Mail,* 14 October 1975.
57 Hogg, *Constitutional Law of Canada,* 435.
58 Campbell, 'From Keynesianism to Monetarism,' 644.
59 Ibid.
60 David A. Wilton, 'An Evaluation of Wage and Price Controls in Canada,' *Canadian Public Policy* 10, 2 (1984): 173-4.
61 Confidential interview, 21 May 1998.
62 Confidential interview, 26 June 1998.
63 Peter A. Hall, 'Policy Paradigms, Social Learning, and the State: The Case of Economic Policymaking in Britain,' *Comparative Politics* 25, 3 (1993): 285.
64 See, for example, John Burton, 'Fifty Years On: Background and Foreground,' in *Keynes's General Theory: Fifty Years On – Its Relevance and Irrelevance to Modern Times* (London: Institute of Economic Affairs, 1986), 7; and James M. Buchanan and Richard E. Wagner, *Democracy in Deficit: The Political Legacy of Lord Keynes* (New York: Academic Press, 1977), 90.
65 Richard Cleroux, 'Mulroney Latest Entry in PC Race,' *Globe and Mail,* 16 October 1975, A13.
66 Turner, *Budget Speech* (1975), 15.
67 Macdonald, *Attack on Inflation,* 8.
68 Donald S. Macdonald, *Budget Speech,* 25 May (Ottawa: Department of Finance, 1976), 21. Reiterating the goal probably had something to do with Ottawa's failure, which Macdonald noted, to meet this spending objective in the 1975-6 fiscal year (22).
69 Ibid.
70 Ibid., 18.
71 Donner and Peters, *The Monetarist Counter-Revolution,* 12.
72 Clarence L. Barber and John C.P. McCallum, *Unemployment and Inflation: The Canadian Experience* (Toronto: Canadian Institute for Economic Policy, 1980), 21-6, 126-7.
73 Ibid., 69-75; Donner and Peters, *The Monetarist Counter-Revolution,* chap. 3.
74 Barber and McCallum, *Unemployment and Inflation,* 26; Donner and Peters, *The Monetarist Counter-Revolution,* 31.
75 Richard French, *How Ottawa Decides: Planning and Industrial Policy Making, 1968-1984,* 2nd ed. (Toronto: James Lorimer, 1984), 67; Savoie, *The Politics of Public Spending,* 75.
76 André C. Drainville, 'Monetarism in Canada and the World Economy,' *Studies in Political Economy* 46 (Spring 1995): 21.
77 Confidential interviews, 21 May 1998; 3 June 1998; 26 June 1998.
78 Macdonald, *Budget Speech* (1976), 23.
79 Gerald K. Bouey, 'Remarks by Gerald K. Bouey, Governor of the Bank of Canada,' *Bank of Canada Review* (October 1975): 28; Gerald K. Bouey, 'Statement by Gerald K. Bouey, Governor of the Bank of Canada,' *Bank of Canada Review* (November 1975): 4.
80 Gordon R. Sparks, 'The Theory and Practice of Monetary Policy in Canada: 1945-83,' in *Fiscal and Monetary Policy,* research coordinator John Sargent, Collected Research Studies Series/Royal Commission on the Economic Union and Development Prospects for Canada, vol. 21 (Toronto: University of Toronto Press, 1986), 137.
81 Ibid., 144.
82 Bruno and Sacks, *Worldwide Stagflation,* 160.

83 Drainville, 'Monetarism in Canada,' 21; Sparks, 'The Theory and Practice of Monetary Policy,' 144-5.

84 See Drainville, 'Monetarism in Canada,' 35 n. 3, for the numbers and the claim that gradualism was 'drastic'; see also Sparks, 'The Theory and Practice of Monetary Policy,' 137-8 on the money supply target range.

85 Bouey, 'Statement,' (November 1975), 4.

86 Drainville, 'Monetarism in Canada,' 15-16; see also p. 30.

87 Donner and Peters, *The Monetarist Counter-Revolution,* 27, 35-6. Monetarism, strictly understood, proscribes discretionary short-term intervention. Donner and Peters provide an excellent overview and critique of monetary gradualism, and of monetarist doctrine more generally.

88 Richard G. Lipsey, Paul N. Courant, and Douglas D. Purvis, *Economics,* 8th Canadian ed. (New York: HarperCollins, 1994), 720.

89 Gonick, *Great Economic Debate,* 115-16. Gonick is a critic of the policy, but he identifies Canadian monetary policy as shadowing the Federal Reserve to protect the exchange rate.

90 See Sparks, 'The Theory and Practice of Monetary Policy,' 141.

91 Allan J. MacEachen, *Budget Papers – Supplementary Information and Notice of Ways and Means Motion on the Budget,* 28 June (Ottawa: Department of Finance, 1982), 1.

92 According to the 'Mundell-Fleming' theorem, if capital is mobile, a country can control its exchange rate or its monetary policy, but not both. With the Federal Reserve's move in 1979, the Bank of Canada gave up control of monetary policy to protect the exchange rate. The bank could have let the dollar slide as capital left the country to seek higher interest rates in the United States. In this sense, monetary policy was not strictly determined by American actions. The bank's 'choice,' however, was certainly profoundly informed by the distorting impact of what was going on south of the border. On the Mundell-Fleming, or 'open economy trilemma' theory, see Louis Pauly, *Who Elected the Bankers?* (Ithaca, NY: Cornell University Press, 1997), 20-9; and Maurice Obstfeld, 'The Global Capital Market: Benefactor or Menace?' *The Journal of Economic Perspectives* 12, 4 (1998): 9-30.

93 For example, debt-service charges rose 37.5 percent due to higher interest rates in 1980-1. Allan J. MacEachen, *The Budget in More Detail,* 12 November (Ottawa: Department of Finance, 1981), 11.

94 Rudiger Dornbusch and Mario Draghi, eds., Introduction to *Public Debt Management: Theory and History* (New York: Cambridge University Press, 1990), 1-2. Dornbusch and Draghi's account is too technical to explain the accompanying politics, but it describes the economic conundrum.

95 Allan J. MacEachen, *Budget Speech,* 28 October (Ottawa: Department of Finance, 1980), 3.

96 Allan J. MacEachen, *Budget Speech,* 12 November (Ottawa: Department of Finance, 1981), 1.

97 MacEachen, *Budget in More Detail* (1981), 3-4.

98 Campbell, *Grand Illusions,* 216.

99 See John Gerard Ruggie, 'International Regimes, Transactions, and Change: Embedded Liberalism in the Postwar Economic Order,' in *International Regimes,* ed. Stephen D. Krasner (Ithaca, NY: Cornell University Press, 1983), 221.

Chapter 4: Persisting Keynesian Conceptualizations of Deficit Finance, 1975-84

1 Pierre Trudeau, *The Essential Trudeau,* ed. Ron Graham (Toronto: McClelland and Stewart, 1998), 31-3.

2 See, for example, Marc Lalonde, *The Federal Deficit in Perspective,* April (Ottawa: Department of Finance, 1983), 7.

3 Ibid.; see also Clarence L. Barber and John C.P. McCallum, *Unemployment and Inflation: The Canadian Experience* (Toronto: Canadian Institute for Economic Policy, 1980), 19, 93.

4 Lalonde, *The Federal Deficit in Perspective,* 5-7; H. Mimoto and P. Cross, 'The Growth of the Federal Debt,' *Canadian Economic Observer* (June 1991): 3.1-3.17.

5 W. Irwin Gillespie, *Tax, Borrow and Spend: Financing Federal Spending in Canada, 1867-1990* (Ottawa: Carleton University Press, 1991), 211-14.

6 In general, a tax expenditure gives preferential treatment by granting relief from the standard provisions of the tax system. Money is spent by not collecting it. Tax expenditures give a picture of less government involvement in the economy than if the measures were on the spending side of the balance sheet, but the spending is real and the resulting deficit the same. G. Bruce Doern, Allan M. Maslove, and Michael J. Prince, *Public Budgeting in Canada: Politics, Economics, and Management* (Ottawa: Carleton University Press, 1988), 60-1.

7 Gillespie, *Tax, Borrow and Spend,* 214-16.

8 David A. Wolfe, 'Politics, the Deficit and Tax Reform,' *Osgoode Hall Law Journal* 26, 2 (1988): 359-61.

9 Ibid., 365; David A. Wolfe, 'The Politics of the Deficit,' in *The Politics of Economic Policy,* research coordinator G. Bruce Doern, Collected Research Studies Series/Royal Commission on The Economic Union and Development Prospects for Canada, vol. 40 (Toronto: University of Toronto Press, 1985), 120-1.

10 Robert M. Campbell, *Grand Illusions: The Politics of the Keynesian Experience in Canada, 1945-1975* (Peterborough, ON: Broadview Press, 1987), 182-3.

11 Douglas D. Purvis and Constance Smith, 'Fiscal Policy in Canada: 1963-84,' in *Fiscal and Monetary Policy,* research coordinator John Sargent, Collected Research Studies Series/Royal Commission on the Economic Union and Development Prospects for Canada, vol. 21 (Toronto: University of Toronto Press, 1986), 23.

12 Confidential interview, 26 June 1998.

13 Confidential interview, 3 June 1998.

14 Lalonde, *The Federal Deficit in Perspective,* 7-8, 60.

15 Arguments were issued at the time that the federal deficit was primarily structural rather than countercyclical in nature. For instance, the government of Ontario calculated that Ottawa would have had a substantial deficit in 1977 even at full employment. See Arthur W. Donner and Douglas D. Peters, *The Monetarist Counter-Revolution: A Critique of Canadian Monetary Policy 1975-1979* (Toronto: James Lorimer, 1979), 32-4. But at the time, this was an argument, not an established fact. Donner and Peters write that 'in retrospect it now appears that stronger economic growth did not yield sufficiently increased revenues and reduced expenditures to markedly reduce government deficits' (32).

16 David A. Dodge, 'Reflections on the Role of Fiscal Policy: The Doug Purvis Memorial Lecture,' *Canadian Public Policy* 24, 3 (1998): 279, emphasis in original.

17 Economists writing in the late 1970s and 1980 thought at least some of the explanation for deficits was the underlying economy. For example, Clarence Barber and John McCallum, writing in 1980, concluded that the deficits of the previous years were mainly the result of lower economic activity, although they also saw discretionary tax moves as a factor (Barber and McCallum, *Unemployment and Inflation,* 93-6). In 1979, Arthur Donner and Douglas Peters attributed increases in the federal deficit both to a lagging domestic economy and to fiscal measures (Donner and Peters, *The Monetarist Counter-Revolution,* 32). According to Mimoto and Cross, the OECD has calculated that had growth and employment remained at pre-1975 levels, the federal government's cyclically adjusted (that is, structural) balance would have been in surplus until 1982 (Mimoto and Cross, 'The Growth of the Federal Debt,' 3.14). However, the source they cite to establish this claim does not offer robust support for their position.

18 Thomas J. Courchene, 'Half-Way Home: Canada's Remarkable Fiscal Turnaround and the Paul Martin Legacy,' *Policy Matters* 3, 8 (2002): 14.

19 Confidential interviews, 21 May 1998; 26 June 1998.

20 Confidential interview, 26 June 1998.

21 Confidential interviews, 21 May 1998; 3 June 1998; 26 June 1998.

22 Confidential interview, 21 May 1998.

23 The Progressive Conservatives, for example, argued that Turner's 1973 budget should be opposed because it was less stimulative than its predecessors. Terrance Wills, 'PCs Call Budget Less Expansionary than Last Year's, Move for Defeat,' *Globe and Mail,* 22 February 1973, A8.

24 John N. Turner, *Budget Speech,* 23 June (Ottawa: Department of Finance, 1975), 5.

25 Ibid., 1.

26 Ibid., 13.
27 Campbell, *Grand Illusions*, 186.
28 Donald S. Macdonald, *Budget Speech*, 25 May (Ottawa: Department of Finance, 1976), 8.
29 Ibid., 8-9.
30 Ibid., 9.
31 Confidential interview, 3 June 1998.
32 Macdonald, *Budget Speech* (1976), 23.
33 Donald S. Macdonald, *Budget Speech*, 31 March (Ottawa: Department of Finance, 1977), 19.
34 Ibid., 10.
35 David A. Wolfe, 'The Rise and Demise of the Keynesian Era in Canada: Economic Policy, 1930-1982,' in *Readings in Canadian Social History*, vol. 5 (Toronto: McClelland and Stewart, 1984), 70.
36 Macdonald, *Budget Speech* (1976), 9.
37 Jean Chrétien, *Economic and Fiscal Statement*, 20 October (Ottawa: Department of Finance, 1977), 4.
38 Ibid., 8-9.
39 Ibid., 5.
40 Jean Chrétien, *The Budget*, 10 April (Ottawa: Department of Finance, 1978), 5-6.
41 Ibid., 6.
42 Ibid., 12-13.
43 John N. Turner, *Budget Speech*, 19 February (Ottawa: Department of Finance, 1973), 20.
44 Donald V. Smiley, *Canada in Question: Federalism in the Eighties*, 3rd ed. (Toronto: McGraw-Hill Ryerson, 1980), 193.
45 William Johnson, Jeffrey Simpson, and Richard Cleroux, 'Quebec Angry but Still Undecided about Federal Sales Tax Reduction,' *Globe and Mail*, 12 April 1978, A1-A2.
46 Smiley, *Canada in Question*, 193.
47 Donald Savoie, *The Politics of Public Spending in Canada* (Toronto: University of Toronto Press, 1990), 151-2; Lawrence Martin, *Chrétien*, vol. 1, *The Will to Win* (Toronto: Lester, 1995), 262-3.
48 Smiley, *Canada in Question*, 177.
49 Ibid.
50 Wayne Cheveldayoff, 'Federal Sales Tax Cut to 9% in a Boost-Business Budget,' *Globe and Mail*, 19 November 1978, A1-A2.
51 Ibid., A2.
52 Jean Chrétien, *Budget Speech*, 16 November (Ottawa: Department of Finance, 1978), 10.
53 Cheveldayoff, 'Federal Sales Tax Cut,' *Globe and Mail*, 19 November 1978, A1.
54 Martin, *Chrétien*, 270.
55 Savoie, *The Politics of Public Spending*, 155-6.
56 Confidential interview, 13 July 1998.
57 Confidential interview, 3 June 1998.
58 Martin, *Chrétien*, 121. Martin argues that Chrétien's political character was and is defined by three features: fiscal conservatism, social policy liberalism, and instinctive federalism.
59 Smiley, *Canada in Question*, 159.
60 Stephen Clarkson and Christina McCall, *Trudeau and Our Times*, vol. 1, *The Magnificent Obsession* (Toronto: McClelland and Stewart, 1990), 179.
61 Clarkson and McCall, *Trudeau and Our Times*, 2:232.
62 Jeffrey Simpson, 'Budget Aimed at Reasserting Ottawa's Power,' *Globe and Mail*, 27 October 1980, A1.
63 The finance minister was politely but firmly candid about the goal of greater fairness regarding the distribution of energy revenues among governments. Allan J. MacEachen, *The Budget*, 28 October (Ottawa: Department of Finance, 1980), 9.
64 Ibid., 4.
65 Ibid., 21.
66 Ibid., 4.
67 Confidential interview, 30 January 2001.

68 MacEachen, *The Budget* (1980), 27.
69 Ibid., 9.
70 Ibid., 30.
71 See Smiley, *Canada in Question,* 193-202.
72 MacEachen, *The Budget* (1980), 6-12.
73 Clarkson and McCall, *Trudeau and Our Times,* 2:170-4.
74 Richard Simeon and Ian Robinson, *State, Society, and the Development of Canadian Federalism,* Collected Research Studies Series/Royal Commission on the Economic Union and Development Prospects for Canada, vol. 71 (Toronto: University of Toronto Press, 1990), 240-1.
75 Clarkson and McCall, *Trudeau and Our Times,* 2:181-3.
76 Ibid., 176.
77 Joseph Quinlan and Marc Chandler, 'The U.S. Trade Deficit: A Dangerous Obsession,' *Foreign Affairs* 80, 3 (2001): 91.
78 Clarkson and McCall, *Trudeau and Our Times,* 2:196.
79 Ian A. Stewart, 'Debt Is Not Proof of Profligacy,' *Globe and Mail,* 13 March 1999, D7.
80 Allan J. MacEachen, *The Budget in More Detail,* 12 November (Ottawa: Department of Finance, 1981), 3.
81 Allan J. MacEachen, *Budget Speech,* 12 November (Ottawa: Department of Finance, 1981), 1-2.
82 Ibid.,1.
83 MacEachen, *Budget in More Detail* (1981), 2-4.
84 Ibid., 50.
85 Confidential interview, 3 June 1998. See also Gillespie, *Tax, Borrow and Spend,* 194-5.
86 Doern, Maslove, and Prince, *Public Budgeting in Canada,* 65-6.
87 Ibid; Clarkson and McCall, *Trudeau and Our Times,* 2:233-40. There is another, deliciously Machiavellian, argument that MacEachen's myriad proposals were a smokescreen designed to allow Ottawa to deindex the tax system. W. Irwin Gillespie, 'The 1981 Federal Budget: Muddling through or Purposeful Tax Reform?' *Canadian Tax Journal* 31, 6 (1983): 975-1002, especially pp. 986-7.
88 Savoie, *Politics of Public Spending,* 75; Clarkson and McCall, *Trudeau and Our Times,* 2:239.
89 Allan J. MacEachen, *The Budget,* 28 June (Ottawa: Department of Finance, 1982), 4-5.
90 Ibid., 4.
91 Ibid., 3.
92 David Langille, 'The Business Council on National Issues and the Canadian State,' *Studies in Political Economy* 24 (Autumn 1987): 59.
93 MacEachen, *The Budget* (1982), 1.
94 Ibid., 2-3.
95 Ibid., 10.
96 Confidential interview, 25 January 2001.
97 Marc Lalonde, *Statement on the Economic Outlook and the Financial Position of the Government of Canada,* 27 October (Ottawa: Department of Finance, 1982), 2.
98 Ibid., 2, 20.
99 Ibid., 8.
100 Ibid.
101 Ibid., 7.
102 Marc Lalonde, *Budget Papers – Supplementary Information and Notices of Ways and Means Motions on the Budget,* 19 April (Ottawa: Department of Finance, 1983), 5.
103 James Rusk, 'Tax Breaks Will Be a Boost for Business,' *Globe and Mail,* 20 April 1983, A10.
104 Ann Silversides, 'Business Groups Like Budget, but Worry about Deficit's Size,' *Globe and Mail,* 20 April 1983, A11.
105 Peter Cook, 'Leak to TV Camera Means More Funds,' *Globe and Mail,* 20 April 1983, A1.
106 Marc Lalonde, *Budget Speech,* 19 April (Ottawa: Department of Finance, 1983), 19.
107 Lalonde, *Federal Deficit in Perspective,* 5-7.
108 Ibid., 8-10.
109 Ibid., 7.
110 Ibid., 10-11.

111 Ibid., 13-15.
112 Ibid., 16.
113 Ibid., 16-17.
114 Ibid., 19.
115 Marc Lalonde, *The Canadian Economy in Recovery,* February (Ottawa: Department of Finance, 1984), 4.
116 Marc Lalonde, *The Budget Speech,* 15 February (Ottawa: Department of Finance, 1984), 5.
117 Ibid., 3.
118 James Rusk, 'Budget No Help in Economic Ills, Opposition Says,' *Globe and Mail,* 16 February 1984, A11.
119 Jeffrey Simpson, 'Budget Burying Major Promises in PC Campaign,' *Globe and Mail,* 12 December 1979, A11.
120 William P. Irvine, 'Epilogue: The 1980 Election,' in *Canada at the Polls, 1979 and 1980: A Study of the General Elections,* ed. Howard R. Penniman (Washington, DC: American Enterprise Institute for Public Policy Research, 1981), 344.
121 John C. Crosbie, *Budget Speech,* 11 December (Ottawa: Department of Finance, 1979), 2.
122 John C. Crosbie with Geoffrey Stevens, *No Holds Barred: My Life in Politics* (Toronto: McClelland and Stewart, 1997), 169.
123 Confidential interview, 27 May 1998.
124 Crosbie, *Budget Speech* (1979), 2.
125 Ibid., 3.
126 Confidential interview, 21 May 1998.
127 Crosbie, *Budget Speech* (1979), 3.
128 Department of Finance, *The Economic Assumptions Underlying the Fiscal Projections of the Budget,* 11 December (Ottawa: Department of Finance, 1979).
129 Savoie, *Politics of Public Spending,* 61.
130 Ibid., 63-6. In addition to Savoie, for another detailed account of the Policy and Expenditure Management System, see Richard French, *How Ottawa Decides: Planning and Industrial Policy Making 1968-1984,* 2nd ed. (Toronto: James Lorimer, 1984), 138-42.
131 MacEachen, *The Budget* (1980), 12.
132 Crosbie, *Budget Speech* (1979), 8.
133 My calculations based on ibid., 34.
134 Ibid., 16.
135 Department of Finance, *Government of Canada Tax Expenditure Account: A Conceptual Analysis and Account of Tax Preferences in the Federal Income and Commodity Tax Systems,* December (Ottawa: Department of Finance, 1979).
136 Robert Sheppard and Mary Trueman, '"Budget that Stole Christmas" Condemned by Opposition Spokesmen,' *Globe and Mail,* 12 December 1979, A12.
137 Crosbie, *No Holds Barred,* 180.
138 See Peter Aucoin, 'Organizational Change in the Management of Canadian Government: From Rational Management to Brokerage Politics,' *Canadian Journal of Political Science* 19, 1 (1986): 691-709.
139 Department of Finance, *Canada's Recent Inflation Experience, November 1978,* One of a Series of Papers on Medium and Long-Term Economic Issues (Ottawa: Department of Finance, 1978), 4.
140 David Wilton argues the AIP did help reduce inflation and concludes that Canada could have done much worse without policy. David A. Wilton, 'An Evaluation of Wage and Price Controls in Canada,' *Canadian Public Policy* 10, 2 (1984), 173-4.
141 See David R. Cameron, 'Social Democracy, Corporatism, Labour Quiescence and the Representation of Economic Interest in Advanced Capitalist Society,' in *Order and Conflict in Contemporary Capitalism: Studies in the Political Economy of Western European Nations,* ed. John H. Goldthorpe (Oxford: Oxford University Press, 1984).
142 See Michael M. Atkinson and William D. Coleman, *The State, Business, and Industrial Change in Canada* (Toronto: University of Toronto Press, 1989).
143 See Robert M. Campbell, *The Full-Employment Objective in Canada, 1945-75: Historical, Conceptual, and Comparative Perspectives,* Study prepared for the Economic Council of

Canada (Ottawa: Supply and Services Canada, 1991), chap. 3, for a thorough comparative analysis of Canada's low institutional capacity for managing unemployment.

144 Atkinson and Coleman, *The State, Business, and Industrial Change*, 40-52.
145 Peter Gourevitch, *Politics in Hard Times: Comparative Responses to International Economic Crisis* (Ithaca, NY: Cornell University Press, 1986), 59.
146 Savoie, *The Politics of Public Spending*, 74-6.
147 John Richards 'Reducing the Muddle in the Middle: Three Propositions for Running the Welfare State,' in *Canada: The State of the Federation 1997 – Non-Constitutional Renewal*, ed. Harvey Lazar (Kingston, ON: Institute for Intergovernmental Relations, 1998), 75-6.

Chapter 5: Restructuring Power Relations
1 Brian Mulroney, 'What's in Free Trade for Canada?' *Globe and Mail*, 17 April 2001, A17.
2 George Perlin, 'Opportunity Regained: The Tory Victory in 1984,' in *Canada at the Polls, 1984: A Study of the Federal General Elections*, ed. Howard R. Penniman (Durham, NC: Duke University Press, 1988), 91.
3 Ibid.
4 Paul McCracken et al. *Towards Full Employment and Price Stability* (Paris: Organisation for Economic Co-operation and Development, 1977).
5 Robert O. Keohane, 'Economics, Inflation, and the Role of the State: Political Implications of the McCracken Report,' *World Politics* 31 (October 1978): 108.
6 McCracken et al., *Towards Full Employment*, 189-206.
7 Ibid., 167-72.
8 Ibid., 210-13.
9 Confidential interview, 26 June 1998.
10 Keohane, 'Economics, Inflation, and the Role of the State,' especially p. 122.
11 Milton Friedman, 'The Role of Monetary Policy,' *The American Economic Review* 58, 1 (1968): 1-17. The literature on the NAIRU is voluminous. Two useful sources are: Canada, Royal Commission on the Economic Union and Development Prospects for Canada (The Macdonald Commission), *Report*, vol. 2 (Ottawa: Minister of Supply and Services, 1985), 269-300, especially pp. 275-86; and Cy Gonick, *The Great Economic Debate* (Toronto: James Lorimer, 1987), 24-7.
12 See Paul Krugman, *Peddling Prosperity: Economic Sense and Nonsense in the Age of Diminished Expectations* (New York: W.W. Norton, 1994), chap. 1, for an account of the evolution in economic theory from Keynes to the Phillips Curve to monetarism to the natural rate of unemployment to rational expectations theory.
13 Ibid., 50.
14 See John Sargent, 'Comment: On Macro Public Finance,' in *Retrospectives on Public Finance*, ed. Lorraine Eden (Durham, NC: Duke University Press, 1991), 344-7.
15 Robert Skidelsky, *John Maynard Keynes: The Economist As Saviour, 1920-1937*, vol. 2 (London: Macmillan, 1992), 344.
16 See Arthur W. Donner and Douglas D. Peters, *The Monetarist Counter-Revolution: A Critique of Canadian Monetary Policy 1975-1979* (Toronto: James Lorimer, 1979), 12, on the affinity between monetarism and what they call 'conservatism.'
17 John Shields and Stephen McBride, *Dismantling a Nation: The Transition to a Corporate Rule in Canada*, 2nd ed. (Halifax: Fernwood Press, 1997), 31-3.
18 See, for example, G. Bruce Doern, Allan M. Maslove, and Michael J. Prince, *Public Budgeting in Canada: Politics, Economics, and Management* (Ottawa: Carleton University Press, 1988), 5.
19 Shields and McBride, *Dismantling a Nation*, 32.
20 See Donald J. Savoie, *Thatcher, Reagan, Mulroney: In Search of a New Bureaucracy* (Toronto: University of Toronto Press, 1994). For more on this theme regarding Reagan and Thatcher, see also Paul Pierson, *Dismantling the Welfare State? Reagan, Thatcher, and the Politics of Retrenchment* (New York: Cambridge University Press, 1994).
21 G. Bruce Doern, Leslie A. Pal, and Brian W. Tomlin, 'The Internationalization of Canadian Public Policy,' in *Border Crossings: The Internationalization of Canadian Public Policy* (Toronto: Oxford University Press, 1996), 3.

22   Ibid.
23   See Eric Hobsbawm, *The Age of Capital, 1848-1875* (London: Abacus, 1975).
24   Stephen Gill, 'Knowledge, Politics, and Neo-Liberal Political Economy,' in *Political Economy and the Changing Global Order,* ed. Richard Stubbs and Geoffrey R.D. Underhill (Toronto: McClelland and Stewart, 1994), 85.
25   Ibid., 78-9.
26   Robert B. Reich, *The Work of Nations* (New York: Vintage Books, 1992), 111.
27   Stephen Gill, 'Globalisation, Market Civilisation, and Disciplinary Neoliberalism,' *Millennium: Journal of International Studies* 24, 3 (1995): 405-6.
28   Geoffrey R.D. Underhill, 'Introduction: Conceptualizing the Changing Global Order,' in *Political Economy,* ed. Stubbs and Underhill, 18.
29   For the tight connections between technological advance and American support for the arms industry, see John Kenneth Galbraith, *The New Industrial State,* 4th ed. (Scarborough, ON: Mentor, 1985), 282, 299, 306-8.
30   See Eric Helleiner, *States and the Reemergence of Global Finance: From Bretton Woods to the 1990s* (Ithaca, NY: Cornell University Press, 1994).
31   For this history, see Sylvia Ostry, *The Post-Cold War Trading System: Who's on First* (Chicago: University of Chicago Press, 1997).
32   See Doern, Pal, and Tomlin, 'The Internationalization of Canadian Public Policy,' 3-6 for a definition of the internationalization of public policy. Their basic point is that public policy becomes internationalized as it becomes influenced by factors beyond national territorial boundaries. The state, by contrast, is internationalized to the extent it participates in, and its functions are operated through, supranational forums.
33   See Benjamin Barber, 'Jihad vs. McWorld,' *The Atlantic Monthly,* March 1992, 53-65. For a fascinating discussion that includes global and economic factors in its rich account of contemporary nationalism, see Eric Hobsbawm, *Nations and Nationalism since 1780: Programme, Myth, Reality,* 2nd ed. (New York: Cambridge University Press, 1992), chap. 6.
34   Michael Wilson, *The Budget,* 20 February (Ottawa: Department of Finance, 1990), 15-16.
35   Michael Wilson, *The Budget Speech,* 10 February (Ottawa: Department of Finance, 1988), 5.
36   Keith G. Banting, 'Social Policy,' in *Border Crossings,* ed. Doern, Pal, and Tomlin, 36-7.
37   Ibid., 37.
38   Ibid., 37-8.
39   For a pessimistic assessment of the relationship between these changes and the human condition, see Darin Barney, *Prometheus Wired: The Hope for Democracy in the Age of Network Technology* (Vancouver: UBC Press, 2000).
40   For a masterful review and argument regarding the limits of the globalization hypothesis, see John F. Helliwell, *Globalization: Myths, Facts, and Consequences,* Benefactors Lecture Series, 23 October (Toronto: C.D. Howe Institute, 2000).
41   William Watson, *Globalization and the Meaning of Canadian Life* (Toronto: University of Toronto Press, 1998), 24.
42   Ibid., chap. 4.
43   Paul N. Doremus, William W. Keller, Louis W. Pauly, and Simon Reich, *The Myth of the Global Corporation* (Princeton, NJ: Princeton University Press, 1998).
44   John Helliwell, 'Canada's National Economy: There's More to It Than You Thought,' in *Canada: The State of the Federation 1998/99: How Canadians Connect,* ed. Harvey Lazar and Tom McIntosh (Kingston, ON: Institute of Intergovernmental Relations, 1999).
45   On the argument generally that the globalization hypothesis is exaggerated and that it is an error to view the global economy as ungovernable, see Paul Hirst, 'The Global Economy – Myths and Realities,' *International Affairs* 73, 3 (1997), 409-25.
46   Robert Cox, 'Global Restructuring: Making Sense of the Changing International Political Economy,' in *Political Economy,* 45-50.
47   Maurice Obstfeld, 'The Global Capital Market: Benefactor or Menace?' *The Journal of Economic Perspectives* 12, 4 (1998): 11.
48   See Helliwell, *Globalization,* 7-11, regarding how mobile capital actually is across national borders.

49 Indeed, Peter Drucker argues that the *only* control on 'fiscal irresponsibility' under float-ing exchange rates is speculative money and the threat of currency runs. See Peter F. Drucker, 'The Global Economy and the Nation-State,' *Foreign Affairs* 76, 5 (1997): 162-4. In my view, Drucker misses other constraints on fiscal largesse. See Chapter 9.

50 See Helleiner, *Reemergence of Global Finance,* 12.

51 Elizabeth Smythe, 'Investment Policy,' in *Border Crossings,* ed. Doern, Pal, and Tomlin, 192.

52 Ibid., 197-8. Smythe points out that by 1994, Ottawa interpreted Canadian foreign invest-ment as part of the globalization of production that maintains competitiveness. In other words, Ottawa became even more comfortable with international capital flows over time.

53 Shields and McBride, *Dismantling a Nation,* 28.

54 Maxwell A. Cameron and Brian W. Tomlin, *The Making of NAFTA: How the Deal Was Done* (Ithaca, NY: Cornell University Press, 2000), 29.

55 Michael Wilson, various budget speeches: (23 May 1985), 21; (18 February 1987), 2-3; (10 February 1988), 11-12; (27 April 1989), 3; (20 February 1990), 15-16; and (26 February 1991), 17; Don Mazankowski, *The Budget Speech,* 25 February (Ottawa: Department of Finance, 1992), 2, 11-12; Don Mazankowski, *The Budget Speech,* 26 April (Ottawa: Depart-ment of Finance, 1993), 3.

56 In this regard Frances Abele misses several years in claiming that 'at least' since the con-clusion of the 1989-90 free trade debates, deficit and debt reduction have been linked to international concern about Canadian competitiveness and Canada's attractiveness to investment. See Frances Abele, 'The Politics of Competitiveness,' in *How Ottawa Spends: The Politics of Competitiveness – 1992-93,* ed. Frances Abele (Ottawa: Carleton University Press, 1992), 12.

57 Gill, 'Globalisation, Market Civilisation,' 411-12.

58 See Neil Bradford, *Commissioning Ideas: Canadian National Policy Innovation in Comparative Perspective* (Toronto: Oxford University Press, 1998), 15-16.

59 The major tenet of Fordism, that high wages ensure demand for products, was accepted in the postwar era not so much because high wages were thought of as good by business as because growth acted as a solvent permitting both meeting wage demands and reason-able profit levels. See Gonick, *Great Economic Debate,* 331-2. There was no urgency to the issue.

60 Harold Chorney, *The Deficit and Debt Management: An Alternative to Monetarism* (Ottawa: Canadian Centre for Policy Alternatives, 1989), 7-24.

61 David A. Wolfe, 'The Crisis in Advanced Capitalism: An Introduction,' *Studies in Political Economy* 11 (Summer 1983): 12.

62 Ibid., 12-13. See also Gonick, *Great Economic Debate,* 327-44.

63 Wolfe, 'Crisis in Advanced Capitalism,' 13-14.

64 Frank Strain and Hugh Grant 'The Social Structure of Accumulation in Canada, 1945-1988,' *Journal of Canadian Studies* 26, 4 (1991-2): 81-3. See also Michael Bruno and Jeffrey D. Sachs, *Economics of Worldwide Stagflation* (Oxford: Basil Blackwell, 1985), 162-4, for comparative and Canadian measures of declining pre-tax returns to manufacturing capi-tal and declining growth of manufacturing capital stock from the early 1960s to the early 1980s.

65 Stephen Clarkson and Christina McCall, *Trudeau and Our Times,* vol. 2, *The Heroic Delusion* (Toronto: McClelland and Stewart, 1994), 111.

66 Stephen Clarkson, 'Disjunctions: Free Trade and the Paradox of Canadian Development,' in *The New Era of Global Competition: State Policy and Market Power,* ed. Daniel Drache and Meric Gertler (Montreal and Kingston: McGill-Queen's University Press, 1991), 113.

67 Ibid., 113-14.

68 David Langille, 'The Business Council on National Issues and the Canadian State,' *Studies in Political Economy* 24 (Autumn 1987): 42-3.

69 Michael M. Atkinson and William D. Coleman, *The State, Business, and Industrial Change in Canada* (Toronto: University of Toronto Press, 1989), 48-9.

70 Langille, 'Business Council on National Issues,' 45.

71 Atkinson and Coleman, *State, Business, and Industrial Change,* 49.

72   G. Bruce Doern and Brian W. Tomlin, *Faith and Fear: The Free Trade Story* (Toronto: Stoddart, 1991), 49.

73   Atkinson and Coleman, *State, Business, and Industrial Change,* 49.

74   Doern and Tomlin, *Faith and Fear,* 53.

75   Bradford, *Commissioning Ideas,* 112. Bradford notes that while the business submissions were criticized by the commissioners for their predictability and shallowness, think tanks like the C.D. Howe Institute and the Economic Council of Canada gave more expert formulations.

76   Doern and Tomlin, *Faith and Fear,* 49.

77   Richard Simeon, 'Inside the Macdonald Commission,' *Studies in Political Economy* 22 (Spring 1987): 173-4.

78   Ibid., 174-6.

79   Neil Bradford, 'The Policy Influence of Economic Ideas: Interests, Institutions and Innovation in Canada,' *Studies in Political Economy* 59 (Summer 1999): 35.

80   Duncan Cameron and Daniel Drache, 'Outside the Macdonald Commission: Reply to Richard Simeon,' *Studies in Political Economy* 26 (Summer 1988): 174-7.

81   Ibid., 180.

82   Simeon, 'Inside the Macdonald Commission,' 168.

83   Doern and Tomlin, *Faith and Fear,* 57; Bradford, *Commissioning Ideas,* 119-20.

84   Bradford, *Commissioning Ideas,* 120.

85   Michael Wilson, *A New Direction for Canada – An Agenda for Economic Renewal* (Ottawa: Department of Finance, 1984), 32-3. See also Doern and Tomlin, *Faith and Fear,* 31.

86   Doern and Tomlin, *Faith and Fear,* 227.

87   Ibid., 31.

88   Ibid., 140-1.

89   See Stephen Clarkson and Timothy Lewis, 'The Contested State: Canada in the Post-Cold War, Post-Keynesian, Post-Fordist, Post-National Era,' in *How Ottawa Spends 1999-2000 – Shape Shifting: Canadian Governance toward the 21st Century,* ed. Leslie A. Pal (Toronto: Oxford University Press Canada, 1999), 298-9, 302-3.

90   Canada, Royal Commission on the Economic Union and Development Prospects for Canada (The Macdonald Commission), *Report,* vol. 1 (Ottawa: Minister of Supply and Services, 1985), 357. Reproduced with the permission of the Minister of Public Works and Government Services, 2002, and Courtesy of the Privy Council Office.

91   On Ontario's evolution in the federation, see David R. Cameron, 'Post-Modern Ontario and the Laurentian Thesis' in *Canada: State of the Federation 1994,* ed. Douglas Brown and Janet Hiebert (Kingston, ON: Institute of Intergovernmental Relations, 1994); Sid Noel, 'Ontario and the Federation at the End of the Twentieth Century,' in *Canada: The State of the Federation 1997: Non-Constitutional Renewal,* ed. Harvey Lazar (Kingston, ON: Institute of Intergovernmental Relations, 1998); Thomas J. Courchene, with Colin R. Telmer, *From Heartland to North American Region State: The Social, Fiscal, and Federal Evolution of Ontario – An Interpretive Essay,* Monograph Series on Public Policy and Public Administration no. 6 (Toronto: University of Toronto, Faculty of Management, 1998); *Ontario: Exploring the Region-State Hypothesis,* Proceedings of a Colloquium held at the University of Toronto, 26 March 1999, University of Toronto, Department of Political Science, 1999.

92   On the incoherence of Mulroney's coalition, see R.K. Carty, 'On the Road Again: The Stalled Omnibus Revisited,' in *Canadian Political Party Systems: A Reader,* ed. R.K. Carty (Peterborough, ON: Broadview Press, 1992), 639. For an excellent history of the Meech Lake round of constitutional reform, see Peter Russell, *Constitutional Odyssey: Can the Canadians Become a Sovereign People?* 2nd ed. (Toronto: University of Toronto Press, 1993), chap. 9.

93   Doern and Tomlin, *Faith and Fear,* 241.

94   H.D. Forbes, 'Absent Mandate 88? Parties and Voters in Canada,' in *Party Politics in Canada,* 6th ed., ed. Hugh Thorburn (Scarborough, ON: Prentice Hall Canada, 1991), 255-70. The view that this election produced a mandate is challenged in Harold D. Clarke, Lawrence Leduc, Jane Jenson, and Jon H. Pammett, *Absent Mandate: Interpreting Change in Canadian Elections* (Toronto: Gage, 1991). By Leduc and others' standards, a mandate

would be almost impossible to obtain. Their criteria are that a person must have (1) voted; (2) identified free trade as the most important election issue; (3) specified that issues were the major reason for their voting decision; (4) had their view on free trade affect their vote at least somewhat; and (5) voted for a party having the same position on free trade as the voter. Since most voters did not meet these criteria, and those who did split pretty evenly, they conclude that 'the existence of such evenly balanced minorities indicates that no policy mandate for the Free Trade Agreement emerged from the voting in the 1988 Canadian federal election' (146-8). So measured, I doubt that it would ever be possible to obtain a mandate regarding a contentious issue. For the rather sunny view that the 1988 election was an instance of citizens democratically determining their country's future, see Richard Johnston, André Blais, Henry E. Brady, and Jean Crête, *Letting the People Decide: Dynamics of a Canadian Election* (Montreal and Kingston: McGill-Queen's University Press, 1992), 15.

95 On the significance of Canadian Royal Commissions, see G. Bruce Doern, 'The Role of Royal Commissions in the General Policy Process and in Federal-Provincial Relations,' *Canadian Public Administration* 10, 4 (1967): 417-33.

96 Langille, 'The Business Council on National Issues,' 59.

97 Michael Ornstein, 'The Social Organization of the Canadian Capitalist Class in Comparative Perspective,' *Canadian Review of Sociology and Anthropology* 26, 1 (1989): 154.

Chapter 6: The Priority of Structural Reform, 1984-93

1 Brian Mulroney, 'Reflections of a Former Prime Minister,' interview by Brian Stewart, *The National,* CBC television, 2 June 1999.

2 In some contrast, the notion of 'punctuated equilibrium' holds that change is not a slow continuous process but rather occurs in short bursts. Stephen D. Krasner, 'Approaches to the State: Alternative Conceptions and Historical Dynamics,' *Comparative Politics* 16, 2 (1984): 242-3.

3 Edward Greenspon and Anthony Wilson-Smith, *Double Vision: The Inside Story of the Liberals in Power* (Toronto: Doubleday Canada, 1996), 54.

4 Confidential interview, 25 January 2001.

5 G. Bruce Doern and Brian W. Tomlin, *Faith and Fear: The Free Trade Story* (Toronto: Stoddart, 1991), 23.

6 Confidential interview, 25 January 2001.

7 Michael Wilson, *A New Direction for Canada – An Agenda for Economic Renewal* (Ottawa: Department of Finance, 1984), 19.

8 Ibid., 1.

9 Ibid., 1-2.

10 Ibid., 2; Michael Wilson, *Economic and Fiscal Statement,* 8 November (Canada: Department of Finance, 1984), 2.

11 Wilson, *A New Direction,* 2-3; Wilson, *Economic and Fiscal Statement,* 2-3.

12 The agenda for renewal recommended reform in nine areas: research and development, innovation, and technology diffusion; export markets and financing; private sector investment; labour markets and human resources; adapting to economic and technological change; the regional dimension to growth and competitiveness; economic regulation and intervention; energy policy; and coordination with the provinces. Wilson, *A New Direction,* 23-66.

13 Michael Wilson, *Reducing the Deficit and Controlling the National Debt,* November (Ottawa: Department of Finance, 1985), iii.

14 Taki Sarantakis, 'Of Deficits and Debt: Rolling Back the Post-Prosperous Canadian State,' unpublished paper, Toronto.

15 Richard Johnston, André Blais, Henry E. Brady, and Jean Crête, *Letting the People Decide: Dynamics of a Canadian Election* (Montreal and Kingston: McGill-Queen's University Press, 1992), 4, 248-9.

16 Wilson, *Economic and Fiscal Statement,* 4.

17 Wilson, *A New Direction for Canada,* 10.

18 Ibid., 16.

19 Ibid., 19.
20 Confidential interview, 25 January 2001.
21 Confidential interview, 25 January 2001; confidential interview, 30 January 2001.
22 Confidential interview, 25 January 2001; confidential interview, 30 January 2001.
23 Confidential interview, 25 January 2001.
24 See Chapter 4 for a more detailed analysis of Marc Lalonde, *The Federal Deficit in Perspective,* 19 April (Ottawa: Department of Finance, 1983).
25 Wilson, *Reducing the Deficit,* 7.
26 The real rate of interest is simply the nominal rate of interest less the rate of inflation.
27 Wilson, *Reducing the Deficit,* 11-12.
28 Ibid., 13.
29 Michael Wilson, *Budget Speech,* 23 May (Ottawa: Department of Finance, 1985), 16.
30 Compare Marc Lalonde, *The Fiscal Plan,* 15 February (Ottawa: Department of Finance, 1984), 5, with Michael Wilson, *The Fiscal Plan,* 23 May (Ottawa: Department of Finance, 1985), 24.
31 Wilson, *Reducing the Deficit,* 17.
32 Richard G. Lipsey, Paul N. Courant, and Douglas D. Purvis, *Economics,* 8th Canadian ed. (New York: HarperCollins, 1994), 720-1.
33 Wilson, *Reducing the Deficit,* 17.
34 Wilson, *A New Direction for Canada,* 84.
35 Wilson, *Budget Speech* (1985), 18.
36 Ibid., 21.
37 Wilson, *Reducing the Deficit,* 20
38 Wilson, *Budget Speech* (1985), 5
39 Wilson, *A New Direction for Canada,* 67, 84.
40 Ibid., 69.
41 Ibid., 14.
42 Ibid., 69.
43 Canadian Press, 'Deficit Numbers Belie Tory Claims,' *Globe and Mail,* 9 November 1984, A11.
44 Lawrence Martin, 'Mulroney Says Turner Hiding Economic Contingency Plans,' *Globe and Mail,* 18 August 1984, A1-A2.
45 House of Commons, *Debates,* 7 November 1984, 22-3.
46 John Richards 'Reducing the Muddle in the Middle: Three Propositions for Running the Welfare State,' in *Canada: The State of the Federation 1997 – Non-Constitutional Renewal,* ed. Harvey Lazar (Kingston, ON: Institute for Intergovernmental Relations, 1998), 76.
47 House of Commons, *Debates,* 7 November 1984, 31-8, especially p. 32.
48 Ibid., 42-3
49 Michael Wilson, *The Budget Speech,* 26 February (Ottawa: Department of Finance, 1986), 16.
50 Michael Wilson, *The Fiscal Plan,* 26 February (Ottawa: Department of Finance, 1986), 16-17.
51 Bruce Little, 'Wilson Says Public Backs Him,' *Globe and Mail,* 25 May 1985, A1-A2.
52 Wilson, *Budget Speech* (1985), 19.
53 Ibid., 6.
54 Wilson, *Fiscal Plan* (1986), 40-1.
55 Bruce Little and Christopher Waddell, 'Dollar's Fall Sets Stage for Deficit-Cutting Budget,' *Globe and Mail,* 26 February 1986, A1, A4.
56 See W. Irwin Gillespie, *Tax, Borrow and Spend: Financing Federal Spending in Canada, 1867-1990* (Ottawa: Carleton University Press, 1991), 202-5.
57 Allan M. Maslove, 'What Really Happened with Tax Reform,' *Policy Options* 10, 1 (1989): 18.
58 Ibid.
59 Gillespie, *Tax, Borrow and Spend,* 223-4.
60 Wilson, *Economic and Fiscal Statement,* 13.
61 Department of Finance, *Budget Papers,* 26 February (Ottawa: Department of Finance, 1986), 23-4.

62 Michael Wilson, *The Agenda for Economic Renewal: Principles and Progress,* 18 February (Ottawa: Department of Finance, 1987), 12.

63 Ross Howard and Cathryn Motherwell, 'What's Good for Toronto Called Bad for East, West,' *Globe and Mail,* 19 February 1987, B10.

64 Donald J. Savoie, *The Politics of Public Spending in Canada* (Toronto: University of Toronto Press, 1990), 177.

65 Robert M. Campbell, 'Jobs ... Job ... Jo ... J ... The Conservatives and the Unemployed,' in *How Ottawa Spends: The Politics of Competitiveness – 1992-93,* ed. Frances Abele (Ottawa: Carleton University Press, 1992), 41.

66 Savoie, *The Politics of Public Spending,* 163-71.

67 Ibid., 171.

68 Donald Savoie, *Governing from the Centre: The Concentration of Power in Canadian Politics* (Toronto: University of Toronto Press, 1999), 170; confidential interview, 25 January 2001.

69 Savoie, *The Politics of Public Spending,* 132-42.

70 Ibid., 348-56.

71 Wilson, *A New Direction for Canada,* 71, 87.

72 Thomas Walkom, 'PM Changes Stand on Social Programs,' *Globe and Mail,* 10 November 1984, A1, A2.

73 Neil Bradford, *Commissioning Ideas: Canadian National Policy Innovation in Comparative Perspective* (Toronto: Oxford University Press, 1998), 118.

74 Greenspon and Wilson-Smith, *Double Vision,* 126.

75 Michael J. Prince, 'From Health and Welfare to Stealth and Farewell: Federal Social Policy, 1980-2000,' in *How Ottawa Spends 1999-2000 – Shape Shifting: Canadian Governance toward the 21st Century,* ed. Leslie A. Pal (Toronto: Oxford University Press Canada, 1999), 170.

76 Peter Aucoin, 'Organizational Change in the Management of Canadian Government: From Rational Management to Brokerage Politics,' *Canadian Journal of Political Science* 19, 1 (1986): 691-709.

77 Savoie, *Governing from the Centre,* 170.

78 See Ken Battle and Sherri Torjman, *Federal Social Programs: Setting the Record Straight* (Ottawa: Caledon Institute for Social Policy, 1993). Battle and Torjman trace and detail all the initiatives the Mulroney government took with respect to social programs, and there was clearly important retrenchment. As they also argue, this was largely done by arcane technical changes that few people understood (7). See also Prince, 'From Health and Welfare to Stealth and Farewell,' 171-2; and Bradford, *Commissioning Ideas,* 121-2, for descriptions of the 'politics of stealth' in the income security field.

79 Don Mazankowski, *The Budget Speech,* 25 February (Ottawa: Department of Finance, 1992), 14-15.

80 Geoffrey York, 'Government Scraps Day-Care Commitment,' *Globe and Mail,* 27 February 1992, A1, A8.

81 Michael Wilson, *The Fiscal Plan: Controlling the Public Debt,* 27 April (Ottawa: Department of Finance, 1989), 39.

82 Doern and Tomlin, *Faith and Fear,* 228-9.

83 Michael Wilson, *The Budget Speech,* 10 February (Ottawa: Department of Finance, 1988), 9-10.

84 Ross Howard, 'Opposition Leaders Say Minister Has Given Them Election Weapon,' *Globe and Mail,* 11 February 1988, B14.

85 Wilson, *Budget Speech* (1985), 3.

86 Wilson, *Budget Speech* (1988), 8.

87 Michael Wilson, *The Budget Speech,* 27 April (Ottawa: Department of Finance, 1989), 3.

88 Ibid.

89 Thomas J. Courchene, with Colin R. Telmer, *From Heartland to North American Region State: The Social, Fiscal, and Federal Evolution of Ontario – An Interpretive Essay,* Monograph Series on Public Policy and Public Administration no. 6 (Toronto: University of Toronto, Faculty of Management, 1998), 100.

90 Jeffrey Simpson, 'Squaring off at Budget Time,' *Globe and Mail,* 20 February 1990, A6.

91 Ibid.

92 Confidential interview, 25 January 2001; confidential interview, 2 June 1998.
93 David A. Dodge, 'Reflections on the Role of Fiscal Policy: The Doug Purvis Memorial Lecture,' *Canadian Public Policy* 24, 3 (1998): 280.
94 Bank of Canada Act, *Revised Statutes of Canada*, 1985, c. B-2.
95 John W. Crow, 'The Bank of Canada and Its Objectives,' *Bank of Canada Review* (April 1987): 21-2.
96 William D. Coleman, 'Monetary Policy, Accountability, and Legitimacy: A Review of the Issues in Canada,' *Canadian Journal of Political Science* 24, 4 (December 1991): 718. Actually, price stability and zero-inflation are not necessarily the same thing. The bank's 'official' goal is the former, which may or may not be defined as the latter. For instance, a one-time price rise would not, after the first year, be counted as inflation, yet prices would not have been stable. As an academic exercise, at least, defining price stability is a task that the bank is beginning to think about seriously. Confidential interviews with Bank of Canada officials, 2 June 1998. See Bank of Canada, *Price Stability, Inflation Targets, and Monetary Policy*, Proceedings of a conference held by the Bank of Canada, May 1997 (Ottawa: Bank of Canada, 1998).
97 Confidential interview, 2 June 1998.
98 Stephen Clarkson and Christina McCall, *Trudeau and Our Times*, vol. 2, *The Heroic Delusion* (Toronto: McClelland and Stewart, 1994), 127-8.
99 Confidential interview, 2 June 1998.
100 Ibid.
101 Ibid. At least one commentator argued that partial deindexation undermined the credibility of the price stability policy. See D. Johnson, 'An Evaluation of the Bank of Canada Zero Inflation Target: Do Wilson and Crow Agree?' *Canadian Public Policy* 16, 3 (1990): 308-25.
102 Dodge, 'Reflections on the Role of Fiscal Policy,' 281; confidential interview, 25 January 2001.
103 Confidential interview, 2 June 1998.
104 Confidential interview, 25 January 2001.
105 Harold Chorney argues that inflation in southern Ontario, particularly Toronto, was caused by real estate speculation and the capital gains exemption. It was therefore preventable without harsh monetary contraction. *The Deficit and Debt Management: An Alternative to Monetarism* (Ottawa: Canadian Centre for Policy Alternatives, 1989), 70-1.
106 Wilson, *Budget Speech* (1989), 4.
107 Paul Jenkins and Brian O'Reilly, 'Monetary Policy and the Economic Well-Being of Canadians,' in *The Review of Economic Performance and Social Progress – The Longest Decade: Canada in the 1990s*, ed. Keith G. Banting, Andrew Sharpe, and France St-Hilaire (Montreal: Institute for Research on Public Policy, 2001), 95.
108 Wilson, *The Fiscal Plan* (1989), 10-11.
109 Wilson, *Budget Speech* (1989), 4.
110 Ibid., 6-13.
111 Ross Howard, 'Budget a Betrayal, Opposition Says,' *Globe and Mail*, 29 April 1989, A1-A2.
112 Michael Wilson, *The Budget*, 20 February (Ottawa: Department of Finance, 1990), 3.
113 Ibid., 10.
114 Ibid.
115 Ibid., 43.
116 Ibid., 12.
117 Confidential interview, 2 June 1998.
118 Pierre Fortin, 'The Great Canadian Slump," *Canadian Journal of Economics* 29, 4 (1996): 783.
119 See Charles Freedman and Tiff Macklem, 'A Comment on "The Great Canadian Slump,"' *Canadian Journal of Economics* 31, 3 (1998): 648-50, 659.
120 OECD data indicates that in the second half of 1990, growth in the United States was 0.3 percent, while growth in Canada was -1.9 percent. Organisation for Economic Co-operation and Development, *OECD Economic Outlook* 49, July (Paris: Organisation for Economic Co-operation and Development, 1991).
121 Pierre Fortin, 'The Canadian Fiscal Problem: The Macroeconomic Connection,' in *Hard*

Money, Hard Times: Why Zero Inflation Hurts Canadians, ed. Lars Osberg and Pierre Fortin (Toronto: James Lorimer, 1998).

122 Freedman and Macklem, 'A Comment on,' 659. A Bank of Canada economist argues that the main difference between the bank and Fortin relates to views of the capacity of the economy. Fortin sees unemployment of 7.5 percent as consistent with potential output through the 1980s. Since unemployment was almost always above this level during the 1980s, in his view policy was too restrictive. The bank view is that unemployment of 7.5 percent was inflationary, and so looser money was inappropriate. Confidential interview, 2 June 1998.

123 The debate continues. See Pierre Fortin, 'The Great Canadian Slump: A Rejoinder to Freedman and Macklem,' *Canadian Journal of Economics* 32, 4 (1999): 1082-92; and Pierre Fortin 'The Canadian Standard of Living: Is There a Way Up?' C.D. Howe Institute Benefactors Lecture, 19 October 1999. Bank economists (nominally writing on their own behalf) and Fortin continue to joust as well regarding the appropriateness of bank policy in the second half of the 1990s, and particularly regarding the precise inflation targets. See Pierre Fortin, 'Interest Rates, Unemployment and Inflation: The Canadian Experience in the 1990s,' and Jenkins and O'Reilly, 'Monetary Policy and the Economic Well-Being,' in *The Review of Economic Performance,* ed. Banting, Sharpe, and St-Hilaire. I would note that the Bank of Canada cannot admit that price stability as implemented was a major error in the late 1980s and early 1990s, because doing so would impugn its continuing policy stance and undermine the anti-inflation credibility the bank built in that era.

124 See Johnson, 'An Evaluation of the Bank of Canada Zero Inflation Target'; R. Lucas, 'The Bank of Canada and Zero Inflation: A New Cross of Gold?' *Canadian Public Policy* 15, 1 (1989): 84-93; Andrew Jackson, *Against John Crow: A Critique of Current Monetary Policy and Proposals for an Alternative* (Ottawa: Canadian Centre for Policy Alternatives, 1990); Fortin, 'The Great Canadian Slump,' and 'The Canadian Fiscal Problem'; and Thomas Courchene, 'Zero Means Almost Nothing: Towards a Preferable Inflation and Macro Stance,' in *Rearrangements: The Courchene Papers* (Oakville, ON: Mosaic Press, 1992).

125 Douglas Curtis, 'Canadian Fiscal and Monetary Policy and Macroeconomic Performance 1984-1993: The Mulroney Years,' *Journal of Canadian Studies* 32, 1 (1997): 151.

126 Daniel Trefler, *The Long and Short of the Canada-U.S. Free Trade Agreement* (Ottawa: Industry Canada Research Publications Program, 1999), 22. See also Andrew Jackson, 'From Leaps of Faith to Lapses of Logic,' *Policy Options* 20, 5 (1999): 16.

127 John McCallum, 'Two Cheers for the FTA,' *Policy Options* 20, 5 (1999): 11.

128 Michael Wilson, *The Fiscal Plan,* 10 February (Ottawa: Department of Finance, 1988), 33; Wilson, *The Fiscal Plan* (1989), 45; Wilson, *The Budget* (1990), 106-7.

129 Dodge, 'Reflections on the Role of Fiscal Policy,' 281.

130 Thomas Courchene, 'Mon pays, c'est l'hiver: Reflections of a Market Populist,' *Canadian Journal of Economics* 25, 4 (1992): 766-7.

131 Canada, Royal Commission on the Economic Union and Development Prospects for Canada (The Macdonald Commission), *Report,* vol. 1 (Ottawa: Minister of Supply and Services, 1985), 316-18.

132 Ibid., 317.

133 Duncan Cameron argues that the adjustment effects, predicted by both critics and advocates of the FTA, were much more swift and severe than anticipated. Whether a one-time adjustment to new market conditions or a trend to permanent weakness due to Canadian incentives to invest in the United States, permanent job loss out of the 1990-1 recession was perhaps 60 percent of total job loss, as opposed to 25 percent after the 1981-2 recession. Cameron also posits that the 'zero-inflation' policy of the Bank of Canada was a culprit, and that it, in conjunction with free trade adjustment, caused the 'made-in-Canada' recession. See Duncan Cameron, Introduction to *Canada under Free Trade,* ed. Duncan Cameron and Mel Watkins (Toronto: James Lorimer, 1993), xiv-xv.

134 See Louis Pauly, *Who Elected the Bankers?* (Ithaca, NY: Cornell University Press, 1997), 20-9; and Maurice Obstfeld, 'The Global Capital Market: Benefactor or Menace?' *The Journal of Economic Perspectives* 12, 4 (1998): 14.

135 Another approach, which would have rescued the government from the problem that,

under conditions of capital mobility, it could control either the exchange rate or monetary policy, but not both, would have been financial re-regulation that put controls on capital. See Andrew Jackson, *Deficit, Debt and the Contradictions of Tory Economics* (Ottawa: Canadian Centre for Policy Alternatives, 1990). But such an approach was politically chimerical in an age of ascendent financial capital and neo-liberal discipline.

136   Alan Freeman, 'Fight Recession, Not Deficit, Liberals, NDP Urge Wilson,' *Globe and Mail,* 25 February 1991, A6.
137   Michael Wilson, *The Budget Speech,* 26 February (Ottawa: Department of Finance, 1991), 5.
138   Drew Fagan, 'Spending Increases Decried,' *Globe and Mail,* 27 February 1991, B1, B6.
139   Wilson, *Budget Speech* (1991), 7.
140   Mazankowski, *Budget Speech* (1992) 12-16.
141   Ibid., 19.
142   Don Mazankowski, *Budget Papers,* 25 February (Ottawa: Department of Finance, 1992), 49.
143   Hugh Winsor, 'Tories Borrow from Reform Party,' *Globe and Mail,* 26 February 1992, A1, A6.
144   Mazankowski, *Budget Papers* (1992), 71.
145   Don Mazankowski, *The Budget Speech,* 26 April (Ottawa: Department of Finance, 1993), 19.
146   Michael Wilson, *The Budget,* 26 February (Ottawa: Department of Finance, 1991), 114.
147   John Maynard Keynes, *The Economic Consequences of the Peace,* vol. 2 of *The Collected Writings of John Maynard Keynes,* ed. Donald Moggridge (1919; reprint, London: Macmillan, 1971), 148-9.
148   See Paul Krugman, *Peddling Prosperity: Economic Sense and Nonsense in the Age of Diminished Expectations* (New York: W.W. Norton, 1994), chap. 10, appendix to chap. 10.
149   Niccolò Machiavelli, *The Prince,* in *The Portable Machiavelli,* ed. Peter Bondanella and Mark Musa (Toronto: Penguin Books Canada, 1979), 159.
150   Karl Polanyi, *The Great Transformation: The Political and Economic Origins of Our Time* (1944; reprint, Boston: Beacon Press, 1957), 36-7.
151   Michael Wilson, *A New Direction for Canada,* 84.

Chapter 7: Economic Insecurity and the Political Conditions for Deficit Elimination

1   Liberal Party of Canada, *Creating Opportunity: The Liberal Plan for Canada* (Ottawa: Liberal Party of Canada, 1993), 91-5. On the improprieties of the Mulroney government, see Stevie Cameron, *On the Take: Crime, Corruption and Greed in the Mulroney Years* (Toronto: Macfarlane Walter and Ross, 1994).
2   Liberal Party of Canada, *Creating Opportunity,* 15-26.
3   Don Mazankowski, *The Budget Speech,* 26 April (Ottawa: Department of Finance, 1993), 19.
4   Liberal Party of Canada, *Creating Opportunity,* 62-89; 96-103.
5   Liberal Party of Canada, *A Record of Achievement: A Report on the Liberal Government's 36 Months in Office* (Ottawa: Liberal Party of Canada, 1996).
6   On the relationship between the budgetary balance and social spending, and particularly the link between deficit elimination and declining social spending, see Ken Battle, 'Relentless Incrementalism: Deconstructing and Reconstructing Canadian Income Security Policy,' in *The Review of Economic Performance and Social Progress – The Longest Decade: Canada in the 1990s,* ed. Keith G. Banting, Andrew Sharpe, and France St-Hilaire (Montreal: Institute for Research on Public Policy, 2001), 191-2.
7   Gordon Betcherman, 'Inside the Black Box: Human Resource Management and the Labor Market,' in *Good Jobs, Bad Jobs, No Jobs: Tough Choices for Canadian Labor Law,* ed. John Richards and William G. Watson (Toronto: C.D. Howe Institute, 1995), 72. For an interpretation of economic insecurity in the American context, see Jerald Wallulis, *The New Insecurity: The End of the Standard Job and Family* (Albany, NY: State University of New York Press, 1998).
8   Lars Osberg and Andrew Sharpe, 'Trends in Economic Well-Being in Canada in the 1990s,' in *The Review of Economic Performance,* 240-1.

9 Frank L. Graves, 'The Economy through a Public Lens: Shifting Canadian Views of the Economy,' in *The Review of Economic Performance*, ed. Banting et al. 72-3. See also Frank L. Graves, 'Rethinking Government As If People Mattered: From "Reaganomics" to "Humanomics,"' in *How Ottawa Spends 1999-2000: Shape Shifting: Canadian Governance Toward the 21st Century*, ed. Leslie A. Pal (Toronto: Oxford University Press, 1999), 43-5. Graves notes that insecurity goes beyond the economic sphere and includes fears regarding identity, culture, and values. It is no coincidence that Reform, the party that spoke most clearly to insecurity in Canadian life, in addition to attacking the deficit and taxes, also had an agenda regarding getting tough on each of crime, Quebec, and affirmative action.
10 Battle, 'Relentless Incrementalism,' 193.
11 For an argument that meaning requires interpretation, see Michael Walzer, *Interpretation and Social Criticism* (Cambridge, MA: Harvard University Press, 1987), especially p. 26.
12 Some of the data I use in this section disaggregate various economic groups, but not along certain demographic lines, such as region, gender, and age. There are no doubt interesting things to learn through these lenses, and there were surely differences in how things broke out between the West and the East, women and men, and the young and old. However, my enterprise is not to argue that this group or that group was objectively particularly insecure and therefore supported certain policies or parties. The broad direction of change regarding the role of the state in the economy is what matters for my purposes, and the argument is located in a generalized experience of economic insecurity given form by parties articulating a concomitant vision of the state's economic role. A very large majority of voters wound up supporting neo-liberal parties that advocated balanced budgets and concomitant policies. For some quantitative evidence of the mass public's rightward shift between 1993 and 1997, see Neil Nevitte, André Blais, Elisabeth Gidengil, and Richard Nadeau, *Unsteady State: The 1997 Canadian Federal Election* (Toronto: Oxford University Press, 2000), chap. 4, especially pp. 52-4 and p. 57.
13 Pierre Fortin, 'The Canadian Fiscal Problem: The Macroeconomic Connection,' in *Hard Money, Hard Times: Why Zero Inflation Hurts Canadians*, ed. Lars Osberg and Pierre Fortin (Toronto: James Lorimer, 1998), 32.
14 Ibid.
15 Pierre Fortin, 'The Great Canadian Slump,' *Canadian Journal of Economics* 29, 4 (1996), 762.
16 Ibid., 761.
17 Ibid., 762.
18 Douglas Curtis, 'Canadian Fiscal and Monetary Policy and Macroeconomic Performance 1984-1993: The Mulroney Years,' *Journal of Canadian Studies* 32, 1 (1997): 137-8.
19 Pierre Fortin, *The Canadian Standard of Living: Is There a Way Up?* Benefactors Lecture Series, 19 October (Toronto: C.D. Howe Institute, 1999), 39.
20 Ibid., 39-40.
21 Charles Freedman and Tiff Macklem, 'A Comment on "The Great Canadian Slump,"' *Canadian Journal of Economics* 31, 3 (1998): 663.
22 Fortin, *The Canadian Standard of Living*, 38.
23 Freedman and Macklem, 'A Comment,' 663.
24 Paul Martin, *The Budget Plan*, 28 February (Ottawa: Department of Finance, 2000), 179-80. The total government sector includes the federal, provincial, and local governments, along with the Canada Pension Plan and Quebec Pension Plan.
25 Roderick Hill, 'Real Income, Unemployment and Subjective Well-Being: Revisiting the Costs and Benefits of Inflation Reduction in Canada,' *Canadian Public Policy* 26, 4 (2000): 399-414.
26 Ken Battle and Sherri Torjman, *Federal Social Programs: Setting the Record Straight* (Ottawa: Caledon Institute for Social Policy, 1993), 7.
27 Fortin, *The Canadian Standard of Living*, 4-6.
28 For individuals, between 1990 and 1995 real incomes declined by 6 percent. For families, real incomes fell by 4.8 percent between 1990 and 1995. See Statistics Canada, *The Daily: 1996 Census: Sources of Income, Earnings and Total Income, and Family Income*, 12 May 1998 (Ottawa), information from the Nation Series, package no. 9, Catalogue no. 93FOO29XDB96000.

29 Fortin, *The Canadian Standard of Living*, 6-10.
30 Statistics Canada, 'Population 15 Years and Over by Sex, Age Groups and Labour Force Activity, for Canada, Provinces and Territories, 1981-1996 Censuses,' selected from Catalogue no. 93F0027XDB96001 in the Nation Series. (Data originally located at <www.statcan.ca>.)
31 W. Craig Riddell, 'Employment and Unemployment in Canada: Assessing Recent Experience,' *Policy Options* 17, 6 (1996): 9-14.
32 Betcherman, 'Inside the Black Box,' 74-5.
33 Fortin, *The Canadian Standard of Living*, 22, 24.
34 Ibid., 15.
35 Betcherman, 'Inside the Black Box,' 74-5.
36 Ibid., 76.
37 See Harvey Krahn, 'Non-Standard Work on the Rise,' *Perspectives on Labour and Income* 7, 4 (1995): 35-8.
38 That 'flexibility' in work was rather more desired by employers than employees is indicated by the decline in self-employment that emerged as the economy picked up steam in the late 1990s and demand for employees rose. Jim Stanford noticed this trend, and argued economic growth suggested that people could now choose between options, and the choice was pretty clear. Self-employment (including self-employed small employers) accounted for 75 percent of net job growth between 1990 and 1997. The self-employed portion of the population, so defined, grew from 14 percent to 18 percent. By the end of 2000, the proportion was 15.7 percent and falling. Small business profits were rising and still people were moving to more stable wage and salary employment. But from 1990 until at least 1997, incentives were structured such that Canadians had to turn to options they experienced as relatively unpalatable. See Jim Stanford, 'I'm the Boss Here, and I'm Firing Myself,' *Globe and Mail*, 2 January 2001, A13.
39 See Peter Stoyko, 'Creating Opportunity or Creative Opportunism? Liberal Labour Market Policy,' in *How Ottawa Spends 1997-98 – Seeing Red: A Liberal Report Card*, ed. Gene Swimmer (Ottawa: Carleton University Press, 1997), 91. The small business sector had 42 to 48 percent of job gains and 37 to 40 percent of job losses between 1978 and 1992.
40 Canada has experienced a polarization in hours of work (Battle, 'Relentless Incrementalism,' 193).
41 Jim Stanford, 'A Fred Astaire Budget,' *Policy Options* 21, 3 (2000): 11; Fortin, *The Canadian Standard of Living*, 58.
42 Stanford, 'A Fred Astaire Budget,' 10-11.
43 Some political scientists argue that value change in the industrial democracies shows decreasing concern with 'material' issues and greater concern with 'post-material' matters. See, for example, Neil Nevitte, *The Decline of Deference: Canadian Value Change in Cross-National Perspective* (Peterborough, ON: Broadview Press, 1996); Ronald Inglehart, *The Silent Revolution: Changing Values and Political Styles among Western Publics* (Princeton, NJ: Princeton University Press, 1977).
44 Donald Savoie, *Governing from the Centre: The Concentration of Power in Canadian Politics* (Toronto: University of Toronto Press, 1999), 173-4.
45 Ken Battle, *Government Fights Growing Gap between Rich and Poor* (Ottawa: Caledon Institute of Social Policy, 1995).
46 Ibid.
47 Robert W. Cox, 'The Global Political Economy and Social Choice,' in *The New Era of Global Competition: State Policy and Market Power*, ed. Daniel Drache and Meric S. Gertler (Montreal and Kingston: McGill-Queen's University Press, 1991), 340, 343-4.
48 See Jim Stanford, 'The Economic and Social Consequences of Fiscal Retrenchment in Canada in the 1990s,' in *The Review of Economic Performance*, 146, 151. In the same volume, see also Battle, 'Relentless Incrementalism,' 190, and Osberg and Sharpe, 'Trends in Economic Well-Being,' 239-40.
49 'Inequality,' *The Economist* 333, 7888 (5 November 1994): 19.
50 Battle, 'Relentless Incrementalism,' 192. Andrew Heisz, Andrew Jackson, and Garnett Picot argue that, unlike in the United States, there was no overall increase in the returns

to education in Canada throughout the 1980s and up to the mid-1990s; rather, the position of the least educated got even worse. See their article 'Distributional Outcomes in Canada in the 1990s,' in *The Review of Economic Performance*, 257.

51 Robert B. Reich, *The Work of Nations* (New York: Vintage Books, 1992), chap. 25.
52 See *Policy Options* 20, 7 (1999), for a range of views on the 'brain drain.'
53 See John F. Helliwell, 'Checking the Brain Drain: Evidence and Implications,' in *Policy Options* 20, 7 (1999): 6-17.
54 Betcherman, 'Inside the Black Box,' 79.
55 On the 'first-past-the-post' electoral system's preference for the party that wins the most votes and parties with regionally concentrated votes, see Alan C. Cairns's classic article, 'The Electoral System and the Party System in Canada, 1921-1965,' *Canadian Journal of Political Science* 1, 1 (1968): 55-80.
56 See Alain Noël, 'The Bloc Québécois as Official Opposition,' in *Canada: The State of the Federation 1994*, ed. Douglas M. Brown and Janet Hiebert (Kingston, ON: Institute of Intergovernmental Relations, 1994), 20-4 on the Bloc's electoral support in 1993. Noël does allow that there may have been elements of an economic protest vote in Bloc support, but this falls short of establishing the Bloc's representativeness of a specific socioeconomic base, as opposed to a base built on language and identity.
57 Tom Flanagan, *Waiting for the Wave: The Reform Party and Preston Manning* (Toronto: Stoddart, 1995), 163.
58 David Laycock, 'Reforming Canadian Democracy? Institutions and Ideology in the Reform Party Project,' *Canadian Journal of Political Science* 27, 2 (1994): 219.
59 Ibid.
60 Preston Manning, *The New Canada* (Toronto: Macmillan, 1992), 321.
61 In 1994, Thérèse Arseneau argued that the opportunities for Reform to influence policy in the manner of earlier third parties were sharply circumscribed by Reform's relationship to the governing Liberals. She said that 'the Liberals are the only major brokerage party left but are ideologically too distant from Reform to adopt many of its policies' ('The Reform Party of Canada: Past, Present and Future,' in *Canada: The State of the Federation 1994*, ed. Brown and Hiebert, 53). Time has proved this assertion to be clearly wrong. It is based on an outdated vision of the current Liberal Party whose brokerage function now takes place along a different part of the ideological continuum.
62 See John Richards and Larry Pratt, *Prairie Capitalism: Power and Influence in the New West* (Toronto: McClelland and Stewart, 1979), chap. 2 for an account of both 'left' and 'right' populism in the West after the turn of the last century.
63 Laycock, 'Reforming Canadian Democracy?' 213-47.
64 Flanagan, *Waiting for the Wave*, 32-3.
65 On the relationships between the Harris Conservatives and Reform, see Sid Noel, 'Ontario and the Federation at the End of the Twentieth Century,' in *Canada: The State of the Federation 1997 – Non-Constitutional Renewal*, ed. Harvey Lazar (Kingston, ON: Institute of Intergovernmental Relations, 1998), 274, 277-8.
66 On the relationships between the Klein Conservatives and Reform, see David Taras and Allan Tupper, 'Politics and Deficits: Alberta's Challenge to the Canadian Political Agenda,' in *Canada: The State of the Federation 1994*, ed. Brown and Hiebert, 66-7.
67 Manning, *The New Canada*, 320.
68 Flanagan, *Waiting for the Wave*, 159-60.
69 Edward Greenspon and Anthony Wilson-Smith, *Double Vision: The Inside Story of the Liberals in Power* (Toronto: Doubleday Canada, 1996), 22, 97-9.
70 Ibid., 22.
71 The Liberals, and particularly the prime minister, described the government's approach as the 'Canadian way.' A paper entitled 'The Canadian Way in the 21st Century' could be found on the prime minister's Web site in 2001.
72 Paul Martin, *Budget Speech*, 6 March (Canada: Department of Finance, 1996), 3.
73 Robert B. Reich, Introduction to *The Power of Public Ideas*, ed. Robert B. Reich (Cambridge, MA: Ballinger, 1988), 5.
74 Confidential interview, 25 January 2001.

75 Evert A. Lindquist, 'The Bewildering Pace of Public Sector Reform in Canada,' in *Public Sector Reform: Rationale, Trends, and Problems,* ed. Jan-Erik Lane (London: Sage, 1997), 53-4.

76 Paul Martin, *Budget Speech,* 27 February (Ottawa: Department of Finance, 1995), 7.

77 See Allan M. Maslove and Kevin D. Moore, 'From Red Books to Blue Books: Repairing Ottawa's Fiscal House,' in *How Ottawa Spends 1997-98 – Seeing Red: A Liberal Report Card,* ed. Gene Swimmer (Ottawa: Carleton University Press, 1997), 33.

78 Paul Martin, *Economic Statement and Budget Update,* 18 October (Ottawa: Department of Finance, 2000), 8. See also Paul Martin, *Economic Update,* 17 May (Ottawa: Department of Finance, 2001), 9.

79 Ronald D. Kneebone and Kenneth J. McKenzie, 'The Characteristics of Fiscal Policy in Canada,' *Canadian Public Policy* 25, 4 (1999): 498-9.

80 Ibid., 498.

81 Greenspon and Wilson-Smith, *Double Vision,* 349-50.

82 David R. Cameron, 'The Faltering Scapegoat: Canadian Federalism and Its Prospects,' in *Politics: Canada,* 8th ed., ed. Paul W. Fox and Graham White (Toronto: McGraw-Hill, 1995), 160.

83 Greenspon and Wilson-Smith, *Double Vision,* 349.

84 Confidential interview, 25 January 2001.

85 Martin, *Budget Speech* (1996), 7.

86 Paul Martin, *The Budget Plan 1998: Building Canada for the 21st Century – Strong Economy and Secure Society,* 24 February (Ottawa: Department of Finance, 1998), 99-121.

87 Jim Stanford argues that EI is nowhere near as effective an automatic stabilizer as it was even in the early 1990s. 'The Economic and Social Consequences,' 148-9. On Employment Insurance reform generally, see Geoffrey E. Hale, 'Reforming Employment Insurance: Transcending the Politics of the Status Quo,' *Canadian Public Policy* 24, 4 (1998): 429-51.

88 On the Stabilization Program, see Thomas J. Courchene with Colin R. Telmer, *From Heart- land to Region State: The Social, Fiscal and Federal Evolution of Ontario – An Interpretive Essay,* Monograph Series on Public Policy and Public Administration no. 6 (Toronto: University of Toronto, Faculty of Management, 1998), 140.

89 Graves, 'The Economy through a Public Lens,' 81.

Chapter 8: Only Nixon Can Go to China, 1993-8

1 Department of Finance, *Agenda: Jobs and Growth – A New Framework for Economic Policy,* October (Ottawa: Department of Finance, 1994), 1.

2 Ibid., 1-2.

3 Ibid., 2.

4 Ibid., 2-3.

5 Ibid., 15-16.

6 Ibid., 43-4.

7 Ibid., 47-8.

8 Ibid., 50-3.

9 Ibid., 61-70.

10 Ibid., 55-6.

11 See Stephen Clarkson, 'Constitutionalizing the Canadian-American Relationship,' in *Canada under Free Trade,* ed. Duncan Cameron and Mel Watkins (Toronto: James Lorimer, 1993), 280-2.

12 For an argument that abrogation was the best course, see Duncan Cameron with Mel Clark, 'Renegotiation and Termination,' in *Canada under Free Trade,* ed. Cameron and Watkins. In my view, Cameron underestimates the political difficulty of abrogating the CUFTA.

13 Bob Rae, *From Protest to Power: Personal Reflections on a Life in Politics* (Toronto: Viking, 1996), 214.

14 Michael Wilson, *The Budget,* 26 February (Ottawa: Department of Finance, 1991), 103-14.

15 Department of Finance, *Agenda: Jobs and Growth – Creating a Healthy Fiscal Climate – The*

Economic and Fiscal Update, October (Ottawa: Department of Finance, 1994), 6. Pierre
Fortin has argued that it appears the bank has aimed not at 2 percent inflation, but rather
for the lower end of the band. 'The Great Canadian Slump,' *Canadian Journal of Economics* 24, 4 (1996): 775.

16 Paul Martin, *Economic Update,* 17 May (Ottawa: Department of Finance, 2001), 12.
17 Edward Greenspon and Anthony Wilson-Smith, *Double Vision: The Inside Story of the Liberals in Power* (Toronto: Doubleday Canada, 1996), 68-70.
18 Department of Finance, *Agenda: Jobs and Growth – Creating,* 6; Department of Finance,
Agenda: Jobs and Growth – A New Framework, 13.
19 Greenspon and Wilson-Smith, *Double Vision,* 70.
20 Department of Finance, *Agenda: Jobs and Growth – A New Framework,* 19-20.
21 Ibid., 23.
22 Greenspon and Wilson-Smith, *Double Vision,* 47-8.
23 Ibid., 37-42.
24 Paul Martin, *The Budget Speech,* 22 February (Ottawa: Department of Finance, 1994), 3.
25 Paul Martin, *The Budget Plan,* 22 February (Ottawa: Department of Finance, 1994), 15.
26 Martin, *Budget Speech* (1994), 19.
27 Ibid., 13.
28 Paul Martin, *Response to Prebudget Consultations – Facing Choices Together,* February
(Ottawa: Department of Finance, 1994), 15. Martin did state in this document that 80
percent of the government's fiscal measures would be on the spending side.
29 Arthur Kroeger, 'Changing Course: The Federal Government's Program Review of 1994-
95,' in *Hard Choices or No Choices: Assessing Program Review,* ed. Armelita Armita and
Jacques Bourgault (Toronto: Institute of Public Administration, 1996), 24.
30 Martin, *Budget Speech* (1994), 3.
31 Greenspon and Wilson-Smith, *Double Vision,* 156; confidential interview, 13 August 1998.
32 Greenspon and Wilson-Smith, *Double Vision,* 153-6; confidential interview, 13 August
1998; confidential interview, 25 January 2001.
33 Confidential interview, 13 August 1998.
34 Greenspon and Wilson-Smith, *Double Vision,* 271.
35 Donald Savoie, *Governing from the Centre: The Concentration of Power in Canadian Politics*
(Toronto: University of Toronto Press, 1999), 173.
36 Ibid., 177-8.
37 Confidential interview, 25 January 2001; see also Paul Jenkins and Brian O'Reilly, 'Monetary Policy and the Well-Being of Canadians,' in *The Review of Economic Performance and
Social Progress – The Longest Decade: Canada in the 1990s,* ed. Keith G. Banting, Andrew
Sharpe, and France St-Hilaire (Montreal: Institute for Research on Public Policy, 2001), 104.
38 Greenspon and Wilson-Smith, *Double Vision,* 235-6.
39 Paul Martin, *Budget Plan,* 27 February (Ottawa: Department of Finance, 1995), 27.
40 Arthur Kroeger argues that late 1994 turbulence in financial markets and shifts in international capital movements created the psychological breakthrough that made Program
Review successful. Kroeger, 'Changing Course,' in *Hard Choices or No Choices,* 24-5.
41 Confidential interview, 13 August 1998. See Savoie, *Governing from the Centre,* 177-8, 183.
42 Confidential interview, 25 January 2001.
43 Ibid; confidential interview, 30 January 2001.
44 Confidential interview, 25 January 2001.
45 Greenspon and Wilson-Smith, *Double Vision,* 195-205
46 Confidential interview, 25 January 2001.
47 See Savoie, *Governing from the Centre,* 170-1, 178-9, 183; Greenspon and Wilson-Smith,
Double Vision, 161-4. This is also confirmed by my interviews: 13 August 1998 and 25
January 2001.
48 Greenspon and Wilson-Smith, *Double Vision,* 157.
49 Confidential interview, 13 August 1998.
50 Savoie, *Governing from the Centre,* 179-80; confidential interview, 25 January 2001.
51 Savoie, *Governing from the Centre,* 186-7.

52 Department of Finance, *Agenda: Jobs and Growth – A New Framework*, 71.
53 Ibid.
54 Department of Finance, *Agenda: Jobs and Growth – Creating*, 5. See Chapter 6 for the Mulroney government's vicious circle argument against deficits.
55 Department of Finance, *Agenda: Jobs and Growth – A New Framework*, 78.
56 Ibid., 76-9.
57 Ibid., 73.
58 Ibid., 86.
59 Ibid., 84.
60 Paul Martin, *Budget Speech*, 6 March (Ottawa: Department of Finance, 1996), 8.
61 As the government quietly anticipated, Michael Wilson's partial deindexation of the tax system, combined with a progressive bracket and rate structure, resulted in low inflation slowly putting more people into higher tax brackets even if their real incomes were not rising. Department of Finance, *Agenda: Jobs and Growth – Creating*, 83. 'Bracket creep' undermined, to a modest degree, the balance the Liberals claimed to strike in favour of spending reductions and against increasing the tax yield.
62 Martin, *Response to Prebudget Consultations* (1994), 14-15.
63 Paul Martin, *The Budget Speech*, 18 February (Ottawa: Department of Finance, 1997), 25-7.
64 Paul Martin, *The Budget Plan*, 28 February (Ottawa: Department of Finance, 2000), 12-14, 79-104; Paul Martin, *Economic Statement and Budget Update*, 18 October (Ottawa: Department of Finance, 2000), 12-15.
65 Martin, *Economic Statement* (2000), 12.
66 Department of Finance, *Agenda: Jobs and Growth – Creating*, 5.
67 Confidential interview, 30 January 2001.
68 Confidential interview, 25 January 2001.
69 Department of Finance, *Agenda: Jobs and Growth – Creating*, 9.
70 Marian Stinson, 'Currency Markets Give Thumbs Up,' *Globe and Mail*, 28 February 1995, A1-A2.
71 Paul Martin, *The Budget Speech*, 27 February (Ottawa: Department of Finance, 1995), 2-3.
72 Ibid., 4.
73 Martin, *Budget Speech* (1995), 4.
74 Ibid., 21-4.
75 Ibid., 8.
76 Ibid., 9-11.
77 Ibid., 16.
78 Ibid., 17-18.
79 Ibid., 18.
80 Greenspon and Wilson-Smith, *Double Vision*, 231.
81 Shawn McCarthy, 'Martin Backs off Seniors Plan,' *Globe and Mail*, 29 July 1998, A1, A4.
82 William Watson, 'Has Neo-Conservatism Failed?' *Policy Options* 22, 2 (2001): 10.
83 Martin, *Budget Speech* (1995), 6.
84 Department of Finance, *Agenda: Jobs and Growth – Creating*, 27-8.
85 Ibid., 56.
86 Savoie, *Governing from the Centre*, 173.
87 Ibid., 174-5.
88 Department of Finance, *Agenda: Jobs and Growth – Creating*, 39.
89 Savoie, *Governing from the Centre*, 183-4; confidential interview, 25 January 2001.
90 Martin, *Budget Speech* (1995), 33; Martin, *Budget Plan* (1995), 111-12.
91 Treasury Board of Canada, *Employment Statistics for the Federal Public Service: April 1, 1996 to March 31, 1997* (Ottawa: Treasury Board of Canada, 1997), 62-3. In the public sector more widely defined, there were further job losses.
92 Some of the lost positions were not filled when they were cut, so the loss of 30,000 positions did not mean that 30,000 people lost their jobs. Tom Courchene states that, in the end, the federal civil service was reduced by 50,000 persons. See Tom Courchene, 'Half-Way Home: Canada's Remarkable Fiscal Turnaround and the Paul Martin Legacy,' *Policy Matters* 3, 8 (2002): 23.

93 Martin, *Budget Speech* (1995), 9.
94 Savoie, *Governing from the Centre,* 182-3.
95 Arthur Kroeger, 'The Central Agencies and Program Review,' an undated paper prepared for the Canadian Centre for Management Development, cited in Savoie, *Governing from the Centre,* 177.
96 Ken Battle, 'Relentless Incrementalism: Deconstructing and Reconstructing Canadian Income Security Policy,' in *The Review of Economic Performance and Social Progress,* ed. Banting, Sharpe, and St-Hilaire, 224.
97 Savoie, *Governing from the Centre,* 181-2.
98 Martin, *Budget Speech* (1995), 9.
99 Ibid., 4.
100 Ibid., 25.
101 See Jane Pulkingham and Gordon Ternowetsky, 'The Changing Landscape of Social Policy and the Canadian Welfare State,' in *Remaking Canadian Social Policy: Social Security in the Late 1990s* (Halifax: Fernwood, 1996), 15; Ken Battle and Sherri Torjman, 'Desperately Seeking Substance: A Commentary on the Social Security Review,' in *Remaking Canadian Social Policy,* ed. Pulkingham and Ternowetsky, 64; and Battle, 'Relentless Incrementalism,' 224.
102 Michael J. Prince, 'From Health and Welfare to Stealth and Farewell: Federal Social Policy, 1980-2000,' in *How Ottawa Spends 1999-2000 – Shape Shifting: Canadian Governance toward the 21st Century,* ed. Leslie A. Pal (Toronto: Oxford University Press Canada, 1999), 191.
103 Susan D. Phillips, 'The Canada Health and Social Transfer: Fiscal Federalism in Search of a Vision,' in *Canada: The State of the Federation 1995,* ed. Douglas Brown and Jonathan Rose (Kingston, ON: Institute of Intergovernmental Relations, 1995), 73.
104 Stefan Dupré states that counting tax points in the value of the then EPF transfer is 'at the top of my list of the Big Lies of Canadian public finance,' because the tax points are provincial own-source revenues for which provinces are politically responsible. J. Stefan Dupré, 'Comment: The Promise of Procurement Federalism,' in *The Future of Fiscal Federalism,* ed. Keith G. Banting, Douglas M. Brown, and Thomas J. Courchene (Kingston, ON: School of Policy Studies, Queen's University, 1994), 250.
105 Courchene, for example, gives these budgetary techniques some credit for deficit elimination. See Courchene, 'Half-Way Home,' 21-3.
106 Department of Finance, *Agenda: Jobs and Growth – Creating,* 9-10.
107 Confidential interview, 25 January 2001.
108 Department of Finance, *Agenda: Jobs and Growth – Creating,* 22.
109 Ibid.
110 Confidential interview, 13 August 1998.
111 Michael Wilson, *The Budget,* 20 February (Ottawa: Department of Finance, 1990), 11-12.
112 Michael Wilson, *The Budget,* 26 February (Ottawa: Department of Finance, 1991), 78.
113 Don Mazankowski, *The Budget Speech,* 25 February (Ottawa: Department of Finance, 1992), 21.
114 Confidential interview, 25 January 2001.
115 Over time, Martin would be subjected to increasing criticism of his approach to budgeting on the grounds he was hoarding funds to ensure his fiscal goals and engaging in ad hoc year-end spending that entailed poorly designed and ill-accounted programs. He would return to five-year fiscal forecasts and adopt private sector consensus forecasts in response.
116 Nova Scotia, House of Assembly, *Speech from the Throne,* 58th General Assembly, 1st session, 7 October 1999, 8-9.
117 Chrétien committed to decentralization, recognition of Quebec as a distinct society, and a veto on constitutional change for Quebec for any amendment affecting its jurisdiction in his Verdun speech of 24 October 1995 and in his address to the nation the next night.
118 The federal government announced it would no longer use its spending power to create new shared cost programs in areas of exclusive provincial jurisdiction without the consent of a majority of the provinces. Those not consenting would be compensated if they operated an equivalent or comparable initiative. Ottawa also promised to withdraw from

labour market training, forestry, mining, and recreation. Partnerships with provinces in other areas were recommended. See the 1996 Speech from the Throne. Canada, House of Commons, *Debates,* 27 February 1996, 35th Parliament, 2nd Session, vol. 133 (Ottawa: Canada Communications Group, 1996).

119 See Harvey Lazar, ed., *Canada: The State of the Federation 1997 – Non-Constitutional Renewal* (Kingston, ON: Institute of Intergovernmental Relations, 1998).

120 For a negative, but accurate, assessment of the Social Union Framework Agreement, see Christopher Dunn, 'FYI: SUFA, DOA,' *Policy Options* 21, 4 (2001): 50-1.

121 Alain Noël, 'Collaborative Federalism – With a Footnote,' *Policy Options* 21, 4 (2001): 44-6.

122 Roger Gibbins, *Shifting Sands: Exploring the Political Foundations of SUFA,* Policy Matters 2, 3 (Montreal: Institute for Research on Public Policy, 2001).

123 For a favourable and a skeptical account, respectively, of the impact of the federal government's approach to the deficit fight, see Don Drummond, 'Deficit Elimination, Economic Performance and Social Progress in Canada in the 1990s,' and Jim Stanford, 'The Economic and Social Consequences of Fiscal Retrenchment in Canada in the 1990s,' in *The Review of Economic Performance and Social Progress,* ed. Banting, Sharpe, and St-Hilaire. Essentially, Drummond and Stanford differ on the appropriateness of eliminating the deficit so quickly. Drummond argues that, given the failures of earlier fiscal tightening to eliminate the deficit, going more slowly in 1995 could have led to confidence losses and worsened economic performance (p. 135). Stanford takes the position that spending cuts weakened the social tapestry, and were unnecessary because Martin still would have balanced the budget within his initial timetable without reducing spending (pp. 154-5).

124 Martin, *Budget Speech* (1995), 15-22.

125 Confidential interview, 13 August 1998.

126 Murray Campbell and Anne McIlroy, 'Liberals Offer To Spend More on Health Care,' *Globe and Mail,* 29 April 1997, A1.

127 Tu Thanh Ha, 'Liberals' Big Pledge a Loner, Martin Says,' *Globe and Mail,* 30 April 1997, A8.

128 Paul Martin, *The Budget Plan 1998: Building Canada for the 21st Century – Strong Economy and Secure Society,* 24 February (Ottawa: Department of Finance, 1998), 53.

129 Ibid., 8.

130 Ibid., 13-16.

131 Liberal Party of Canada, *Securing Our Future Together: Preparing Canada for the 21st Century* (Ottawa: Liberal Party of Canada, 1997), 29.

132 Martin, *Budget Speech* (1997), 19-24.

133 Michael Wilson, *The Budget Speech,* 10 February (Ottawa: Department of Finance, 1988), 8-10.

134 Don Mazankowski, *The Budget Speech,* 26 April (Ottawa: Department of Finance, 1993), 19.

135 Paul Martin, *Budget in Brief,* 18 February (Ottawa: Department of Finance, 1997), 9.

136 Gene Swimmer, 'Seeing Red: A Liberal Report Card,' in *How Ottawa Spends 1997-98 – Seeing Red: A Liberal Report Card,* ed. Gene Swimmer (Ottawa: Carleton University Press, 1997), 19.

137 Richard Nadeau, André Blais, Neil Nevitte, and Elisabeth Gidengil, 'It's Unemployment, Stupid! Why Perceptions about the Job Situation Hurt the Liberals in the 1997 Election,' *Canadian Public Policy* 26, 1 (2000): 86.

138 Ibid.

139 Ibid., 82.

140 The Liberals ran on fiscal and administrative competence in 1963, for example, to differentiate themselves from the 'allegedly incompetent' Diefenbaker Tories. Robert M. Campbell, *Grand Illusions: The Politics of the Keynesian Experience in Canada, 1945-1975* (Peterborough, ON: Broadview Press, 1987), 143-4.

141 Nadeau et al., 'It's Unemployment, Stupid!' 82, 87.

142 Scott Feschuk, 'Cutting Debt, Taxes Top Canadians' List,' *Globe and Mail,* 1 November 1997, A1.

143 Nadeau et al., 'It's Unemployment, Stupid!' 88.

144 Department of Finance, *The Budget Chartbook 1998,* 24 February (Ottawa: Department of Finance, 1998), 65.

145 Greenspon and Wilson-Smith, *Double Vision,* 134, 270-1.

146 Martin, *Budget Speech* (1995), 6.

147 Neil Bradford, *Commissioning Ideas: Canadian National Policy Innovation in Comparative Perspective* (Toronto: Oxford University Press, 1998), 119.

148 Martin, *Budget Speech* (1995), 7.

149 John Locke, *Second Treatise of Government,* ed. C.B. Macpherson (1690; Indianapolis: Hackett, 1980), 111, emphasis in original.

150 Such legislation included British Columbia's Tax and Consumer Rate Freeze Act, *Revised Statutes of British Columbia,* 1996, c. 447, and Balanced Budget Act, *Statutes of British Columbia,* 2000, c. 21; Alberta's Alberta Taxpayer Protection Act, *Statutes of Alberta,* c. A-37.8, and Balanced Budget and Debt Retirement Act, *Statutes of Alberta,* c. B-0.5 (both introduced in 1995); Saskatchewan's Balanced Budget Act, *Statutes of Saskatchewan,* 1995, c. B-0.01; Manitoba's Balanced Budget, Debt Repayment and Taxpayer Protection Act, *Statutes of Manitoba,* 1995, c. 7; Ontario's Balanced Budget Act, *Statutes of Ontario,* 1999, c. 7, Sch. B, and Taxpayer Protection Act, *Statutes of Ontario,* 1999, c. 7, sch. A; Quebec's Act Respecting the Elimination of the Deficit and a Balanced Budget, *Statutes of Quebec,* 1996, c. 55; New Brunswick's Balanced Budget Act, *Statutes of New Brunswick,* 1995, c. 23; and Nova Scotia's Expenditure Control Act, *Statutes of Nova Scotia,* 1993, c. 4. Like all efforts to formalize fiscal control, this type of legislation was usually more about symbolism than substance.

151 John Porter, *The Vertical Mosaic: An Analysis of Social Class and Power in Canada* (Toronto: University of Toronto Press, 1965), 367-8.

152 Ibid., 368-9.

153 See Anthony Giddens, *The Third Way: The Renewal of Social Democracy* (Cambridge: Polity Press, 1998).

Chapter 9: Maynard Where Art Thou?

1 For a notable exception, see Paul Pierson, *Dismantling The Welfare State? Reagan, Thatcher, and the Politics of Retrenchment* (New York: Cambridge University Press, 1994).

2 For a detailed exegesis of the notion of the relative autonomy of the state, see Gregory Albo and Jane Jenson, 'A Contested Concept: The Relative Autonomy of the State,' in *The New Canadian Political Economy,* ed. Wallace Clement and Glen Williams (Montreal and Kingston: McGill-Queen's University Press, 1989).

3 Kathleen Thelen and Sven Steinmo, 'Historical Institutionalism in Comparative Politics,' in *Structuring Politics: Historical Institutionalism in Comparative Analysis,* ed. Sven Steinmo, Kathleen Thelen, and Frank Longstreth (New York: Cambridge University Press, 1992), 14-15.

4 See Donald Savoie, *Governing from the Centre: The Concentration of Power in Canadian Politics* (Toronto: University of Toronto Press, 1999), 162-72.

5 Robert W. Cox, 'The Global Political Economy and Social Choice,' in *The New Era of Global Competition: State Policy and Market Power,* ed. Daniel Drache and Meric S. Gertler (Montreal and Kingston: McGill-Queen's University Press, 1991), 337.

6 Keith G. Banting, 'Social Policy,' in *Border Crossings: The Internationalization of Canadian Public Policy,* ed. G. Bruce Doern, Leslie A. Pal, and Brian W. Tomlin (Toronto: Oxford University Press, 1996), 40.

7 James O'Connor, *The Fiscal Crisis of the State* (New York: St. Martin's Press, 1973), 5-10; Alan Wolfe, *The Limits of Legitimacy: Political Contradictions of Contemporary Capitalism* (New York: Free Press, 1977), 6-7; Ralph Miliband, *Marxism and Politics* (Oxford: Oxford University Press, 1977), 97. In some formulations, certain social programs are categorized as serving the accumulation function by reducing the costs of reproducing labour power. Other social programs serve the legitimation function by maintaining social peace among the unemployed. See O'Connor, *Fiscal Crisis,* 7.

8 Louis W. Pauly, 'Capital Mobility, State Autonomy and Political Legitimacy,' *Journal of International Affairs* 48, 2 (1995): 369-88.

9 See James M. Buchanan and Richard E. Wagner, *Democracy in Deficit: The Political Legacy of Lord Keynes* (New York: Academic Press, 1977), 50-1, chap. 7.

10 See Richard Simeon, *In Search of a Social Contract: Can We Make Hard Decisions As If Democracy Matters?* Benefactors Lecture Series, 13 September (Toronto: C.D. Howe Institute, 1994), especially 5-8.

11 See David Robertson Cameron, 'Half-Eaten Carrot, Bent Stick: Decentralization in an Era of Fiscal Restraint,' *Canadian Public Administration* 37, 4 (1994): 439; and Richard Simeon, 'The Political Context for Renegotiating Fiscal Federalism,' in *The Future of Fiscal Federalism*, ed. Keith G. Banting, Douglas M. Brown, and Thomas J. Courchene (Kingston, ON: School of Policy Studies, Queen's University, 1994), 143.

12 David A. Stockman, *The Triumph of Politics: How the Reagan Revolution Failed* (New York: Harper and Row, 1986), 376-80. Indeed, in keeping with the accumulation/legitimation dichotomy, Stockman argues that there is a trade-off between capitalist prosperity and social security (391). Americans opted rather more for the latter than he would have preferred.

13 This is Simeon's opposition. See *In Search of a Social Contract*, 5-8.

14 Paul Pierson, 'The New Politics of the Welfare State,' *World Politics* 48, 2 (1996): 143-4, emphasis in original.

15 Polls taken for the Liberals' Social Security Review in 1994 and 1995 found that a majority of Canadians were of the view that social programs required substantial change. See Ken Battle, 'Relentless Incrementalism: Deconstructing and Reconstructing Canadian Income Security Policy,' in *The Review of Economic Performance and Social Progress – The Longest Decade: Canada in the 1990s*, ed. Keith G. Banting, Andrew Sharpe, and France St-Hilaire (Montreal: Institute for Research on Public Policy, 2001), 194.

16 See, for example, O'Connor, *Fiscal Crisis*, 8, 25-9.

17 I recognize that this is a limited notion of democracy, one in which robust democratic concerns are circumscribed by liberal capitalist imperatives. Alan Wolfe has argued that liberalism upholds accumulation, that democracy supports legitimation, and that the two are contradictory. Wolfe, *Limits of Legitimacy*, 7. He wrote, in 1977, that 'if a choice has to be made between liberalism and democracy, it is my hope that the overwhelming majority of people in late capitalist societies will pick the latter' (346-7). In Canada, things did not work out as Wolfe desired. Contradictions between liberalism and democracy have largely been resolved by collapsing democratic concerns into support for liberalism's capitalist accumulation. This is 'democratic' insofar as it seems, of late, to reflect the desires of the majority of the Canadians. But it will not satisfy those with aspirations for a democratic experience organized around participation and equality, and may contain the seeds of its own destruction.

18 Pauly, 'Capital Mobility, State Autonomy,' 384.

19 Robert Skidelsky, *John Maynard Keynes: The Economist As Saviour, 1920-1937*, vol. 2 (London: Macmillan, 1992), 220-1.

20 I am not arguing that this was a robust experiment in democratic participation and equality. Rather, the neo-liberal turn restored the legitimacy of parliamentary government, at least in the short and medium terms. The centralization of power and the disciplining of society that neo-liberalism encourages may create, over time, their own legitimacy issues.

21 Paul Martin, *Economic Statement and Budget Update*, 18 October (Ottawa: Department of Finance, 2000), 9.

22 Battle, 'Relentless Incrementalism,' 194.

23 Michael Hart, *Fifty Years of Canadian Tradecraft: Canada at the GATT, 1947-1997* (Ottawa: Centre for Trade Policy and Law: 1998), 191.

24 Neil Nevitte, André Blais, Elisabeth Gidengil, and Richard Nadeau, *Unsteady State: The 1997 Canadian Federal Election* (Toronto: Oxford University Press, 2000), chap. 4.

25 William Watson, 'Has Neo-Conservatism Failed?' *Policy Options* 22, 2 (2001): 6. For another assessment of neo-conservatism's successes and failures, see Jim Stanford, 'The Revolution Is Dead. Long Live the Revolution,' *Policy Options* 22, 3 (2001): 34-43.

26 Watson, 'Has Neo-Conservatism Failed?' 15.

27 Aristotle, *The Politics*, trans. Carnes Lord (Chicago: University of Chicago Press, 1984), 37.

28 A.F.W. Plumptre, *Three Decades of Decision: Canada and the World Monetary System, 1944-1975* (Toronto: McClelland and Stewart, 1977), 20.

29 For a history and analysis of federal and provincial roles in housing policy since the Second World War, including federal withdrawal from social housing, see Barbara Wake Carroll and Ruth J.E. Jones, 'The Road to Innovation, Convergence, or Inertia: Devolution in Housing Policy in Canada,' *Canadian Public Policy* 26, 3 (2000): 277-93.

30 See Maxwell A. Cameron and Brian W. Tomlin, *The Making of NAFTA: How the Deal Was Done* (Ithaca, NY: Cornell University Press, 2000), 29, on the greater responsiveness of weaker (i.e., asymmetrically interdependent) states to the demands of stronger states than to domestic constituents in international negotiations.

31 On the substantial remaining Canadian policy autonomy in the face of North American integration, see George Hoberg, 'Canada and North American Integration,' *Canadian Public Policy* 26, supplement 2 (2000): S35-S50.

32 Peter F. Drucker, 'The Global Economy and the Nation-State,' *Foreign Affairs* 76, 5 (1997): 164.

33 Ibid., 162-4.

34 Geoffrey E. Hale, 'Managing the Fiscal Dividend: The Politics of Selected Activism,' in *How Ottawa Spends 2000-2001 – Past Imperfect, Future Tense,* ed. Leslie A. Pal (Toronto: Oxford University Press, 2000), 59.

35 William Watson, 'How the Budget Is Made: An Interview with Scott Clark, Deputy Minister of Finance,' *Policy Options* 20, 1 (1999): 17.

36 Thomas J. Courchene, 'Half-Way Home: Canada's Remarkable Fiscal Turnaround and the Paul Martin Legacy,' *Policy Matters* 3, 8 (2002): 32.

37 Paul Martin, *Economic Update,* 17 May (Ottawa: Department of Finance, 2001), 13; Canada, House of Commons, *Debates,* 30 January 2001, 37th Parliament, 1st Session, vol. 137 (Ottawa: Canadian Government Publishing, 2001), 10; Paul Martin, *The Budget Plan,* 28 February (Ottawa: Department of Finance, 2000), 45.

38 David A. Dodge, 'Reflections on the Role of Fiscal Policy: The Doug Purvis Memorial Lecture,' *Canadian Public Policy* 24, 3 (1998): 284.

39 Department of Finance, *Annual Financial Report of the Government of Canada: Fiscal Year 2000-2001,* September (Ottawa: Department of Finance, 2001), 6.

40 Martin, *Economic Statement* (2000), 15.

41 Jim Stanford 'A Fred Astaire Budget,' *Policy Options* 21, 3 (2000): 7. Of course, if it is permanent, can it really be a crisis?

42 Canada, House of Commons, *Debates,* 30 January 2001, 37th Parliament, 1st Session, vol. 137.

43 See Canada, Industry Canada, *Achieving Excellence: Investing in People, Knowledge and Opportunity: Canada's Innovation Strategy,* February (Ottawa: Industry Canada, 2002); and Canada, Human Resources Development Canada, *Knowledge Matters: Skills and Learning for Canadians: Canada's Innovation Strategy,* February (Hull, QC: Human Resources Development Canada, 2002).

44 With economic policy focusing increasingly on investing in human capital, the distinction between economic and social policy is becoming increasingly blurred. Thomas J. Courchene, 'Glocalization: The Regional/International Interface,' *Canadian Journal of Regional Science* 18, 1 (1995): 7.

45 New Keynesian economics holds that nominal variables, such as changes in the money supply, can have real effects and that real market imperfections are crucial for understanding economic fluctuations. Real market imperfections mean that prices are sticky. Sticky prices, in turn, mean that changes in nominal variables can have real consequences. New Keynesian economics aspires to provide the microfoundations of Keynesian macroeconomics. See, for example, N. Gregory Mankiw and David Romer, eds., *New Keynesian Economics* (Cambridge, MA: MIT Press, 1991), especially pp. 1-3; Jeff Frank, *The New Keynesian Economics: Unemployment, Search and Contracting* (Brighton, UK: Wheatsheaf Books, 1986). For an excellent literature review by a legal scholar rather than an economist, see Gillian Lester, 'Careers and Contingency,' *Stanford Law Review* 51, 1 (1998): 129-45.

46 Robert Skidelsky, 'Ideas and the World,' *The Economist* 357, 8189 (25 November-1 December 2000): 85.

47 Watson, 'How the Budget Is Made,' 18.
48 Watson, 'Has Neo-Conservatism Failed?' 14.
49 Martin, *Economic Update* (2001), 13.
50 Department of Finance, News Release 2001-049, '*Economic Update* Announces Continued Budgetary Surpluses and Further Debt Reduction,' 17 May 2001; Heather Scoffield, 'Martin Aiming to Deliver February Budget,' *Globe and Mail,* 17 August 2001, A5; Shawn McCarthy, 'Job Losses, Rate Cuts Predicted,' *Globe and Mail,* 1 September 2001, A1, A4.

Bibliography

Abbott, D.C. *Budget Speech*. 29 April. Ottawa: Queen's Printer, 1947.
–. *Budget Speech*. 18 May. Ottawa: Queen's Printer, 1948.
–. *Budget Speech*. 22 March. Ottawa: Queen's Printer, 1949.
–. *Budget Speech*. 28 March. Ottawa: Queen's Printer, 1950.
–. *Budget Speech*. 10 April. Ottawa: Queen's Printer, 1951.
–. *Budget Speech*. 8 April. Ottawa: Queen's Printer, 1952.
Abele, Frances. 'The Politics of Competitiveness.' In *How Ottawa Spends: The Politics of Competitiveness – 1992-93*, ed. Frances Abele, 1-22. Ottawa: Carleton University Press, 1992.
Albo, Gregory, and Jane Jenson. 'A Contested Concept: The Relative Autonomy of the State.' In *The New Canadian Political Economy*, ed. Wallace Clement and Glen Williams, 180-211. Montreal and Kingston: McGill-Queen's University Press, 1989.
Arendt, Hannah. *The Origins of Totalitarianism*. New York: Harcourt Brace, 1973.
Aristotle. *The Politics*. Trans. Carnes Lord. Chicago: University of Chicago Press, 1984.
Arseneau, Thérèse. 'The Reform Party of Canada: Past, Present and Future.' In *Canada: The State of the Federation 1994*, ed. Douglas M. Brown and Janet Hiebert, 37-57. Kingston, ON: Institute of Intergovernmental Relations, 1994.
Atkinson, Michael, and William D. Coleman. *The State, Business, and Industrial Change in Canada*. Toronto: University of Toronto Press, 1989.
Aucoin, Peter. 'Organizational Change in the Management of Canadian Government: From Rational Management to Brokerage Politics.' *Canadian Journal of Political Science* 19, 1 (1986): 691-709.
Axworthy, Thomas S., and Pierre Elliott Trudeau, eds., *Towards a Just Society: The Trudeau Years*. Markham, ON: Viking, 1990.
Bank of Canada. *Price Stability, Inflation Targets, and Monetary Policy*. Proceedings of a conference held by the Bank of Canada, May 1997. Ottawa: Bank of Canada, 1998.
Banting, Keith G. 'Social Policy.' In *Border Crossings: The Internationalization of Canadian Public Policy*, ed. G. Bruce Doern, Leslie A. Pal, and Brian W. Tomlin, 27-54. Toronto: Oxford University Press, 1996.
Barber, Benjamin. 'Jihad vs. McWorld.' *The Atlantic Monthly,* March 1992, 53-65.
Barber, Clarence L. *Theory of Fiscal Policy As Applied to a Province*. Study prepared for the Ontario Committee on Taxation. Toronto: Queen's Printer, 1966.
Barber, Clarence L., and John C.P. McCallum. *Unemployment and Inflation: The Canadian Experience*. Toronto: Canadian Institute for Economic Policy, 1980.
Barney, Darin. *Prometheus Wired: The Hope for Democracy in the Age of Network Technology*. Vancouver and Toronto: UBC Press, 2000.
Battle, Ken. *Government Fights Growing Gap between Rich and Poor*. Ottawa: Caledon Institute of Social Policy, 1995.
–. 'Relentless Incrementalism: Deconstructing and Reconstructing Canadian Income Security Policy.' In *The Review of Economic Performance and Social Progress – The Longest*

Decade: Canada in the 1990s, ed. Keith G. Banting, Andrew Sharpe, and France St-Hilaire, 183-229. Montreal: Institute for Research on Public Policy, 2001.

Battle, Ken, and Sherri Torjman. 'Desperately Seeking Substance: A Commentary on the Social Security Review.' In *Remaking Canadian Social Policy: Social Security in the Late 1990s,* ed. Jane Pulkingham and Gordon Ternowetsky, 52-66. Halifax: Fernwood, 1996.

–. *Federal Social Programs: Setting the Record Straight.* Ottawa: Caledon Institute for Social Policy, 1993.

Benson, Edgar. *Budget Speech.* 22 October. Ottawa: Queen's Printer, 1968.

–. *Budget Speech.* 18 June. Ottawa: Department of Finance, 1971.

Betcherman, Gordon. 'Inside the Black Box: Human Resource Management and the Labor Market.' In *Jobs, Bad Jobs, No Jobs: Tough Choices for Canadian Labor Law,* ed. John Richards and William G. Watson, 70-102. Toronto: C.D. Howe Institute, 1995.

Beveridge, William. *Full Employment in a Free Society.* London: George Allen and Unwin, 1944.

Bienefeld, Fred, Duncan Cameron, Harold Chorney, Bob Dale, Andrew Jackson, Tom Naylor, Mario Seccareccia, Monica Townson, and Mel Watkins. *'Bleeding the Patient': The Debt/Deficit Hoax Exposed.* Ottawa: Canadian Centre for Policy Alternatives, 1993.

Bliss, Michael. *Right Honourable Men: The Descent of Canadian Politics from Macdonald to Mulroney.* Toronto: HarperCollins, 1994.

Bossons, John. 'Issues in the Analysis of Government Deficits.' In *Fiscal and Monetary Policy,* research coordinator John Sargent, 85-112. Collected Research Studies Series/Royal Commission on the Economic Union and Development Prospects for Canada. Vol. 21. Toronto: University of Toronto Press, 1986.

Bouey, Gerald K. 'Remarks by Gerald K. Bouey, Governor of the Bank of Canada.' *Bank of Canada Review* (October 1975): 23-30.

–. 'Statement by Gerald K. Bouey, Governor of the Bank of Canada.' *Bank of Canada Review* (November 1975): 3-7.

Bradford, Neil. *Commissioning Ideas: Canadian National Policy Innovation in Comparative Perspective.* Toronto: Oxford University Press, 1998.

–. 'The Policy Influence of Economic Ideas: Interests, Institutions and Innovation in Canada.' *Studies in Political Economy* 59 (Summer 1999): 17-60.

Bruce, Neil, and Douglas D. Purvis. 'Consequences of Government Budget Deficits.' In *Fiscal and Monetary Policy,* research coordinator John Sargent, 43-84. Collected Research Studies Series/Royal Commission on the Economic Union and Development Prospects for Canada. Vol. 21. Toronto: University of Toronto Press, 1986.

Bruno, Michael, and Jeffrey D. Sachs. *Economics of Worldwide Stagflation.* Oxford: Basil Blackwell, 1985.

Buchanan, James M., and Richard E. Wagner. *Democracy in Deficit: The Political Legacy of Lord Keynes.* New York: Academic Press, 1977.

Burton, John. 'Fifty Years On: Background and Foreground.' In *Keynes's General Theory: Fifty Years On – Its Relevance and Irrelevance to Modern Times,* 3-24. London: Institute of Economic Affairs, 1986.

Cairns, Alan C. 'The Electoral System and the Party System in Canada, 1921-1965.' *Canadian Journal of Political Science* 1, 1 (1968): 55-80.

Cameron, David R. 'The Growth of Government Spending: The Canadian Experience in Comparative Perspective.' In *State and Society: Canada in Comparative Perspective,* research coordinator Keith G. Banting, 21-51. Collective Research Studies Series/Royal Commission on the Economic Union and Development Prospects for Canada no. 31. Toronto: University of Toronto Press, 1986.

–. 'Social Democracy, Corporatism, Labour Quiescence and the Representation of Economic Interest in Advanced Capitalist Society.' In *Order and Conflict in Contemporary Capitalism: Studies in the Political Economy of Western European Nations,* ed. John H. Goldthorpe, 143-78. Oxford: Oxford University Press, 1984.

Cameron, David Robertson. 'The Faltering Scapegoat: Canadian Federalism and Its Prospects.' *Politics: Canada,* 8th ed., ed. Paul W. Fox and Graham White, 157-65. Toronto: McGraw-Hill, 1995.

–. 'Half-Eaten Carrot, Bent Stick: Decentralization in an Era of Fiscal Restraint.' *Canadian Public Administration* 37, 4 (1994): 431-44.

–. 'Post-Modern Ontario and the Laurentian Thesis.' In *Canada: State of the Federation 1994*, ed. Douglas Brown and Janet Hiebert, 109-32. Kingston, ON: Institute of Intergovernmental Relations, 1994.

Cameron, Duncan. Introduction to *Canada under Free Trade*, ed. Duncan Cameron and Mel Watkins, ix-xxiii. Toronto: James Lorimer, 1993.

Cameron, Duncan, and Daniel Drache. 'Outside the Macdonald Commission: Reply to Richard Simeon.' *Studies in Political Economy* 26 (Summer 1988): 173-80.

Cameron, Duncan, with Mel Clark. 'Renegotiation and Termination.' In *Canada under Free Trade*, ed. Duncan Cameron and Mel Watkins, 277-82. Toronto: James Lorimer, 1993.

Cameron, Maxwell A., and Brian W. Tomlin. *The Making of NAFTA: How the Deal Was Done*. Ithaca, NY: Cornell University Press, 2000.

Cameron, Stevie. *On the Take: Crime, Corruption and Greed in the Mulroney Years*. Toronto: Macfarlane Walter and Ross, 1994.

Campbell, Murray, and Anne McIlroy. 'Liberals Offer to Spend More on Health Care.' *Globe and Mail*, 29 April 1997, A1.

Campbell, Robert M. 'From Keynesianism to Monetarism.' *Queen's Quarterly* 88, 4 (1981): 635-50.

–. *The Full-Employment Objective in Canada, 1945-85: Historical, Conceptual, and Comparative Perspectives*. Study prepared for the Economic Council of Canada. Ottawa: Supply and Services Canada, 1991.

–. *Grand Illusions: The Politics of the Keynesian Experience in Canada, 1945-75*. Peterborough, ON: Broadview Press, 1987.

–. 'Jobs ... Job ... Jo ... J ... The Conservatives and the Unemployed.' In *How Ottawa Spends: The Politics of Competitiveness – 1992-93*, ed. Frances Abele, 23-55. Ottawa: Carleton University Press, 1992.

–. 'Post-Keynesian Politics and the Post-Schumpeterian World.' *Canadian Journal of Political and Social Theory* 8, 1-2 (1984): 72-91.

Canada. Department of Finance. *Agenda: Jobs and Growth – A New Framework for Economic Policy*. October. Ottawa: Department of Finance, 1994.

–. *Agenda: Jobs and Growth – Creating a Healthy Fiscal Climate – The Economic and Fiscal Update*. October. Canada: Department of Finance, 1994.

–. *Annual Financial Report of the Government of Canada: Fiscal Year 2000-2001*. September. Ottawa: Department of Finance, 2001.

–. *The Budget Chart Book 1998 – Building Canada for the 21st Century: A Strong Economy and a Secure Society*. 24 February. Ottawa: Department of Finance, 1998.

–. *Budget Papers*. 26 February. Ottawa: Department of Finance, 1986.

–. *Canada's Recent Inflation Experience, November 1978*. One of a series of papers on medium- and long-term economic issues. Ottawa: Department of Finance, 1978.

–. *The Economic and Fiscal Update: Strong Economy and Secure Society*. 14 October. Ottawa: Department of Finance, 1998.

–. *The Economic Assumptions Underlying the Fiscal Projections of the Budget*. 11 December. Ottawa: Department of Finance, 1979.

–. *Government of Canada Tax Expenditure Account: A Conceptual Analysis and Account of Tax Preferences in the Federal Income and Commodity Tax Systems*. December. Ottawa: Department of Finance, 1979.

–. News Release 2001-049, '*Economic Update* Announces Continued Budgetary Surpluses and Further Debt Reduction.' 17 May 2001.

Canada. Department of Reconstruction. *Employment and Income with Special Reference to the Initial Period of Reconstruction*. Ottawa: Department of Reconstruction, 1945.

Canada. House of Commons. *Debates,* 7 November 1984. 33rd Parliament, 1st Session. Vol. 1. Ottawa: Canada Communications Group, 1984.

–. House of Commons. *Debates,* 27 February 1996. 35th Parliament, 2nd Session. Vol. 133. Ottawa: Canada Communications Group, 1996.

–. House of Commons. *Debates,* 30 January 2001. 37th Parliament, 1st Session. Vol. 137. Ottawa: Canadian Government Publishing, 2001.

Canada. Human Resources Development Canada. *Knowledge Matters: Skills and Learning for Canadians: Canada's Innovation Strategy.* Hull, QC: Human Resources Development Canada, 2002.

Canada. Industry Canada. *Achieving Excellence: Investing in People, Knowledge and Opportunity: Canada's Innovation Strategy.* Ottawa: Industry Canada, 2002.

Canada. Royal Commission on the Economic Union and Development Prospects for Canada. (The Macdonald Commission.) *Report.* Vols. 1 and 2. Ottawa: Minister of Supply and Services, 1985.

Canadian Press. 'Deficit Numbers Belie Tory Claims.' *Globe and Mail,* 9 November 1984, A11.

–. 'Program Goes beyond PC '74 Plan, Stanfield Says.' *Globe and Mail,* 15 October 1975, B4.

Carroll, Barbara Wake, and Ruth J.E. Jones. 'The Road to Innovation, Convergence, or Inertia: Devolution in Housing Policy in Canada.' *Canadian Public Policy* 26, 3 (2000): 277-93.

Carty, R.K. 'On the Road Again: The Stalled Omnibus Revisited.' In *Canadian Political Party Systems: A Reader,* ed. R.K. Carty, 624-40. Peterborough, ON: Broadview Press, 1992.

Cheveldayoff, Wayne. 'Federal Sales Tax Cut to 9% in a Boost-Business Budget.' *Globe and Mail,* 19 November 1978, A1-A2.

–. 'Stanfield Says Liberals Deserve "Honor" of Defeat over Budget.' *Globe and Mail,* 9 May 1974, A1.

Chorney, Harold. *The Deficit: Hysteria and the Current Economic Crisis.* Ottawa: Centre for Policy Alternatives, 1985.

–. *The Deficit and Debt Management: An Alternative to Monetarism.* Ottawa: Canadian Centre for Policy Alternatives, 1989.

Chorney, Harold, John Hotson, and Mario Seccareccia. *'The Deficit Made Me Do It!' The Myths about Government Debt,* ed. Ed Finn. Ottawa: Canadian Centre for Policy Alternatives, 1992.

Chrétien, Jean. *The Budget.* 10 April. Ottawa: Department of Finance, 1978.

–. *Budget Speech.* 16 November. Ottawa: Department of Finance, 1978.

–. *Economic and Fiscal Statement.* 20 October. Ottawa: Department of Finance, 1977.

Clarke, Harold D., Lawrence Leduc, Jane Jenson, and Jon H. Pammett. *Absent Mandate: Interpreting Change in Canadian Elections.* Toronto: Gage, 1991.

Clarkson, Stephen. 'Constitutionalizing the Canadian-American Relationship.' In *Canada under Free Trade,* ed. Duncan Cameron and Mel Watkins, 3-20. Toronto: James Lorimer, 1993.

–. 'Disjunctions: Free Trade and the Paradox of Canadian Development.' In *The New Era of Global Competition: State Policy and Market Power,* ed. Daniel Drache and Meric Gertler, 103-26. Montreal and Kingston: McGill-Queen's University Press, 1991.

Clarkson, Stephen, and Christina McCall. *Trudeau and Our Times.* Vol. 1, *The Magnificent Obsession.* Toronto: McClelland and Stewart, 1990.

–. *Trudeau and Our Times.* Vol. 2, *The Heroic Delusion.* Toronto: McClelland and Stewart, 1994.

Clarkson, Stephen, and Timothy Lewis. 'The Contested State: Canada in the Post-Cold War, Post-Keynesian, Post-Fordist, Post-National Era.' In *How Ottawa Spends 1999-2000 – Shape Shifting: Canadian Governance Toward the 21st Century,* ed. Leslie Pal, 293-340. Toronto: Oxford University Press, 1999.

Cleroux, Richard. 'Mulroney Latest Entry in PC Race.' *Globe and Mail,* 16 October 1975, A13.

Coleman, William. 'Monetary Policy, Accountability, and Legitimacy: A Review of the Issues in Canada.' *Canadian Journal of Political Science* 24, 4 (1991): 711-34.

Cook, Peter. 'Leak to TV Camera Means More Funds.' *Globe and Mail,* 20 April 1983, A1.

Cooper, Barry. *The Klein Achievement.* Monograph Series on Public Policy and Public Administration no. 1. Toronto: University of Toronto, 1996.

Co-operative Commonwealth Federation. 'The Regina Manifesto.' In *Canadian Political Thought,* ed. H.D. Forbes, 241-50. Toronto: Oxford University Press, 1987.

Courchene, Thomas J. 'Glocalization: The Regional/International Interface.' *Canadian Journal of Regional Science* 18, 1 (1995): 1-20.
–. *Half-Way Home: Canada's Remarkable Fiscal Turnaround and the Paul Martin Legacy.* Policy Matters 3, 8. Montreal: Institute for Research on Public Policy, 2002.
–. 'Mon pays, c'est l'hiver: Reflections of a Market Populist,' *Canadian Journal of Economics* 25, 4 (1992): 759-91.
–. 'Zero Means Almost Nothing: Towards a Preferable Inflation and Macro Stance.' In *Rearrangements: The Courchene Papers.* Oakville: Mosaic Press, 1992.
Courchene, Thomas J., with Colin R. Telmer. *From Heartland to North American Region State: The Social, Fiscal and Federal Evolution of Ontario – An Interpretive Essay.* Monograph Series on Public Policy and Public Administration no. 6. Toronto: University of Toronto, Faculty of Management, 1998.
Cox, Robert. 'The Global Political Economy and Social Choice.' In *The New Era of Global Competition: State Policy and Market Power,* ed. Daniel Drache and Meric S. Gertler, 335-50. Montreal and Kingston: McGill-Queen's University Press, 1991.
–. 'Global Restructuring: Making Sense of the Changing International Political Economy.' In *Political Economy and the Changing Global Order,* ed. Richard Stubbs and Geoffrey R.D. Underhill, 45-59. Toronto: McClelland and Stewart, 1994.
Crosbie, John C. *Budget Speech.* 11 December. Ottawa: Department of Finance, 1979.
Crosbie, John C., with Geoffrey Stevens. *No Holds Barred: My Life in Politics.* Toronto: McClelland and Stewart, 1997.
Crow, John. 'The Bank of Canada and Its Objectives.' *Bank of Canada Review* (April 1987): 21-7.
Curtis, Douglas. 'Canadian Fiscal and Monetary Policy and Macroeconomic Performance 1984-1993: The Mulroney Years.' *Journal of Canadian Studies* 32, 1 (1997): 135-52.
de Bever, Leo. 'International Impact of the Federal Budget.' In *The 1995 Federal Budget: Retrospect and Prospect,* ed. Thomas J. Courchene and Thomas A. Wilson, 3-10. Policy Forum Series no. 33. Kingston, ON: John Deutsch Institute for the Study of Economic Policy, 1995.
Deutsch, J.J. 'War Finance and the Canadian Economy, 1914-20.' *Canadian Journal of Economics and Political Science* 6, 4 (1940): 525-42.
Dodge, David A. 'Reflections on the Role of Fiscal Policy: The Doug Purvis Memorial Lecture.' *Canadian Public Policy* 24, 3 (1998): 275-89.
Doern, G. Bruce. 'The Role of Royal Commissions in the General Policy Process and in Federal-Provincial Relations.' *Canadian Public Administration* 10, 4 (1967): 417-33.
Doern, G. Bruce, Allan M. Maslove, and Michael J. Prince. *Public Budgeting in Canada: Politics, Economics, and Management.* Ottawa: Carleton University Press, 1988.
Doern, G. Bruce, and Brian W. Tomlin, *Faith and Fear: The Free Trade Story.* Toronto: Stoddart, 1991.
Doern, G. Bruce, Leslie A. Pal, and Brian W. Tomlin. 'The Internationalization of Canadian Public Policy.' In *Border Crossings: The Internationalization of Canadian Public Policy,* ed. G. Bruce Doern, Leslie A. Pal, and Brian W. Tomlin, 1-26. Toronto: Oxford University Press, 1996.
Donner, Arthur, and Douglas D. Peters. *The Monetarist Counter-Revolution: A Critique of Canadian Monetary Policy 1975-1979.* Toronto: James Lorimer, 1979.
Doremus, Paul, William W. Keller, Louis W. Pauly, and Simon Reich. *The Myth of the Global Corporation.* Princeton, NJ: Princeton University Press, 1998.
Dornbusch, Rudiger, and Mario Draghi. Introduction to *Public Debt Management: Theory and History,* ed. Rudiger Dornbusch and Mario Draghi, 1-13. New York: Cambridge University Press, 1990.
Drache, Daniel. 'Introduction – Celebrating Innis: The Man, the Legacy, and Our Future.' In *Staples, Markets, and Cultural Change,* by Harold A. Innis, xii-lv. Montreal and Kingston: McGill-Queen's University Press, 1995.
Drainville, André C. 'Monetarism in Canada and the World Economy.' *Studies in Political Economy* 46 (Spring 1995): 7-42.
Drucker, Peter F. 'The Global Economy and the Nation-State.' *Foreign Affairs* 76, 5 (1997): 159-71.

Drummond, Don. 'Deficit Elimination, Economic Performance and Social Progress in Canada in the 1990s.' In *The Review of Economic Performance and Social Progress – The Longest Decade: Canada in the 1990s*, ed. Keith G. Banting, Andrew Sharpe, and France St-Hilaire, 131-40. Montreal: Institute for Research on Public Policy, 2001.

Dunn, Christopher. 'FYI: SUFA, DOA.' *Policy Options* 21, 4 (2001): 50-1.

Dupré, J. Stefan. 'Comment: The Promise of Procurement Federalism.' In *The Future of Fiscal Federalism*, ed. Keith G. Banting, Douglas M. Brown, and Thomas J. Courchene, 249-54. Kingston, ON: Queen's University, School of Policy Studies, 1994.

Editorial. 'A Patchwork War.' *Globe and Mail*, 14 October 1975, A6.

–. 'When the Deficit War Was Over.' *Globe and Mail*, 11 February 1997, A14.

Eichner, Alfred S. Introduction to *A Guide to Post-Keynesian Economics*, ed. Alfred S. Eichner. New York: M.E. Sharpe, 1978.

Evans, Peter B., Dietrich Rueschemeyer, and Theda Skocpol, eds., *Bringing the State Back In*. New York: Cambridge University Press, 1985.

Fagan, Drew. 'Spending Increases Decried.' *Globe and Mail*, 27 February 1991, B1, B6.

Feschuk, Scott. 'Cutting Debt, Taxes Top Canadians' List.' *Globe and Mail*, 1 November 1997, A1.

Flanagan, Tom. *Waiting for the Wave: The Reform Party and Preston Manning*. Toronto: Stoddart, 1995.

Fleming, Donald. *Budget Speech*. 20 December. Ottawa: Queen's Printer, 1960.

–. *Budget Speech*. 20 June. Ottawa: Queen's Printer, 1961.

–. *Budget Speech*. 10 April. Ottawa: Queen's Printer, 1962.

Forbes, H.D. 'Absent Mandate 88? Parties and Voters in Canada.' In *Party Politics in Canada*, ed. Hugh Thorburn, 255-69. 6th ed. Scarborough, ON: Prentice Hall Canada, 1991.

Fortin, Pierre. 'The Canadian Fiscal Problem: The Macroeconomic Connection.' In *Hard Money, Hard Times: Why Zero Inflation Hurts Canadians*, ed. Lars Osberg and Pierre Fortin, 26-38. Toronto: James Lorimer, 1998.

–. *The Canadian Standard of Living: Is There a Way Up?* Benefactors Lecture Series, 19 October. Toronto: C.D. Howe Institute, 1999.

–. 'The Great Canadian Slump.' *Canadian Journal of Economics* 29, 4 (1996): 761-87.

–. 'The Great Canadian Slump: A Rejoinder to Freedman and Macklem.' *Canadian Journal of Economics* 32, 4 (1999): 1082-92.

–. 'Interest Rates, Unemployment and Inflation: The Canadian Experience in the 1990s.' In *The Review of Economic Performance and Social Progress – The Longest Decade: Canada in the 1990s*, ed. Keith G. Banting, Andrew Sharpe, and France St-Hilaire, 113-30. Montreal: Institute for Research on Public Policy, 2001.

Foucault, Michel. *Power/Knowledge: Selected Interviews and Other Writings*. Ed. Colin Gordon. New York: Pantheon Books, 1980.

Frank, Jeff. *The New Keynesian Economics: Unemployment, Search and Contracting*. Brighton, UK: Wheatsheaf Books, 1986.

Freedman, Charles, and Tiff Macklem. 'A Comment on "The Great Canadian Slump."' *Canadian Journal of Economics* 31, 3 (1998): 646-65.

Freeman, Alan. 'Fight Recession, Not Deficit, Liberals, NDP Urge Wilson.' *Globe and Mail*, 25 February 1991, A6.

French, Richard. *How Ottawa Decides: Planning and Industrial Policy Making 1968-1984*. 2nd ed. Toronto: James Lorimer, 1984.

Friedman, Milton. 'The Role of Monetary Policy.' *The American Economic Review* 58, 1 (1968): 1-17.

Galbraith, John Kenneth. *The Age of Uncertainty*. Boston: Houghton Mifflin, 1977.

–. *Economics and the Public Purpose*. Boston: Houghton Mifflin, 1973.

–. *A View from the Stands: Of People, Politics, Military Power, and the Arts*. Boston: Houghton Mifflin, 1986.

–. *The New Industrial State*. 4th ed. Scarborough, ON: Mentor, 1985.

Gerth, H.H., and C. Wright Mills. 'Introduction: The Man and His Work.' In *From Max Weber: Essays in Sociology*, ed. H.H. Gerth and C. Wright Mills, 3-74. London: Kegan Paul, Trench, Trubner, 1947.

Gibbins, Roger. *Shifting Sands: Exploring the Political Foundations of SUFA.* Policy Matters 2, 3. Montreal: Institute for Research on Public Policy, 2001.

Giddens, Anthony. *The Third Way: The Renewal of Social Democracy.* Cambridge: Polity Press, 1998.

Gilbert, J.C. *Keynes's Impact on Monetary Economics.* Toronto: Butterworths, 1982.

Gill, Stephen. 'Globalisation, Market Civilisation, and Disciplinary Neoliberalism.' *Millennium: Journal of International Studies* 24, 3 (1995): 399-423.

–. 'Knowledge, Politics, and Neo-Liberal Political Economy.' In *Political Economy and the Changing Global Order,* ed. Richard Stubbs and Geoffrey R.D. Underhill, 75-88. Toronto: McClelland and Stewart, 1994.

Gillespie, W. Irwin. 'The 1981 Federal Budget: Muddling through or Purposeful Tax Reform?' *Canadian Tax Journal* 31, 6 (1983): 975-1002.

–. 'Postwar Canadian Fiscal Policy Revisited, 1945-1975.' *Canadian Tax Journal* 27, 3 (1979): 265-76.

–. *Tax, Borrow and Spend: Financing Federal Spending in Canada, 1867-1990.* Ottawa: Carleton University Press, 1991.

Goldstein, Judith. *Ideas, Interests, and American Trade Policy.* Ithaca, NY: Cornell University Press, 1993.

Goldstein, Judith, and Robert O. Keohane. 'Ideas and Foreign Policy: An Analytical Framework.' In *Ideas and Foreign Policy: Beliefs, Institutions, and Political Change,* ed. Judith Goldstein and Robert O. Keohane, 3-30. Ithaca, NY: Cornell University Press, 1993.

Gonick, Cy. *The Great Economic Debate.* Toronto: James Lorimer, 1987.

Gordon, H. Scott. 'A Twenty Year Perspective: Some Reflections on the Keynesian Revolution in Canada.' In *Canadian Economic Policy since the War,* ed. S.F. Kalisky, 23-46. Montreal: Canadian Trade Committee, 1966.

Gordon, Walter. *Budget Speech.* 13 June. Ottawa: Queen's Printer, 1963.

–. *Budget Speech.* 16 March. Ottawa: Queen's Printer, 1964.

Gourevitch, Peter. *Politics in Hard Times: Comparative Responses to International Economic Crisis.* Ithaca, NY: Cornell University Press, 1986.

Graves, Frank L. 'The Economy through a Public Lens: Shifting Canadian Views of the Economy.' In *The Review of Economic Performance and Social Progress – The Longest Decade: Canada in the 1990s,* ed. Keith G. Banting, Andrew Sharpe, and France St-Hilaire, 63-86. Montreal: Institute for Research on Public Policy, 2001.

–. 'Rethinking Government As If People Mattered: From "Reaganomics" to "Humanomics."' In *How Ottawa Spends 1999-2000: Shape Shifting: Canadian Governance toward the 21st Century,* ed. Leslie A. Pal, 37-73. Toronto: Oxford University Press, 1999.

Greenspon, Edward, and Anthony Wilson-Smith. *Double Vision: The Inside Story of the Liberals in Power.* Toronto: Doubleday Canada, 1996.

Ha, Tu Thanh. 'Liberals' Big Pledge a Loner, Martin Says.' *Globe and Mail,* 30 April 1997, A8.

Hale, Geoffrey E. 'Managing the Fiscal Dividend: The Politics of Selected Activism.' In *How Ottawa Spends 2000-2001 – Past Imperfect, Future Tense,* ed. Leslie A. Pal, 59-94. Toronto: Oxford University Press, 2000.

–. 'Reforming Employment Insurance: Transcending the Politics of the Status Quo.' *Canadian Public Policy* 24, 4 (1998): 429-51.

Hall, Peter A. 'Conclusion: The Politics of Keynesian Ideas.' In *The Political Power of Economic Ideas: Keynesianism across Nations,* ed. Peter A. Hall, 361-91. Princeton, NJ: Princeton University Press, 1989.

–. 'Policy Paradigms, Social Learning, and the State: The Case of Economic Policymaking in Britain.' *Comparative Politics* 25, 3 (1993): 275-96.

Harris, Richard G. 'The Public Debt and the Social Policy Round.' In *Paying Our Way: The Welfare State in Hard Times,* ed. Richard G. Harris, John Richards, David M. Brown, John McCallum, 1-31. Toronto: C.D. Howe Institute, 1994.

Harris, Walter. *Budget Speech.* 5 April. Ottawa: Queen's Printer, 1955.

Hart, Michael. *Fifty Years of Canadian Tradecraft: Canada at the GATT, 1947-1997.* Ottawa: Centre for Trade Policy and Law, 1998.

Hartle, Douglas G. *The Federal Deficit.* School of Policy Studies Discussion Paper Series no. 93-30. Kingston, ON: Queen's University, 1993.

Heclo, Hugh. 'Ideas, Interests, Institutions.' In *The Dynamics of American Politics: Approaches and Interpretations,* ed. Lawrence C. Dodd and Calvin Jillson, 366-92. Boulder, CO: Westview Press, 1994.

–. *Modern Social Politics in Britain and Sweden.* New Haven, CT: Yale University Press, 1974.

Heisz, Andrew, Andrew Jackson, and Garnett Picot. 'Distributional Outcomes in Canada in the 1990s.' In *The Review of Economic Performance and Social Progress – The Longest Decade: Canada in the 1990s,* ed. Keith G. Banting, Andrew Sharpe, and France St-Hilaire, 247-72. Montreal: Institute for Research on Public Policy, 2001.

Helleiner, Eric. *States and the Reemergence of Global Finance: From Bretton Woods to the 1990s.* Ithaca, NY: Cornell University Press, 1994.

Helliwell, John F. 'Canada's National Economy: There's More to It Than You Thought.' In *Canada: The State of the Federation 1998/99: How Canadians Connect,* ed. Harvey Lazar and Tom McIntosh, 87-100. Kingston, ON: Institute of Intergovernmental Relations, 1999.

–. 'Checking the Brain Drain: Evidence and Implications.' *Policy Options* 20, 7 (1999): 6-17.

–. *Globalization: Myths, Facts, and Consequences.* Benefactors Lecture Series, 23 October. Toronto: C.D. Howe Institute, 2000.

Hill, Roderick. 'Real Income, Unemployment and Subjective Well-Being: Revisiting the Costs and Benefits of Inflation Reduction in Canada.' *Canadian Public Policy* 26, 4 (2000): 399-414.

Hirst, Paul. 'The Global Economy – Myths and Realities.' *International Affairs* 73, 3 (1997): 409-25.

Hoberg, George. 'Canada and North American Integration.' *Canadian Public Policy* 26, supplement 2 (2000): S35-S50.

Hobsbawm, Eric. *The Age of Capital, 1848-1875.* London: Abacus, 1975.

–. *Nations and Nationalism since 1780: Programme, Myth, Reality.* 2nd ed. New York: Cambridge University Press, 1992.

Hogg, Peter W. *Constitutional Law of Canada, Student Edition.* Toronto: Thomson Canada, 1999.

Howard, Ross. 'Budget a Betrayal, Opposition Says.' *Globe and Mail,* 29 April 1989, A1-A2.

–. 'Opposition Leaders Say Minister Has Given Them Election Weapon.' *Globe and Mail,* 11 February 1988, B14.

Howard, Ross, and Cathryn Motherwell, 'What's Good for Toronto Called Bad for East, West.' *Globe and Mail,* 19 February 1987, B10.

Ilsley, J.L. *Budget Speech.* 12 September. Ottawa: King's Printer, 1939.

–. *Budget Speech.* 12 October. Ottawa: Queen's Printer, 1945.

–. *Budget Speech.* 27 June. Ottawa: Queen's Printer, 1946.

'Inequality.' *The Economist* 333, 7888 (5 November 1994): 19-21.

Inglehart, Ronald. *The Silent Revolution: Changing Values and Political Styles among Western Publics.* Princeton, NJ: Princeton University Press, 1977.

Irvine, William P. 'Epilogue: The 1980 Election.' In *Canada at the Polls, 1979 and 1980: A Study of the General Elections,* ed. Howard R. Penniman, 337-98. Washington, DC: American Enterprise Institute for Public Policy Research, 1981.

–. 'An Overview of the 1974 Federal Election in Canada.' In *Canada at the Polls: The General Election of 1974,* ed. Howard R. Penniman, 29-55. Washington, DC: American Enterprise Institute for Public Policy Research, 1975.

Jackson, Andrew. *Against John Crow: A Critique of Current Monetary Policy and Proposals for an Alternative.* Ottawa: Canadian Centre for Policy Alternatives, 1990.

–. *Deficit, Debt and the Contradictions of Tory Economics.* Ottawa: Canadian Centre for Policy Alternatives, 1990.

–. 'From Leaps of Faith to Lapses of Logic.' *Policy Options* 20, 5 (1999): 12-18.

Jenkins, Paul, and Brian O'Reilly. 'Monetary Policy and the Economic Well-Being of Canadians.' In *The Review of Economic Performance and Social Progress – The Longest Decade: Canada in the 1990s,* ed. Keith G. Banting, Andrew Sharpe, and France St-Hilaire, 89-111. Montreal: Institute for Research on Public Policy, 2001.

Jenson, Jane. '"Different" but Not "Exceptional": Canada's Permeable Fordism.' *Canadian Review of Sociology and Anthropology* 26, 1 (1989): 69-94.

Johnson, D. 'An Evaluation of the Bank of Canada Zero Inflation Target: Do Wilson and Crow Agree?' *Canadian Public Policy* 26, 3 (1990): 308-25.

Johnston, Richard, André Blais, Henry E. Brady, and Jean Crête. *Letting the People Decide: Dynamics of a Canadian Election.* Montreal and Kingston: McGill-Queen's University Press, 1992.

Johnson, William. 'Lewis Says Budget Is Cruel, Hypocritical, Can't Be Supported.' *Globe and Mail,* 8 May 1974, A1.

Johnson, William, Jeffrey Simpson, and Richard Cleroux. 'Quebec Angry but Still Undecided about Federal Sales Tax Reduction.' *Globe and Mail,* 12 April 1978, A1-A2.

Kalecki, Michael. 'Political Aspects of Full Employment.' In *Collected Works of Michael Kalecki,* ed. Jerzy Osiatynski. Vol. 1, *Capitalism: Business Cycles and Full Employment,* 347-56. Oxford: Clarendon Press, 1990.

Kenen, Peter. *The International Economy.* 3rd ed. New York: Cambridge University Press, 1994.

Keohane, Robert. 'Economics, Inflation, and the Role of the State: Political Implications of the McCracken Report.' *World Politics* 31 (October 1978): 108-28.

Keynes, John Maynard. *The Collected Writings of John Maynard Keynes.* Vol. 2, *The Economic Consequences of the Peace,* ed. Donald Moggridge. 1919. Reprint, London: Macmillan, 1971.

–. *The Collected Writings of John Maynard Keynes.* Vol. 4, *A Tract on Monetary Reform,* ed. Donald Moggridge. 1923. Reprint, London: Macmillan, 1971.

–. *The Collected Writings of John Maynard Keynes.* Vols. 5 and 6, *A Treatise on Money,* ed. Donald Moggridge. 1930. Reprint, London: Macmillan, 1971.

–. *The General Theory of Employment Interest and Money.* 1936. Reprint, New York: St. Martin's Press, 1957.

–. 'How to Pay for the War.' In *The Collected Writings of John Maynard Keynes.* Vol. 9, *Essays in Persuasion,* ed. Donald Moggridge, 367-439. 1940. Reprint, London: Macmillan, 1971.

Kneebone, Ronald D., and Kenneth J. McKenzie. 'The Characteristics of Fiscal Policy in Canada.' *Canadian Public Policy* 25, 4 (1999): 483-501.

Krahn, Harvey. 'Non-Standard Work on the Rise.' *Perspectives on Labour and Income* 7, 4 (1995): 35-42.

Krasner, Stephen D. 'Approaches to the State: Alternative Conceptions and Historical Dynamics.' *Comparative Politics* 16, 2 (1984): 223-46.

Kroeger, Arthur. 'Changing Course: The Federal Government's Program Review of 1994-95.' In *Hard Choices or No Choices: Assessing Program Review,* ed. Armelita Armita and Jacques Bourgault, 21-8. Toronto: Institute of Public Administration, 1996.

Krugman, Paul. *Peddling Prosperity: Economic Sense and Nonsense in the Age of Diminished Expectations.* New York: W.W. Norton, 1994.

Lalonde, Marc. *Budget Papers – Supplementary Information and Notices of Ways and Means Motions on the Budget.* 19 April. Ottawa: Department of Finance, 1983.

–. *Budget Speech.* 19 April. Ottawa: Department of Finance, 1983.

–. *The Budget Speech.* 15 February. Ottawa: Department of Finance, 1984.

–. *The Canadian Economy in Recovery.* February. Ottawa: Department of Finance, 1984.

–. *The Economic Outlook for Canada.* 19 April. Ottawa: Department of Finance, 1983.

–. *The Federal Deficit in Perspective.* April. Ottawa: Department of Finance, 1983.

–. *Statement on the Economic Outlook and the Financial Position of the Government of Canada.* 27 October. Ottawa: Department of Finance, 1982.

Langille, David. 'The Business Council on National Issues and the Canadian State.' *Studies in Political Economy* 24 (Autumn 1987): 41-85.

Laxer, Gordon. *Open for Business: The Roots of Foreign Ownership in Canada.* Toronto: Oxford University Press, 1989.

Laycock, David. 'Reforming Canadian Democracy? Institutions and Ideology in the Reform Party Project.' *Canadian Journal of Political Science* 27, 2 (1994): 213-47.

Lazar, Harvey, ed. *Canada: The State of the Federation 1997 – Non-Constitutional Renewal.* Kingston, ON: Institute of Intergovernmental Relations, 1998.

Leduc, Lawrence, and J. Alex Murray. 'Survey Shows More Public Support of Curbs.' *Globe and Mail,* 25 May 1976, B1.

Lester, Gillian. 'Careers and Contingency.' *Stanford Law Review* 51, 1 (1998): 73-145.

Lewis, Timothy. 'How Keynes Came to Canada: Keynesian Indeterminacy and the Canadian Interpretation of Keynesianism.' Paper presented at the Annual Meeting of the Canadian Political Science Association, St. Catharines, ON, June 1996.

Liberal Party of Canada. *Creating Opportunity: The Liberal Plan for Canada.* Ottawa: Liberal Party of Canada, 1993.

–. *A Record of Achievement: A Report on the Liberal Government's 36 Months in Office.* Ottawa: Liberal Party of Canada, 1996.

–. *Securing Our Future Together: Preparing Canada for the 21st Century.* Ottawa: Liberal Party of Canada, 1997.

Lindquist, Evert A. 'The Bewildering Pace of Public Sector Reform in Canada.' In *Public Sector Reform: Rationale, Trends, and Problems,* ed. Jan-Erik Lane, 47-63. London: Sage, 1997.

Lipsey, Richard G., Paul N. Courant, and Douglas D. Purvis, *Economics.* 8th Canadian ed. New York: HarperCollins, 1994.

Little, Bruce. 'Wilson Says Public Backs Him.' *Globe and Mail,* 25 May 1985, A1-A2.

Little, Bruce, and Christopher Waddell. 'Dollar's Fall Sets Stage for Deficit-Cutting Budget.' *Globe and Mail,* 26 February 1986, A1, A4.

Locke, John. *Second Treatise of Government.* Ed. C.B. Macpherson. 1690. Indianapolis: Hackett, 1980.

Lucas, R. 'The Bank of Canada and Zero Inflation: A New Cross of Gold?' *Canadian Public Policy* 25, 1 (1989): 84-93.

McBride, Stephen. 'The Continuing Crisis of Social Democracy: Ontario's Social Contract in Perspective.' *Studies in Political Economy* 50 (Summer 1995): 65-93.

McCallum, John. 'Two Cheers for the FTA.' *Policy Options* 20, 5 (1999): 6-11.

McCarthy, Shawn. 'Job Losses, Rate Cuts Predicted.' *Globe and Mail,* 1 September 2001, A1, A4.

–. 'Martin Backs off Seniors Plan.' *Globe and Mail,* 29 July 1998, A1, A4.

McCracken, Paul, Guido Carli, Herbert Giersch, Attila Karaosmanoglu, Ryutaro Komiya, Assar Lindbeck, Robert Marjolin, and Robin Matthews. *Towards Full Employment and Price Stability.* Paris: Organization for Economic Co-operation and Development, 1977.

Macdonald, Donald. *Attack on Inflation – A Program of National Action.* 14 October. Ottawa: Department of Finance, 1975.

–. *Budget Speech.* 25 May. Ottawa: Department of Finance, 1976.

–. *Budget Speech.* 31 March. Ottawa: Department of Finance, 1977.

MacEachen, Allan J. *The Budget.* 28 October. Ottawa: Department of Finance, 1980.

–. *The Budget.* 28 June. Ottawa: Department of Finance, 1982.

–. *The Budget in More Detail.* 12 November. Ottawa: Department of Finance, 1981.

–. *Budget Papers – Supplementary Information and Notice of Ways and Means Motion on the Budget.* 28 June. Ottawa: Department of Finance, 1982.

–. *Budget Speech.* 12 November. Ottawa: Department of Finance, 1981.

Machiavelli, Niccolò. *The Prince.* In *The Portable Machiavelli,* ed. Peter Bondanella and Mark Musa, 77-166. Toronto: Penguin Books Canada, 1979.

McKenzie, Kenneth J. *A Tragedy of the House of Commons: Political Institutions and Fiscal Policy Outcomes from a Canadian Perspective.* Benefactors Lecture Series, 8 November. Toronto: C.D. Howe Institute, 2001.

Mackintosh, W.A. 'The White Paper on Employment and Income in Its 1945 Setting.' In *Canadian Economic Policy Since the War,* ed. S.F. Kalisky, 9-21. Montreal: Canadian Trade Committee, 1966.

McQuaig, Linda. *Shooting the Hippo: Death by Deficit and Other Canadian Myths.* Toronto: Viking, 1995.

Mankiw, N. Gregory, and David Romer, eds. *New Keynesian Economics.* Cambridge, MA: MIT Press, 1991.

Manning, Preston. *The New Canada.* Toronto: Macmillan, 1992.

Martin, Lawrence. *Chrétien.* Vol. 1, *The Will to Win.* Toronto: Lester, 1995.
–. 'Mulroney Says Turner Hiding Economic Contingency Plans.' *Globe and Mail,* 18 August 1984, A1-A2.
Martin, Paul. *Budget in Brief.* 18 February. Canada: Department of Finance, 1997.
–. *The Budget Plan.* 22 February. Ottawa: Department of Finance, 1994.
–. *Budget Plan.* 27 February. Ottawa: Department of Finance, 1995.
–. *Budget Plan.* 28 February. Ottawa: Department of Finance, 2000.
–. *The Budget Plan 1998: Building Canada for the 21st Century – Strong Economy and Secure Society.* 24 February. Ottawa: Department of Finance, 1998.
–. *The Budget Speech.* 22 February. Ottawa: Department of Finance, 1994.
–. *Budget Speech.* 27 February. Ottawa: Department of Finance, 1995.
–. *Budget Speech.* 6 March. Ottawa: Department of Finance, 1996.
–. *Budget Speech.* 18 February. Ottawa: Department of Finance, 1997.
–. *Economic Statement and Budget Update.* 18 October. Ottawa: Department of Finance, 2000.
–. *Economic Update.* 17 May. Ottawa: Department of Finance, 2001.
–. *Response to Prebudget Consultations – Facing Choices Together.* February. Canada: Department of Finance, 1994.
Maslove, Allan M. 'What Really Happened with Tax Reform.' *Policy Options* 10, 1 (1989): 18-24.
Maslove, Allan M., and Kevin D. Moore. 'From Red Books to Blue Books: Repairing Ottawa's Fiscal House.' In *How Ottawa Spends 1997-98 – Seeing Red: A Liberal Report Card,* ed. Gene Swimmer, 23-49. Ottawa: Carleton University Press, 1997.
Mazankowski, Don. *Budget Papers.* 25 February. Ottawa: Department of Finance, 1992.
–. *The Budget Speech.* 25 February. Ottawa: Department of Finance, 1992.
–. *The Budget Speech.* 26 April. Ottawa: Department of Finance, 1993.
Miliband, Ralph. *Marxism and Politics.* Oxford: Oxford University Press, 1977.
Mimoto, H., and P. Cross. 'The Growth of the Federal Debt.' *Canadian Economic Observer* (June 1991): 3.1-3.17.
Mintz, Jack M., and Ross S. Preston. *Capital Budgeting in the Public Sector.* Policy Forum Series no. 30. Kingston, ON: Queen's University, John Deutsch Institute for the Study of Economic Policy, 1993.
Moggridge, Donald. *Keynes.* Toronto: University of Toronto Press, 1993.
–. *Keynes and the Contemporary World.* Toronto: Ryerson Department of Economics, 1984.
Mulroney, Brian. Interview by Brian Stewart. 'Reflections of a Former Prime Minister.' *The National.* CBC Television, 2 June 1999.
–. 'What's in Free Trade for Canada?' *Globe and Mail,* 17 April 2001, A17.
Nadeau, Richard, André Blais, Neil Nevitte, and Elisabeth Gidengil. 'It's Unemployment, Stupid! Why Perceptions about the Job Situation Hurt the Liberals in the 1997 Election.' *Canadian Public Policy* 26, 1 (2000): 77-91.
Nevitte, Neil. *The Decline of Deference: Canadian Value Change in Cross-National Perspective.* Peterborough, ON: Broadview Press, 1996.
Nevitte, Neil, André Blais, Elisabeth Gidengil, and Richard Nadeau. *Unsteady State: The 1997 Canadian Federal Election.* Toronto: Oxford University Press, 2000.
Noël, Alain. 'The Bloc Québécois As Official Opposition.' In *Canada: The State of the Federation 1994,* ed. Douglas M. Brown and Janet Hiebert, 19-35. Kingston, ON: Institute of Intergovernmental Relations, 1994.
–. 'Collaborative Federalism – With a Footnote.' *Policy Options* 21, 4 (2001): 44-6.
Noel, Sid. 'Ontario and the Federation at the End of the Twentieth Century.' In *Canada: The State of the Federation 1997 – Non-Constitutional Renewal,* ed. Harvey Lazar, 271-93. Kingston, ON: Institute of Intergovernmental Relations, 1998.
Nova Scotia. House of Assembly. *Speech from the Throne.* 58th General Assembly. 1st Session. 7 October 1999. <www.gov.ns.ca/legislature/hansard/han58-1/i99oct07.htm>. 20 January 2003.
Obstfeld, Maurice. 'The Global Capital Market: Benefactor or Menace?' *The Journal of Economic Perspectives* 12, 4 (1998): 9-30.
O'Connor, James. *The Fiscal Crisis of the State.* New York: St. Martin's Press, 1973.

Ontario: Exploring the Region-State Hypothesis. Proceedings of a Colloquium held at the University of Toronto, 26 March 1999. University of Toronto, Department of Political Science, 1999.

Organisation for Economic Co-operation and Development. *OECD Economic Outlook* 49. July. Paris: Organisation for Economic Co-operation and Development, 1991.

Ornstein, Michael. 'The Social Organization of the Canadian Capitalist Class in Comparative Perspective.' *Canadian Review of Sociology and Anthropology* 26, 1 (1989): 151-77.

Osberg, Lars, and Andrew Sharpe. 'Trends in Economic Well-Being in Canada in the 1990s.' In *The Review of Economic Performance and Social Progress – The Longest Decade: Canada in the 1990s,* ed. Keith G. Banting, Andrew Sharpe, and France St-Hilaire, 233-45. Montreal: Institute for Research on Public Policy, 2001.

Ostry, Sylvia. *The Post-Cold War Trading System: Who's on First?* Chicago: University of Chicago Press, 1997.

Pauly, Louis. 'Capital Mobility, State Autonomy and Political Legitimacy.' *Journal of International Affairs* 48, 2 (1995): 369-88.

–. *Who Elected the Bankers?* Ithaca, NY: Cornell University Press, 1997.

Pekkarinen, Jukka. 'Keynesianism and the Scandinavian Models of Economic Policy.' In *The Political Power of Economic Ideas: Keynesianism across Nations,* ed. Peter A. Hall, 311-45. Princeton, NJ: Princeton University Press, 1989.

Perlin, George. 'Opportunity Regained: The Tory Victory in 1984.' In *Canada at the Polls, 1984: A Study of the Federal General Elections,* ed. Howard R. Penniman, 79-96. Durham, NC: Duke University Press, 1988.

Perry, J. Harvey. *Taxes, Tariffs, and Subsidies: A History of Canadian Fiscal Development.* Vols. 1 and 2. Toronto: University of Toronto Press, 1955.

Phillips, A.W. 'The Relation between Unemployment and the Rate of Change in Money Wage Rates in the United Kingdom, 1951-1957.' *Economica* 25, 100 (November 1958): 283-99.

Phillips, Susan D. 'The Canada Health and Social Transfer: Fiscal Federalism in Search of a Vision.' In *Canada: The State of the Federation 1995,* ed. Douglas Brown and Jonathan Rose, 65-96. Kingston, ON: Institute of Intergovernmental Relations, 1995.

Pierson, Paul. 'The Deficit and the Politics of Domestic Reform.' In *The Social Divide: Political Parties and the Future of Activist Government,* ed. Margaret Weir, 126-78. Washington, DC: Brookings Institution Press, 1998.

–. *Dismantling the Welfare State? Reagan, Thatcher, and the Politics of Retrenchment.* New York: Cambridge University Press, 1994.

–. 'The New Politics of the Welfare State.' *World Politics* 48, 2 (1996): 143-79.

Piva, Michael J. *The Borrowing Process: Public Finance in the Province of Canada, 1840-1867.* Ottawa: University of Ottawa Press, 1992.

Plumptre, A.F.W. *Three Decades of Decision: Canada and the World Monetary System, 1944-1975.* Toronto: McClelland and Stewart, 1977.

Polanyi, Karl. *The Great Transformation: The Political and Economic Origins of Our Time.* Boston: Beacon Press, 1944.

Porter, John. *The Vertical Mosaic: An Analysis of Social Class and Power in Canada.* Toronto: University of Toronto Press, 1965.

Prince, Michael J. 'From Health and Welfare to Stealth and Farewell: Federal Social Policy, 1980-2000.' In *How Ottawa Spends 1999-2000 – Shape Shifting: Canadian Governance toward the 21st Century,* ed. Leslie A. Pal. Toronto: Oxford University Press Canada, 1999.

Pulkingham, Jane, and Gordon Ternowetsky. 'The Changing Landscape of Social Policy and the Canadian Welfare State.' In *Remaking Canadian Social Policy: Social Security in the Late 1990s,* ed. Jane Pulkingham and Gordon Ternowetsky, 2-29. Halifax: Fernwood, 1996.

Purvis, Douglas D., and Constance Smith. 'Fiscal Policy in Canada: 1963-84.' In *Fiscal and Monetary Policy,* research coordinator John Sargent, 1-42. Collected Research Studies Series/Royal Commission on the Economic Union and Development Prospects for Canada. Vol. 21. Toronto: University of Toronto Press, 1986.

Quinlan, Joseph, and Marc Chandler. 'The U.S. Trade Deficit: A Dangerous Obsession.' *Foreign Affairs* 80, 3 (2001): 87-97.

Rae, Bob. *From Protest to Power: Personal Reflections on a Life in Politics.* Toronto: Viking, 1996.

Reich, Robert. Introduction to *The Power of Public Ideas,* ed. Robert B. Reich. Cambridge, MA: Ballinger, 1988.

–. *The Work of Nations.* New York: Vintage Books, 1992.

Richards, John. 'Reducing the Muddle in the Middle: Three Propositions for Running the Welfare State.' In *Canada: The State of the Federation 1997 – Non-Constitutional Renewal,* ed. Harvey Lazar, 71-104. Kingston, ON: Institute for Intergovernmental Relations, 1998.

Richards, John, and Larry Pratt. *Prairie Capitalism: Power and Influence in the New West.* Toronto: McClelland and Stewart, 1979.

Riddell, W. Craig. 'Employment and Unemployment in Canada: Assessing Recent Experience.' *Policy Options* 17, 6 (1996): 9-14.

Robinson, Joan. 'What Has Become of the Keynesian Revolution?' In *Essays on John Maynard Keynes,* ed. Milo Keynes, 123-31. London: Cambridge University Press, 1975.

Robson, William, and William M. Scarth. 'Debating Deficit Reduction: Economic Perspectives and Policy Choices.' In *Deficit Reduction: What Pain, What Gain?* Policy Study no. 23, ed. William B.P. Robson and William M. Scarth, 1-41. Toronto: C.D. Howe Institute, 1994.

Rorty, Richard. *Contingency, Irony, and Solidarity.* New York: Cambridge University Press, 1989.

Ruggie, John Gerard. 'Embedded Liberalism Revisited: Institutions and Progress in International Economic Relations.' In *Progress in Postwar International Relations,* ed. Emanuel Adler and Beverly Crawford, 201-34. New York: Columbia University Press, 1991.

–. 'International Regimes, Transactions, and Change: Embedded Liberalism in the Postwar Economic Order.' In *International Regimes,* ed. Stephen D. Krasner, 195-231. Ithaca, NY: Cornell University Press, 1983.

–. 'Trade, Protectionism and the Future of Welfare Capitalism.' *Journal of International Affairs* 48, 1 (1994): 1-11.

Rusk, James. 'Budget No Help in Economic Ills, Opposition Says.' *Globe and Mail,* 16 February 1984, A11.

–. 'Tax Breaks Will Be a Boost for Business.' *Globe and Mail,* 20 April 1983, A10.

Russell, Peter. *Constitutional Odyssey: Can the Canadians Become a Sovereign People?* 2nd ed. Toronto: University of Toronto Press, 1993.

Sabatier, Paul A. 'Policy Change over a Decade or More.' In *Policy Change and Learning: An Advocacy Coalition Approach,* ed. Paul A. Sabatier and Hank C. Jenkins-Smith, 13-39. Boulder, CO: Westview Press, 1993.

Salant, Walter S. 'The Spread of Keynesian Doctrines and Practices in the United States.' In *The Political Power of Economic Ideas: Keynesianism across Nations,* ed. Peter A. Hall, 27-51. Princeton, NJ: Princeton University Press, 1989.

Samuelson, Paul A. 'Fiscal and Financial Policies for Growth.' In *The Collected Scientific Papers of Paul A. Samuelson.* Vol. 2, ed. Joseph Stiglitz, 1387-403. Cambridge, MA: MIT Press, 1966.

Sarantakis, Taki. 'Of Deficits and Debt: Rolling Back the Post-Prosperous Canadian State.' Unpublished paper, Toronto.

Sargent, John. 'Comment: On Macro Public Finance.' In *Retrospectives on Public Finance,* ed. Lorraine Eden, 344-7. Durham, NC: Duke University Press, 1991.

Savoie, Donald. *Governing from the Centre: The Concentration of Power in Canadian Politics.* Toronto: University of Toronto Press, 1999.

–. *The Politics of Public Spending in Canada.* Toronto: University of Toronto Press, 1990.

–. *Thatcher, Reagan, Mulroney: In Search of a New Bureaucracy.* Toronto: University of Toronto Press, 1994.

Scoffield, Heather. 'Martin Aiming To Deliver February Budget.' *Globe and Mail,* 17 August 2001, A5

Seccareccia, Mario. 'Keynesianism and Public Investment: A Left-Keynesian Perspective on the Role of Government Expenditures And Debt.' *Studies in Political Economy* 46 (Spring 1995): 43-78.

Sharp, Mitchell. *Budget Speech.* 29 March. Ottawa: Queen's Printer, 1966.
–. *Budget Speech.* 1 June. Ottawa: Queen's Printer, 1967.
Sheppard, Robert, and Mary Trueman, '"Budget That Stole Christmas" Condemned by Opposition Spokesmen.' *Globe and Mail,* 12 December 1979, A12.
Shields, John, and Stephen McBride, *Dismantling a Nation: The Transition to a Corporate Rule in Canada.* 2nd ed. Halifax: Fernwood Press, 1997.
Silversides, Ann. 'Business Groups Like Budget, but Worry about Deficit's Size.' *Globe and Mail,* 20 April 1983, A11.
Simeon, Richard. 'Inside the Macdonald Commission.' *Studies in Political Economy* 22 (Spring 1987): 167-79.
–. 'The Political Context for Renegotiating Fiscal Federalism.' In *The Future of Fiscal Federalism,* ed. Keith G. Banting, Douglas M. Brown, and Thomas J. Courchene, 135-48. Kingston, ON: Queen's University, School of Policy Studies, 1994.
–. *In Search of a Social Contract: Can We Make Hard Decisions As If Democracy Matters?* Benefactors Lecture Series, 13 September. Toronto: C.D. Howe Institute, 1994.
Simeon, Richard, and Ian Robinson. *State, Society, and the Development of Canadian Federalism.* Collected Research Studies Series/Royal Commission on the Economic Union and Development Prospects for Canada. Vol. 71. Toronto: University of Toronto Press, 1990.
Simpson, Jeffrey. 'Budget Aimed at Reasserting Ottawa's Power.' *Globe and Mail,* 27 October 1980, A1.
–. 'Budget Burying Major Promises in PC Campaign.' *Globe and Mail,* 12 December 1979, A11.
–. 'Remorseless Arithmetic: The Citizen and the State in Canada.' *Queens Quarterly* 101, 4 (1994): 781-99.
–. 'Squaring off at Budget Time.' *Globe and Mail,* 20 February 1990, A6.
Skidelsky, Robert. 'Ideas and the World.' *The Economist* 357, 8189 (25 November-1 December 2000): 83-5.
–. *John Maynard Keynes: The Economist As Saviour, 1920-1937.* Vol. 2. London: Macmillan, 1992.
–. *John Maynard Keynes: Fighting for Britain, 1937-1946.* Vol. 3. London: Macmillan, 2000.
–. *John Maynard Keynes: Hopes Betrayed, 1883-1920.* Vol. 1. Toronto: Penguin Books, 1983.
Slater, David W. *War Finance and Reconstruction: The Role of Canada's Department of Finance, 1939-1946.* Ottawa: David W. Slater, 1995.
Smiley, Donald V. *Canada in Question: Federalism in the Eighties.* 3rd ed. Toronto: McGraw-Hill Ryerson, 1980.
Smythe, Elizabeth. 'Investment Policy.' In *Border Crossings: The Internationalization of Canadian Public Policy,* ed. G. Bruce Doern, Leslie A. Pal, and Brian W. Tomlin, 188-208. Toronto: Oxford University Press, 1996.
Sparks, Gordon R. 'The Theory and Practice of Monetary Policy in Canada: 1945-83.' In *Fiscal and Monetary Policy,* research coordinator John Sargent, 119-47. Collected Research Studies Series/Royal Commission on the Economic Union and Development Prospects for Canada. Vol. 21. Toronto: University of Toronto Press, 1986.
Stanford, Jim. 'The Economic and Social Consequences of Fiscal Retrenchment in Canada in the 1990s.' In *The Review of Economic Performance and Social Progress – The Longest Decade: Canada in the 1990s,* ed. Keith G. Banting, Andrew Sharpe, and France St-Hilaire, 141-60. Montreal: Institute for Research on Public Policy, 2001.
–. 'A Fred Astaire Budget.' *Policy Options* 21, 3 (2000): 7-13.
–. 'I'm the Boss Here, and I'm Firing Myself.' *Globe and Mail,* 2 January 2001, A13.
–. 'The Revolution Is Dead. Long Live the Revolution.' *Policy Options* 22, 3 (2001): 34-43.
Statistics Canada. *The Daily: 1996 Census: Sources of income, earnings and total income, and family income,* 12 May 1998. Ottawa. Information from the Nation Series, Package no. 9, Catalogue no. 93FOO29XDB96000.
–. 'Population 15 Years and over by Sex, Age Groups and Labour Force Activity, for Canada, Provinces and Territories, 1981-1996 Censuses.' Nation Series, Catalogue no. 93F0027XDB96001.
Stewart, Ian A. 'Debt Is Not Proof of Profligacy.' *Globe and Mail,* 13 March 1999, D7.

Stinson, Marian. 'Currency Markets Give Thumbs Up.' *Globe and Mail,* 28 February 1995, A1-A2.

Stockman, David A. *The Triumph of Politics: How the Reagan Revolution Failed.* New York: Harper and Row, 1986.

Stoyko, Peter. 'Creating Opportunity or Creative Opportunism? Liberal Labour Market Policy.' In *How Ottawa Spends 1997-98 – Seeing Red: A Liberal Report Card,* ed. Gene Swimmer, 85-110. Ottawa: Carleton University Press, 1997.

Strain, Frank, and Hugh Grant. 'The Social Structure of Accumulation in Canada, 1945-1988.' *Journal of Canadian Studies* 26, 4 (1991-2): 75-93.

Swimmer, Gene. 'Seeing Red: A Liberal Report Card.' In *How Ottawa Spends 1997-98 – Seeing Red: A Liberal Report Card,* ed. Gene Swimmer, 1-22. Ottawa: Carleton University Press, 1997.

Taft, Kevin. *Shredding the Public Interest: Ralph Klein and 25 Years of One-Party Government.* Edmonton: University of Alberta Press, 1997.

Taras, David, and Allan Tupper. 'Politics and Deficits: Alberta's Challenge to the Canadian Political Agenda.' In *Canada: The State of the Federation 1994,* ed. Douglas M. Brown and Janet Hiebert, 61-83. Kingston, ON: Institute of Intergovernmental Relations, 1994.

Thelen, Kathleen, and Sven Steinmo. 'Historical Institutionalism in Comparative Politics.' In *Structuring Politics: Historical Institutionalism in Comparative Analysis,* ed. Sven Steinmo, Kathleen Thelen, and Frank Longstreth, 1-32. New York: Cambridge University Press, 1992.

Treasury Board of Canada. *Employment Statistics for the Federal Public Service: April 1, 1996 to March 31, 1997.* Ottawa: Treasury Board of Canada, 1997.

Trefler, Daniel. *The Long and Short of the Canada-U.S. Free Trade Agreement.* Ottawa: Industry Canada Research Publications Program, 1999.

Trudeau, Pierre. *Approaches to Politics.* Toronto: Oxford University Press, 1970.

–. *The Essential Trudeau.* Ed. Ron Graham. Toronto: McClelland and Stewart, 1998.

Turner, John N. *Budget Speech.* 19 February. Ottawa: Department of Finance, 1973.

–. *Budget Speech.* 6 May. Ottawa: Department of Finance, 1974.

–. *Budget Speech.* 23 June. Ottawa: Department of Finance, 1975.

Underhill, Geoffrey. 'Introduction: Conceptualizing the Changing Global Order.' In *Political Economy and the Changing Global Order,* ed. Richard Stubbs and Geoffrey R.D. Underhill, 17-44. Toronto: McClelland and Stewart, 1994.

Walkom, Thomas. 'PM Changes Stand on Social Programs.' *Globe and Mail,* 10 November 1984, A1-A2.

Wallulis, Jerald. *The New Insecurity: The End of the Standard Job and Family.* Albany: State University of New York Press, 1998.

Walzer, Michael. *Interpretation and Social Criticism.* Cambridge, MA: Harvard University Press, 1987.

Watson, William. *Globalization and the Meaning of Canadian Life.* Toronto: University of Toronto Press, 1998.

–. 'Has Neo-Conservatism Failed?' *Policy Options* 22, 2 (2001): 6-17.

–. 'How the Budget Is Made: An Interview with Scott Clark, Deputy Minister of Finance.' *Policy Options* 20, 1 (1999): 12-18.

Weber, Max. 'The Social Psychology of World Religions.' In *From Max Weber: Essays in Sociology,* ed. H.H. Gerth and C. Wright Mills, 267-301. London: Kegan Paul, Trench, Trubner, 1947.

Weir, Margaret. 'Ideas and Politics: The Acceptance of Keynesianism in Britain and the United States.' In *The Political Power of Economic Ideas: Keynesianism across Nations,* ed. Peter A. Hall, 53-86. Princeton, NJ: Princeton University Press, 1989.

Whitaker, Reginald. *A Sovereign Idea: Essays on Canada As a Democratic Community.* Montreal and Kingston: McGill-Queen's University Press, 1992.

Will, Robert. *Canadian Fiscal Policy 1945-63.* Studies of the Royal Commission on Taxation no. 17. Ottawa: Queen's Printer, 1967.

Williams, Glen. *Not for Export: The International Competitiveness of Canadian Manufacturing.* 3rd ed. Toronto: McClelland and Stewart, 1994.

Wills, Terrance. 'Lapel Daisies a Reply to PM.' *Globe and Mail,* 9 May 1974, A1.
–. 'PCs Call Budget Less Expansionary Than Last Year's, Move for Defeat.' *Globe and Mail,* 22 February 1973, A8.
Wilson, Michael. *The Agenda for Economic Renewal: Principles and Progress,* 18 February. Ottawa: Department of Finance, 1987.
–. *The Budget.* 20 February. Ottawa: Department of Finance, 1990.
–. *The Budget.* 26 February. Ottawa: Department of Finance, 1991.
–. *The Budget Speech.* 23 May. Ottawa: Department of Finance, 1985.
–. *The Budget Speech.* 26 February. Ottawa: Department of Finance, 1986.
–. *The Budget Speech.* 18 February. Ottawa: Department of Finance, 1987.
–. *The Budget Speech.* 10 February. Ottawa: Department of Finance, 1988.
–. *The Budget Speech.* 27 April. Ottawa: Department of Finance, 1989.
–. *The Budget Speech.* 26 February. Ottawa: Department of Finance, 1991.
–. *Economic and Fiscal Statement.* 8 November. Ottawa: Department of Finance, 1984.
–. *The Fiscal Plan.* 23 May. Ottawa: Department of Finance, 1985.
–. *The Fiscal Plan.* 26 February. Ottawa: Department of Finance, 1986.
–. *The Fiscal Plan: Controlling the Public Debt.* 27 April. Ottawa: Department of Finance, 1989.
–. *A New Direction for Canada – An Agenda for Economic Renewal.* 8 November. Ottawa: Department of Finance, 1984.
–. *Reducing the Deficit and Controlling the National Debt.* November. Ottawa: Department of Finance, 1985.
Wilton, David A. 'An Evaluation of Wage and Price Controls in Canada.' *Canadian Public Policy* 10, 2 (1984): 167-76.
Winsor, Hugh. 'Tories Borrow from Reform Party.' *Globe and Mail,* 26 February 1992, A1, A6.
Wolfe, Alan. *The Limits of Legitimacy: Political Contradictions of Contemporary Capitalism.* New York: Free Press, 1977.
Wolfe, David A. 'The Crisis in Advanced Capitalism: An Introduction.' *Studies in Political Economy* 11 (Summer 1983): 7-26.
–. "The Delicate Balance: The Changing Economic Role of the State in Canada." Vol. 1. PhD diss., University of Toronto, 1980.
–. 'The Politics of the Deficit.' In *The Politics of Economic Policy,* research coordinator G. Bruce Doern, 111-62. Collected Research Studies Series/Royal Commission on the Economic Union and Development Prospects for Canada. vol. 40. Toronto: University of Toronto Press, 1985.
–. 'Politics, The Deficit and Tax Reform.' *Osgoode Hall Law Journal* 26, 2 (1988): 347-66.
–. 'The Rise and Demise of the Keynesian Era in Canada: Economic Policy, 1930-1982.' In *Readings in Canadian Social History,* vol. 5, ed. Michael S. Cross and Gregory S. Kealey, 46-78. Toronto: McClelland and Stewart, 1984.
Workman, Thom. *Banking on Deception: The Discourse of Fiscal Crisis.* Halifax: Fernwood Publishing, 1996.
–. 'The Discourse of Fiscal Crisis.' *Studies in Political Economy* 59 (Summer 1999): 61-89.
York, Geoffrey. 'Government Scraps Day-Care Commitment.' *Globe and Mail,* 27 February 1992, A1, A8.

Index